Alias
Frank
Canton

Joe Horner, alias Frank Canton, as he looked in 1895.
Courtesy Wyoming State Museum.

Alias Frank Canton

by
Robert K. DeArment

Illustrated Maps by Rosemary DeArment Walter

UNIVERSITY OF OKLAHOMA PRESS : NORMAN AND LONDON

Also by Robert K. DeArment

Bat Masterson: The Man and the Legend (Norman, 1979)
Knights of the Green Cloth: The Saga of the Frontier Gamblers
(Norman, 1982)
*George Scarborough: The Life and Death of a Lawman
on the Closing Frontier* (Norman, 1992)
(ed.) *Early Days in Texas: A Trip to Hell and Heaven,*
by Jim McIntire (Norman, 1992)

Library of Congress Cataloging-in-Publication Data
DeArment, Robert K., 1925–
Alias Frank Canton / by Robert K. DeArment.
p.   cm.
Includes bibliographical references and index.
ISBN 0-8061-2828-3 (alk. paper)
1. Canton, Frank, 1849–1927. 2. Pioneers—Oklahoma—Biography. 3. Pioneers—
Wyoming—Biography. 4. Pioneers—Alaska—Biography. 5. Frontier and pioneer
life—Oklahoma. 6. Frontier and pioneer life—Wyoming. 7. Frontier and pioneer
life—Alaska. 8. Oklahoma—Biography. 9. Wyoming—Biography. 10. Alaska—
Biography. I. Title.
F699.C36D43   1996
973—dc20   95-39758
[B]   CIP

The paper in this book meets the guidelines for permanence and durability of the
Committee on Production Guidelines for Book Longevity
of the Council on Library Resources, Inc.

∞

Contents

Part Five. The State of Oklahoma Years

Illustrations

Maps

Acknowled

THE FOLLO

helpful to me in developing this biography, and I
gratitude: Gary C. Anderson, Jim Gatchell Mem
Wyoming; Billy Birmingham, Texas Department of
tutional Division, Huntsville; Jean Brainard, Wyomin
merce, Cheyenne; Jim Browning, Charleston, South C
Ripley, Oklahoma; Jack DeMattos, North Attlebor
Dillinger, Buffalo, Wyoming; H. D. English, Chief Depu
County, Lawton, Oklahoma; Robert Ernst, Stillwater, C
American Heritage Center, University of Wyoming, La
Kirkland, Washington; Elnora Frye, Laramie, Wyomin
Historian, Wyoming Department of Commerce, Cheyenn
Fort Collins, Colorado; John Hutchins, Lakewood, Colora
Zionsville, Indiana; John R. Lovett, Librarian, Western H
University of Oklahoma, Norman; Bob McCubbin, El Pa
McDermott, Sheridan, Wyoming; Patty Myers, Johnson
Buffalo, Wyoming; Chuck Parsons, Smiley, Texas; Nar
Eastford, Connecticut; William B. Secrest, Fresno, Californi
Alton Museum of History and Art, Alton, Illinois; the lat
Cheyenne, Wyoming; Carol Williams, Texas and Southweste
ers Foundation, Fort Worth.

Alias
Frank
Canton

Introduction

"No more lovable a character was produced, or a more fearless
or conscientious champion of law and order than Frank M. Canton.
If he ever knew fear, even his most intimate friends could see
no trace of it."

Cattleman, November 1927

His death on September 27, 1927,
was front-page news across the state of Oklahoma. The Associated Press
wire service picked up the story, and newspapers throughout the nation reported that General Frank M. Canton—picturesque frontiersman, veteran
law enforcement officer of the Old West, colorful soldier of fortune, first
adjutant general of the state of Oklahoma, and the prototype for the fictional western heroes of novelists Owen Wister and Rex Beach—was dead.[1]

The body lay in state in the capitol building at Oklahoma City as eulogies
filled the press. Interment was performed on September 29 with full military rites. High-ranking military and civilian state officials in attendance
included a former governor of the state, judges, U.S. congressmen, and university professors. Pioneers of the territorial days and celebrated frontier
peace officers paid their last respects.

Few of the dignitaries attending that funeral knew that the true name of
the man they honored was Joe Horner and not Frank Canton, or that his
"picturesque, colorful" history included a criminal career marked by convictions for bank and highway robbery, desperate jail escapes, and indictments for cold-blooded murder. The life of the man they knew as Frank
Canton was one of almost constant conflict and controversy. His tempestu-
ous history, a career "wrapped in mystery,"[2] was directly attributable to his
own complex and often contradictory character. A self-confessed and convicted armed robber and accused back-shooting assassin, he misrepresented
himself for fifty years. He had a weakness for alcohol, but he was also a

loving family man to whom his wife and daughter were completely devoted. After a wild youth as a vicious desperado, he transformed himself into a frontier lawman and chased felons for almost a half century. He proved to be an intelligent, ambitious, and hard-working peace officer who demonstrated exceptional courage on numerous occasions as he dealt with some of the toughest and most dangerous outlaws in the West. But controversy also clouded his long career in law enforcement. As an officer, he has been called a "Jekyll and Hyde of the Plains,"[3] who followed "his chosen calling, the killing of marked men for valuable consideration."[4] Other historians of the West have termed him "a merciless, congenital, emotionless killer,"[5] a "mysterious and somewhat sinister" character, "taciturn and calculating, with an unfortunate tendency to become vicious when drinking,"[6] and "one of the most incredible figures in the Wild West . . . [who] left dead men and legends from Wyoming to the Klondike."[7] His friends, however, thought he was a remarkably "steadfast man and a true comrade, the sort one could tie to,"[8] and "a great character and a splendid officer [who] was for law and order as he saw it and did not know the meaning of 'compromise.'"[9]

Little compromise can be found in the views of critics and defenders. The man known as Frank Canton stirred passions during his lifetime, and the controversy continues among admirers and detractors today. In his final years Joe Horner, alias Frank Canton, with his fingers gnarled by arthritis, laboriously penned an autobiography, which was published after his death. Well written and packed with exciting adventures, the book is nonetheless disappointing. All autobiography tends to be selectively self-serving, but *Frontier Trails*, as it was titled by the editor, was especially so, omitting almost as much as it included.

Told here, for the first time, is the complete story of the life of Joe Horner, alias Frank Canton, and the role he played in the history of the turbulent western frontier that produced him.

Part One

The
Texas
Years

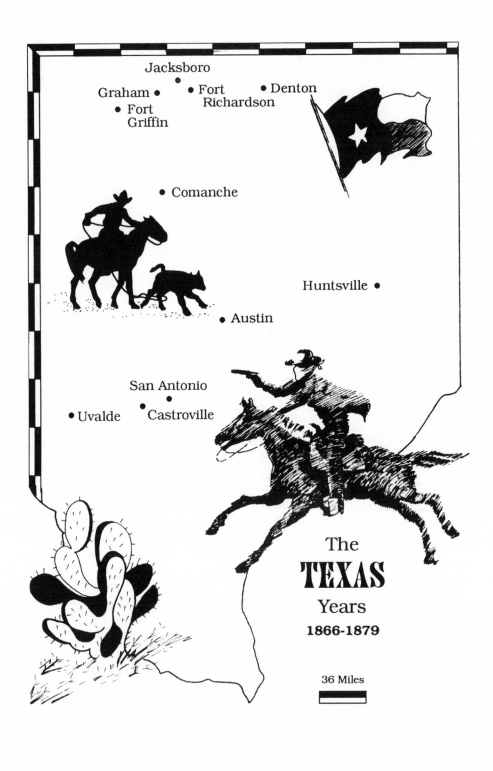

Jacksboro

Graham •
• Fort
Griffin

• Fort
Richardson

• Denton

• Comanche

Huntsville •

• Austin

San Antonio
•
• Castroville

• Uvalde

The
TEXAS
Years
1866-1879

36 Miles

Chapter 1

The Cowboy, 1849-1873

"Much of Canton's career is wrapped in mystery and some of the significant events of his life no doubt will never come to light."

—Dan L. Thrapp, *Encyclopedia of Frontier Biography*

Frank Canton was accused of killing a number of men. But he spent most of his life trying to kill Joe Horner, the man he had been in his youth. Once he became Frank Canton, he lied about his name, his age, and even his place of birth in an effort to expunge Joe Horner from history. He was so successful that almost another half century passed after his death before the story of Horner came to light.

Joe Horner was the son of John W. Horner, born in 1812, one of five sons and a daughter of a Virginia physician of Scottish descent who was said to have fought in the Revolutionary War.[1] John Horner was a farmer and Methodist preacher who also practiced medicine. According to family tradition, he had only six months of formal schooling but educated himself through reading and kept an extensive library. He married twice and fathered twelve children.

John Horner had wanderlust. In the early 1830s he left Virginia for the frontier country of Ohio, where he married. The couple had three daughters: Mary, born in 1834, Virginia in 1836, and Eliza Ann in 1838.[2] John's wife died in about 1840, and he returned east and married Mary Jane Clemmons, a twenty-four-year-old woman of English and Irish heritage, in Baltimore. Nine children—four boys and five girls—were born to this union. Josiah W. ("Joe") Horner was the middle child, with four older and four younger siblings. In 1849, the year of Joe Horner's birth, William and Josiah Clemmons, brothers of Mary Jane, joined the great rush to the California goldfields. Josiah, for whom Joe Horner was named, died during the return trip and was buried at sea.[3]

After his second marriage, John Horner led his family to Keokuk, Iowa, where Margaret was born in 1841, Martha in 1843, and John Wesley in 1844. The Horners next settled in Harrison Township, Henry County, Indiana. Here daughter Mary Jane (Mollie) was born in 1847, Josiah on September 15, 1849, and George in 1852. By 1854 the Horners were located near Kansas City, Missouri, and the following year were in Topeka, Kansas, where Allen joined the family in 1855 and Kate in February 1857. The next stop was Huntsville, Arkansas, where the last child, Minnie Belle, was born in January 1859. The Horners in 1860 were back in Missouri, living at Ozark, in the southwestern corner of the state.[4] Despite the constant uprootings, the Horner children were evidently well provided for. "He must have been a wonderful financier," mused a daughter, "to have transported such a boodle of children (most times in a prairie schooner) & but a few of us could claim the same state for our birthplace. . . . We could not have appeared shoddy as we were well clothed & had no thot [sic] but what we were as good as anybody."[5]

At the outbreak of the Civil War, the Horners were living at Ozark. Although almost fifty years old, with a wife and a flock of children, Horner went off to fight for the Confederacy. On August 20, 1862, the Confederate secretary of war had authorized Colonel H. E. Clark to recruit and equip a regiment of Missouri volunteers. Within ten days John W. Horner had joined the unit as a private in the company of Captain A. F. Jones.[6] Three months later the oldest son, John Wesley, also enlisted in the Confederate army, joining Company C of the 34th Regiment under General Sterling Price. Despite wounds received at the Battle of Prairie Grove, Arkansas, he fought for the Confederacy until Robert E. Lee's surrender in 1865.[7]

In early 1863 the elder John Horner became a military surgeon. Wounded and captured at the battle of Mount Vernon, Missouri, in 1864, he was taken by Union forces to Alton, Illinois, and confined in the former state penitentiary as a prisoner of war. He died there in 1865. There are two versions of Horner's death in the family tradition. According to one, the doctors at Alton, recognizing that Horner could not recover from his wounds, permitted him to be taken to an aunt's home nearby, where he died.[8] The other has it that Doctor Horner treated a Union officer's wife, who had pneumonia, and that he died after contracting the disease from his patient.[9] It is more likely that Horner was one of the last victims of the smallpox epidemic that raged in the Alton prison during the winter of 1863 and did not abate until late in 1864. At the peak of the scourge, the dead mounted up so fast that prison officials gave up trying to keep accurate records. Estimates of prisoner deaths from the disease ranged from one thousand to five thousand; the army officially listed 1,354.[10]

herds never seemed to diminish in numbers. At the same time, the Cooper family of Cottontail Thicket was losing cattle. The inference was clear. The Coopers accused Horner, charging him with the theft of three head of cattle from Ann Cooper and of one cow, the property of Harvey Cooper.[21]

Many years later, writing as the respected lawman Frank Canton, Joe Horner would consistently blame buffalo hunters for the introduction of cattle rustling into Texas. "Before the days of the buffalo hunters cattle stealing was almost unknown in Texas," he said, adding that they "were the first cattle thieves to operate in an organized way." He noted, "The day of systematic theft in Texas can be traced to the time when the government forbade further slaughter of the buffalo."[22]

In 1874 Jacksboro harbored many hunters forced off the buffalo ranges by the Red River war raging that year. Some of them may well have fallen in with the Horner-Cotnam crowd and influenced Horner to take up this line of criminal activity, but it was Horner, a cattleman, who was indicted.

On July 10 a warrant was issued for Horner's arrest on the assault charge. By prior arrangement with Horner and his supporters, Sheriff Crutchfield delayed making the arrest until August 24, when warrants in the cattle theft cases were also issued and served. Horner was released the same day on bond of $150 in each case. Bondsmen were Joe himself, R. J. Henson, and Stanley Cooper. Trials in the three cases were scheduled for the October term of the district court. Horner was represented by Attorney H. H. Sams.[23]

Ironically, the grand jury of June 1874, which had cleared Henry Strong in the Jeffries shooting, was the same body that handed down all three indictments against Joe Horner. This was an especially active session, and its work reflects the turmoil then rampant in Jack County. Bills of indictments were also issued in two murder cases that had aroused great excitement that year. In the first, former Sheriff Michael McMillan was indicted for the murder of Johnny Alexander, the man Strong had employed to nail Jeffries in the mail robbery case. McMillan's trial resulted in a hung jury, and he escaped before he could be retried. Apprehended about fifteen years later, he was returned to Jacksboro, tried again, and acquitted.[24] The second sensational murder case involved a black man named Eli Bly, charged with the murder and robbery of his white employer, Thomas Carmichael. Bly was indicted, tried, convicted, sentenced, and executed within two months.[25] The case contributed to the highly charged racial tensions then building in Jacksboro, tensions that were to embroil Joe Horner and significantly affect his future.

Racial bitterness engendered by the Civil War was only exacerbated in Texas by the "Carpetbag Constitution" government of Governor Edmund J. Davis during the Reconstruction period. Jack County had many "unreconstructed rebels," who resented blacks and their newly won freedom, but for several years friction between blacks and whites on the northern frontier had been ameliorated by the constant danger presented by a third race—the Indian. Indian raids threatened both blacks and whites, and together they fought the common enemy.

For his bravery during the Indian conflicts, a black man named Brit Johnson had become a local hero on the frontier. Johnson, a freedman, scouted for the army out of Fort Belknap and distinguished himself in many clashes with Indians during the 1860s. Kiowas killed his son and carried off his wife and two other children in 1864. Johnson worked determinedly to rescue his family. He was finally successful and managed also to save three whites from Indian captivity. Settlers of the northern Texas counties, both black and white, were genuinely shocked and saddened when Johnson and three other blacks were killed by the Kiowas in January 1871 on Salt Creek Prairie between Forts Richardson and Griffin.[26]

Since Jacksboro's inception, blacks had lived peaceably in a segregated area near Lost Creek. There they managed their own affairs and avoided confrontation with whites. A violent and bloody episode in August 1872, however, embittered and alienated both races. Two white soldiers of the Eleventh Infantry, Sergeant William Lawrence and Corporal Zachery Ringiron, attempted to disrupt a dance in the black district. The blacks resisted, gunfire erupted, and both soldiers were shot. Lawrence died, and Ringiron was severely wounded. The presumed gunman, a black man named Charles Copelan, disappeared from Jacksboro that night. The next morning eight or nine well-armed soldiers from the fort, accompanied by a Jacksboro blacksmith named McGinnis, stormed into the area with the announced purpose of "killing every Negro man they could find." All the black men had fled except an old man named George Mosely, who was shot dead on the spot. The civil authorities arrested, tried, and convicted McGinnis of being accessory to the murder of Mosely, but he broke out of jail and was never recaptured. The soldiers were not prosecuted, and no one was ever tried for the murder of Sergeant Lawrence.[27]

Racial tensions escalated in the spring of 1873 when three companies of the Tenth Cavalry, composed of black troopers, arrived at Fort Richardson. These were the "Buffalo Soldiers," as the Indians called them. The sight of ex-slaves, wearing blue uniforms and carrying weapons, was not pleasing to former Confederates and their sympathizers in Jacksboro. Half a century later Joe Horner expressed his contempt for the black soldiers of Fort Richardson: "The Indians called them the 'buffalo soldier.' They were of no benefit to the settlers, and absolutely no protection to them. I never knew a negro soldier to kill an Indian while they were in the country, but I have known them to kill some pretty good white men. The cowboys did not get along with them very well. A cowboy could never understand what a negro soldier was good for unless it was to practice on occasionally when they were not fighting Indians."[28]

Actually, the buffalo soldiers did much to protect the settlers during this period. According to official reports, between September and December 1873, detachments of the Tenth Cavalry had a dozen engagements with the Indians, inflicting an undetermined number of casualties. They also killed four white horse thieves and captured seventeen others. In the process they recovered nearly twelve hundred head of stolen animals.[29]

But Horner's jaundiced view of the black troopers was almost universally shared by whites in the area. Jim McIntire, a cowboy on Jim Loving's Lost Valley Ranch, was also a member of the local company of Texas Rangers and thus participated in several pitched battles with the Indians during this period. He wrote: "There was a lot of colored troops at Fort Jacksboro [sic]. . . . They made so much noise while on the march that we could not hope to surprise the Indians. . . . We had all kinds of trouble in keeping the 'niggers' quiet, as they would rather have frightened the Indians away by their noise than have defeated them in battle."[30] According to H. H. McConnell, a former soldier who lived in Jacksboro after retirement, the bias against black troopers was not confined to white civilians but extended to white military men as well. "The citizens here had little use for the [black soldiers], and, in fact, the white soldiers hadn't either; they looked upon them as an unnecessary evil."[31]

Not surprisingly, the black troopers resented the prejudice held by the very people they were there to defend. But their behavior in town, if reported accurately, aggravated the situation. "They were haughty, impudent and insulting," wrote Thomas Horton. "They usually came over to town in bunches of from thirty to forty. The private citizens had no protection from them, if one happened to say Negro in the hearing of one of these groups he was grossly insulted and against such numbers had to endure their scoffing."[32]

Beyond the racial factor, the constant tension between civilians and soldiers also manifested itself occasionally in Jacksboro. When the white Fourth Cavalry was stationed at Fort Richardson, a major conflict was narrowly averted following the killing of Trooper Burke in a Jacksboro bawdy house. Angry members of his troop burned the brothel to the ground, and a rumor quickly spread through Jacksboro that soldiers from the fort were preparing to burn the entire town the next night. Armed citizens assembled from the countryside, and the military officers had a difficult job convincing them that the report was false.[33]

This, then, was the emotionally charged atmosphere in Jacksboro on Saturday, October 10, 1874, when Joe Horner, facing trial on three counts in two weeks and carrying a personal animus, rode into town. He and Frank Lake, one of his cowboys, had driven a small bunch of cattle to Fort Richardson in fulfillment of Horner's government contract. Lake, twenty years old and a native of Tennessee, had come to the northern Texas cattle ranges from Washington County in northwestern Arkansas, near Horner's old stamping grounds in southwestern Missouri. The two had another common bond: their fathers had both been confined as Confederate prisoners of war at the Alton, Illinois, penitentiary.[34]

Leaving Lake with the cattle about a half mile from the fort, Horner rode in to make arrangements with the commissary sergeant for the delivery of the beeves. But first he stopped in a saloon to slake his habitual thirst. There he confronted two black troopers who, according to the story as it was later remembered in Jacksboro, demanded that he buy them drinks. Horner indignantly refused, and insults were exchanged. Hot words led to hot lead. Horner shot one of the soldiers, Private George Smith, and the other fled. There was no evidence that either trooper fired a weapon at Horner or that they were even armed.

Horner left Smith bleeding on the floor, walked up the street, and entered another saloon. Alerted by the fleeing trooper, a party of soldiers came with a cart and removed Smith to the post hospital, where it was found that his wound was severe but not life-threatening. A second detail of six black troopers and a white sergeant also entered the town to arrest Smith's assailant.

But Horner, now thoroughly aroused, was not in a mood to submit to arrest. He and young Joe Watson, who had joined him in the saloon, opened fire with six-shooters on the approaching cavalrymen. The detail took cover behind a log building and returned the fire with rifles. Slugs from the guns of Horner and Watson knocked chunks off the corners of the log house and soon routed the squad. According to Thomas Horton, who witnessed the battle, Horner and Watson "walked out to the curb and squatted down and whipped the detail off of them."[35]

Hearing the shots, other soldiers ran from the fort, took positions along the bank of Lost Creek, and began shooting down Main Street with rifles. Horner's Winchester was in a saddle scabbard on his hitchracked horse. He ran to the animal, jerked out the rifle, and swung into the saddle. Watson, meanwhile, ran to the house of his grandfather, Joe Henson, to get his rifle, but Grandmother Henson threw her arms around him and prevented him from returning to the battle.

Horner engaged the soldiers in a long-range rifle duel, "moving his horse slowly east and west across the road, shooting back all the time at the Negroes, hitting one Negro between the eyes, killing him instantly."³⁶ Finally a bullet struck Horner's horse, passing completely through the body, and the animal dropped dead on the sidewalk. "The ball went through the sweat-leather on each side just where Horner's knees apparently should have been, yet he was unhurt," Thomas Horton remembered.³⁷

Horner then ran to Ed Eastburn's hardware and gun shop to replenish his supply of ammunition. As he came out he was hailed by Frank Lake, who had ridden into town to investigate the sounds of battle. Lake was holding his horse behind the Island Saloon. Leaping into the saddle, he swung by Horner, who jumped up behind him, and they galloped out of town.

A detachment of soldiers pursued them and soon overtook Lake's laboring horse. Horner and Lake dismounted, and another gunfight erupted, Horner's third of the day. Lake took a bullet through the meat of his right thigh. Leaving him to the ministrations of the military, Horner mounted the horse and escaped.

The soldiers took Lake to the post hospital, where he was treated and released without charge. Horner rode hard for his brother's ranch near Graham, which he reached at about midnight. There he lay low for a few days, waiting for the army's next move. Hearing nothing from the fort, he rode back into Jacksboro and requested the legal advice of U.S. Commissioner Moses Wiley, a former army officer with experience in dealing with the military. Together Horner and Wiley called on Colonel William Wood, the post commander. According to Thomas Horton, a treaty was made, "Mr. Horner agreeing not to kill any more Negroes if the Negroes would not kill any more of him."³⁸

Horner had wounded Trooper George Smith in the original saloon skirmish and presumably had killed another soldier in the street fight. The post returns, medical reports, and muster rolls of Companies E, I, and L, Tenth Cavalry, for October 1874, make no direct reference to either of these casualties, although Private George Smith of Company I was reported "Sick in Hospital."³⁹ According to a later report in a local newspaper, the dead black man was an innocent bystander, "a discharged soldier who, at the time of the fight, was standing [around] to see the fun."⁴⁰ The unfortunate spectator may have been James H. Roberson, who had been discharged from Company I at Fort Richardson on October 3, a week before the street fight.⁴¹

Horton's account suggests that many Jacksboro residents felt that the actions taken by Joe Horner against the "haughty, impudent and insulting" blacks that day were understandable, even heroic. The Horner family certainly held that view. John Wesley Horner told his daughter that Joe was accosted by "two drunk negroes that insulted him. He shot one but did not kill him."⁴² Another niece, as late as 1972, almost one hundred years after the event, defended his actions, saying, "Uncle Joe had trouble over at Jacksboro with some Negro soldiers in 1874 or 1875 and had to shoot his way out in self-defense."[43]

Joe Horner himself was closemouthed about his Jacksboro experiences for many years, but his version as finally recounted to friends fifty years later was colored considerably. While admitting that he and his partner, Cotnam, "were young and inclined to 'toot 'em up' a little" in Jacksboro, Horner said the trouble began when the black troopers killed Cotnam. Since his own "reputation as a trouble maker was pretty well established," Horner said the soldiers knew they had to kill him or he "would kill as many of them as he could." The scene of the initial confrontation, according to Horner's account, was a Jacksboro restaurant rather than a saloon. He was eating when three black troopers came in. "Gun play started immediately," and he "killed two or three negro soldiers." He told of the fight in the street, where "the troops in a mob" charged and shot the horse out from under him. He "crouched back of the carcass and stopped the charge." No mention was made of the fight on the prairie and the wounding and abandonment of Frank Lake.[44]

Horner's story, though self-serving, is interesting in that it is the first and only mention of Bill Cotnam's death at the hands of the black soldiers. Although none of the histories of the town or fort refer to the killing of Cotnam or of any other white civilian by the troopers, the story cannot be totally disregarded. Cotnam disappeared from the Jack County scene at about this time. It is not impossible that a party of buffalo soldiers tangled with him somewhere on the prairie, killed him, buried the body, and failed to report the incident for fear of military or civilian reprisal. This could not have happened before the Horner gunfight, however. W. W. Cotnam was still alive four months after the battle, when he was summoned as a defense witness in one of Horner's court cases in February 1875.[45]

Although the army chose not to press charges against Horner for the shootings of October 10, S. W. T. Lanham, district attorney for the Thirteenth Judicial District, did. When Horner appeared in court later that month to plead successfully for continuances in the three cases pending against him, he found that the new grand jury had indicted him for "assault with intent to murder one George Smith." The foreman of the new grand jury was Stanley Cooper, one of Horner's bondsmen in the earlier cases, an ironic touch perhaps lost on Horner. Sheriff Crutchfield arrested Horner on the new assault charge on November 27. Horner was released the same day on a four-hundred-dollar bond provided by Horner himself, W. B. Strumer, and Asa Henson. Trial was scheduled for February 1875.[46]

In the midst of Joe Horner's mounting legal problems, his brother Wes, who stood stoutly at Joe's side throughout the ordeal, was married. In December 1874 Wes Horner and Ann Noah Sandifer, of Denton County, were wed.[47]

Jacksboro was incorporated on January 9, 1875. The first mayor was L. P. Anderson, who appointed Bill Gilson town marshal.[48] Gilson was described by a contemporary as "a huge man, cool, brave, quick and powerful, and possessing every element necessary to cope with the 'toughs' who sought to 'run the town.' Joe Horner and his followers were the typical 'bad men' of that day, but Gilson took them all in alike, and they knew their man enough to let him alone."[49]

Big Bill Gilson may have slowed down Horner in town, but apparently the increasingly notorious desperado was still up to his old tricks in the outlying districts. On January 15, 1875, he reportedly stole a cow belonging to George Rogers, and he was accused of stealing another from George Dalton on February 21, four days before he was to appear in court to answer charges already pending against him.[50] When he appeared at that February term of court, he faced a total of six bills of indictment, two for assault and four for cattle theft. All cases were continued while Sheriff Crutchfield tried to locate and serve summons papers on state and defense witnesses. Among those Horner requested to be called in his defense were Joe Watson, Frank Lake, Nate Brumbelow, and Bill Cotnam. Eventually Crutchfield served papers on all but Lake, who had returned to his Arkansas home to nurse his gunshot wound.

Horner still had not spent a day in jail, but as his notoriety mounted, keeping his liberty became increasingly more difficult. He and his bondsmen were already committed to $850 on the first four cases. Now he learned that bail bond was set at one thousand dollars on each of the new cases. His bondsmen balked at pledging these amounts, and Horner had to look elsewhere for men of property to back him. Eventually he found them: H. Cooper in Jack County, his brother Wes in Young County, and J. L. Harding in Wise County. So that he could remain free, the sheriff did not arrest him until July 10, 1875, when the commitments of the bondsmen were certain.

In September all this sparring with the law came to a sudden end. H. Cooper withdrew his surety commitment, and Sheriff Crutchfield ordered the arrest of Horner. "The notorious Joe Horner was gobbled up by Deputy Sheriff [S. R.] Hartley on Tuesday evening and was consigned to apartments in the Gilson House," announced the *Frontier Echo* on September 11. "As his stay may be protracted, we trust that the agents of the house will take good care of him. This house seems to be doing a good business, and has more permanent guests than anybody." The lockup, jocularly called the "Gilson House" after the popular town marshal, was a small building on the town square. Horner now faced confinement within these walls for more than five months; trials on his various charges were not scheduled to be held until the district court met in February 1876.

But the Gilson House held him less than a week. At four o'clock on the morning of September 13, four men silently approached a guard who sat in a chair outside the building. They covered him with pistols, disarmed him, and awakened a second guard who had been sleeping. Two gunmen held the jailers at gunpoint at the rear of the building while the others passed files and saw blades through the grating to the prisoners. Five of the six prisoners inside began working on the leg-irons chaining them to the floor. One, a black man named Henderson, either refused to take part in the escape or was not offered the opportunity. When the leg chains were severed, the prisoners attacked the door hasps, and in a few minutes Joe Horner and four other men stepped out of the building.[51] A saddled horse stood waiting for Horner. He rode off with his rescuers, heading west. Outside of town they cut the telegraph line to Graham in two places.

As newspaper accounts reported, there was no doubt that the escape was "planned and carried out by the confederates of Joe Horner."[52] Identifying the rescuers is more risky, but the four probably included Joe's brothers, Wes, George, and Allen. George, twenty-two years old in 1875, is known to have come from Denton County to join Joe at about this time. Twenty-year-old Allen was staying with Wes at his place in Young County. Based on these facts and subsequent events, it is believed that the three Horner brothers and Joe's outlaw pal Bill Redding pulled off the Jacksboro breakout.

A nineteen-year-old telegraph operator and lineman named Floyd Shock set out from Graham at this time to repair the line to Jacksboro. "The line was cut somewhere east of Graham," he recalled many years later. "I went to repair it. Possibly eight or ten miles east of Graham, I met Wes and Allen Horner. They stopped me and we had quite a chat and they told me that they thought I would find the trouble a mile or so west of Jacksboro, which I subsequently did."[53] Wes and Allen were able to pinpoint the location of the break so accurately probably because they had been in the party that cut the line after the jailbreak. It is also likely that somewhere between Jacksboro and Graham the others in the party took another trail, and those others were Joe and George Horner and Bill Redding.

When Joe Horner cut his shackles and walked out of the Gilson House, he also cut all ties to his former life. After Monday, September 13, 1875, he would no longer be considered just another reckless cowboy, a little quick with a rope and a six-shooter, perhaps, but basically a decent fellow in a little legal trouble. From that day forward he would be an outlaw. Somewhere on the road between Jacksboro and Graham his brothers made a decision. John

Wesley and Allen chose to let Joe go his way; George Horner elected to ride the outlaw trail with his brother.

In the following months the Horner Gang was blamed for much of the criminal activity across the northern counties of Texas. Newspapers as far away as Houston took note of the outlaw Joe Horner and erroneously reported that there were several indictments against him for murder.[54] The *San Antonio Daily Express* charged Horner "with heading a band of desperadoes and out-laws" who had been "operating between Sherman and Griffin for a long time." The paper added: "We understand that there is a reward offered by the Governor for the capture of Joe Horner, who is charged with murder. Sherman, Jacksboro, Richardson, Griffin, Comanche and all points in that section of the State are familiar with their outrages, and honest and peaceable citizens dread their presence as they do death. We might occupy this entire page of our paper in giving details of robberies, thefts and murders which they have committed, and even then not present one-half."[55] The following February, Texas Ranger Lieutenant D. W. Roberts would allege in his reports that Joe and George Horner went "on a robbing and murdering expedition" that fall in the country around Fort McKavett in Menard County, some two hundred miles southwest of Jacksboro.[56]

No record of rewards offered for Horner or of murder indictments filed against him have been found in Texas, but a persistent rumor that he was responsible for the vicious murder of an elderly couple during this period has become part of his legend.[57] Several robberies in remote frontier communities, however, were attributed to Horner and his cohorts. A saloonkeeper of the area, when asked many years later if he had ever heard of Joe Horner, exclaimed: "Hear of him! He came into my saloon one night, held us all up and left with the bar receipts and the bank roll."[58] An article in the *New York Sun* in the 1890s said that Horner had been a "terror" in West Texas twenty years before. "There'll be few Texans 40 years old who won't recognize that name the minute they see it," a Texas old-timer was quoted as saying. "Joe was for a number of years the hardest man in West Texas. He wasn't any imitation bad man, but the real thing."[59]

In January 1876 the Horner band attempted a major heist, an effort that would bring down the leader and cause the breakup of the gang. The gang's old nemesis, Henry Strong, was the key contributor to the debacle. Convinced that he was marked for death by Joe Horner, Strong again turned detective, hoping to nail the gang before Horner killed him. He traced Joe and George Horner and Bill Redding to Comanche, the seat of Comanche County. On the morning of January 10, 1876, he was concealed in the alley behind the H. R. Martin bank of Comanche watching the Horner brothers and Redding hitch their horses in the alley and enter the bank.

Inside were the cashier, Charles B. Mason, and the bookkeeper, K. E. Hoy. One of the three men approached Mason and requested change for a large-denomination bill. As the cashier turned to the safe, the men suddenly leaped over the counter. Two leveled revolvers at Mason and Hoy, while the third cleaned out the safe, taking about fifty-five hundred dollars in cash. The robbers then herded the bank employees out the back door at gunpoint.

Strong saw Mason and Hoy, their hands raised, exiting the building. Horner and his companions followed, brandishing pistols. Strong ducked behind a building, watching as the three mounted their horses and said, "Now squeal if you want to." Then they released their hostages, put spurs to their horses, and galloped off. "Charge this to the James Boys," one of them yelled. As Mason and Hoy, shouting the alarm, rushed back to the bank, Strong went around to the front. People were excitedly converging on the bank. Among them Strong recognized Boss Green, the Comanche town marshal. "I told Boss Green that I knew the robbers well," said Strong, "and that if a half dozen good men would go with me we could catch them."[60]

At the head of a hastily gathered posse, the veteran government scout tracked the bandits south almost two hundred miles but lost the trail near San Antonio. The men in the posse returned to Comanche, but Strong stayed on, hoping for a new lead. He contacted the Bexar County officers and provided full descriptions of the men and their horses. He identified the three as Joe Horner, Tom Wagman, and Bill Redding. Actually, "Tom Wagman" was another alias of Redding's.[61]

As he suspected, the bank robbers had remained in the area and were camped two miles west of the city near the Castroville road. Newspapers later reported that the men visited the town frequently, spending "several hundreds of dollars [in] the shooting galleries and other places of amusement."[62]

On the morning of February 2 Joe Horner rode into San Antonio and tied his horse just off Main Plaza. He visited several stores including a gun shop where he reportedly inquired about having a steel breastplate made.[63] While he was gone, two sheriff's deputies, Thomas P. McCall and Fred Bader, spotted the horse, which matched the description furnished by Strong, and waited nearby for the owner's return. When Horner came back and prepared to mount, the deputies closed in. The arrest was dramatically described in the pages of the San Antonio Daily Express: "Just as [Horner] was placing the bridle reins over the horses's head . . . , both sprang at him, each seizing him firmly by one arm, and at the same time presenting a cocked pistol. Horner then [shouted] 'stand back,' while he attempted to draw a revolver [from] his bosom. But the deputies had him—he could not help himself. When he found that all hope of escape was gone, he showed evidences of brutal rage,

The Main Plaza, San Antonio, as it looked at about the time the Horner brothers were arrested there. *Courtesy Western History Collections, University of Oklahoma.*

gritting his teeth like a mad boar. They promptly relieved him of his arms, and escorted him to the county jail."[64] The evidence against Horner was powerful. He and his horse fit descriptions provided by bank robbery eyewitness Henry Strong. Included in the $147.50 found in his pockets was a one-hundred-dollar bill whose number matched that of one stolen from the Comanche bank.

On the afternoon of the same day, officers spotted George Horner, who also fit Strong's description of one of the robbers. He was mounted when Sheriff Dan Bonnett and Deputies McCall, Bader, and Andrew Bonnett approached. One of the deputies walked up and extended his right hand in greeting. George took it, and the officer held him "in a firm and unrelinquishing grip." Then "three six-shooters, in the hands of the Sheriff and his other two deputies, covered the man on horseback." When told he was under arrest, George "made an effort to get his revolver. . . . One of the deputies near by told him to draw back, or he would kill him. . . . He made no further efforts to protect himself. The Sheriff then took his revolver from him, whereupon the man remarked that this was a h——ll of a town, not to give a man a chance to fight. The Sheriff responded that elections cost too much here to have one every six months."[65] George insolently gave his name as "Treedle" to the arresting officers. Only later did they learn his true identity. When searched, he was found to have $980 in currency and $102.50 in gold. Several of the bills were from the Comanche bank.

Redding was seen in town after dark that evening but slipped away before he could be arrested. He quickly departed the San Antonio area, taking with him a fine horse belonging to a man named George Schroeder. Alerts went out to officers throughout the region, and within a month Redding was nabbed at Lockhart. Arrested as "Louis Johnson," he was brought back to San Antonio by Deputies Bader and Bonnett and placed in the Bexar County jail, where "he was warmly greeted by the Comanche bank robbers, the Horners, of whom he appeared to be an old friend."[66] It was soon learned that "Louis Johnson" was William Z. Redding, alias Tom Wagman, alias John Wagner, the third suspect in the Comanche bank robbery case. On March 1 all three suspects were indicted in Comanche County on bank robbery charges, and bail was set at twenty-five hundred dollars each.[67]

Frontier Echo Editor G. W. Robson in Jacksboro reported the arrests with no surprise. The Horner brothers, he said, were "desperate characters, well known to our people," and Joe was the "unmoving spirit in the Comanche bank robbery." A month later the paper printed a rumor that a party of masked men had taken the Horner brothers from the Comanche County sheriff as they were being transferred to Comanche for trial and had hanged them on a black oak tree. "Needs confirmation," Robson added ruefully.[68] In the absence of Joe Horner, the six cases against him on the February docket of the district court at Jacksboro were continued. Eventually all charges against him were dropped in Jack County, with the exception of Cause No. 327, the assault on Ed Harris, for which he was convicted in absentia. He was fined one hundred dollars, and his bond was forfeited.[69]

Officers took Bill Redding to Austin and confined him in the Travis County lockup to answer murder charges pending against him in Llano County. On September 14, 1876, with T. S. Redding and A. H. Murchison acting as his sureties, he made the twenty-five-hundred-dollar Comanche County bail and walked out of jail. When he failed to appear for trial on the twenty-seventh, his bond was forfeited and warrants were issued for him and his bondsmen. Comanche County officials were still looking for them nine years later.[70] Bill Redding became a major participant in the Hoodoo war raging in Mason County in the 1870s. He climbed high on the list of the state's most sought-after criminals; the Texas fugitive list for 1878 showed him as wanted in Comanche County on the bank robbery charge, in Lampasas County for aiding prisoners to escape, and in Llano County for cattle theft and related charges. He was described as about thirty years old and six feet tall, with a slender build, a light complexion, light hair, blue eyes, and a light, thin beard. As late as 1886 he was still wanted in Lampasas County for jailbreaking and

San Saba County on charges of cattle theft. He never went to trial for the Comanche bank robbery.[71]

For more than a year the Horner brothers languished in the "Bat Cave," a large, two-story, stone building on Military Plaza that housed the Bexar County courthouse and jail, while their attorney, Leslie Thompson of the San Antonio law firm of Teal and Thompson, sought to develop some kind of defense. During this period, activities of a criminal group identified in the press as "the Horner Gang" continued in northern Texas. Citizens of the region were greatly alarmed in February when a gang stormed into Fort Griffin with pistols ablaze, so frightening the government telegraph operator that he could not provide a coherent account of the affair, other than "he heard bullets whistle, and dropped flat on the floor for his own safety." The outlaws raided the government arsenal, making off with carbines, revolvers, and ammunition. "They are supposed to be the Horner gang," said the dispatch, "taking this method of arming themselves for committing further depredations."[72] The raid reminded one San Antonio newspaperman of the Civil War: "Two of the Horner brothers are in our county jail, charged with robbing a bank in Comanche county, and it will doubtless cheer them up to hear that the boys are doing so well, and amusing themselves so much. But this attacking the forts and arsenals of the United States once led to a serious internecine struggle, and the Horner boys are liable to be involved in complications if it is kept up. They have not got out of the Comanche bank scrape yet."[73]

Joe Watson, a member of the Horner Gang, took up with Mrs. Wolf, a notorious Jacksboro prostitute, who then became known as Sally Watson. In April 1876 the gang's old enemy, Henry Strong, helped to bring Watson's criminal career to an abrupt end. After the theft of some horses near Fort Griffin, a party that included Strong, Shackelford County Sheriff John M. Larn, cattleman J. M. Matthews, Lieutenant Edward P. Turner, and several Tonkawa scouts trailed the thieves to a location on Stinking Creek. In a sharp gunfight, Watson and two others, identified only as "Reddy" and "Larapie Dan," were wounded and captured. Sally Watson and a buffalo hunter who had camped with the horse thieves were taken into custody, but the posse wasted no time on Joe Watson, Reddy, and Larapie Dan. The men tied ropes around their necks and strung them to trees on the spot. News of the lynching was greeted in Jacksboro with "much rejoicing among the good citizens," according to the *Frontier Echo,* "as the men were notorious desperadoes and the country is better off without than with them." A letter from a Fort Griffin correspondent to the *Fort Worth Democrat* echoed this opinion: "Watson was a noted desperado here and at Jacksboro; and the community feels relieved at the assurance that his pistol shots and yells will no more be heard in our streets."[74]

On March 15, 1877, Joe Horner finally went to trial in the district court
at San Antonio for the Comanche bank robbery. The indictment, which identified many of the bills taken in the robbery by the issuing bank and serial
number, was eight pages long.[75] Judge George Henry Noonan presided, the
prosecution was led by M. J. ("Mack") Anderson, and Henry Strong was
chief witness for the state. According to the *San Antonio Daily Express:*
"[The defendant] scarcely looks the daring desperado he has proven himself
to be. He listened to the proceedings of the trial and heard the verdict pronounced with the most stolid indifference." That verdict was reached by the
jury after only twenty-five minutes of deliberation. Horner was convicted
and was sentenced to ten years of hard labor at the state penitentiary. He
remained in the Bat Cave as his attorney filed appeals.[76]

The following day San Antonio prosecutors entered a nolle prosequi in
the case against George Horner, but Comanche County officers appeared
with a capias and escorted George to Comanche for trial. The jail there was
insecure, and George was transferred to the lockup at Austin in Travis County.
This jail, described as "a series of iron cages, dark and poorly ventilated,"
where the prisoners dripped sweat in the summer heat and, lacking beds,
"slept on quilt pallets on the sheet-iron floor," housed from sixty to ninety
prisoners, including some of the most notorious Texas criminals and feud-
ists of the turbulent 1870s.[77]

In July, George was returned to Comanche, and his case was scheduled
for the September session of court. His attorneys, W. J. S. Adams and G. R.
Hart, requested a bail bond reduction and a continuance on the grounds that
certain defense witnesses had not been located. Both requests were granted.
Trial was rescheduled for March 1878, and bond was reduced to one thousand dollars. George's brother Wes Horner, his brother-in-law P. C. Sams,
and his attorneys Adams and Hart signed the bond, and for the first time in
twenty months George was released from custody.

The following spring his attorneys requested court attachments for a
number of defense witnesses, one of whom, surprisingly, was Henry Strong,
the man most responsible for the breakup of the Horner gang. Served with
the papers at Cambridge, Texas, Strong wrote Judge J. R. Fleming of the
district court at Comanche:

> As I was the means of the Commanche bank robers [sic] being
> arrested, I believe the attachments are issued for the sole purpose of
> killing me. They . . . have repeatedly threatened my life and have
> shot at me nine times since the 23rd day of June 1874. Two of the
> Horner boys came here to this county with an attachment and tried
> to get the sheriff of this county to turn me over to them. . . . I was
> forced . . . to kill a bosom friend of theirs and the Horner party have

Horner's second escape was from the Bat Cave in San Antonio. *Courtesy Western History Collections, University of Oklahoma.*

sworn to kill me. I believe for me to come to Commanche would be certain death at their hands. . . . I know of no possible good that I could do the defendant.[78]

A series of court continuances delayed George's case until October 1879, more than three and a half years after the original indictment. Prosecutors finally gave up and recommended that the case be retired from the docket.[79]

While George Horner fought his legal battle, brother Joe had battles of his own. His attorneys filed the usual appeals after his conviction in March 1877, but Joe, still confined in the old Bat Cave in San Antonio, had little hope for their success. Even before his sentencing he was laboring to escape. Somehow he obtained a case knife and worked sawteeth into its blade. He and three other prisoners sawed through the two-inch oak planking lining their cell, removed a section large enough for the passage of a man's body, and went to work on the stone wall beyond. They hid debris from each night's work under a blanket in a corner and concealed evidence of their work with a mixture of soap and sand. Using the same makeshift saw blade, they also cut their leg-irons almost through.

Only two weeks after his trial, Horner was ready to go. With his cellmates—a black man named Perry Upson, jailed on a minor theft offense, Bob Peel, a convicted rapist, and Charles Brown, an accused horse thief—he made his bid for freedom on the night of Sunday, April 1. Breaking free from their shackles, they pushed out the last rocks in the wall and squeezed through the opening. Upson, the tallest and strongest, boosted the others to the top of the outer wall. A blanket and pants had been knotted together for the purpose of pulling Upson up, but once on top, the three escapees dropped to the ground beyond the wall, leaving Upson standing in the yard. A passerby saw the breakout, sounded an alarm, and soon officers, blowing shrill whistles, converged on the area. The escapees ran to Erastus Reed's livery stable nearby, quickly saddled horses, and galloped off into the night.[80]

Horner disappeared for a couple of weeks, and officers believed he had taken "a straight shute for Mexico."[81] Then, in the early hours of April 17, he appeared with an accomplice near Blanco Creek in Uvalde County and stopped the eastbound stage going from Eagle Pass to Castroville. A heavy rain was falling as Horner and his companion, brandishing revolvers, rode up to the coach and signaled the driver, Henry Green, to stop. One guarded the driver while the other pulled back the window curtains of the coach, announced that a holdup was in progress, and ordered the passengers out. John Melifont of Fort Clark, E. W. Cole of New York, and an army sergeant named Sullivant obeyed. From Melifont the bandits took eighty dollars in gold coins and currency and a pistol valued at seven dollars. They permitted the others to keep the small pocket change they carried and returned a small pistol and silver watch to Cole. The frightened passengers fumbled nervously with their belongings. Cole dropped a knife to the ground, and some small coins slipped through Melifont's fingers. Melifont stooped to pick up the silver, and one of the robbers, covering everyone with a brace of pistols as his partner collected the loot, instantly fired a shot, narrowly missing the man's head and plowing up mud between his feet. The robber explained to the terrified passenger that he had thought Melifont was reaching for the knife. Described as "very tall, probably over six feet in height, [with] dark hair, eyes, and complexion," the gunman was probably Joe Horner, whose slender build made him appear taller than his height of just under six feet. After finishing their work, the road agents waved the stagecoach on. Mounting a pair of fine horses, a dark brown one and a bright sorrel, and leading another pony, they vanished into the darkness. Soon afterward they cut the telegraph wires, an old trick of Horner's.[82]

The *San Antonio Daily Express* announced on April 19, "It is almost certain that Joe Horner, who escaped from our jail a short time ago, was one of the robbers, and that they rode the horses stolen from Mr. Erastus Reed the night of the jail delivery." Later that day San Antonio received additional news: Horner and his companion, later identified as Jim Jones, alias Williams, had been recognized in Uvalde County, and Horner had been captured.

This "sent a thrill of joy to the hearts of the Sheriff and his corps [and] they wanted to ring the big bell and sound aloud the tom-tom."[83]

Ironically, Horner was brought to bay by a local unit of minutemen, the volunteer guardians of the peace to which he had once belonged. Five Uvalde County minutemen—Captain J. J. H. Patterson,[84] Henry Patterson, W. B. Nichols, Tom Leakey, and John Collins—had closed in on Horner and Jones and engaged them in a lively firefight. The minutemen reportedly fired forty shots, but no one was hit. "Horner and his companion fought as long as they could," said a news dispatch, but Horner finally surrendered as Jones "made his escape amid a perfect shower of bullets." The minutemen also recovered Reed's stolen horses and captured Horner's weapons, a rifle and two six-shooters.[85]

Authorities took Joe Horner to Uvalde and gave him a speedy trial for the stage holdup. On April 23, four days after his capture and only six days after the crime, he was indicted for robbery in the court of the Twenty-Fourth Judicial District. He entered a guilty plea before Judge Thomas M. Paschal and was tried and convicted on the same day. The jury sentenced him to ten years' imprisonment, the time to run concurrently with the ten years already imposed on him in Bexar County.[86]

Four days later Horner also pleaded guilty to the charge of "breaking telegraph wire" after the holdup. "You will assess his penalty," Judge Paschal instructed the jury, "at imprisonment for a term not to exceed five years or for any period less than that, or you may fine him not less than one hundred dollars nor more than two thousand dollars." The jury apparently felt that Horner had been adequately punished already; it sentenced him to only one additional day in the penitentiary.[87]

On April 30 Horner made another effort to escape. He managed to cut his shackles with an old razor, but guards discovered the attempt before he could proceed further.[88] Judge Paschal, recognizing Horner's notoriety, ordered special precautions for transfer of the prisoner: "It appearing to the Court that there is danger of rescuing the Defendant Joe Horner from the custody of the Sheriff of Uvalde County while conveying him to the Penitentiary at Huntsville, it is ordered that he be allowed a guard of three men to convey him from Uvalde to San Antonio and from San Antonio to Huntsville he be allowed a guard of two."[89]

Uvalde County Sheriff George P. Johnson and two deputies took Horner to San Antonio for formal sentencing by Judge Noonan in the bank robbery case. The same officers escorted the prisoner to Huntsville Penitentiary, where jailers received him on May 5, 1877. Sheriff Johnson later told reporters that Horner expressed no remorse for his crimes but boasted of his exploits. He was already planning an escape and a criminal future, hinting that a return visit to San Antonio might be profitable, for with "two good men" he could "clean out any bank" there.[90]

At Huntsville, Horner was assigned inmate number 5920. For the records he said he had been born in Indiana, was twenty-seven years old, was unmarried, and had a "common" education. His habits were "intemperate," and he used tobacco. Physically he was five feet, eleven and a half inches tall and weighed 138 pounds. He was fair-complected, with blue eyes and light hair, and had no scars, marks, or tattoos.[91]

Horner entered the penitentiary at a critical time in the history of the Texas prison system. The prison at Huntsville, almost thirty years old in 1877, had been operated under a lease arrangement with a private contractor for the previous six years. Under the terms of the arrangement, the contractor received whatever benefits accrued from the prison labor in return for paying the state a specified monthly amount per inmate and agreeing to feed, clothe, and guard the convicts. With the great influx of immigrants into Texas following the Civil War, the chaotic conditions under the despised Reconstruction government, and the lawlessness of the 1870s, the prison population had exploded. In 1860 there were 182 inmates at Huntsville; when Horner entered in the spring of 1877, there were 1,588.[92] In 1876 the prison lessees, Ward, Dewey, and Company, came under severe criticism in the newspapers and in Austin. The firm was accused of gross mismanagement and of brutal treatment of inmates. In August 1876 the Texas legislature abrogated the Dewey-Ward contract, to become effective as soon as an interim contractor could be found. On April 2, 1877, only a month before the prison gates slammed shut on Horner, the Galveston firm of Burnett and Kilpatrick took over the lease on a temporary basis.[93]

Under a law enacted by the Texas legislature in 1866, prisoners were divided for work purposes into two categories. "First-class" prisoners, those convicted of murder, arson, rape, horse stealing, burglary, perjury, or robbery, were to be kept confined within the prison walls; "second-class" convicts, serving time for lesser crimes, could be employed on "works of public utility" outside the prison.[94] Horner, of course, qualified as "first-class" and was put to work in one of the prison industries, which included furniture, wheelwright, and shoe and harness shops and a mill for the production of cotton and woolen cloth.

Under the temporary lessees, Burnett and Kilpatrick, and later under the firm of Cunningham and Ellis, which was awarded a five-year contract to manage the prison beginning January 1, 1878, conditions improved for the inmates, but punishment for intractable convicts still included the stocks, the dark cell, the ball and chain, and whipping. The notorious gunman John Wesley Hardin, who entered Huntsville on October 5, 1878, was an incorrigible prisoner and later wrote graphically of the brutal whippings he received.[95]

The Sixteenth Texas Legislature in March 1879 amended the state penal code and enacted new legislation designed to reform the prison system. One of the new provisions discarded the former "first-class" and "second-class" prisoner distinction for work assignments within or outside the walls and allowed the superintendent and directors to establish the rules for those assignments. It was decided that all inmates could be used on outside work details except those with over fifteen years to serve, those with special work skills required in the prison shops, those considered "notoriously bad," and those considered physically unfit for outside labor.[96]

For Joe Horner, who had less than fifteen years to serve and had no special skills or infirmities, this policy change meant that he could now be reassigned to an outside labor gang, as long as he was not branded "notoriously bad." Horner's life up to this point had been characterized by recklessness and arrogance. Perhaps, like Wes Hardin, in his first months of incarceration he defied the prison officials and spent time in the dark hole, the stocks, and the whipping blocks. No record of his prison behavior has survived, and he never wrote of his imprisonment later, but clearly, at some point the harsh reality of prison life sobered him and caused him to consider deeply the direction his life had taken.

Horner greatly respected power and those who wielded it. He had tried to exert his own power as an outlaw but had failed because, even on the unstable frontiers of Texas, the law and its enforcers were powerful enough to strike him down. At some point during his incarceration he decided to take a different path. He resolved that once he regained his freedom, he would ally himself with the powerful instead of defying them. He would take a new name and go to a new land and, by making himself useful to those who wielded power, would be protected by them and perhaps acquire some of that power for himself.

But first he had to free himself from the prison that held him. The thought of escape, foremost in his mind when he entered Huntsville, had never left.[97] Horner knew that a breakout from within the walls would be very difficult but that chances of escape while on an outside work detail were much better. Under the provisions of the new policy, if he behaved himself, he could get an outside assignment and a shot at freedom and the new life he envisioned. He was careful not to be deemed "notoriously bad."

By mid-1879 more than 80 percent of Huntsville convicts were working outside the walls. Only three hundred of the total prison population of seventeen hundred remained inside. The prison lessees contracted out the others as laborers on sugar and cotton plantations or assigned them to railroad

construction or wood-chopping gangs.[98] But this arrangement was temporary; a new law stipulated that by January 1, 1880, "or as soon thereafter as
possible," all prisoners should be behind walls.[99]

Horner, who in the summer of 1879 was working on one of the outside
gangs, knew that he would never have a better opportunity to escape. Time
was running out. Of course, the prison officials were aware of the potential
for escape presented by working the prisoners outside, especially at remote
lumber camps or railroad grading sites. The major objection to continuing
the practice, Prison Superintendent Thomas J. Goree said in his 1878 bien-
nial report, was "the temptation offered to convicts to escape, and the great
number of escapes" that occurred. He recommended that white prisoners
working at isolated locations be fitted with the "spur," a tight-fitting iron
collar riveted around the ankle. Sharp prongs that pointed down toward the
foot permitted the wearer to work or walk slowly but prevented running.[100]

On August 4, 1879, Joe Horner disappeared from one of these work gangs.
His escape went unnoticed in the press, and details, other than the date, were
not recorded in the prison files. Stories circulated years later that his "escape" had been arranged with prison officials by people of influence in Texas.[101]
Perhaps this was true. Newspapers that had previously printed every rumor
of a Horner escape were strangely silent when he actually took flight. Stranger
still, in 1886 the adjutant general's office of the state of Texas published a list
purporting to enumerate every escaped convict from the Texas state penitentiaries from the beginning of the system. The list contained names, numbers, and descriptions of 1,752 escapees, but Joe Horner was not included.[102]

In a sense Joe Horner died in August 1879. The desperado and outlaw
disappeared, not only from the Texas penal system but from the earth itself.
The man who had murdered him, a man calling himself Frank M. Canton,
would spend the remainder of his days trying to eradicate the memory of
Joe Horner forever.

Part Two

The Wyoming Years

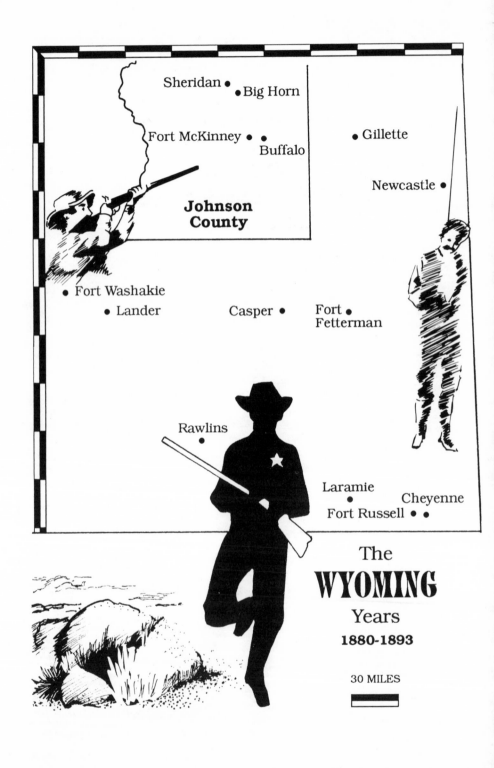

Sheridan • • Big Horn

Fort McKinney • • Buffalo

• Gillette

Newcastle •

Johnson County

• Fort Washakie

• Lander   Casper •   Fort • Fetterman

Rawlins •

Laramie •   Cheyenne

Fort Russell • •

The
WYOMING
Years
1880-1893

30 MILES

Chapter 3

The Sheriff, 1880-1886

"Johnson County at that time had a good sheriff, Frank Canton, who was by far the best sheriff the county ever had up to that time."

Joe LeFors, *Wyoming Peace Officer*

It is not known how or why Canton chose the name he assumed. Perhaps he reversed the name of his friend Milton Franklin Lake to come up with "Frank M." He may have taken his last name from the town of Canton in Van Zandt County, Texas, or he may simply have liked the sound of it. He never used a full middle name, only the initial, but his widow reported it as "Melvin" at his death.[1]

In his memoirs Canton never indicated that he had lived the first thirty years of his life under another name. There were many falsehoods in that account, both of omission and of commission, for, like most liars, he found that one lie begets another. To explain his departure from Texas, he wrote: "By the year 1878, Texas was comparatively quiet, too quiet to suit me, so I decided to try the Northwest territory once more. I had had a desire to return to that country ever since I had gone north with Burk Burnett in sixty-nine."[2]

He said he left in the early summer of 1878 in charge of a herd of twenty-five hundred cattle bound for Ogallala, Nebraska. To establish the year as 1878, he described an encounter with the Dull Knife band of Northern Cheyenne Indians who left their Indian Territory reservation in September of that year. But Frank Canton personally saw no part of the Dull Knife Raid, as it was called, for during the entire year of 1878 he was still in the clutches of the Texas penal system.

Following his escape in August 1879, Canton went north and may even have worked as a trail herder part of the way. But August was late in the year to start a herd north from Texas. It is more likely that after his escape, he put a thousand miles between himself and Huntsville as quickly as possible. Once he felt safe in Wyoming, he may have joined an outfit moving a herd of longhorns into Montana.

Canton claimed that at Ogallala he was hired by the Wyoming Stock Raisers Association as field inspector and was assigned to the Yellowstone River country of Montana.[3] He said he went to Miles City, where he was also appointed a deputy sheriff by Custer County Sheriff Thomas H. Irvine. It was in this capacity, he said, that he accompanied Montana Stock Growers Association Detective W. D. Smith into the Crow Indian reservation to bring back two Indians charged with killing cattle and selling the beef for elk meat.[4] If this happened, it was the first of innumerable similar arrests Canton would make over the next forty years. But records in Wyoming and Montana do not confirm his employment either as a stock inspector or as a deputy sheriff at this time.[5]

Canton in late 1879 and early 1880 was working as a cowboy. But even as he punched cattle at thirty-five dollars a month, the determination he had formed at Huntsville to align himself with those who held the levers of power took shape. Soon after his arrival on the northern ranges he grasped every opportunity to seek out and ingratiate himself with the important cattlemen of the region, men like twenty-eight-year-old, English-born Moreton Frewen, manager of the huge Powder River Cattle Company. He also cultivated the friendship of well-known lawmen: Tom Irvine, of Miles City; Sheriff John J. Healy, of Chouteau County, Montana; Thomas Jefferson Carr, city marshal of Cheyenne; and Sheriff Nathaniel K. Boswell, of Laramie.

In 1880 Canton was in Colorado, cowboying for rancher Sie Doty on the South Platte River. The next spring he helped drive a herd to the Y Cross, OW, and Goldie Ranches in Wyoming. While working roundups in the Cheyenne area he met Charles Warren Bard, a young Minnesotan who had recently arrived on the cattle ranges and who was employed as roundup cook. Bard later remembered that Canton joined the roundup with no bedroll and that the two shared a bed. Canton then worked as a drover stocking the ranges of Hackney, Holt, and Williams on Crazy Woman Creek in Johnson County.[6]

In 1875 the Fourth Legislative Assembly of Wyoming had created Johnson County, a huge area extending east of the Bighorn River to beyond the Powder and from the Montana line on the north to the southern reaches of the Rattlesnake Mountains. The county was organized in May 1881, and the town of Buffalo, near Fort McKinney, became the seat.[7]

As more ranches were established in the county and more cattle brought in, it became apparent to the officers of the Wyoming Stock Growers Association (WSGA), based in Cheyenne, that they needed a man in Johnson County to look after the interests of their expanding membership there. In August 1881 Canton's contacts with the big ranchers and lawmen of Wyoming and Montana bore fruit. He was called to Cheyenne and interviewed by Thomas Sturgis, secretary of the WSGA. It was plain that Canton knew the cattle industry and a great deal about the methods and practices of rustlers and outlaws. Sturgis did not inquire into how he had acquired that knowledge. Most of the cowboys of Wyoming were Texans, and many had come north after scrapes with the law. Sturgis was not concerned with past history; he was looking for a man who was range-wise, resourceful, aggressive, and above all, loyal to his employers. Sturgis found Canton to be "quick and active in his movements, with light hair, blue eyes that were always looking at you and good, clean-cut features. In manners he was exceedingly quiet and unassuming, with a low, distinct voice that [was] never heard raised above an ordinary conversational tone. There was no limit, however, to his nerve, even if his ways were modest."[8] Impressed, Secretary Sturgis employed Canton on August 22, 1881.

As a WSGA inspector, Canton was expected to move around the county and keep an eye out for any signs of rustling activity, to assist in the settling of ownership disputes at roundups, and to verify ownership of cattle at shipping points. For this he was to receive a salary of ninety dollars a month, half to be paid by the county and half by the association. When he attempted to bill the WSGA for his expenses soon after he started, Sturgis reproached him gently: "The understanding with the principal stockmen about Powder River, when you were sent up there, was that the board of yourself and horse should be borne by the various ranches wherever you might be working. It is not expected that you will be constantly in one place."[9]

To cover his territory, Canton certainly had to keep on the move. His range extended "from Fetterman to the Montana line, from the Little and Upper End of the Belle Fourche on the east, and to the Tongue River on the west."[10] It was wild country, sparsely populated and full of game. For Canton, "it was the best rendezvous for outlaws" that he had ever seen, "and they were there, plenty of them."[11]

Moreton Frewen and other ranchers of the area formed the Johnson County Stock Growers Association, an affiliate of the WSGA, in November 1881. Friction developed between some of the smaller cattlemen and Frewen during the organizational meetings, and Canton made sure his loyalty to Frewen and the WSGA was recognized. "A certain cattle man of this county told me that if I worked for Frewen's interests the other stock men would have nothing to do with me," he wrote Sturgis. "I informed him that I was working under instructions of the Cheyenne Association and supposed for stock men generally and would ride as far for Frewen's cows as any one elses unless ordered not to do so."[12]

As an association inspector, Canton was expected to obtain an appointment as deputy sheriff to enable him to make arrests. The first sheriff of Johnson County, Nat James, was elected in April 1881. His chief deputy was a crony named Tom Farrell. Both were former Frewen cowboys—good, well-meaning fellows but ineffective. As one Buffalo resident put it: "The high life in our little adolescent city was altogether too much for both Nat and Tom. The County Commissioners could not put them out of office so they put in Frank Canton as deputy sheriff and stock inspector. He called to him a little sawed off Texan of the name of Jim Enochs, and they hung a man or two and then things settled down nice and quiet."[13]

Deputy Sheriffs Canton and Enochs hanged no one, but Canton assumed much of the responsibility of the sheriff's office during the remaining year of James's term. For example, when Dr. Samuel Phillips, the father of a young man murdered in the county, came to Buffalo to verify the identity of the victim, it was Deputy Canton who received him. "I took him to the grave of the murdered man," Canton reported. "We dug him up and the Dr. recognized the remains without a doubt as being that of his son."[14]

In his autobiography, Canton claimed that also at this time he "secured four hundred and eighty acres of land twelve miles southwest of Buffalo at the foot of the Big Horn Mountains and commenced farming and stock raising."[15] The homestead actually came later, but on December 12, 1881, he registered his own horse brand, a circle on the right shoulder.[16]

Canton's efforts in behalf of the big cattlemen were quickly appreciated. In early 1882 the executive committee of the Johnson County Stock Growers Association requested that the WSGA and the county commissioners raise his salary to $150 a month. W. D. Smith, the Montana cattle detective, was now in Wyoming, and his appointment as stock inspector in Johnson County at the same salary was also requested. Both requests were approved.[17]

The ranchers urged Canton to run for sheriff in the forthcoming elections. He accepted but noted in a letter to Sturgis, "I expect to have a very heavy race to run, as my opponent is a granger and that element has the majority in this county." Despite the opposition of the farmers, or "grangers" as they were called, on November 7, 1882, Canton was elected to a two-year term. The election was contested but was finally decided in his favor.[18]

When he took office, Canton was required to resign his position as stock inspector, but his outstanding work was officially recognized in a resolution that was proposed by WSGA attorney Charles W. Wright and that was unanimously adopted at the association's annual meeting in Cheyenne in April 1883: "Resolved, that we, the Wyoming Stock Growers Association, desire

The handsome young sheriff of Johnson County, Wyoming, Frank M. Canton. *Courtesy Western History Collections, University of Oklahoma.*

hereby publicly to express our appreciation of, and thanks for, the valuable aid and assistance rendered to every stock grower in Wyoming by the Honorable F. M. Canton, Sheriff of Johnson County, in pursuit and capture of persons charged with the violation of the criminal laws of the Territory."[19] As he basked in that fulsome praise and the title "Honorable," an appellation never attached to the name Joe Horner, Canton also took comfort in the sizable salary increase he received; as sheriff, he would be paid $250 a month.[20]

Having some personal experience regarding jail security and the lack thereof, he quickly moved to improve the county lockup. At his insistence the county commissioners approved the erection of a stockade around the building. Constructed of pointed eight-inch logs, sixteen feet in length, and implanted in a four-foot trench, the wall was set back ten feet from the building. Sheriff Canton also purchased two pairs of handcuffs and two pairs of shackles. Later in the year he installed in the jail "two steel cages of the most approved pattern," eight feet wide, eleven feet long, and seven feet in height.[21]

Despite these improvements, preventing prisoner escapes required the constant vigil of guards. "Sheriff Canton and his men never seem to sleep," wrote a Buffalo correspondent to the *Laramie Boomerang.* "There have been no escapes from our apology for a jail this winter."[22]

Charley Bard, who had shared his bedroll with Canton in 1881, was living with his wife and two young sons, Floyd and Tode, near the courthouse in Buffalo at this time. Floyd was only about four, but he remembered Canton well, for the tall sheriff frightened him so. "One day as Tode and I were playing alongside the jail, digging in the sand by the foundation, along came Canton," Bard recalled. "He sure looked mad. He said, 'If you boys don't quit that digging, I'm going to put you both in jail.' After that we were both scared of Canton."[23]

Among Canton's deputies during his term of office were the "little sawed off Texan," Jim Enochs, and W. D. Smith, the stock inspector. Others included Tom Adams, H. A. Bennett, G. G. Hopkins, Chris Gross, Ed Lloyd, and Tom Farrell, as well as J. H. Drummond, who served as jailer, and Charles H. Burritt, a lawyer and later the mayor of Buffalo. Canton appointed John A. McDermott, "an excellent clerical man and a brave and loyal officer," as undersheriff.[24]

McDermott was a shrewd choice as an office man to handle paperwork and details, but he was not a man of action like Canton. A story illustrating this was told for years around Buffalo. One day in the early 1880s McDermott was in the lobby of the Occidental Hotel when the undersheriff noticed that the liveryman across the street was backed against the wall with his hands raised. A man held him at gunpoint. McDermott crossed the street to investigate and soon found himself, hands in the air, up against the wall with the liveryman. Just then Sheriff Canton happened by. Slipping his right hand into his coat pocket, Canton walked straight up to the gunman and ordered him to hand over his pistol. One glance at the face of the sheriff convinced the holdup man he had better comply, and he meekly gave up the weapon.[25] The incident was embarrassing for McDermott, and he was ribbed about it for years, but he proved to be an efficient officer and later served as U.S. marshal for the state of Wyoming and as sheriff of Converse County.[26] It also was a good example of how Canton was able to intimidate men with a look. "When Canton got his steel gray eye on a man that settled it," said one Johnson County pioneer. "Sheriff Canton rules the boys that 'turn themselves loose' with an iron hand, and it carries a lot of weight," agreed the *Laramie Daily Sentinel.*[27]

Although Canton was making more money than he had ever made before, he had little to show for it. The Johnson County tax assessment rolls for 1883 listed him as single and living in Buffalo, with $275 in assets, con-

Buffalo, Wyoming, on Clear Creek, as it looked when Canton was sheriff there. *Courtesy American Heritage Center, University of Wyoming.*

sisting of two horses valued at $175, clocks, watches, and jewelry valued at $75, and $25 in other property.[28]

Sheriff Canton's first notable arrests were made in the winter of 1883–84, when he took in Jim Baker and Tee Haines, two members of the E. O. Stewart horse-stealing gang. Canton and a deputy trailed the thieves for weeks before catching up with them at a remote ranch in the Black Hills of Dakota Territory. The outlaws fled when the officers entered the house. "The mercury stood at 40 degrees below zero," Canton said. "We followed them and found them pretty well frozen and captured them without resistance."[29] The *Cheyenne Daily Leader* announced the arrests, reporting that Haines and Baker were charged with stealing seventy head of horses from the Little Venture Cattle Company on Powder River the previous summer.[30] Canton and J. M. Enochs testified against gang leader E. O. "Eb" Stewart when he was tried for cattle theft at Cheyenne in November 1884, but he beat that charge. In September 1885, Stewart was included by the WSGA on a blacklist of thieves believed to be operating in Johnson County.[31]

"During those days," Canton later wrote, "the worst criminals we had to deal with were the stage robbers, or road agents, as they were called in that country."[32] The leader of the highwaymen was George Francis Warden, alias Big Nose George Parrott, who was notorious in the region before Canton came north. Captured at Miles City, Montana, on July 19, 1880, Parrott was taken to southern Wyoming by Carbon County Sheriff M. Wilson Rankin. He was tried for the murders of two men, convicted, and sentenced to death, but on March 22, 1881, before the law could hang him, a mob took him from the jail at Rawlins and lynched him.[33] Canton claimed no role in the demise of Big Nose George, but he did say in his autobiography that "shortly after" the death of the bandit leader, he captured "the notorious stage robber, Bill Brown, and his partner."[34] Actually, Brown was arrested by Canton in January 1891, ten years after Big Nose George died.[35]

In an 1885 interview, Canton said that the capture of a horse thief named Alonzo Edenfield was his most difficult arrest up to that time. Members of the Edenfield gang stole six horses from Canton's former employers, Hackney, Holt, and Williams, on Crazy Woman Creek in 1883. Canton, riding alone, later came on Edenfield at a place called the "Nine Mile Water Holes." The outlaw's horse was jaded, and Edenfield was attempting to steal a replacement when Canton appeared. Edenfield resisted, and to make the arrest, Canton "almost had to kill him," but the sheriff finally got the outlaw's feet tied beneath his horse's belly and brought him in. Later Canton and his deputies rounded up two other gang members, Joseph Walters and John Henry Muldoon. After their conviction for horse theft in July 1884, Sheriff Canton conveyed them to the prison at Joliet, Illinois.[36]

Canton was building a reputation as a resourceful and relentless pursuer of criminals. The *Big Horn Sentinel* of September 27, 1884, noted his arrival in town in search of thieves who had stolen some horses and mules belonging to a rancher named Hyatt near Buffalo. "The sheriff has sent one party in the direction [of Billings, Montana] and another towards Deadwood, and is himself on the lookout for the thieves," the paper reported. "It is very likely that they will be overhauled, as Sheriff Canton is not much of a man to 'monkey' with them when he gets started." Jack Knight and Harry Arable were arrested a week or so later by Deputy Sheriff Tom Adams and were returned to Buffalo, where they were convicted of stealing Hyatt's stock and sentenced to three years' imprisonment.[37] Canton's greatest challenge as sheriff was the apprehension of horse thieves; thirteen of the sixteen criminals he and his deputies conveyed to the Illinois State Prison at Joliet were convicted of horse stealing.[38]

Canton was the unanimous choice for reelection when the Democratic Party held its county convention at Buffalo on October 13, 1884. On No-

A group of young folks in the early 1880s. Frank Canton is standing at
the far right and his wife-to-be, Annie Wilkerson, is sitting at the far left.
Courtesy American Heritage Center, University of Wyoming.

vember 4 he defeated the Republican candidate, W. E. Jackson, and began his
second term.[39]

During his travels around Johnson County, Canton arranged to stop as
often as possible at the ranch of George T. Beck. The attraction was not the
company of Beck but that of the pretty seventeen-year-old daughter of Bill
Wilkerson, the ranch foreman. Anna May Wilkerson, daughter of William
H. and Julia A. Wilkerson, was born May 1, 1867, at Metamora, Woodford

County, Illinois. She was no doubt flattered by the attention she received from the handsome county sheriff with his tall, slender figure, clear blue eyes, strong jaw and chin, and long, curling mustache. Although he was more than twice her age, she agreed to his offer of marriage.[40]

On the evening of January 20, 1885, Canton arrived at the Wilkerson home near Big Horn accompanied by Harvey A. Bennett, the mayor of Buffalo, and Congregationalist Minister Josiah P. Sparrow, who the following day united Canton and Anna in marriage.[41] Just when Canton revealed to his bride and the Wilkersons the dark history of the Texas desperado Joe Horner is not known, but they came to know the story in time and, despite this knowledge, never wavered in their support for Frank Canton during the difficult and dangerous days that lay ahead.

Canton took his bride to Buffalo and the small cottage in which he had been living on the courthouse square while carpenters enlarged his house. Canton's deputies had often bunked with him, and the *Sentinel* of January 24 remarked, "This will oblige Undersheriff McDermott and friends from Big Horn who frequently visit him to rustle for sleeping apartments in future."[42]

Canton had little to offer his teenaged wife in the way of worldly goods. The 1884 tax assessment rolls showed that at the age of thirty-five he had accumulated property totaling only $640 in value. His house in town and a ranch he was homesteading were valued at $500. His only other assets were a fine horse valued at $100 and other property worth $40.[43] The only dwelling on the 480-acre ranch was a tiny shack housing a man Canton kept there to establish permanent residency for homesteading purposes. While he held the office of sheriff the Cantons lived in Buffalo.

In February Sheriff Canton was called to quell a riot in Sheridan but found that the "riot" was simply the drunken debauch of a notorious saloon character and cowtown ruffian known as Dick Buckley. Among other transgressions, Buckley, whose real name was William Peyton, had deserted the army. Buckley had then fled from town when officers from Fort McKinney arrived to arrest him, but he later returned, vowing to "paint the streets of Sheridan red with blood before night, and conducted himself throughout the day with the utmost recklessness, drinking heavily, shooting dogs and firing several shots at persons at long range, and when no desirable mark presented itself, discharging his pistol promiscuously, without regard to the personal safety of anyone."[44]

The town officers disappeared, and Sheriff Canton was summoned by wire. He arrived to find the town quiet. Buckley had attempted to bulldoze Pete Jones, a tough bartender in the Keesee and Company Saloon. Jones had pulled a shotgun from behind the bar and with one blast brought the rampage and the Buckley career to an abrupt halt. A coroner's jury quickly returned a verdict of justifiable homicide. "The death of the notorious Dick Buckley at Sheridan at the hands of Pete Jones is very little lamented in Buffalo," said a newspaper, "the general verdict here being that his death was well merited." Canton's only comment was that by the time the sheriff reached Sheridan, "the boys had laid him out."[45]

But a violent death occurring a month later was viewed a great deal differently by the citizens and officers of Johnson County, and its aftermath would concern Canton for many months to come.[46] In late March an elderly German settler named Jacob Schmerer disappeared from his small hay farm in the Red Hills six miles southeast of Buffalo. A neighbor stopping by Schmerer's Dry Creek Ranch in early April found the large log house deserted. The owner's wagon was in the barn, but three of his horses, including a beautiful team consisting of a large bay and a buckskin with a black streak running from withers to tail, were missing. There were dried bloodstains in the living quarters. Suspecting foul play, the neighbor informed the authorities at Buffalo. After viewing the scene, Canton announced that he believed Schmerer had been murdered by Bill Booth, a young man who had been poisoning wolves with Schmerer that winter and had since disappeared. The sheriff offered a one-hundred-dollar reward to Burrell Madden, a black man familiar with the surrounding country, if he could find the body of Schmerer. At the same time he announced a five-hundred-dollar reward for the apprehension of Booth. Madden discovered Schmerer's body in a canyon two miles from the log house a few days later. The old man's skull was crushed, and a cord was fastened tightly around his throat. The hunt for Booth intensified.

As was afterwards learned, Bill Booth had murdered Schmerer after an argument, secreted the body, and left with the old man's horses. He went to the Black Hills, where he sold the prize team and traded the other horse for a mule. He then went to Miles City and Billings, Montana, where, closely following the newspaper reports of the officers on his trail, he remained for about a month. In late May he was back in Miles City. There Deputy Sheriff W. D. Smith recognized him and made the arrest. On a requisition issued by Governor Francis E. Warren, Canton and Undersheriff McDermott on June 1 returned Booth to Johnson County for trial. At Canton's request, the governor a few days later authorized payment of the arrest reward to W. D. Smith.[47] Emotions ran high in Buffalo when Booth was lodged in the county jail. A lynch mob surrounded the jail, but Canton persuaded the leaders to let the law take its course.[48]

At first Booth denied that he had killed Schmerer. He admitted taking the old man's horses but claimed they had been given to him as payment for back wages. Later he changed his story, saying that he had killed Schmerer in self-defense. Indicted for first-degree murder on June 25, he went on trial before Judge Jacob B. Blair five days later. H. S. Elliott conducted his defense and C. H. Burritt prosecuted the case, which was publicized widely across the territory. A jury found Booth guilty, and on July 3 Judge Blair sentenced him to death by hanging at Buffalo, with the date of execution set for October 2, 1885. "Booth has weakened a good deal lately, having been confirmed by a priest," Sheriff Canton remarked in a September interview.[49] But, as Canton was to learn, Bill Booth had not so "weakened" that he could not make repeated escape attempts.

His attorney, H. S. Elliott, appealed the conviction to the Wyoming Supreme Court, and pending review, the scheduled execution date came and went. In late November Booth took his first shot at freedom. A jail inmate named Leo Lambrigger, serving out a term in default of payment of a fifty-dollar fine, was not considered dangerous and was given the run of the jail corridor. For reasons unknown, "or for pure cussedness," Lambrigger let Booth and a prisoner named Carson out of their cells, and they concealed themselves in the large water tank mounted above the cages. When Canton looked in before locking up for the night, he noticed that the two inmates were missing from their cells.

> The sheriff then crawled up to their hiding place, getting in rather narrow quarters, and discovered his would-be ex-jailbirds sitting in the water tank, in about a foot of water, with the lid of the tank closed. When the order was given for them to return to their cell, Booth made a move as though he intended to resist the officer by force, when he was laid out by a blow with a six-shooter, and Carson was covered at the same time by a pistol held in the other hand of the sheriff. They both then begged the officer to spare their lives, and no further trouble was had in getting them back to their quarters.[50]

A month later Canton again thwarted an escape attempt by Booth. During a routine inspection he found that the bars on the bottom of Booth's cage had been sawed through. Further investigation turned up a steel spring taken from a boot sole and nicked to form a saw blade. Another blade was found in the lining of Booth's coat collar. Canton ordered the prisoner shackled in his cell.[51]

A grand jury report, submitted in December, found that, with four prisoners in a cell, the jail was much too crowded. Construction of another tier of cells with a surrounding corridor and steel-shuttered windows was recommended. "The prisoners," said the report, "are carefully and humanely treated; everything necessary for the health and comfort is furnished. We have investigated the recent attempt to release prisoners from the jail, and

Canton called on Thomas Jefferson Carr, who had previously hanged two men at Cheyenne, for advice in the execution of Bill Booth. *Courtesy American Heritage Center, University of Wyoming.*

are of the opinion that the sheriff is entirely blameless in the affair. . . . We exonerate the sheriff from all blame in this matter."[52] The county commissioners acted on the recommendations the following year, and new jail cells were installed at a cost of more than four thousand dollars.[53]

On January 27, 1886, the Wyoming Supreme Court rejected Booth's appeal and set March 5 as a new execution date. Within a week an increasingly desperate Booth attempted escape again. Inmate Carson alerted Canton on February 5 that Booth had sawed through his irons and intended to overpower the sheriff when he entered the cell. Canton took Booth from the cage and found that he had severed the shackles with pen nibs fashioned into tiny saws. Canton had a blacksmith rivet new irons on the prisoner's legs and secure the shackles to the floor bars with a heavy chain.[54]

Following this failure, Booth accepted his fate. A few days before his hanging, he confessed to the murder. His real name, he said, was John Owens. He was born in Ohio and moved to Illinois, where he married and fathered a child, but both wife and baby contracted smallpox and died. He drifted on to Kansas, Indian Territory, Texas, and Colorado before coming to Wyoming. He said that the murder of Schmerer "was the first crime of this character he had committed," and although "he had frequently been in saloon rows," he had never "previous to this occasion taken the life of another." He expressed his gratitude to Attorney Elliott for his efforts to save him from the gallows and "also wished to be remembered kindly to Mr. Canton, the sheriff, for that gentleman's many kind favors shown toward him during the period of his confinement, though, considering, he confessed to being a very badly behaved guest of the jail."[55]

As the date approached for the only legal hanging ever held in Johnson County, Canton made his preparations.[56] Never having hanged a man before, he undoubtedly sought advice and guidance from his friend T. Jeff Carr, who, as Laramie County sheriff, had hanged two men previously at Cheyenne. Carr, now U.S. marshal for the Territory of Wyoming, had appointed Canton a deputy U.S. marshal on October 1, 1885. It was the first of many such appointments Canton would receive in his lifetime.[57]

Canton had the gallows built behind the courthouse. The traditional thirteen steps led to a platform ten feet square. A trapdoor was centered beneath an overhead beam from which the noose dangled. The tying of the noose itself and the calculation of the slack required to break the neck cleanly were problems for Canton. Carr's experience must have proved invaluable. The gallows stood almost in the shadow of the Canton residence on the courthouse grounds. As the time of execution neared, Annie moved in with friends in the south end of town to get away from the somber scene.[58]

The hanging itself went off without a hitch. At 7:30 on the morning of March 5 Canton was somewhat surprised to find the prisoner sleeping soundly in his cell. He awoke Booth and remained as the condemned man ate a hearty breakfast and dressed in the black suit provided for the occasion. He read the death warrant to Booth and then left as the prisoner and a Catholic priest spent a half hour together in prayer. Promptly at eleven Canton led a procession that included Booth, the priest, and several sheriff's deputies to the scaffold. The noose was placed around Booth's neck, and his legs were tied. Asked if he had anything to say, Booth replied in a strong voice that he did not. The black velvet death hood was fitted over his head, Canton nodded, the trap flew open at precisely 11:05, and Bill Booth took "the necktie route for a warmer clime."[59] Twelve minutes later Dr. J. H. Lott pronounced the man dead. Canton turned the body over to the coroner and swore in the eighteen spectators as a coroner's jury, which quickly determined that John Owens, alias Bill Booth, had met his death as a result of a legal execution. Canton was lauded in the press for his efficiency: "In this case Sheriff Canton showed his usual coolness in fulfilling the duties of his office, and much credit is due him for the very systematic arrangement made regarding the execution."[60]

During the year of the Schmerer murder investigation and the Bill Booth case, Sheriff Canton made several other important arrests. In February 1885 the last charges against Frank James, the Missouri bandit, were dropped, and the papers were full of stories of the James Brothers Gang. Among the gang members who had scattered was a man named Jim Cummins. Learning that

Harvey Gleason, alias Teton Jackson, was the most notorious outlaw captured by Canton during his tenure as Johnson County sheriff. *Author's collection.*

an inoffensive Buffalo shoemaker was in fact Jim Cummins, Canton jailed him and wired the sheriff of Clay County, Missouri. "I never did anything worse than Frank James did, and if they have reprieved him they surely will me," Cummins said. The Missouri authorities evidently agreed with this reasoning: they refused to send a requisition for Cummins, and Canton turned him loose.[61]

The most notorious outlaw captured by Sheriff Canton during this period was the redoubtable Teton Jackson, leader of a gang of horse thieves who had plagued the northern country for years.[62] Jackson, whose real name was Harvey Gleason, had taken his pseudonym from the Teton Mountains and Jackson Hole, his base of operations. A loosely knit criminal organization under his leadership developed a systematic horse-stealing operation, taking ponies from ranges in Idaho, Nevada, and Utah to hidden pastures in Jackson Hole. There brands were altered, and the stolen stock was driven to markets in Wyoming, Montana, and Dakota. Rewards for Jackson had been offered, but until the fall of 1885 he had managed to elude lawmen seeking him.

On October 10 Canton received a telegram from William F. Hosford, an officer at Blackfoot, Idaho, and detective for the Wyoming Stock Growers Association. Hosford had information that Jackson was moving a herd of stolen horses through the Bighorn Basin. Canton and two of his deputies, Chris Gross and Ed Lloyd, immediately set out for the Paint Rock Canyon cabin of Lee Lucas, a man Canton suspected of being in league with the thieves. After a hard, all-night ride, the officers reached the Lucas place shortly before daybreak. Smoke curled from the chimney, and candlelight flickered in the single window, through which Jackson could be seen.

Silently approaching the cabin, Canton posted Lloyd at the window and whispered to Gross to stick the muzzle of his rifle through a hole in the log wall and cover Jackson. With revolver drawn he then burst into the room. The bandit chief, partially dressed, squatted by the fire, lighting his pipe with a glowing splinter. Lucas was slicing venison for breakfast. Two other men were still in their bunks. Canton ordered everyone to line up with hands held high. All quickly complied except Jackson, who remained unmoving for several moments, drawing on his pipe and eyeing the distance to his holstered pistol hanging several feet away. "Canton," he said, finally, "I ain't afraid of you or your guns. I'd fight that out, but what's been a-bothering me is the end of that rifle that's been trained on my head for the last five minutes."[63]

Canton handcuffed Jackson and sent Lucas and his deputies to round up the horses in the canyon. The other two men turned out to be wolf hunters and were allowed to leave. Canton then was alone in the cabin with Teton Jackson. "He was not a pleasant companion," said Canton.

> I have never seen a man of his description before or since. He was about forty-five, over six feet in height, weight a hundred and ninety, stubby beard, raw-boned, coarse features, flaming red hair, red face, and eyes as black as a snake's. . . . I had taken a seat about six feet from him with my revolver in my hand. He began to complain that the handcuffs were so tight that the blood could not circulate and that he was in great pain, and that if I would take them off he would keep quiet and promise not to hurt me. I told him that I was not the least bit uneasy about his hurting me, and that I had no objection to granting his request, but that he was the one taking all the chances, for if he made the slightest move I would kill him. He said he understood the situation. I then threw the keys over to him, and he unlocked the handcuffs and pitched the keys and cuffs back to me.
>
> After he removed the cuffs he began rubbing his wrists and said that I would never take him to Buffalo and that he wanted to serve notice on me right there and then that he was a better man than I was, even without a six-shooter. He began to talk very abusive. I told him I would take him to Buffalo and that he was worth as much to me dead as alive. I told him I would prefer to take his dead body as it would be less trouble to handle than a live one. I then threw the open handcuffs on the floor at his feet and told him that if he did not snap them on his wrists in ten seconds, he could take his medicine. I think he put them on in less time than I had given him.[64]

The horses brought in by the deputies were identified as having been stolen from the Idaho ranch of High and Stout. The officers placed Jackson on one of the ponies, tied his legs together under the horse's belly, and driving the other horses ahead, started back for Buffalo. Canton recalled a perilous moment on the return trip as they crossed a mountain meadow.

> The sod was underlaid with mud, six to eight feet deep. It would bear up a horse, crossing singly, but the bunch being ahead cut the turf enough so that my horse broke through. I jumped off and broke through the bog with one foot, so it threw me down and my horse struggled and floundered around until he got on the turf again before I got to my feet. Teton was watching me while I was having this trouble and when my horse got on his feet again, he trotted ahead leaving me afoot, and went right up to the side of Jackson. My Winchester was in the scabbard, and Teton saw his opportunity at once and was just reaching down for it when I called to the deputies to look out. Ed Loyd [sic] drew his six-shooter just in time to make the desperate outlaw let the gun alone. As I got on my horse again, Teton said, "If I could have got that gun I would have settled with you anyway."
> It was a close call, but "an inch of a miss is as good as a mile."[65]

The night of October 11, after forty sleepless hours spent mostly in the saddle, the officers arrived back in Buffalo with their prisoner and the stolen horses. Jackson was kept in jail until October 24, when Bill Hosford and A. T. Stout arrived from Blackfoot with extradition papers and took him to Bingham County, Idaho, where he was convicted and sentenced to fourteen years in prison. On November 5, 1885, he entered the U.S. penitentiary at Boise City.

Jackson wrote Canton from prison, saying he held no grudge against the officer who had collared him, and humbly requested a few dollars with which to purchase tobacco. Canton responded with a short note and enclosed a twenty-dollar bill. He felt generous, perhaps, because he had just received his share of the reward money for the capture of the noted outlaw.[66]

Territorial newspapers praised Canton for his capture. "When Canton starts [after a criminal]," it was said, "he does not come back empty-handed." A Blackfoot paper reported: "Hosford and Stout speak very highly of Sheriff Frank Canton for the manner in which he treated them, and also speak very highly of his courage and bravery. They say that country contains lots of hard characters, but that Sheriff Canton has got them so that they are afraid to attempt anything desperate and that he will probably be the means of breaking up several more gangs of horse thieves soon."[67]

That prophecy was fulfilled within weeks when Deputy Sheriff Chris Gross shot a Jackson gang member to death and arrested another. On December 1 Gross located "Big George" Stevens, alias "Red Cloud," and his partner, Frank Lamb, in a cabin on Spring Creek in the No Wood country. With Dave Hart and Billy Burnett, he broke into the cabin at first light, surprising the outlaws in their bunks. Stevens, however, showed fight. "Hot words passed between Gross and Stevens," reported the *Big Horn Sentinel*, "which resulted in a shot being fired by Gross, the ball taking effect in Stevens' head, killing him instantly."[68]

Hart and Burnett went on ahead with Lamb while Gross followed with the body of Stevens. It was bitterly cold. As darkness fell, Gross stopped at the ranch house of Edward Burnett at the mouth of Crazy Woman Canyon. "We were just setting down to supper and Chris walked in," recalled Edward Burnett. "'Unsaddle,' I said. 'Come and help me unpack a horse,' said Chris. I got a lantern. . . . When I shone the lantern on the pack I dropped right there." The body of Stevens was draped over a saddle and tied head to feet with a double diamond hitch. "Chris persuaded me to hold the lantern and he undid the pack rope, but he couldn't make me help lift the dead h. t. [horse thief] off the saddle, so he rolled him off like a cowboy unloading his bed and he fell with a thud, frozen solid, round as a horseshoe. I ate no supper that night." Burnett believed that Stevens would have surrendered without a fight to the sheriff because Canton's "steel gray eyes" would have cowed him. Gross could not be blamed, he said. "It was not his fault that he had the playful, joyous, jolly blue eyes of [the Swedish] race. The face does not count. Bat Masterson had a round, jolly face, but he had the eye. Canton had the face and the eye. What a howling success he would have been as a banker."[69]

Frank Lamb was placed in the county jail while Canton and his deputies rounded up other associates of Teton Jackson's. In November, A. J. ("Jack") Slack, alias Frank Cook, was nabbed in Miles City, and Canton, armed with a requisition issued by Governor Warren, returned him to Johnson County. J. H. ("Hank") Dunbar, charged with stealing four horses from a stagecoach stop at Forty Mile Ranch, was nabbed and joined the others in Canton's calaboose.

"Sheriff Canton and his deputies are making it warm for the combination of thieves operating on the Wyoming and Montana line," commented the *Big Horn Sentinel* of December 6. "The evidence of Frank Lamb in the coroner's inquest of 'Big George' shows that a notorious band of horse thieves is [being] broken up." Lamb, Slack, and Dunbar were indicted, tried, and convicted on grand larceny charges at the December term of district court. Judge Blair imposed sentences ranging from three to six years for each defendant. On January 7, 1886, Undersheriff McDermott, assisted by special sheriff's deputy H. A. Bennett, started for the prison at Joliet with six men in shackles. In addition to Lamb, Slack, and Dunbar were Orin Cook, a deranged man to be delivered to the insane asylum at Jacksonville, Illinois, and a pair of Arapaho Indians named Samuel and Beaver who had been convicted of killing beef.[70]

The story of these two Arapahos always intrigued Canton, and he eventually wrote a long, dramatic account of their arrest, which was published several times.[71] As sheriff, Canton was not an official employee of the Wyoming Stock Growers Association, but he kept the organization informed regarding conditions on the ranges. In the summer of 1885 he reported that game was scarce and that Arapaho and Shoshone hunting parties from the Fort Washakie reservation were killing cattle. Indian agents and the military, with primary responsibility for control of the Indians, were tied up in red tape and were ineffectual, in his opinion. Only the arrest, conviction, and incarceration of one or more Indians by the civil authorities would bring a halt to the cattle losses. He asked for funds to employ witnesses to help him build a case against the Indians. The WSGA guaranteed the necessary money, and Canton enlisted two hunters, "Bear George" McClellan and Bill Glass, at five dollars a day each to scout out the country.[72]

In August the hunters rode into Buffalo with an Indian pinto and a cowhide carrying the CY brand. They told Canton they had surprised two young Arapahos in the act of butchering a freshly killed cow. The Indians fled, double-mounted on a black horse. McClellan and Glass finished skinning the animal and brought the hide and the other Indian pony to Buffalo. They also brought an old Stetson hat and a medicine bag left by the Indians at the scene. The medicine bag was Arapaho, and the name "Samuel" was faintly inscribed on the brim of the hat. With this scant evidence Canton secured arrest warrants and set out with McClellan, Glass, and Deputy Chris Gross to find the culprits.

They tracked the Indians to the camp of Arapaho chieftain Black Coal. There Canton learned that a young man called "Samuel" belonged to the band of Sharp Nose, a subchief with a reputation for troublemaking. The agency clerk described Samuel as a handsome, good-hearted Indian, with plenty of nerve and "really too fine to be under such an old scoundrel as Sharp Nose." Samuel had married a young woman called "Mollie," a graduate of Carlisle Indian School, who "spoke good English, wrote a beautiful hand, and was noted for being the handsomest squaw in the Arapahoe tribe."[73]

Late that night the clerk accompanied Canton's party to the camp of Sharp Nose, and they began a tepee-to-tepee search for Samuel. In the fifth one they found him, wrapped in the arms of Mollie. Canton slapped cuffs on the man, and the party made a run for their horses as the camp erupted. "It was

bedlam turned loose," Canton remembered. "Indians running in every direction catching and saddling horses, dogs howling and barking, squaws chant-
ing war songs, and with war whoops mingled with the rest of the noise. I had
taken the precaution to set saddles back on the horses and tighten the cinches
before leaving them, and I now put Samuel on the pinto pony, which we had
brought along for that purpose, tied his feet together under the horse . . . ,
and started on a fast ride for Fort Washakie, twenty miles away."[74]

Canton jailed Samuel at the fort. The next morning a large body of Indians appeared outside the post. Canton estimated their number at five hundred or more and said many wore warbonnets and all were excited. "Washakie,
with perhaps a dozen of the head men of the Shoshones, and Black Coal with
about the same number of his band of Arapahoes had come into the post,
and were standing in two groups near the flagstaff." Canton shook hands
with the chiefs and explained through an interpreter that he had warrants
for the arrest of two Indians for cattle theft. One, Samuel, was already under
guard, and he wanted the other. If Black Coal cooperated, Canton promised
to make the punishment as light as possible, but if he interfered, "the Great
Father at Washington" would no longer recognize him as chief of the Arapahos.[75]

Black Coal dispatched six men to fetch Beaver, who was identified by
McClellan and Glass as the other cow-killer. The chief further sealed Beaver's
fate by claiming the pinto pony and the medicine bag. Beaver joined Samuel
in the post guardhouse.

Canton had a tense confrontation with Sharp Nose at the agency later
that day. The subchief tried to barter horses for the freedom of his men and
was infuriated by Canton's refusal. Sharp Nose stepped toward Canton threat-
eningly as his companions encircled the whites. "I put my hand on my six-
shooter," Canton said, "and Gross and Glass pulled theirs clear from the
scabbards." Sharp Nose stopped, considered, and looking Canton straight in
the eye, said, "If you try to take Samuel and Beaver off the reservation I will
kill and scalp you, and all your party." Canton responded that he intended to
start with them in the morning and that if Sharp Nose interfered, he would
kill the two prisoners and then fight to the last cartridge. Sharp Nose, scowl-
ing, stalked out of the council house. Canton and his men followed to find
Black Coal waiting with a hundred men to escort him back to the fort. The
meeting was like sitting on a powder keg, Canton said. A false move "would
have been the spark that would have fired the powder, which would have
meant death to us as well as the death of many of the Indians. Black Coal's
act in being at the council house with his men showed how well he appreciated the situation and how binding he considered his promise."[76]

The next day Canton and his party started back to Buffalo with their prisoners. Mollie, the wife of Samuel, insisted on going along and convinced a reluctant Canton that she would be valuable as an interpreter. Angry Arapahos paralleled the trail for twenty miles, and Sharp Nose himself, according to Canton's account, suddenly appeared in a canyon and caught the reins of the sheriff's horse. "As soon as I saw who it was," said Canton, "I gave him a jab in the face with my Winchester, spurred my horse, and literally rode him down. Sharp Nose rolled over out of the trail and the party rode by in single file, Glass and Gross, who were bringing up the rear, being ready to kill him if he made a threatening motion. But he did not. He seemed to be completely cowed. After we were well past Sharp Nose, the whole camp commenced a mournful chant, which Mollie explained was the death song for Samuel and Beaver."[77]

The rest of the two-hundred-mile trip was uneventful. In early September Canton lodged his young Arapaho prisoners—Samuel was twenty, Beaver only seventeen—in the Buffalo jail, where they remained until the December session of court. They were indicted, tried, and convicted, but Judge Blair, honoring Canton's promise that they would receive light sentences, imposed the minimum prison term of one year each.

Mollie remained in Buffalo throughout that fall and early winter, living in the Canton home, visiting with Samuel at every opportunity, and serving as interpreter at court proceedings. When Undersheriff McDermott left for Joliet with his prisoners in January, she was inconsolable. The Cantons, especially Annie, admired her steadfastness and devotion to her husband and became quite fond of her. The affection was returned, and after Mollie returned to the reservation, she came back to Buffalo about every six weeks, making the long trip alone to visit with the Cantons and receive any news of Samuel. She never failed to bring a gift for Annie, said Canton. "At one time she brought a beautiful buffalo robe with Indian pictures worked in porcupine quills. The next trip she gave a fine saddle pony, which Mrs. Canton rode for years. At another time she brought handsome beadwork, and often a string of mountain trout caught at her last camp in the mountains a few miles from town, all simple tokens of good will."[78]

Samuel and Beaver served ten months and seventeen days and were released from prison on November 29, 1886. In his memoirs Canton wrote that Major McClaughrey, warden of the Illinois State Prison, bought the two Indians a suit of clothes and a railroad ticket to Rawlins, Wyoming. The press reported at the time, however, that Canton, after requesting that the Arapaho agent arrange return transportation for the Indians and receiving no response, went to Joliet and brought them back at his own expense.[79]

According to the *Big Horn Sentinel* of February 13, 1886, Samuel and Beaver were "the first full-blooded Indians" ever incarcerated at the Illinois penitentiary. But the same week that Undersheriff McDermott escorted them to prison, an Indian named Bad Belly, said to be a chief of the Crow tribe, was arrested in Buffalo and eventually joined the Arapahos at Joliet. Canton collared Bad Belly on January 2, 1886, and charged him with stealing horses from the Stoddard and Howard Live Stock Company. During the six months the Crow Indian languished in the Canton calaboose awaiting trial, he proved to be a difficult and obstreperous jailbird. In March, after engaging in a vicious fight with inmate Leo Lambrigger, he was threatened with a diet of bread and water. Bad Belly had no funds, and the county paid M. L. Andrews twenty-five dollars to defend him. In July he was convicted, sentenced to a year in prison, and conveyed to Joliet, along with two other horse thieves, by Frank Canton and Jim Enochs.[80]

On September 16, 1885, Canton was interviewed by Ashley Bancroft, who was gathering personal information from prominent Wyoming residents for California historian Hubert Howe Bancroft's monumental history of the region. That interview is an early example of the dissembling that would characterize Canton's public image for the remainder of his life. For the interview he fabricated an early Frank Canton history to replace the actual past of the vanished Joe Horner. He said he was born in Virginia in 1854, was educated there, and came west to Missouri with his father in 1861. He and his father went to Colorado in 1868 and engaged in stock raising at "a point just southwest of Denver." Later he moved to Montana, where he was in the stock business with a man named William Jamison. He said that in 1877 he went to Cheyenne, where he stayed until employed as a detective by the Wyoming Stock Growers Association in 1881, a position that led to his election as Johnson County sheriff in 1882. Bancroft noted at the end of the interview: "Mr. Canton stands very high. Is a man of iron nerve and a typical frontiersman."[81] The substance of the interview appeared in H. H. Bancroft's history, which was published in 1890 and has been used ever since as a source for the misinformation Canton generated.[82]

That same month Canton hitched a horse to the new buggy he had purchased and drove his bride out to look over his ranch property and to visit with some of his neighbors. Early settlers on Kelly and Crazy Woman Creeks, near Canton's property, included D. A. Kingsbury, J. T. Burkhart, George Clayton, Edward Burnett, A. L. Brock, and Charlie Basch. Canton had probably known Charles Franklin Basch longer than any of the others. A native of Birmingham, Connecticut, Basch was one year younger than the sheriff. As a small child he had moved with his parents to Wisconsin, where he attended school. Leaving home at the age of seventeen, he went west and drove Sanderson stagecoaches between Santa Fe, New Mexico, and Walsenburg, Colorado. He later drove coaches on the western slope of Colorado and worked for a transfer company in Denver. When Fort McKinney was established on Clear Creek in the late 1870s, Basch freighted in some of the first supplies. He stayed in the area, taking a job with Moreton Frewen hauling supplies between Rock Creek and Frewen's "76" Ranch on Crazy Woman. He later homesteaded there.[83] Basch would figure largely in the future of Frank Canton.

A. L. and Julia Brock and their two-year-old son were newcomers from Missouri, having arrived only the summer before. Annie Canton wrote a letter to that son, J. Elmer Brock, sixty-two years later:

> The first time I saw you was on the ranch in September of '85. My husband and I drove out to our ranch to see how the man was doing and drove by your father's ranch to call. We only had a little shack boarded up for the man to stay in and your folks had just built a one room log house, had nothing in it but a log bedstead and a fireplace to cook in and no chairs but the seat from the wagon and some boxes. You were running around in a little gingham dress with long ties that would not stayed tied. Your mother and father would not let us leave and we stayed all night and your mother cooked a kettle of beans over the fire and baked some biscuits in an oven that she put on the coals and we had a grand visit.[84]

Annie Canton and Julia Brock had a strong common bond: both were six months pregnant. On December 8, 1885, a daughter, Genevra, was born to the Brocks, and early the next morning Annie gave birth to an eight-and-a-half-pound girl. Annie and Frank named her Ruby. "Sheriff Canton was noticed on the streets during the snow storm Wednesday wearing a smile of contentment a foot deep," reported the *Big Horn Sentinel* of December 12. "Upon inquiry it was learned that a little girl visitor had made her appearance at his house early that morning and had come to stay. The sheriff was kept pretty busy during the day 'setting 'em up' to the boys."[85]

The 1885 tax assessment showed a decided improvement in Canton's financial picture. His total taxable assets had increased by more than one thousand dollars over the previous year. In addition to his ranch property, he now owned three contiguous town lots and four horses. Other belongings were suggestive of his new domesticity: a $50 carriage, household furniture worth $250, and musical instruments valued at $25.[86]

Acting on a telegram received from the governor's office in Texas, Canton in December took into custody the foreman of the Sugg Brothers Ranch on Powder River, a man known as John McFarland. Governor John Ireland said he was sending a requisition for McFarland, whose true name was Alf Rushing and who was wanted for murder, and that the sheriff of Navarro County, Texas, would come to Buffalo to take him back. Canton made the

arrest on December 13 by means of "a very cleverly laid scheme," according
to the *Big Horn Sentinel*. Finding the man in a saloon, Canton "asked him to
indulge in a little of the stimulants kept therein," after which the sheriff led
McFarland to the sheriff's office, where Canton produced the telegram, disarmed him, and locked him up.[87]

McFarland was held for more than two weeks awaiting the appearance of
the Texas sheriff. During that period a number of his cowboy friends from
Powder River, concerned about his fate, drifted into Buffalo. When Judge
Blair held an arraignment hearing on December 29, the friends were all in
attendance. Noting that the Texas authorities had had ample time to appear
and take custody during McFarland's seventeen days in jail, Blair discharged
him. "Cheer after cheer went up in the court room at this instant," said the
Sentinel, "and McFarland's friends picked him up and carried him out of the
court house, 'heeling' him with a couple of six-shooters as they pushed their
way through the crowd."[88]

The day that news account appeared, Sheriff Canton wrote a letter to a
sister of the accused. Mrs. Josie Newman of Sweetwater, Texas, had wired
Canton, inquiring about the fate of her brother. Canton's response shows a
certain contempt he held for Texas lawmen and a confidence, bordering on
arrogance, that he had acquired after two years in the sheriff's office. "Your
telegram reached me today and I answered it at once," Canton said.

> In reply I will say that I have arrested your Bro. Alf Rushing on
> requisition from the Gov. of Texas. I held him sufficient over the
> length of time for the officers to come after him but they failed to
> put in an appearance so I released him.
>
> J. L. Wallace of Corsicana, Texas, is the man who was sent after
> him. He came as far as Cheyenne, Wyoming. I think he was to [*sic*]
> cowardly to come any further for he stopped there ten or twelve
> days and I think he went back to Texas, if he wants any more men in
> this country arrested he can come up here and arrest them himself. I
> am sure I will not arrest another man on his order.[89]

In March, Canton received a telegram that a man he wanted was being
held for him at Fredonia, Wilson County, in southeastern Kansas. Harvey
H. Holmberg had disappeared from Johnson County the previous August,
and a horse belonging to E. Curran had turned up missing at the same time.[90]
A Kansas sheriff had recognized Holmberg from Canton's notices and made
the arrest. Canton stopped in Cheyenne to obtain extradition papers and
went on to Denver, where he boarded a Union Pacific train for Kansas. At
Fredonia he found, to his surprise, that Holmberg was not under arrest but
"under surveillance." When Holmberg learned of Canton's arrival, he arranged with a friendly judge for the issuance of a quick writ of habeas corpus

after Canton made the arrest. Knowing that the next westbound train would not arrive until the following day, he confidently walked into the sheriff's office and submitted to Canton's arrest.

But the Wyoming sheriff knew a few tricks himself, as Holmberg soon learned. Canton hired a horse and buggy and took his prisoner some thirty miles to another railroad point. Finding that the next train headed west was not due for twenty-four hours, he rented another rig and went on to a station of the Atchison, Topeka, and Santa Fe and caught the cars for Colorado. "While the 'fly' lawyers of Fredonia were searching high and low for Sheriff Canton and his captive in Kansas," reported the *Big Horn Sentinel*, "that much tried officer rested in hard-earned security in Colorado."[91]

The trip was an expensive one for the taxpayers of Johnson County; Canton submitted bills totaling $378 to the county commissioners, who in April reluctantly approved payment. It all went for naught, since the case against Holmberg was dismissed later that month.[92]

Canton's inability to get a conviction in the Holmberg case was part of a pattern he saw developing in Johnson County in 1886. It became increasingly difficult to obtain indictments and convictions against those charged with stock theft as jurors became less and less sympathetic to the plight of the large ranchers. Nevertheless, Canton had a list of suspected rustlers and horse thieves and worked diligently to build cases against them.

One of these was a cowboy named Ed Cherpolloid, better known as "One-Eyed Tex" and described by a newspaper as an "unscrupulous rascal, devoted to thieving."[93] Cherpolloid was suspected when Joe LeFors, then cowboying for the Murphy Cattle Company, had a favorite horse stolen. LeFors, later to achieve fame as a stock detective and lawman in Wyoming and Montana, had trailed cattle north and remembered One-Eyed Tex as a horse thief operating down around Mobeetie in Wheeler County, Texas. He never saw his horse again but could not prove Cherpolloid had stolen it.[94]

Canton also was unable to get sufficient evidence to sustain charges of stock theft against Tex, but when the "unscrupulous rascal" liquored up in Buffalo, the sheriff arrested him on a charge of "committing a public indecency." The *Sentinel* hoped that the arrest would serve as a warning that bad men visiting Buffalo "with their hide filled with 'forty-rod'" could not with impunity "insult respectable women." Cherpolloid pled guilty in police court and was fined ten dollars.[95]

Elias R. Smith, alias Sam Brown, was another hard character that Canton badly wanted to collar. Brown ostensibly was a professional gambler who plied his trade in the Powder River cow camps, but Canton was sure he "stood in" with horse thieves and abetted them in their crimes. Brown was known as a dangerous gunman who had been involved in several shooting scrapes, the last being a gunfight in which both he and another tough, named Davis, had been severely wounded.

In late June 1886, Canton captured a suspected horse thief named Duroc ("Rock") Blevens and got him to confess and implicate Brown. Armed with a warrant for Brown's arrest, Deputy Sheriff Ed Lloyd and two specially deputized assistants named Hays and Wagner rode to Brown's Powder River home on the night of June 27. Lloyd approached the house, was met at the doorway by Brown's wife, and stepped inside. Brown shot him without warning. The officer, mortally wounded, fell backward into the yard and died there as Hays and Wagner retreated. In the morning Drew Smith, the agent for the stage company at Powder River and an associate of Brown's, offered to act as a mediator. Brown submitted to arrest, and Hays and Wagner returned to Buffalo with their prisoner and Lloyd's body.

Brown was charged with murder. Canton also filed horse-stealing charges against Brown, "Rock" Blevens, and Drew Smith. Blevens was convicted in July and given a three-year sentence at Joliet, but the theft charges against Brown and Smith did not stick. Brown entered a "not guilty" plea at his murder trial in December, claiming he had thought Lloyd and the others were part of a lynch mob. A jury accepted this story and acquitted him.[96]

Canton never lost a prisoner from his jail while he was sheriff, but one man did escape from his custody. In May 1886, he arrested U. G. ("Roach") Chapman, foreman of the Frontier Land and Cattle Company, one of the enterprises of English cattle baron Sir Horace Plunkett. Canton claimed to have evidence that Chapman had been involved in four horse-stealing cases and also that the ranch foreman was wanted in Idaho for murder.

Because of his position and employer, Chapman received special treatment. "The sheriff allowed Mr. Chapman to remain in the sheriff's office in custody of an officer, to enable him to straighten out and settle his ranch accounts and books," reported the *Sentinel*. After "being assured by Chapman that he would not attempt an escape," Canton kept him in the office rather than a jail cell. Later Chapman "asked Canton for a change of underclothing and was taken to Mr. Canton's house to procure them. Mr. Canton was called away for a few minutes, left Chapman alone, and on his return 'the bird had flown.'"[97]

A Cheyenne newspaper reported that Chapman rode off "well armed on a valuable horse," and one later writer has suggested that perhaps Canton's culpability was more than negligence.[98] But there was no hint of suspicion of Canton in the local press. The *Sentinel* said that "men were sent out in every direction" for Chapman but that all returned empty-handed. Canton the next day arrested Billy Burnett and filed a complaint against him for assisting Chapman in the escape, but on May 11 the charges were dropped for lack of evidence, and Burnett was released. Although the *Sentinel* thought Chapman's recapture was "only a question of time," he was never apprehended and was never seen again in the Wyoming cattle country.[99]

Later that month in Miles City, Jim Conley, a deputy sheriff the *Sentinel* called a "terror to horsethieves," nabbed Bill Howell, indicted three years before for horse theft.[100] Canton brought Howell back, and the next month he was convicted and sentenced to two and a half years in prison. In July Canton and Jim Enochs transferred him to Joliet along with Bad Belly and Rock Blevens. These prisoners joined more than one hundred other Wyoming convicts confined at Joliet and the Nebraska State Prison at Lincoln.[101]

In September a horse kicked Canton, inflicting an injury severe enough to prevent him from performing his duties for weeks. He was confined to his home for several days and then appeared on the streets using crutches.[102]

At about this time he learned that Teton Jackson had escaped from the prison at Boise. Canton later wrote that the outlaw left in his cell a note containing the names of "a dozen different men whom he was going to kill on sight" and that Canton's name headed the list. However, the two men never met again.[103]

As the November elections neared, there was speculation about whether Canton would seek a third term. As early as July the *Sentinel* floated the names of other possible candidates. John McDermott, E. U. Snider, C. W. Morgareidge, Richard E. Kennedy, and J. M. Enochs were mentioned.[104] In September the paper reported that there had been "a great squabble for the office of sheriff," that Jim Enochs was "on a hot trail for the democratic nomination," and that the incumbent had withdrawn from contention. "Canton would have made a strong candidate had he continued in the race, but it is now definitely understood that he is entirely out of the field."[105]

At the Democratic convention on September 27 McDermott narrowly defeated Enochs for nomination as sheriff by a vote of 23 to 21. McDermott was then defeated in the November election by E. U. Snider, the candidate of the People's Party, in a close vote, 787 to 748.[106] Canton's four-year record in office was praised by the *Sentinel*. "A more efficient sheriff than Mr. Canton in the pursuit, detection and capture of criminals will not be expected."[107]

Within a few days the Cantons moved to a rented home in town, leaving what the *Sentinel* editor described as "the shack yclept [called] the 'sheriff's residence'" apparently in poor condition. "We suggest," said the editor, "that there are a good many repairs needed on that house to make it a suitable residence, and that Mr. Canton is the proper party to whom the commissioners should delegate the job."[108]

Chapter 4

The Detective, 1887-1890

"No man better serves to exemplify the range detective than the mysterious and somewhat sinister Frank M. Canton."

Frank Richard Prassel, *The Western Peace Officer*

Frank Canton wrote in his memoirs that he chose not to run for reelection in order to devote his time to his ranch. "The next two years I spent at home with my family," he said. "I think those were the happiest days of my life.... [I] accumulated about five hundred head of cattle and made a success of farming."[1] It is true that after leaving the sheriff's office, Canton built a home at the ranch to replace the shack his hired man had occupied and moved in with his wife and baby, but Frank Canton was too restless and adventurous a soul to devote his days to agriculture.

His decision not to run for reelection was based on his sense of a changing political and economic climate in Johnson County. He knew it was becoming increasingly difficult to seat juries who would indict and convict horse and cattle thieves—his failure at getting H. H. Holmberg, Sam Brown, and Drew Smith put behind bars still rankled—and he noted a tendency on the part of the citizenry to wink at theft of stock as long as the animals belonged to wealthy, nonresident ranchers. He also knew that there had been grumbling over the cost of the sheriff's office and that pressure was being exerted to reduce salaries. He could see nothing but headaches and frustration ahead for a sheriff determined to wage war on stock thieves.

His views proved quite correct. As he anticipated, shortly after he left office the pay of the sheriff and undersheriff was cut in half by the county commissioners.[2] Arrests, indictments, and convictions of horse and cattle thieves dropped precipitously. Nineteen men had been sent to prison from Johnson County during the four years Canton held the office of sheriff, and all but one had been convicted of horse or cattle theft; during the tenures of E. U. Snider and W. G. ("Red") Angus in the next four years, only five defendants went to prison for these crimes.[3] Canton recognized the growing antipathy of the county's residents for the large ranchers, the men whose favor he had determined to cultivate. As sides were formed for a coming clash, there was no question where Frank Canton's loyalty lay.

In July 1883 the Wyoming Stock Growers Association had established a Detective Bureau to protect their range holdings and had appointed veteran Laramie lawman N. K. Boswell as chief. Under Boswell's leadership, Ben Morrison, J. J. Hamlin, John F. Finkbone, George B. Henderson, Frank Brainard, Jim Murray, Sam Moses, and other tough cattle detectives harassed the criminal element on the ranges, to the great satisfaction of their employers. "Much of their work is of such a nature as cannot be properly discussed in detail," reported Secretary Thomas Sturgis at the annual meeting of the WSGA in April 1884. "It is sufficient to say that their efforts have been . . . remarkably successful. [Many thieves] are now in arrest, and under indictment, some having been overtaken in Texas and Arkansas. The expenditure has been large but results fully justify it. The committee [members] are satisfied with the work of the bureau and believe that it need only be continued with equal energy for a reasonable time to free the country of the men who make a profession of cattle stealing."[4]

Two years later, at the April 1886 meeting, the work of the Detective Bureau was again praised and note was taken of the contribution of a particular Wyoming sheriff: "A decided decrease in new criminal cases is noted. The committee acknowledges its indebtedness to Mr. Boswell, and desires also to recognize the great service of Sheriff Canton of Johnson County."[5]

When it became evident in the fall of that year that Canton would not seek reelection, Sir Horace Plunkett of the Frontier Land and Cattle Company urged the association to utilize Canton's abilities and recommended his employment to handle detective work in the Bighorn country. At the October 21, 1886, executive committee meeting, Secretary Sturgis was directed to correspond with Canton in this regard.[6] A letter to Canton went out the following day:

Dear Sir:

At a meeting of the Executive Committee of this Association, held on yesterday, Mr. Plunkett brought forward the unsatisfactory state of the Big Horn Basin, as regards the interests of the stockmen there. He stated that he had had some conversation with you on the subject, and that he had unofficially asked you whether you would undertake to organize a system of detective work in the Basin.

It was the opinion of the Executive Committee that you are the

best qualified person to take the matter in hand, and I was instructed
to invite you to make some proposition to the Committee about
undertaking the work, stating terms as regards remuneration, etc.

In the event of our undertaking the proposed work, you would
be given entire authority to act in whatever manner seemed to you
to be best under the circumstances. The Committee considers that it
would be best that your special connection with the Association
should be kept secret.

Awaiting your reply,

Yours truly, Thomas Sturgis.[7]

Canton replied on October 30:

Dear Sir:

I returned yesterday from a trip over the mountains and found
in my office your letter of Oct. 22. In reply I will say that I had a
conversation not long since with Mr. Plunkett in regard to the
situation in the Big Horn Basin, and I fully agree with him in saying
that the matter should be looked after, for I believe there will be a
more complete system of stealing organized over there than we have
ever had in Johnson County. In regard to your proposition to employ my services to look after this particular case, I will say that I
retire from the Sheriff's office here on Jan. 1st and I will have my
personal affairs to look after for some time. Therefore I could not
undertake this work for the Association unless the position you offer
me be permanent. I think there is a great deal of work that could be
done in different parts of the Territory that would be beneficial to
the interest of your Association, but of course you are the best
judges of that matter. In case you should want to employ me perma-
nently to take charge of this work, I am at your service provided we
could agree upon terms as regards remuneration, the system of
handling the Detective work, etc. But I would not agree to go into
this business unless I could give it all my attention. I would be glad
to hear from you again more fully about this matter. In the meantime I will keep myself well informed as to movements of parties in
the Big Horn Basin until Jan. 1st. Thanking you for the proposition
made to me, I remain,

Yours very truly,

F. M. Canton.[8]

Three days later U.S. Marshal T. Jeff Carr reappointed Canton deputy
U.S. marshal.[9] Then, on November 20 Sturgis wrote Canton that the Executive Committee was "ready to enter into any reasonable agreement" with

him. "They have requested me to communicate with you and to ask what your ideas are in regard to remuneration, provided your employment is permanent. You would be expected to take the position of Chief of Detectives for the northern part of the Territory, to conduct the work in your own way, of course keeping within certain limits as regards expenses."[10]

After additional correspondence Canton proposed in a letter, dated January 22, 1887, that he be paid twenty-five hundred dollars yearly plus expenses. This amount was agreed to, and Canton's official employment began April 1, 1887. His responsibility extended over the northern parts of Laramie, Albany, Carbon, Uinta, and Fremont Counties, and the whole of Johnson and Crook Counties, a vast territory larger than several eastern states. He was free to conduct the work in his own way and was authorized to act in whatever manner he deemed appropriate to the circumstances.[11]

The latitude for appropriate action that field employees were permitted by the WSGA is exemplified in an exchange of letters between Inspector E. P. Philbrick and Secretary Sturgis in the summer of 1886. Philbrick reported that seven heavily armed men camped near Soda Springs were rustling cattle and bragging that they would not be taken alive. "If the outfit were stealing stock and did not want to be taken alive," he wrote, "[then] I thought it would be a good plan to kill them all and arrest them afterward." Sturgis answered: "If you want to go up there and inspect the outfit referred to, you are at liberty to do so. If necessary you may carry out your plan of killing them and then arresting them. I do not think they will be a loss to the community."[12]

Although Sturgis had urged that Canton's "special connection with the Association should be kept secret," it was not long before his appointment was widely publicized. Following the WSGA meeting in April, Sturgis announced the creation of the new job and said it had been awarded to a man "conceded to be second to none in ability, courage and experience."[13] The Big Horn Sentinel on April 23 identified Canton as the man, saying, "The office is an important one and reflects much credit upon Mr. Canton as a gentleman well fitted to fill the position." The Sundance Gazette congratulated "ex-Sheriff Frank M. Canton, whose success during office in the apprehension of criminals" had "marked him as the most efficient detective in the west."[14]

During the remaining months of 1887 Canton traveled widely throughout Wyoming, assisting WSGA detectives and stock inspectors in investigations. Often he left the territory after a wanted man, as in August when he captured a man named Hopkins near Ogden, Utah, and brought him to Buffalo to face indictment in the district court for unlawfully branding cattle.[15] In September he arrested a man named Charles V. Nelson near the Canton ranch on Crazy Woman Creek on a horse-stealing charge filed in Crook County. But before Nelson came to trial, Sweetwater County claimed him on a manslaughter indictment. He was tried, convicted, and sentenced to eight years' imprisonment at Joliet.[16]

That summer Canton reported that Indians were again preying on the cattle herds. "I find there is new large bands of Indians camped on the top of the Big Horn Mountains," he wrote Thomas B. Adams, the new WSGA secretary. "They pretend to be hunting deer and elk, but game is very scarce, and cattle is plenty. I am satisfied they will kill beef. Several of their agents have promised me that they would not allow them to come in this country any more. Yet some of the Indians have showed me passes given them by their agents this summer. I hardly know what steps to take to get them out of the country. Can get no assistance from the military authorities and the Sheriff pays no attention to it."[17]

The situation was further complicated when a county judge ruled that any person—white or red—committing a crime on the Indian reservation could not be prosecuted under territorial law and that civil detectives had no jurisdiction there at all. The reservations thus became sanctuaries for thieves and rustlers. Secretary Adams complained to U.S. Senator Joseph M. Carey, president of the WSGA, but the Indian problem never was resolved.[18]

The winter of 1886–87, marked by blizzards and long spells of subzero temperatures, had been the worst in the memory of western cattlemen. It was not until the summer of 1887 that they realized how badly their herds had been devastated by that killer winter. The economic hardship of the members was reflected in a precipitous drop in per-head assessment contributions to their association treasury. It became obvious to the executive committee that reductions in expenditures were necessary, and the Detective Bureau was an immediate target. At the September meeting of the WSGA, Secretary Adams was instructed to reduce the salary of the association detectives. Frank Canton was requested to take a fifty-dollar-a-month cut.[19]

In October N. K. Boswell resigned, pleading ill health, and many of the detectives working under him were dismissed. Canton was given responsibility for detective work in the entire territory, but the days of the Detective Bureau were numbered. At the executive committee meeting in December 1887 the bureau was terminated and all employees were discharged effective with the completion of pending cases.[20]

The demise of the WSGA Detective Bureau resulted only partly from lack of funding; the operation had proved to be ineffective. In 1884 the WSGA had pushed through the Wyoming territorial legislature the so-called Maverick Bill, giving the association sole authority to conduct roundups in the territory and claim mavericks. This bill, "one of the worst pieces of legislation

Canton succeeded Nathaniel K. Boswell as chief of the Detective Bureau of the Wyoming Stock Growers Association. *Courtesy Wyoming State Museum.*

ever inflicted on the West,"[21] was bitterly resented, flagrantly violated, and practically unenforceable. Maverickers arrested by association detectives were routinely acquitted by juries across the territory, although oft-repeated tales of "hundreds of indictments" resulting in few if any convictions have been shown to be fabrications of a biased press.[22] The detectives continued to identify stock thieves, develop evidence of their guilt, and arrest them, but it became increasingly difficult to obtain indictments and convictions because of a rising tide of resentment against the Maverick Bill, the big cattlemen, and especially the detectives themselves. "We have found from bitter experience," wrote Secretary Adams to an association member, "that wherever evidence of cattle stealing is obtained through the Association inspectors or detectives, it is almost impossible to obtain a conviction in the courts. . . . Detective work, such as would be necessary to stop the trouble . . . , must be undertaken by private enterprise."[23]

The very word "rustlers" took on new meaning in Wyoming as detectives, officials, and members of the WSGA began to apply the term to anyone who opposed them. They believed that in Johnson County especially there were only two classes of citizens: "ranchers, who rustled on the side; and rustlers, who ranched on the side."[24] Those opposed to the "cattle barons," as the big ranchers came to be called, began to accept the appellation "rustlers" as a term of honor.

Canton was paid as chief of detectives through the end of March 1888 and in May was appointed a stock inspector by the Board of Livestock Commissioners, a territorial agency controlled by the WSGA.[25] No longer were half the wages of the local inspector paid by Johnson County. Nor did Canton accept a deputy sheriff's appointment, as had been the practice of former inspectors. The cooperative effort to control cattle theft by county and stock association was a thing of the past. Canton had been well paid as sheriff and detective chief, but, as always, he was short of cash, as shown in a letter he wrote to Tom Irvine in May. Irvine had some money due him from a man named Sines and had written Canton on May 7 asking for help in collecting it. "Old man Sines left some money in the bank here and authorized me to use it," Canton answered, "but in the last letter I rec'd from him he requested me to let the balance of this money stay in the bank until he came which would be about the middle of April. I haven't heard from him since nor don't know where the devil he is. As soon as I find out I will write him and get authority to send you this bill of $21.00. Would pay you myself but I haven't a dollar to save my life that I can use now."[26]

On August 20, 1888, a second daughter was born to Frank and Anna Canton and named Helen. The family was living at the ranch, but as the time approached for delivery, Annie took Ruby, then two and a half, and went to stay with her parents, who had moved to Sheridan. Soon after Helen was born, Annie and the children became very ill. Canton stayed with them at Sheridan until their health improved and he could bring them home.[27]

With the approach of the November elections, Canton again eyed the office of sheriff. Everyone recognized that E. U. Snider had been a failure, and Canton no doubt was confident the Democrats would nominate him for another term. But he did not reckon with the shift in the political mood of the county. He was now viewed as a tool of the powerful ranchers, whom the voters saw as their adversaries. Led by party leaders Oscar H. ("Jack") Flagg, of the Hat Ranch, sheepman D. A. Kingsbury, and Buffalo merchant Robert Foote, the Democrats nominated Red Angus for sheriff, and he handily defeated Republican Delos Babcock at the polls.[28]

William Galispie ("Red") Angus, two months younger than Canton and a native of Ohio, had come west as an enlisted man in the U.S. Army. Taking his discharge at Fort McKinney, he settled in nearby Buffalo and made his living as a professional bartender, pimp, and gambler. Part owner of a saloon and gambling house called the Gold Room, he was known in Buffalo as the mayor of Laurel Avenue, the red-light district.[29] Angus also dabbled in stock raising and, according to Wyoming lawman Malcolm Campbell, was careless in his cattle acquisitions. In 1882, Campbell said, Angus "drove a herd of cattle through the western country, and took the cows of a Mr. Pomeroy along with him as he passed. Angus refused to return the cattle, and court action was necessary before restitution was made."[30]

William Galispie ("Red") Angus, according to Canton, "lived in a saloon and house of prostitution all his life" and associated with "thieves and cutthroats of the worst type." *Author's collection.*

Canton was enraged by being passed over for a man who had "lived in a saloon and house of prostitution all his life." In a letter to the WSGA, Canton added that Angus's associates were "thieves and cutthroats of the worst type."[31] His opinion of Angus was apparently confirmed when the newly elected sheriff appointed Thad Cole, a well-known mavericker, as his chief deputy.

Canton's unvented spleen may have contributed to a severe attack of inflammatory rheumatism he suffered that winter. Struck by the painful malady while staying with his inlaws at Sheridan in January, he was confined to his room and incapacitated for weeks. He did not return to Buffalo until March, and as late as April he still felt the effects of the siege.[32]

For Frank Canton, recovering from his rheumatic attack, a future in law enforcement looked bleak. He still held a commission as deputy U.S. marshal, but there was very little federal work in Johnson County. He also retained his appointment as stock inspector for the WSGA, but without a deputy sheriff's badge—and there would be no appointment as deputy with Red Angus in office—he had no arrest powers. He turned his attention to his ranch. In early 1889, with the financial backing of William Heywood, a Buffalo attorney and "an English writer of note," he bought some cattle in partnership and ranged them along Crazy Woman Greek.[33]

That spring Joe LeFors worked with Canton and Heywood at foreman

Bar C roundup in 1884. Standing left to right: foreman H. W. ("Hank")
Devoe, Ray Peters, George Gordon, Chester Morris, Nate Champion, Joe
Vincent. Seated left to right: Buck Jackson, Jack Donahue, W. H. Hall, Rice
McCarty, Sig Donahue, Al Allison, Bill Rankin, Jack Flagg. When war
erupted, Devoe remained a Canton supporter, Jack Donahue was a deputy
under Sheriff Angus, Champion was killed, and Gordon, Allison, and
Flagg were on the cattlemen's death list. *Courtesy American Heritage
Center, University of Wyoming.*

Charley Ford's "TA" wagon roundup on Poison Creek. LeFors recorded an
incident that probably did much to convince Canton that he could not rest
until the rustling problem in Johnson County was resolved. At the roundup
one morning Canton received a message from his wife, telling him that two
suspicious-looking men had driven a bunch of cattle past the Canton ranch.
They drove at night, a very unusual procedure, and when approached, they
left the cattle and took to the timber.

     "Canton showed me his wife's letter," recalled LeFors, "and said he could
not very well get away as he and Heywood were tallying their cattle. Since I
was only branding calves he insisted that I go and follow those cattle up."
LeFors went by the Canton house, talked to Annie, and got Canton's Winchester. He then followed the trail for some twenty-two miles before he
overtook the cattle, driven by two men he recognized as Powder River rus-

tlers. "One of them tried to make himself mad when I came up," LeFors said. "I was already mad so I could not see that he had anything on me."[34]

LeFors rode into the herd and saw that "every animal they had was burnt, brands defaced and ears cut off close to the head." At a nearby ranch LeFors found a cowboy who said he was heading for the roundup. LeFors gave the man a message for Canton explaining what he had found; meanwhile, he stayed close to the cattle, awaiting Canton's arrival. When Canton did not show up, LeFors rode back to the roundup and found that Canton had not received the message until it was too late. Heywood was sent to Buffalo to report the matter to Sheriff Angus and his deputy, Thad Cole. LeFors noted: "No officer would even come out to see them. The sheriff's office would not do a thing although there was, and is still, a statute against defacing brands. The sheriff's office showed us very plainly that we could expect no help from that direction. How could we hope from help with the deputy sheriff owning a maverick brand himself?"[35]

The incident made it clear to Canton that he had a choice to make: he had to either join the rustlers or attack them. But he had been down the outlaw route once before with disastrous results; he chose the latter course.

Throughout the spring and summer of 1889 a large ad ran in every issue of the *Big Horn Sentinel*:

$1,500 Reward

We the undersigned agree to pay the sum of $1,500 for the conviction of each and every person caught stealing, unlawfully killing, defacing or altering the brands of cattle or horses belonging to any or all of us anywhere. Also for the unlawful branding of mavericks on our respective ranges. [signed] Murphy Cattle Co.; Powder River Cattle Co.; Pratt & Ferris Cattle Co.; Peters & Alston; DesMoines Cattle Co.; Wm. Harris; Wm. Heywood; Conrad & Clarke; Wyoming Cattle Co.; Henry Blair; Frontier Land and Cattle Co.; Stoddard & Howard Live Stock Co.[36]

In June, Canton made a bid for that reward. He worked up a case against six men he considered the worst thieves in Johnson County and at the June session of district court got them indicted on a count of stealing "one head of neat cattle" and on seven counts of branding mavericks. Heading the list of the accused was O. H. ("Jack") Flagg, a twenty-eight-year-old native of West Virginia who came to Wyoming by way of Texas in 1882 and worked on Powder River ranches until he was blacklisted by the WSGA in 1887. He then established his own ranch on the Red Fork of the Powder and stocked it largely with what Canton always claimed was stolen beef. Flagg has been described by one historian as "a highly intelligent man, a cowboy, schoolteacher, editor, author, and politician of exceptional ability" who was also "a rebel who twisted the tails of the big outfits by all means—fair or foul."[37] But to Frank Canton, he was just a thief, albeit a very clever one. Canton's assessment of the man appeared in a letter he wrote to the WSGA two years before:

> I know Jack Flagg very well. I am confident that the Gentleman is Crooked. He bought about 12 head of immigrant cattle last fall from W. E. Hathaway on Powder Riv. I had expected Flagg to commence branding Mavericks this spring for I am satisfied that he bought this little bunch for that purpose. But I was not aware that he had branded any as yet. I think there is two others who intend to go into this business with him. I will investigate the matter at once and see what there is in it. Jack Flagg is an old timer here and is a hard man. He is cunning and it will take some good work to send him over the road.[38]

The five other men indicted were Martin Allison Tisdale, Tom Gardner, L. A. ("Lew") Webb, William Diamond, and "Black" Billy Hill. Tisdale, alias Al Allison, was indicted under the name "Martin Allison." He was the brother of John A. Tisdale, a neighbor of Flagg's on the Red Fork. The Tisdales, Texans who had come north with trail herds in 1884, were better educated than most others of their kind, having attended the Texas Military Institute at Austin. A Cheyenne paper characterized Al Allison as a fugitive and alleged that he had been run out of Texas for horse stealing. Gardner had come up from Texas with one of the Searight brothers' trail herds. He had attended the military school at Austin with the Tisdale brothers and was always close to them. A Cheyenne paper described him as "a tough from Round Rock." Webb was reputed to be from a wealthy Victoria, Texas, family that had spawned a bunch of wild sons and had been bankrupted defending one of them in a murder case. Diamond, indicted under the name William Carroll, had come to Wyoming from Nebraska and was said to have taken up rustling in the Sheridan area. The last of the six was Black Billy Hill, a cowboy who had come into the country in 1886 and worked on Henry Blair's Hoe Ranch, fifty miles south of Buffalo.[39]

With the dozen "immigrant" cattle purchased from Hathaway, Jack Flagg in 1887 established the Hat Ranch on the Red Fork. The following year he sold one-fifth shares in the ranch to Allison, Webb, Gardner and Hill. Although the Hat recorded no more stock purchases, by the spring of 1889 the original dozen longhorns had grown to several hundred.

Flagg and his confederates secured continuances of their cases at the July 1889 session of the district court and were released on bail of eighteen hundred dollars each. That fall the cases were quietly dropped, adding to Canton

Al Allison is in the center, flanked by Joe Coslett, left, and Tom Gardner, right. Coslett and Gardner have often been incorrectly identified as Dudley and Nate Champion. *Courtesy American Heritage Center, University of Wyoming.*

and the big cattlemen's conviction that they could not find justice in the Johnson County courts.[40]

Others agreed. District Court Judge Micah C. Saufley, after the acquittal of four accused stock thieves, expressed his indignation at the breakdown of the judicial system in Johnson County. "Each of these four men who have been tried is guilty of the crime charged," he thundered on the courthouse steps, "and it has been as clearly proved as in any case that has ever come within my knowledge, and yet the jury has in each case turned the prisoner free. I refuse to go on with any more of these cases; it might as well be understood that there is no protection for property in Johnson County."[41]

But even as Judge Saufley—and doubtless Frank Canton—fumed at the seeming impossibility of obtaining rustler convictions, a story broke that riveted everyone's attention. On July 20, 1889, a man named Jim Averell— saloonkeeper, store owner, and postmaster in the Sweetwater country of Carbon County—and Ellen Watson, believed by some to be his wife, were dragged from their homes by a party of men, taken to a canyon of the Sweetwater River, and hanged. Averell and Watson, outspoken adversaries of the big cattlemen, had been accused of harboring and abetting rustlers. The lynchings, called "probably the most revolting crime in the entire an- nals of the West,"[42] was the first major incidence of violence in what was to become an all-out war for the range, a struggle in which Frank Canton would be deeply involved.

There were witnesses to the lynching, and a coroner's jury named several Carbon County cattlemen as the perpetrators, but when a grand jury con- sidered the case three months later, witnesses had mysteriously died or dis- appeared. The cattlemen were never indicted.

Canton's main interest in the affair was probably the involvement of George B. Henderson, a close friend who had worked for Canton as a WSGA detective. When the bureau had been disbanded, John Clay, president of the WSGA, had hired Henderson as foreman of the "71" outfit. Henderson had broad experience, ranging from fighting Mollie Maguires in his native Penn- sylvania to work as a Pinkerton operative. He had been to Europe and had run down a famous criminal in South America. He and Canton were out of the same mold, even to the use of an alias: Henderson's real name was said to have been John Powers. Clay's description of his foreman could very well have applied to Canton also: "He was a silent, shrewd, able man, unfortu- nately giving way to drink occasionally, when he was garrulous and unreli- able. . . . He was a born sleuth, and it had become the mania of his life. He would rather hunt a thief than eat. He had no thought of fear. It was left out of his make-up, and yet he was the most tender of men, with fine instincts."[43]

Henderson was not named as one of the men who lynched Jim Averell and Ellen Watson, but he was close to those who were, and some believed it was he who disposed of the witnesses by murder or intimidation. After the lynching there were several attempts on his life. Finally, on October 8, 1890, he was shot and killed at the Sheehan ranch on the Sweetwater by John Tregoning, alias Jack Smith, and Samuel H. Berry, two cowboys who had worked for him on the 71. The gunmen claimed the shooting resulted from a dispute over wages, but Frank Canton marked it down as revenge for the Averell-Watson lynchings.

Canton testified for the prosecution at the trial of Tregoning and Berry held at Lander, Fremont County, in July of the following year. Tensions ran high. "The court room was crowded with men, many of whom were armed to the teeth, and wearing their guns openly and without rebuke." The jury was out for twenty-seven hours, with eleven standing for a first-degree murder conviction but with one holding out. A compromise verdict of second-degree murder was finally reached. Tregoning was sentenced to life imprisonment and Berry to twenty-five years.[44]

Even as Henderson's killers stood trial, a new lynching outrage was on everybody's mind. In newly formed Weston County, east of Johnson, on the morning of June 4, 1891, three men rode up to the cabin of Thomas J. Waggoner, handcuffed him, placed him on a horse, and rode off. Eleven days later his body was found hanging from a tree in a canyon two miles away.

Waggoner had arrived from Nebraska a few years before and started a very successful horse-raising operation. By 1891 he had a bank account of seventeen thousand dollars and a ranch on which he ran more than a thousand horses. Some claimed he was too successful, that his horse herds were built with stolen stock, and that his place was a way station for horse thieves operating in Montana and Wyoming. When he was lynched, suspicion immediately fell on his accusers, foremost of whom were Joe Elliott and Thomas G. Smith, two WSGA detectives who had worked for Canton. A Weston County deputy sheriff named Fred Coates was believed to be the third man.

Since the men who took Waggoner had worn disguises and masks, his wife could not identify them. No one was ever formally charged in the lynching, but those who hated the big cattlemen were certain it was another example of the high-handed brutality of the WSGA and its detective force, and the affair added fuel to the flames soon to explode in the conflagration known as the Johnson County Cattle War.[45]

But even as these events unfolded, events that would lead to the conflict that would dramatically change Frank Canton's future, life went on. His economic situation had improved, as evidenced by the tax assessment rolls for 1889. He now had five town lots valued at $450. His ranchland and improvements were assessed at $2,400. He had horses and livestock with a total value of $875 and other property worth $857. His taxable assets totaled $4,582, almost triple what he had only three years before.[46] In terms of worldly goods, this was probably the high point in his life.

Canton's "ranch" originally consisted of 160 acres patented as "desert land" by Frank Lake, who had followed him to Wyoming and lived on the property. On December 1, 1887, Lake gave Canton a warranty deed for this plot. In 1889 Canton patented an additional 320 acres and in 1890 was taxed on the total 480 acres.[47] He disposed of three of his town lots and much of his livestock that year, and the value of his total property was assessed at $2,700.[48]

Edward Burnett, a neighbor of Canton's on Crazy Woman Creek, related an amusing story illustrative of Canton's impulsiveness with regard to criminal evidence:

Cattle stealing and killing beef got bad. I used to dig our coal about two miles away. One morning Frank—riding "Curlew"—came over. "A beef has been killed in those hills where you dig your coal. Let's go and look it up."

I saddled up "Angel Eyes" and off we went. We found the head and hide of the beef. Then we circled around, looking for trail signs. When we got together I said, "Have you found anything?"

He produced the sleeve of an old shirt and said, "When we find the rest of this shirt, there will be a hanging."

I looked at it and said: "That's a piece of an old shirt of mine. My wife tied up a lunch for me the last load of coal I dug. The rest of the shirt is at home."[49]

Burnett told another story showing Canton's dogged determination. Canton, Burnett, and a man named Williams were appointed by the county commissioners to evaluate a tract of land for tax purposes. They were to be paid ten dollars a day each, but when the job was completed after three days no pay was forthcoming. A letter from the county attorney convinced Burnett and Williams to forget the matter, but Canton growled, "I'll show them." He did show them too, said Burnett. "We got our pay, $30.00 each, and it was a very pleasant trip."[50]

In 1890 some members of the WSGA urged Canton to run again for sheriff and suggested the association fund his campaign. Secretary Adams thought it was a bad idea. "I doubt very much the wisdom of attempting to raise an 'election fund' on Canton's behalf as an Association," he wrote a member. The association had been accused by its enemies of political interference, he said, but WSGA money had never been spent in the interest of a political aspirant, and he wanted to maintain that record. "The matter is of importance enough to be carefully considered," he said, "and I believe that we can help Canton as individuals, without laying ourselves open to blame."[51] But despite the efforts of individual members on Canton's behalf, Red Angus was again nominated by the Democrats and reelected in November.

That month Canton received a new deputy appointment issued by Joseph P. Rankin, who had replaced Jeff Carr as U.S. marshal for Wyoming.[52] Canton was acting in his capacity as a federal officer when he made an important arrest in early 1891. Two bandits had robbed a stagecoach near Baggs, Wyoming, in December 1889 and ransacked the mail pouches. Federal rewards were offered for their capture and conviction. The following September a man giving his name as Tom Ricketts but later identified as Daniel S. Parker, brother of the notorious outlaw Butch Cassidy, was captured near Moab, Utah, and charged with the robbery.[53]

In January 1891 Canton learned that a man known in Buffalo as Dolph Lusk was actually Bill Brown, the partner of Dan Parker. He confronted Brown at the Flying E Ranch, twenty miles from Buffalo. The outlaw "was heavily armed and did not propose to be taken, but Canton was too quick for him by a few seconds [and] got the drop on him."[54] Brown still "showed fight," reported a contemporary paper. "Although two six-shooters were held at his head he attempted to draw his revolver," but he was persuaded to surrender by Canton, who made the arrest without firing a shot.[55]

Described as "red-headed and eagle-eyed, one of the coolest and self-possessed highwaymen of recent years," Brown was held in the Buffalo jail as a federal prisoner until April, when Canton and Marshal Rankin conveyed him to Cheyenne to be tried with Parker. The two were convicted and given life sentences in the Detroit House of Corrections. Canton reportedly received a reward of one thousand dollars for Brown's capture.[56]

In June 1891 Owen Wister, on the verge of fame as a western novelist, rode into Buffalo, a town he described in a letter to his mother as "something horrible beyond words." With the condescension of an eastern snob he wrote: "If you want some impression of Buffalo's appearance and all the other towns too, think of the most sordid part of Atlantic City you can remember. A general litter of paltry wood houses back to back and side to back at all angles that seem to have been brought and dumped out from a wheelbarrow."[57]

In later years Frank Canton's admirers would claim that he was Wister's inspiration for the hero of the famous novel *The Virginian*. Wister was in Johnson County when Canton was there and certainly heard tales of his bravery and prowess, but there basis for the claim ends. Others believed they were the model for the Wister character, including, most amazingly, Edwin B. Trafton, a horse thief who was once a member of the Teton Jackson gang. Wister himself never publicly disputed any of the claimants, but his acquaintanceship with Canton was fleeting, and it is doubtful he was even aware the lawman claimed to be a Virginian.[58] Wister's only known meeting with Canton occurred when the young writer was riding into Buffalo that June. On the road he passed "Mr. Canton, Deputy U.S. Sheriff [sic]." He

Owen Wister met Canton in Wyoming, but did not model his famous character, The Virginian, on Canton. *Courtesy American Heritage Center, University of Wyoming.*

described Canton as having a "very quiet, very even voice." Wister added, "Does less shooting than any officer in his position, but is feared by all hands."[59]

Wister's letters and notebooks suggest that in Wyoming he was more interested in "the motley blackguards" he met. One who particularly fascinated him was "Black Henry" Smith, a notorious Johnson County rustler who had come up the trail in 1884 after a killing at Henrietta, Texas. Wister described Smith as "the real thing, [an] unabridged 'bad man.'" He had, said the writer, "the worst eyes" that Wister had "ever looked at. Perfectly fearless and shrewd, and treacherous." Wister added: "He is just bad through and through, without a scruple and without an effection. His face is entirely cruel, and you hear cruelty in his voice."[60]

A few days after Canton's meeting with Wister, Annie Canton and her daughters were involved in an accident that injured Annie and seriously endangered the lives of all three. On June 27 Annie set out from Buffalo in the family's light road-buggy, drawn by a gentle team, on the twelve-mile drive to the ranch. With her were Ruby, four and a half years old, and Helen, almost three. A mile from the house a crossbar blocked the entrance to a lane leading to the dwelling. Annie got out of the buggy, raised the bar, and led the horses through. She was replacing the bar when Helen clucked to the team, which started off at a walk.

Annie called to the horses to stop, but with no check on the reins, the animals quickened their pace to a trot. Annie ran to the side of the buggy and tried to climb in as the horses, now thoroughly frightened, broke into a gallop. Partly in and partly out, Annie desperately held fast to the buggy for a half mile. Finally her ankle-length skirts became entangled in a wheel, and she was thrown to the ground and dragged behind until her clothes were ripped from her. She lay unconscious on the ground as the team and buggy rolled on. Ruby was thrown out and escaped with only a few bruises and scrapes, but little Helen clung to the seat throughout the wild ride.

It happened that a children's party was being held at neighbor Edward Burnett's home, and guests spotted the runaway. Charlie Basch and his son-in-law, George Washbaugh, rode hard to head off the team and finally overtook and stopped the buggy three-quarters of a mile beyond the Canton home. Others from the Burnett party found Annie Canton lying unconscious in the lane and carried her to her house. Washbaugh, starting for Buffalo to seek medical help, met Canton on the road, told him of the accident, and continued on. Reported the *Buffalo Bulletin:* "Mr. Canton put spurs to his horse, reached home, saw that his wife's condition was critical, saddled up 'Old Fred' and told Charlie Basch to annihilate space with him, and Basch came very near doing so, as he made the 12 miles to town in exactly thirty-five minutes, arriving here almost simultaneously with George Washbaugh,

The Canton ranch on Crazy Woman Creek. An Arapaho woman, Mollie, drives the wagon. Note the tipis in the left background. *Courtesy Jim Gatchell Memorial Museum, Buffalo, Wyoming.*

who had left the scene of the accidents some minutes before Basch started."[61]

When a doctor arrived and examined Annie, he found that miraculously no bones were broken. She had many bruises and abrasions and had received several severe blows to the head as she bounced along the stony lane. It was feared she had suffered a brain concussion, but by the following day she had regained all her faculties, and the doctor announced that she was out of danger. Annie's mother stayed with her for a week as she mended. On July 4 Annie was moved to Buffalo, where the Wilkersons now lived. She remained under her mother's care until recovery was complete. Through the pages of the *Buffalo Bulletin* Canton expressed his gratitude to those who had rushed to the aid of his wife and children.[62]

By a strange twist of fate, both Charlie Basch, who made the swift run into town after the doctor, and Canton's prize horse "Fred," which he rode, would soon figure prominently in the most controversial event in Frank Canton's life. These next months were filled with misfortune and tragedy for Canton and his family. The accident in the ranch lane seemed to set off a chain of calamity lasting a half year and mounting in severity.

Frank Canton with his horse "Fred," which would figure prominently in two dramatic events. *Courtesy American Heritage Center, University of Wyoming.*

The first difficulty was simply irritating and frustrating. On July 7, as Annie lay resting at the home of the Wilkersons, Canton started for Lander to testify in the trial of Tregoning and Berry, the killers of his friend George Henderson. He was accompanied by Charles Burritt and F. H. Eggleston, who had also been subpoenaed to testify. The three men went in a wagon by way of Crazy Woman Hill, a difficult route even under ordinary conditions. A storm broke as they went up the hill, and a water spout struck the steep slope. The ascent became "absolutely appalling," rather like "crossing Niagara Falls with a locomotive on a slack wire," said the *Buffalo Bulletin*. "The cuts and washouts were fearful, and the mud worse than anything ever experienced." Despite this, the travelers made progress until they came to a yawning chasm impossible to cross. In attempting to turn the wagon, they mired the horses. The *Bulletin*, finding the affair amusing, reported: "After much labor they succeeded in extricating the outfit. Eggleston herded the horses to the bottom of the hill with a thunderbolt, while Burritt declares that he carried four thousand pounds of wagon and freight on his left shoulder two miles down the mountain before there was space enough in the path to turn

Johnson County cowboys. Nate Champion has been identified as the second figure from the left, with the white horse, white neckerchief, and white-handled pistol. *Courtesy American Heritage Center, University of Wyoming.*

around. Canton in the meantime was at the helm, holding by the tongue, casting off the stern sheets and sitting on the counterboard." The party returned to Buffalo, "weary, worn and wet, muddy, moist and mad." The next day they secured a four-horse outfit and started for Lander by the longer route around the mountain.[63]

The following month, perhaps as an aftermath of the Lander trip ordeal, Canton was struck down again by a debilitating rheumatic attack. "Frank Canton is quite seriously ill at Mr. Wilkerson's," reported the *Bulletin.* "It is Frank's old enemy, the rheumatism, which has him in its grip. . . . It is hoped that he will be spared the repetition of the terrible suffering he had two years ago." He was slow in improving and on September 12 left for Hot Springs, South Dakota, hoping to gain some relief from the baths there.[64]

As Canton sought relief from his debilitating rheumatic attacks, the conflict known as the Johnson County Cattle War was heating up. Three major episodes of violence that had already occurred were leading up to full-scale war: the lynching of Jim Averell and Ellen Watson in July 1889, the killing of George Henderson in October 1890, and the hanging of Tom Waggoner in June 1891. Early on the morning of November 1, 1891, the next major incident occurred, incensing many in Johnson County, who viewed it as another outrageous assault on innocent citizens by the minions of the cattle barons.

Central to the story was Nathan D. ("Nate") Champion, described by one lawman as a round-faced, graying, strongly built man of medium height, "fearless in the face of any odds and with the reputation for being the quickest man with a sixgun in the country."[65] Champion, who had been foreman for the EK Ranch before being blacklisted, was now believed to be a leader of the rustlers. He was a close friend of Tom Gardner's and the Tisdale brothers', John A. and Martin A. (Al Allison), who all came from the same part of Texas.[66]

What happened on the morning of November 1 was first reported in the *Buffalo Bulletin* of November 5 but was later described in some detail by Champion himself in an interview published in the Buffalo paper. Champion said he and Ross Gilbertson, another cowboy, were sleeping in an isolated one-room cabin high up on the headwaters of the Middle Fork of the Powder, when they were rudely awakened as the cabin door suddenly burst open. Said Champion:

> The light in the cabin from the open doorway gave me a full view of everything beyond the open door, but I was lying in the darkest part of the room. Two men were standing at the lower corner of the bed, their guns in their hands and pointed directly at me, while a third person stood behind the door, his head just showing over its top. One of the men cried, "Give up, boys; give up, boys." I asked, "Who are you, and what do you want?" at the same time reaching over the side of the bed and taking hold of my revolver. "Oh, we've got you; you might as well give up," said one of the intruders.
>
> With that they began shooting. The first shot just missed my head, the powder burning my face, the ball going through my pillow. As I raised my right arm from the side of the bed I fired at the men. They answered the shot and made a hasty exit, I firing a second shot as they went out the door. The first thing I saw was a Winchester standing against the corner of the cabin and another lying on the ground a few feet away. I took the first gun in my left hand, and just as I grasped it, a man jumped around the corner and threw down on me, but did not attempt to shoot. I jumped inside the door and fired a shot through the chinking of the cabin. When I got outside again, I saw a man going through the brush some distance from the cabin, but he disappeared before I had time to get a shot at him.[67]

Champion said he and Gilbertson followed tracks to a spot some seventy-five yards away where they found four overcoats, a meerschaum pipe, three silk handkerchiefs, and a gray cloth cap. Later Champion discovered a deserted camp where six horses were tethered. The two men found the remains of a pair of goggles in the ashes of the camp fire, together with a lead pencil and some papers. A tarpaulin-wrapped bed was nearby. Another tarpaulin, spattered with blood, was spread out as if to dry.

"I am pretty well convinced," said Champion, "that this crowd came to my cabin to kill Gilbertson and myself, but met with the wrong kind of reception to suit them. Their intention was good enough, but they were scared off. We have all the property enumerated above, which the owners can have by calling for it. All the horses are branded and belong in Johnson county with one exception."[68]

Of the major incidents leading up to the Johnson County Cattle War, this was the first in which the name of Frank Canton has been associated. No direct charge was made against him at the time, however. Officially Champion claimed to have recognized only one of his assailants, and that man was Joe Elliott. Warrants were issued for the arrest of Elliott and of Fred Coates, although apparently the only evidence against the latter was his suspected involvement with Elliott in the Waggoner hanging five months before.[69] Although Elliott and Coates were the only ones officially charged in the Champion assault, Frank Canton and others were identified as participants in a story that soon swept through the county and contributed to the mounting hatred of those believed to be the minions of the cattle barons.

Ross Gilbertson seems to have disappeared soon after the attack. Nate Champion then teamed up with a new partner, a big cowboy named Reuben ("Nick") Ray.[70] Reportedly wanted for two murders in Texas, Ray had drifted into Wyoming from Nebraska in 1889. According to William Irvine of the Ogallala Land and Cattle Company, he "was notorious as a thief" who had several times driven herds of stolen yearlings out of the country.[71] According to a story circulated by rustler sympathizers, several days after the assault, Champion, Ray, and John A. Tisdale ran into Mike Shonsey, foreman of the EK Ranch and a staunch supporter of the big cattlemen's cause. Champion, suspecting that Shonsey was one of the assault party, pulled a gun and demanded that the EK foreman name the others. "I know who they were but I want to hear you say it," he roared. "Don't lie to me or I'll kill you."[72]

A completely cowed Shonsey, so goes the story, admitted taking part in the raid and named his accomplices: Frank Canton, Joe Elliott, Bill Lykens, and a man remembered to history only as "Woodbox Jim." With the exception of Woodbox Jim, all were current or former WSGA detectives, and all were outspoken enemies of those who defied the association. It was the blood of Bill Lykens on the tarpaulin. Hit by one of Champion's snap shots, he had been taken to Casper by fast team for medical treatment that night but never

Mike Shonsey, a range detective who worked for Canton, played a large role in the Johnson County Cattle War. *Courtesy American Heritage Center, University of Wyoming.*

fully recovered and died in Missouri shortly afterward. The story had it that additional proof of Canton's involvement was provided by one of the Winchester rifles left at the scene: it was his property.[73]

All of this folklore grew and expanded in the aftermath of later events. Under oath at the preliminary hearing, Champion could identify only Elliott as one of the men who had attacked him. The later story, as it has evolved, is highly implausible. The men named as Champion's attackers—Canton, Elliott, Lykens, and Shonsey—were all tough, experienced range detectives whose courage and skill with firearms had been well demonstrated. It is difficult to believe that such men would have surprised Champion in his bed, fired at him at point-blank range without hitting him, and then run away, leaving their rifles, their overcoats, and their horses. If an attempt was made on Nate Champion's life in the manner described, it must have been undertaken by a remarkably inept bunch of assassins.

It should be remembered that Nate Champion is the sole source for the story of the dawn assault; Ross Gilbertson's testimony has not survived. Other than Joe Elliott, who vehemently denied involvement, the accused had no comment. In his memoirs, Canton completely ignored the attack on Champion. Shonsey lived into his nineties and apparently never recorded his version of the tale. Lykens, who had resigned his position as WSGA detective long before to take an investigative job with the railroad, had not been active in Johnson County for years. And Woodbox Jim was never identified, let alone interviewed.[74]

There is another possibility. Instead of a cowardly assassination attempt, perhaps there was a gunfight that morning on the remote Middle Fork, matching a party of WSGA detectives that included Canton, Elliott, and Shonsey against Champion, sided by Gilbertson, Nick Ray, and John A. Tisdale, all of whom Champion stated were in the area, and by Orley E. ("Ranger") Jones, another small rancher from the Red Fork. And perhaps Champion, coached by the clever Jack Flagg, simply invented the bed attack to arouse sympathy and make the WSGA gunmen appear more craven. This scenario would help explain the otherwise incomprehensible assassinations of John A. Tisdale and Ranger Jones one month later.

Chapter 5

The Accused, 1891

"Frank Canton lived on to follow his chosen calling, the killing of marked men for valuable consideration."

William H. Kittrell, introduction to A. S. Mercer,
The Banditti of the Plains

The Champion assault was a portent of momentous events to transpire that month. In Buffalo, court was in session, and the town was full of settlers from outlying sections. Cowboys, out of work for the season, crowded the saloons. Everywhere the talk was of the high-handed tactics of the cattle barons in general and the attempt to kill Champion in particular. Openly defying the powerful WSGA, the disgruntled small operators of Johnson County met in Buffalo on November 21 and formed a rival organization, called the Northern Wyoming Farmers' and Stock Growers' Association. Significantly, all but members were barred from Hasbrouck's Hall, where the bylaws and a constitution were drawn up.[1]

The very day of the meeting Frank Canton put his wife and children in a wagon driven by his father-in-law, W. H. Wilkerson, and sent them out of Buffalo. Whether he sensed in the mood of the town an impending explosion or whether he was planning to detonate that explosion himself is not known, but the decision to get his family away from Buffalo at this particular moment could not have been a coincidence. Wilkerson drove Annie and her daughters 110 miles through bitter cold—the temperature in Buffalo had dropped to seventeen below zero only five days before—to Gillette, where they caught a train for Chicago to visit Wilkerson relatives.[2] Little Helen would never return to Buffalo, and it would be almost a year before Annie and Ruby came back.

Among the many visitors to town that month were John A. Tisdale and Orley E. ("Ranger") Jones. According to one account, they were in Buffalo

John A. Tisdale, whose murder triggered an explosion in Johnson County and whose name would be forever linked with that of Frank Canton. *Courtesy American Heritage Center, University of Wyoming.*

to testify before the grand jury in the Champion assault case; if so, this may be a clue that they were indeed present that morning.[3] Neither of these men could be called "rustlers" as the term had been used for years on the range. They were not outlaws who ran off cattle and sold them, nor had they ever been charged with altering brands or branding mavericks to enlarge their own small herds. Their names had never even appeared on the WSGA blacklist of cowboys who were not to be hired. But they were representative of a rapidly growing group that found the hated maverick law and its enforcement by the cattle barons intolerable and that supported the mavericers, who were becoming increasingly open in their defiance of the big cattlemen. Tisdale and Jones had homesteads on the Red Fork near the Hat Ranch and were friendly with Jack Flagg, Tom Gardner, Billy Hill, Lew Webb, Nate Champion, and Nick Ray, all blacklisted by the WSGA.

Tisdale was thirty-six, a solid family man with a wife, two children, and another child on the way. After a good education in Texas he bossed three cattle drives up the trail and managed ranches in the Dakotas. For a time he was foreman of the Elkhorn Ranch of Theodore Roosevelt, who presented him with a high chair when his first son, Martin A. Tisdale, was born. He managed the Northern Pacific stockyards at Mandan before settling in Johnson County in 1889.[4]

A story has persisted through the years in Johnson County that Tisdale knew Canton as Joe Horner in Texas and that two of Tisdale's friends, an elderly couple, had been slain by Horner there. According to this account: "The first time Tisdale laid eyes on Canton, on the streets of Buffalo, he recognized him as the killer of his friends. Tisdale's first impulse was to avenge these deaths forthwith. With this intent, he followed Canton into a store; Canton went out the back door as Tisdale went in the front."[5] No evidence has surfaced to support this tale, either in Texas or Wyoming, but it has been "repeated by the fireside through many evenings over many years and passed on by local note-takers."[6]

"Ranger" Jones, a twenty-three-year-old cowboy with some local celebrity as a bronc-buster, had a small place on the Red Fork with his brother John. He was soon to be married and while in Buffalo bought lumber for a house he planned to construct for his bride. On Thanksgiving Day he attended a dance at Piney, north of Buffalo. While in town he also was said to have had a loud argument with Fred Hesse, with whom he had had a previous run-in on the range.[7]

Fred George Samuel Hesse, born in England in 1852, had arrived in Texas at the age of twenty-one and there learned the cattle business. He went to Wyoming in 1876 and became manager of Moreton Frewen's Powder River Cattle Company. Hesse was the owner of his own spread, the 28, on Crazy

Fred G. S. Hesse, a close friend of
Canton's, fled with him from Buf-
falo. *Courtesy American Heritage
Center, University of Wyoming.*

Woman Creek but made his home in Buffalo and was a close friend and
strong supporter of Frank Canton's.[8]

On Saturday, November 28, Jones pulled out for the Red Fork with his
load of lumber. D. A. Kingsbury passed him on the road near Muddy Creek,
fifteen miles south of town. He was never seen alive again.

Two days later John A. Tisdale drove his wagon out of Buffalo on the
same road. In town he had bought groceries for the winter and purchased
Christmas gifts for his wife and children. His friends later said that he had
spent time drinking in the saloons, unusual behavior for Tisdale, who was
not known as a drinking man, and that he had seemed to have a premonition
of danger. There were rumors that on his way to town he had been fired at
and that he had paid up all his debts, not expecting to reach home alive.[9]
There were stories that he had overheard Frank Canton remark to Fred Hesse
that Canton would "take care of Tisdale."[10] Significance has been attached to
the fact that Tisdale purchased a double-barreled shotgun while in Buffalo,
but a rifle would surely have been a better choice as a weapon of defense if
Tisdale truly feared an attack on the road.

It was late in the afternoon, a strange time to begin a sixty-mile trip by
wagon, when Tisdale left town on Monday, November 30. His wagon—drawn
by a pair of horses, a gray named Eagle and a brown named Coalie—was
loaded with provisions and Christmas presents.[11] Atop the pile was a female
hound dog and her pup given to him by George Munkres, the hardware
dealer, when he had bought his shotgun. Four miles from town Tisdale stopped
for the night with Elmer Freeman at the Cross H Ranch. Freeman would

later testify that Tisdale "was uneasy" and that he "asked to have the curtains pulled down before going to bed."[12]

On Tuesday, December 1, exactly one month after the alleged attack on Nate Champion, Tisdale resumed his journey. At nine o'clock he met and talked with Sam Stringer, the mail carrier, about two miles north of a deep dip in the road called Haywood's Gulch (now Tisdale Gulch). Stringer would be the last to see Tisdale alive.

As Tisdale's wagon dropped down into the draw and started up the other side, a rifle shot rang out. A bullet struck the revolver Tisdale carried in a shoulder holster, ricocheted, and severed the jugular of Eagle, the gray horse. Tisdale grabbed for the shotgun on the seat beside him, but a second rifle shot pierced his side, and he fell back dead. The murderer walked to his horse picketed a hundred yards away, mounted, and led Tisdale's team farther down the draw, out of sight of the road. There he shot and killed the horses and galloped off.

Charlie Basch, the Canton ranch neighbor who had helped save Annie and the girls at the time of the runaway accident the previous summer, was riding a saddle horse toward Buffalo that morning. Approaching Haywood's Gulch from the south at a little after ten o'clock, he met and spoke briefly to mail carrier Stringer. Basch rode through the gulch moments after the killer had done his deadly work. What Basch saw and heard has been the subject of controversy ever since that December morning more than a century ago.

Continuing on toward Buffalo, Basch met Elmer Freeman near the Cross H and told him he had seen something strange at Haywood's Gulch: a man leading a team and wagon off the road. Spotting Basch, the man had drawn his revolver, but no words were exchanged, and Basch rode on. Later he heard shots and in a few minutes saw the man riding hard across country toward Buffalo. Basch believed the man was Frank Canton, because he was riding Fred, the fine sorrel Basch had raced to Buffalo at the time of Annie Canton's accident. Aware that Canton was a deputy U.S. marshal, Basch attributed his strange behavior to some sort of police work in which he was engaged.

Freeman, concerned for Tisdale's safety after his nervous remarks of the previous night, came to a quick conclusion. "I bet Canton has killed Tisdale!" he blurted.[13] Basch and Freeman rode on into Buffalo, which they reached at twenty-five minutes to twelve by Basch's watch.

In light of what he had just told Freeman, Basch's actions on reaching town were peculiar. He did not report to the authorities or to anyone else what he had witnessed but instead had a meal and a couple of drinks and rode on northward to Rock Creek to attend to some cattle business. Years later he would give two conflicting reasons for his strange behavior, neither of which he testified to at the time. In one version he said that shortly after he arrived in town Sheriff Red Angus asked him if he had seen Canton at the gulch and that when he answered yes, Angus told him "not to say anything about it."[14] In another interview, Basch would ascribe his behavior to fear of Canton. "He was the first man that I spoke to in Buffalo," he said.

> He came right down and talked to me. And he says, "Did you see me out at the gulch?"
> I said, "Yes."
> "Well," he said, "that wasn't me that you saw out at the gulch."
> I said, "It wasn't?"
> He said, "No."[15]

Freeman meanwhile was excitedly telling everyone in town, including Sheriff Red Angus and Town Marshal Dan Mitchell, that Tisdale had met with disaster on the road and that Frank Canton had been on the scene. At about noon Angus dispatched Deputy Sheriffs Howard Roles and Jack Donahue to investigate. Freeman and Tom Gardner went along. At Haywood's Gulch they found a large pool of blood and Tisdale's shotgun lying on the road. A trail of blood led to the wagon several hundred yards away, where Tisdale's body lay sprawled across his purchases. The horses were dead in their traces. Later the body of a black hound with yellow legs was found some distance from the scene. It had evidently tried to follow the killer and been shot to death. Only the pup, wrapped in an overcoat in the wagonbed, was alive. The officers examined tracks, left in the snow and mud at the scene, of an unshod horse and a man wearing a Number 8 shoe, but they overlooked other clues in an investigation that has been called "as slovenly and incompetent as was ever seen in any part of the country, East or West."[16]

Freeman rode hard for Buffalo again to spread the news of the murder and to fetch County Coroner Frank H. Eggleston while Tom Gardner carried the sad information to the Tisdale family on the Red Fork. That afternoon another team of horses brought the wagon back to Buffalo. Tisdale's body was taken to a small log building near the courthouse.

The next day Eggleston presided over a coroner's inquest in which Charlie Basch, having returned from Rock Creek, was the star witness. This was the first time Basch publicly told the story that he would later repeat, with varying degrees of accuracy and detail, over many years. His testimony at the inquest was confusing, to say the least. Although admitting he told Freeman that he had seen Frank Canton and the horse Fred with the wagon at Haywood's Gulch, he now denied recognizing either one. He said Deputy Sheriff Roles met him on the way back from Rock Creek, told him of finding Tisdale's body, and said that he was needed for questioning at the inquest. Basch was driving a few head of cattle, which he took to Round's Livery and put in the corral. There he met Canton, who requested a few words with him in the privacy of the barn.

The conversation, as described by Basch under oath a few days later, was innocuous. Canton asked Basch if he had said he recognized Canton's horse at the scene of Tisdale's murder. When Basch answered that he had, Canton "said he could prove the horse had been under lock and key all morning [and] further said that it was a very serious matter for such a thing to get out on a person." In response to a direct question, Basch said that he and Canton were alone during this exchange.[17]

But Basch told the story differently years later. Howard Roles followed them into the barn, Basch said, and stood nearby as Canton questioned him about what he had seen at the gulch. "Howard was watching him, afraid that he was going to do something. . . . I wouldn't say what [Canton] would have done if I had been alone."[18] For whatever reason, Basch did not admit to recognizing either Canton or his horse at the inquest proceedings, and Coroner Eggleston found that Tisdale had come to his death by gunshots fired by a person or persons unknown.

The town was still in an uproar over Tisdale's murder when it was struck another blow. Johnny Jones had not seen or heard from his brother Ranger, who had left for home days before. Alarmed by the news of the Tisdale murder, Jones came into Buffalo and rounded up a search party to help him look for his brother. On the morning of December 3, the day after the Tisdale inquest, a dozen men rode out to comb the draws and gullies along the road to the south. Late that afternoon at Muddy Creek, only three miles from the spot where Tisdale had been killed, Billy Rinker followed the track of a wagon leading off the main road. Several hundred yards away, concealed from the road, he found a wagon and the stiffened body of Ranger Jones slumped over the dashboard. Jones had been dead several days. His horses had been released and were grazing in a nearby pasture.

Rinker raced to Buffalo with the news, and Coroner Eggleston and a party rode out to inspect the scene as well as they could in the darkness and bring the body back to town. The next day a coroner's jury and Dr. Park Holland examined the body in Jones's undertaking establishment. "Five bullet marks were found, one of the missiles having passed through the body, coming out at the right nipple. The deceased wore two coats, under which were belts holding rifle and six-shooter cartridges, and a revolver. On the seat of the buckboard was found a rifle. Neither weapon had been placed in position for instant use, which indicates that the attack was a total surprise."[19]

News of this second brutal murder turned Buffalo into an armed camp ready to explode in violence. Under the headline, "Horrors Accumulate," editor Joe DeBarthe of the *Buffalo Bulletin* gave details of the Jones murder and in an editorial said that people were "terribly worked up [and] trouble was anticipated [as] every man who came to town carried a Winchester rifle."[20]

Of course everyone was sure that these two very similar assassinations were the work of the same man or men. Because of Basch's allegations, Canton was the prime suspect, but some recalled Fred Hesse's difficulties with Ranger Jones. Canton's alleged remark to Hesse that he "would take care of Tisdale," his close friendship with Hesse, and the well-known loyalty of both men to the big cattlemen's interests, as well as other circumstantial evidence, made it easy to conclude that Canton and Hesse, separately or together, had perpetrated the murders. Tension mounted as armed and angry men grumbled that if the law did not take care of these killers, they would do it themselves.

Jack Flagg later wrote:

> Frank Canton and Hesse did not show themselves on the street but remained concealed. Finally word was sent to Canton that the boys wanted to see him and have him explain about his horse having been ridden by the murderer.
>
> Canton sent word down that he would not come; but if I would come to where he was he would talk to me and explain. I went to see him and he told me that he had not been out of town and neither had his horse, and asked me if his life would be safe in case he went out and saw the boys.
>
> I told him I could not answer for the whole crowd but that I would bring five or six of them up to see him and could answer for them that he would not be hurt.
>
> The boys came up to see him and had a talk, but Canton could not satisfy them as to his innocence.[21]

As might be expected, Canton's version of this story is a little different. "The rustlers and their friends," he wrote, "decided on a plot to assassinate me, which failed to materialize. I then called upon a bunch of the leaders of the rustlers and demanded that they prefer charges against me. This, after considerable hesitation, was done."[22]

The *Buffalo Echo* reported that the meeting was called on Canton's initiative and was held in a rear room of the John H. Conrad and Co. general store on Friday, December 4. Appearing with Canton were two of his friends, H. W. ("Hank") Devoe, a respected early settler and roundup foreman, and George W. Munkres, the hardware dealer. With Jack Flagg were John Tisdale's brother Al Allison, Lew Webb, Tom Gardner, and Cullen Watt. Canton "told them he would prefer that they should make formal charges in order that he might have a chance to clear himself in court."[23]

The following Monday Al Allison filed a complaint charging Canton with the murder of his brother. Sheriff Angus arrested Canton the same day and

Carroll H. Parmelee conducted the hearings into the Tisdale murder. *Courtesy American Heritage Center, University of Wyoming.*

held him in custody in the little building by the courthouse that had been Canton's home for four years. According to one story: "A plot to shoot him through the window of the sheriff's room, where he passed the night, was formed, but did not materialize, although the assassin remained up all night trying to screw up his courage."[24]

The hearing before Justice of the Peace Carroll H. Parmelee began on Tuesday morning, December 8. County Attorney Alvin Bennett, assisted by J. Walter Wilson of Sheridan County, prosecuted the case, and Buffalo Mayor Charles H. Burritt represented Canton. Fourteen witnesses were called by the prosecution and fifteen by the defense. Their testimony and the remarks of Justice Parmelee were taken down in shorthand by a Miss Webster, the court stenographer, and reproduced in entirety in both Buffalo papers.[25]

Thirteen of the prosecution witnesses merely filled in the story of Tisdale's movements on the day of the murder and before and provided a description of the murder scene. None of their testimony implicated Canton. It was left for the key witness, Charlie Basch, to make that connection, and as he took the stand, his testimony "was listened to with breathless interest."[26]

In response to questions, Basch said that he was on good terms with Canton, whom he had known about nine years. He said that as he approached Haywood's Gulch on the morning of December 1 he saw a team and wagon stopped in the road and a man leading a horse into the gulch. Topping another rise, he saw the man, mounted now, leading the team off the road. The horse the man rode was a light sorrel with two white hind feet, a white

forehead, and weighed about 950 pounds. "It was, to the best of my knowledge and belief, Mr. Canton's horse," he said. Basch said he was well acquainted with the horse, whose name was Fred, for he had once raced it
twelve miles into Buffalo. "Few horses can go 14 or 15 miles quicker than
that horse," he said in admiration. Although he testified to approaching within
fifty or sixty yards of the man in the gulch, Basch swore that he had not
recognized him. The man, he said, was dressed in a drab-colored overcoat
and a black hat, folded down the middle and pulled low over the eyes. A red-
and-brown scarf, worn around the neck, covered the man's face above the
mustache. Canton usually wore an overcoat and hat similar to the ones described, Basch said, but Basch had never seen him wear a scarf. Basch did not
speak to the man or approach him. He said, "I never ride up on a man carrying a gun in his hand." He thought whatever was going on was none of his
business. After he had ridden some distance down the road he heard two
shots back at the gulch. On cross-examination Basch admitted that his prior
testimony had been different. He said that he "wouldn't swear positive about
the horse" at the coroner's inquest but was "willing to so swear now." He
stated: "The horse I saw this man riding I am positive about. I know whose
horse it was; it was Mr. Canton's horse Fred."[27]

Writing some months later, Jack Flagg would say that the testimony of
Charlie Basch was supported by that of T. B. Hutton, who "swore that he
saw Canton come in on his horse, that he spoke to him; that the horse was
covered with sweat and foam," and by the testimony of Mrs. Olive S. Conrad,
"who swore that she saw a man riding a sorrel horse at tremendous speed
coming from the direction of the gulch."[28] This was a deliberate distortion of
the testimony, however. Hutton said he had seen Canton on a horse that
appeared to have been ridden fast between 1:00 and 2:30 on the afternoon of
Monday, November 30; this was before Tisdale left Buffalo. The horse Mrs.
Conrad saw "was too far away for identification, but looked as though he
was on a run."[29]

Frank Canton took the stand in his own defense. He said neither he nor
his horse left Buffalo on the day of Tisdale's murder. Since returning from
his trip to Hot Springs, South Dakota, he had been staying at the home of
his in-laws, the Wilkersons, he said. He still suffered from rheumatism and
did little horseback riding because he found it painful. He had not been to his
ranch south of town since Thanksgiving, November 26.

Step by step, almost minute by minute, from the hour of 6:00 A.M., when
he arose, until the afternoon, Canton accounted for his movements on that
fateful Tuesday, December 1. He had first fed and watered his horse, which
was kept in a locked stall at Carwile's Stable across the alley from Wilkerson's.
Only he and Wilkerson held keys to the stall. He recounted his stops and the

people with whom he had conversed. He had been to the post office, Dr. J. H. Lott's office, the City Drug Store of F. H. Eggleston, John H. Conrad's Trading Store, Holt's General Store, and the hardware store of George W. Munkres. He had read his mail and the newspapers in the Buffalo Club and had had a drink in the Jones Liquor Store before going to the courthouse and visiting with Sheriff Angus. He had stopped in the Occidental Hotel. At about two in the afternoon he had taken Fred to C. J. Hogerson's Wagon and Blacksmith Shop to be shod. He had not been feeling well at all, he said, since he "still felt pretty lame with rheumatism."[30]

A dozen witnesses, including some of the most respected and influential professionals and businessmen of the town, testified to seeing Canton in Buffalo that Tuesday morning. Most of them had conversed with him, and most could establish the times almost to the minute by their schedules. The testimony of Sam Stringer and Charles Basch fixed the hour of Tisdale's murder at 10:00 or very close to it. Tracks at the scene showed that the killer had waited some time for Tisdale's wagon to appear and had walked from his place of concealment to higher ground several times, looking for his victim's approach. After the shooting, the killer spent more time leading the team away and shooting the horses. It was a twenty-five-minute ride from Buffalo to Haywood's Gulch even on a speedy horse like Fred. To have committed the murder, Canton would have had to have been gone from Buffalo for at least an hour and ten minutes, or from 9:25 to 10:35. Seven reputable men—physicians J. H. Lott and Park Holland, hardware dealer George W. Munkres, druggist Frank H. Eggleston, rancher James T. Craig, Buffalo Club steward I. N. Pearson, and Robert Dunn, clerk at Hasbrouck's Clothing Store—all testified to seeing Canton in Buffalo between the hours of nine and eleven. Munkres and Holland swore to seeing him at or very near 10:00, the critical hour of the murder.

Testimony was taken well into the evening of December 8. Parmelee heard the last witness at 10:00 P.M. and took the matter under advisement, saying that he would announce his decision at 9:30 the following morning. At that time he addressed a packed courtroom:

> I was satisfied of one thing last night, as I think every one in the court room must have been, that the testimony adduced was very far from being sufficient to warrant a conviction before a jury, and in fact that no conviction could ever be had upon the testimony produced in that manner. However, my duties are very different from those of a jury, and it is not for me to decide upon a question of that kind, but the only question that is submitted to me which calls for my opinion and my decision is whether there is sufficient probable cause to think that the crime has been committed and that the

person accused is the one that committed it, to render it my duty to refer the matter to a higher tribunal for final trial and disposition. The testimony thoroughly satisfied me, and I think it could not have but satisfied others and every one that heard it all, that this defendant was not present at the time and place that the deed was committed. . . . I can not bring my mind to think that the horse that has been spoken of, and that is acknowledged to be the property of the defendant, was the horse that Basch saw at that time and place. . . . I can not see upon the whole, in reflecting upon this matter from every stand point, that there is sufficient ground to hold this defendant to answer to the district court, and that will be my decision.[31]

The hearing brought no calm to Buffalo. Not mollified by the Parmelee decision, those outraged by the murders thronged into town carrying guns. Al Allison and Johnny Jones, the brothers of the two murdered men, plotted to confront Canton on the street for a shootout, but knowing "Canton was a dangerous man to mix up with [and] a miss meant certain death," they lost their nerve.[32]

Canton did not lack supporters. Most of the businessmen of Buffalo believed him to be innocent. H. S. Elliott, the former prosecuting attorney of Johnson County who had moved to Chehalis, Washington, wrote Canton that he and his wife were "surprised and horrified" to learn that he had been arrested for the murder of Tisdale.

We know nothing of the circumstances against you nor do we care what they are or how strong they may appear to be, neither of us would ever believe that you had killed a man under such circumstances unless we heard it from your own lips. I know that you are absolutely incapable of committing such a crime under such circumstances, for no brave man could commit such a deed and brave I have every reason to know you to be. I trust and pray that you will not only be immediately released but that every imputation which may rest against you may be speedily cleared up. I only wish that I were present that I might use what talent God has seen fit to give me in a cause I know to be just.[33]

Canton would not receive this letter for some time because before it was delivered, he had departed Buffalo. On December 17 he and Fred Hesse rode out of town. Canton would later say that his decision to leave at that particular time was prompted by the receipt of a telegram from his wife, who said that she was ill in Chicago, but there was an additional reason for his precipitate departure. He learned that the friends of Tisdale had what they claimed was "new" evidence and were taking their case against Canton before a different justice of the peace, Joseph Reimann, to get a warrant issued for his arrest. Hesse, who Canton believed "would be in great danger if he remained in Buffalo alone," left as well.[34]

They began the long ride to the railroad terminus at Gillette on the morning of December 17, accompanied by Sam Sutherland, Hesse's brother-in-law, who would return with the horses when Canton and Hesse boarded the Burlington train. In his memoirs Canton described an exciting ride in which they were pursued by a band of seven rustlers; only the use of a shortcut through the Red Hills and the superior speed and endurance of their horses saved them from falling into the hands of their enemies.[35] He later told a newspaper reporter that they had covered the 110 miles in twenty-four hours.[36]

Buffalo Bulletin editor Joe DeBarthe, increasingly antagonistic to Canton and the ranching interests he represented, alleged almost two months later that the pursuers of Hesse and Canton were not "rustlers" but were, in fact, a posse led by Deputy Sheriff Howard Roles and Special Deputy John Round, who were attempting to serve the warrant issued by J. P. Reimann.[37]

Canton in his memoirs said that from Gillette he went on to Chicago, where he remained all winter with his wife and daughters, but contemporary newspaper stories show clearly that he was back in Wyoming within a week of his hasty departure from Buffalo.[38] Interviewed by Cheyenne newspaper reporters on Christmas Day, he said that at Gillette he had taken the train as far as Crawford, Nebraska, where he first learned that another warrant had been issued for his arrest. Hesse continued on to Chicago, but Canton went to Denver and then to Cheyenne. He arrived on Christmas Eve and checked into the Inter Ocean Hotel.

He had originally planned, he said, to spend Christmas with his family in Chicago and then go for a hot springs rheumatism treatment, but he returned to Wyoming because he wanted to face his accusers. However, he would not go to Buffalo as a prisoner of Sheriff Angus or his deputies, since he did not intend "to go into that country unarmed in the custody of a friend of the rustlers and a personal enemy." He stated, "It would be suicidal." He would return, he said, only "with an escort furnished by the state." He described the law-and-order situation in Johnson County as "deplorable." He could offer no theory to explain the killing of Tisdale and Jones but hinted that they were murdered by the rustlers. There was, he said, "trouble among the rustlers." He added, "Half a dozen [were] carrying Winchesters for others."[39]

The real purpose of Canton's trip to Cheyenne was to confer with the powerful members of the Wyoming Stock Growers Association, in whose service he had toiled so diligently and whose help he now needed to extricate himself from this serious trouble. Assistance came quickly in the appointment of Lacey and Van Devanter, counsel for the WSGA, to defend him. John

W. Lacey and Willis Van Devanter, both former chief justices of the Wyoming Supreme Court, were considered the best legal minds in the state. Canton, never flush with money, could hardly afford such legal talent, but the big ranchers appreciated loyalty and protected their own.

On advice of his counsel, Canton wrote letters to County Attorney Alvin Bennett and Sheriff Angus, saying that it would "only be necessary to send him word that he [was] wanted in Buffalo to secure his presence there" but that he was beginning a trip to pay "visits to friends in different eastern localities." He then boarded a train for Chicago.[40] Canton was described in the press as being in poor physical condition in December 1891. At the time of the Parmelee hearing, according to one story, he was so debilitated that it was "a farce" to charge him with the murder of Tisdale. "He has been in this condition for weeks past and paid a visit to Hot Springs, South Dakota, from which he obtained but little relief. He has been totally unable to mount a horse and little more than able to crawl around."[41] At the time of his visit to Cheyenne later in the month he was still described as being "in poor health."[42]

These stories may have been the basis for the repeated fiction that Canton was tubercular. John K. Rollinson, a Wyoming rancher, wrote that Canton had "a tubercular condition."[43] Bill Walker, who would play a role in upcoming dramatic events, said that "he was a lunger, and at that time I didn't think he would live the year out."[44] And a newspaper columnist in 1941 wrote that Canton's universally recognized fearlessness was due to "the misery of consumption gnawing at his vitals [which] doubtless made him more implacable to those against whom he set his official or private hand."[45]

Canton was not tubercular, nor was he, after the attacks of late 1891, greatly afflicted with inflammatory rheumatism during the remainder of a long and vigorous life. It apparently never occurred to the Cheyenne newspaperman to question how a man who had "been totally unable to mount a horse and little more than able to crawl around" only a few weeks before could, in the dead of winter, accomplish the difficult and arduous 110-mile horseback ride from Buffalo to Gillette in twenty-four hours. Canton was undoubtedly in better physical condition than had been depicted.

Shortly after his arrival in Chicago, however, serious illness struck his family. Annie and both daughters contracted diphtheria and were in critical condition for about ten days. Gradually Annie and six-year-old Ruby recovered, but little Helen, three and a half years old, weakened and died on January 16, 1892.[46]

The new year brought no lessening of the tensions in Johnson County. Prominent in the two Buffalo papers was a notice of a five-thousand-dollar reward offered by the county commissioners "for the arrest and conviction of the murderer or murderers of John A. Tisdale and Orley E. Jones." The editors of the papers were lined up on opposite sides of the fight between the cattle barons and the rustlers, with Joe DeBarthe of the *Bulletin* espousing the cause of the grangers and small ranchers and with Thomas J. Bouton of the *Echo* defending the big cattlemen. Editorials in the papers in the wake of the Parmelee hearing of December 8 illustrate the opposite viewpoints.

DeBarthe praised the restraint exhibited by the murdered men's friends, who had "been here in great numbers and [had] won the respect, confidence and sympathy of this community by the law-abiding manner in which they [had] conducted themselves," whereas Bouton found more threatening the visitors who, "justly filled with wrath, armed themselves, and flocked to town thirsting for vengeance." DeBarthe lauded Sheriff Angus, who, he said, "lulled and quieted [the] angry men who came here crying for vengeance [and] made himself master of the situation by a gentle firmness, not by fear or favor." Bouton found in the sheriff's actions nothing to compliment; he criticized the perfunctory investigation of the murders by the sheriff's office: "The conduct of our peace officers has been reprehensible."[47]

With warrants for the arrest of Joe Elliott and Fred Coates in the alleged dawn attack on Nate Champion, Sheriff Angus in the first week of February went to Merino, Wyoming, and arrested Elliott. Coates had gone to Kentucky on business, he was told. Angus took his prisoner by train to Gillette, from which point he would have to go overland to Buffalo. Elliott's account of that trip reveals the disquiet gripping the country. At Gillette he was tipped by friends that rustlers planned a lynching party for him in Suggs. Elliott said he "didn't like the sound of that," so he asked Jim Swisher, a Gillette officer, for a Colt .45 and a box of cartridges. Elliott recalled:

He got them for me, but made this specification: that I tell Angus, in his presence, that I had them. So when we got on the stage—a sleigh, it was—I told Angus that I was going to Buffalo with him, all right, but that a friend had slipped me a .45, and I wanted to know if he'd let me keep it. Angus looked at me a minute and said yes.

Going down Spotted Horse Creek, the sleigh upset. There was a woman passenger, and she was hurt a little, I believe. Angus's Winchester fell out into the snow, and he asked me to go back and find it. I did, went back and got it, and I carried the Winchester from there on. When we got down to Suggs I went into the eating house, carrying the Winchester, with the .45 sticking out of my pocket. The sheriff just went in there with me, and then went out again. When I got ready to go Angus wasn't there. I figured he was talking to those thieves who wanted to hang me, telling them they couldn't do it.

A woman from Suggs later told Elliott that a bunch of rustlers came in the next morning and said they had lost the trail of the sleigh. "I believe Angus talked them out of it," Elliott said, "though maybe the fact that I had that .45 and the Winchester had something to do with it."[48]

Elliott was released on a one-thousand-dollar bond. At a preliminary hearing Champion positively identified him as the attacker who had "jumped around the corner and threw down" on him but had not fired. Elliott swore he had never seen Champion before and asked: "Does that make sense? What the hell was I there for? If I was going to run why didn't I run? If I was waiting there to shoot him why didn't I shoot him?" Despite his protestations, Elliott was bound over for trial on a charge of assault with intent to murder and jailed at Buffalo for several weeks until he could raise a five-thousand-dollar bail. On March 8 four Newcastle bondsmen were certified in that amount, and Elliott was freed. In the light of later events the case against him was quietly dropped.[49]

On March 26 the Northern Wyoming Farmers' and Stock Growers' Association, which the WSGA did not recognize and considered illegal, met in Buffalo and made plans for spring roundups to be held before the officially sanctioned WSGA roundup. Committee members appointed by President John R. Smith to make arrangements were Tom Gardner, Ed Tway, Robert Foote Jr., Nate Champion, Lew Webb, and Al Allison.[50] All of these men, including Smith, were blacklisted by the WSGA and branded as rustlers.

From faraway Chicago, Frank Canton kept a close eye on these developments. The early months of 1892 were a strange and dangerous time for Canton. During his visit to Cheyenne in December he had discussed with his rancher friends the problems in Johnson County and the deteriorating state of affairs from the cattlemen's perspective. He was told that at a meeting in Omaha the leading members of the WSGA had voted to take decisive action against the rustlers in the spring. Momentous events were afoot, and Canton would play an important part in them.[51] But before that could happen, something had to be done about this bothersome Tisdale murder case. In Chicago, Canton mourned the death of his daughter and awaited developments.

On March 8, 1892, an information was filed in the Second District Court at Buffalo, charging Frank Canton with first-degree murder in the death of John A. Tisdale. County Attorney Bennett that same day wrote Dr. Amos W. Barber, a physician and acting governor, advising him of the information filed and requesting that a requisition be issued for Canton's return from Illinois.[52]

Two days later John W. Blake, judge for the Second Judicial District, wrote Bennett from Laramie, where he was about to open the regular spring term of court. A very large docket faced him, said Judge Blake, and he could not possibly go to Buffalo before June. Although he assured Bennett he was anxious to see the parties guilty of the recent crimes in Johnson County brought to justice, he added a word of caution. "Be sure," he said, "that you are on the right track, as every time you arrest or pursue the wrong parties you are giving the guilty ones greater advantages for escape. I understand there is another warrant and a requisition out for Canton's arrest, and also for Coates of Weston county. I hope you have proof enough to make these steps advisable, for as you will see no trial can be had for some time to come."[53]

Bennett answered on the sixteenth. "There was another warrant issued for Canton's arrest before I arrived home from the Sheridan district court," he said. "At that time I was not aware of any more evidence than was adduced upon the preliminary examination before Judge Parmelee; since then sworn statements have been presented and filed in my office which strongly corroborate the theory claimed by the State at that time. A certified copy of an information was some time ago sent to Cheyenne, asking that a requisition be issued, but as yet has not been granted." In regard to the charges against Joe Elliott and Fred Coates in the Champion assault case, Bennett said that he had "not a single doubt as to their implication." He added, "We have direct proof of their complicity." He was well aware that in Johnson County and throughout the state there were two factions, "strongly and determinedly opposed to each other." He noted, "The waves of public opinion are strong and at times run wild." But he professed to favor neither side. "No one perhaps detests crime more than I do," he assured the judge, "and I believe it right and proper to prosecute the criminal, whether he be a large cattle man, a small cattle man, or no cattle man at all."[54]

When he penned this letter, Bennett had not as yet received a response to his request to the acting governor for a requisition for Canton, but he must have gotten it soon thereafter. Barber's answer was dated March 12:

I am reliably informed,

First: That Canton was arrested upon this same charge in your county during the month of December, 1891, and that a preliminary examination was had upon the charge before a justice of the peace at Buffalo, upon which hearing Canton was discharged, the evidence not being sufficient to justify the justice of the peace in holding him for trial in the district court.

Second: That afterwards a second complaint was filed against Canton, charging him with this same offense; that upon learning of this second charge Canton wrote letters to you and to the sheriff of your county stating that he was ready to meet the charge at any time, and that he would voluntarily return to Buffalo for that purpose whenever you requested his presence there, and further informing you and the sheriff of his whereabouts; and that you and the sheriff, in answer to those letters, wrote to Canton that you would inform him when his presence in Buffalo was necessary, so that he might return voluntarily.

Third: That ever since that time Canton has been openly staying with his family at Chicago, Illinois, and that his whereabouts have been well known to you and the sheriff of your county.

Fourth: That neither you nor the sheriff of your county have indicated to Canton any desire for his return.

Fifth: That Canton has at no time shown any disposition to evade or avoid an arrest, examination or trial upon this charge.

If this be true it cannot be well claimed that Canton is a fugitive from justice, and in the entire absence of any request for his return it does not seem right for your county to be put to the considerable expense of bringing Canton to Buffalo on a requisition.

Under these circumstances it is but right to your county that you should first request Canton to return to Buffalo to answer the charge.[55]

The acting governor's refusal to cooperate in forcing Canton's return was seen by the rustler element as proof that Dr. Barber was a tool of the cattle barons, a view confirmed by later developments. For Canton, Barber's refusal ensured his continued freedom beyond the boundaries of Wyoming. But, if he was to assist in any action of the cattlemen against the rustlers, it would be necessary for him to move within the state. A warrant for his arrest, spiced with a five-thousand-dollar reward, was still outstanding. Canton may not have feared a trial, but he definitely wanted to avoid any possibility of confinement at Buffalo until his case could be heard by Judge Blake in June. Spending months in the jail he once supervised was an unpleasant prospect in itself, but he also had little confidence in Sheriff Angus's ability or desire to protect him from his enemies in Johnson County.

Following notification of the information filing in March, Canton's attorneys began negotiations for a bail-bond agreement. It took several weeks, but on April 4, in Judge Blake's court at Laramie, they succeeded in getting bail fixed and bondsmen qualified. The amount, thirty thousand dollars, was enormous for the time, and the list of sureties included many of the wealthiest and most powerful ranchers of the state. There were twenty-one names in all, every one a prominent member of the Wyoming Stock Growers Association.

The roll call included the following: George W. Baxter, former governor of Wyoming and an executive committeeman of the WSGA; Hiram B. Ijams, secretary of the organization; R. S. Van Tassell, also a member of the executive committee; E. S. Rouse Boughton, vice-president of the Frontier Land and Cattle Company; Joseph G. Pratt, of the huge U Cross Ranch in Johnson County; and James W. Hammond, another member of the WSGA executive committee. Within hours of the finalization of the bail-bond agreement, thir-teen of the bondsmen, all prominent ranchers, would embark with Canton on the ill-advised and ill-fated "cattlemen's invasion" of Johnson County.[56] Because of that invasion and its legal aftermath, the case of the state of Wyoming versus Frank M. Canton, charged with the murder of John A. Tisdale, would not be resolved for another year.

Chapter 6

The Warrior, 1892-1893

"Canton is acknowledged to be the nerviest man on Wyoming soil.
The rustlers wanted to get him out of the way and skin him alive,
but no ten would dare give him battle."

Chicago Herald, April 25, 1892

Smarting from cattle losses they attributed to the work of rustlers, alarmed at the prospect of a spring roundup in which they were sure they would lose *all* mavericks, and angry at the inability of the legal system to control what they considered a total breakdown of the concept of property rights, the big cattlemen of Wyoming prepared for war in the winter of 1891–92. Montana ranchers, led by pioneer cattleman Granville Stuart, in 1884 had conducted a successful campaign to sweep stock thieves from their ranges, reportedly killing many, and the Wyoming cattlemen undoubtedly took that operation as their model.[1] Their plan was simple: with a force of tough fighting men and a death list, they would mount a swift punitive raid into rustler-infested Johnson County. As they found the listed men, they would kill them. After a dozen or so had been eliminated, the rest of the thieving rabble would panic and flee the country.[2]

The number of names on that death list, men who "should die for the good of the country," has been reported as low as nineteen and as high as seventy.[3] The original list, "neatly typewritten in a column," is not extant, but from contemporary sources it is possible to identify most of the names that certainly would have appeared.[4] On April 19, at the height of the invasion excitement, the *Chicago Herald* published a story attempting to justify the actions of the cattlemen and appended a list of the supposed rustlers of Johnson County. The thirty-four-name roster, probably provided by Secretary Hiram Ijams of the WSGA, was headed by Jack Flagg and included his close associates on the hated Hat Ranch: Al Allison, Tom Gardner, Billy Hill, Lew Webb, William Diamond, Ross Gilbertson, Nate Champion, and Nick Ray. Other old enemies of Frank Canton's such as Edward ("One-Eyed Tex") Cherpolloid, Andrew S. ("Arapaho") Brown, and Thad Cole were named, as well as Johnny Jones, brother of the murdered Ranger Jones. Buffalo merchant Robert Foote and County Treasurer W. E. Williams were listed, along with notorious outlaws Charlie Taylor and "Black Henry" Smith. The rest were cowboys and settlers suspected of mavericking: Sanford ("Zang") Thompson; Will ("Hump-backed Kid") Donnelly; Lee Moore; H. S. ("Jumbo") McKenzie; Johnson Long; George Gordon; Jack Toddy; Tom Hathaway; Jack Bell; Ed ("Eat-Em-Up-Jake") Tway; John R. Smith and his son, Al; Frank Smith, alias Gus Johnson; Andy Kennedy; George ("Chips") Peterson; Jim Huff; and Terence ("Coyote") Smith. An injunction to block the renegade roundup in Johnson County was issued on May 4. The names of those enjoined closely approximated the published list.[5]

With his unique knowledge of Johnson County and its residents, Frank Canton was probably the author of the infamous death list; when the "cattlemen's invasion" ended in disaster, it was in Canton's valise that the list was reportedly found.[6] In his memoirs Canton attempted to depict the invasion as legal. The cattlemen, he said, "secured warrants for some ten or twelve of the leaders of the rustler band" and requested Canton "to join the party and take charge of the criminal warrants," but there were no warrants, and the raid had no justification in law at all.[7] Yet Canton was assured by the mission planners that the state's most influential and powerful figures— men like Acting Governor Amos W. Barber, U.S. Senators Joseph M. Carey and Francis E. Warren, Canton's attorney Willis Van Devanter, Union Pacific Railroad officials, and many of the region's prominent cattlemen—supported the plan.[8]

Preparations were to be conducted in the utmost secrecy. Ranchers had to be enlisted and fighting men recruited. Horses, wagons, provisions, guns, and ammunition had to be procured and arrangements made for transportation by special railroad cars. Canton's enemies have charged that he went to Texas to enlist gunmen, but he had good reason not to show his face in Texas, where it might be recognized as that of Joe Horner, convicted felon and escaped convict.[9] Another former Texan, WSGA detective Tom Smith (not the Thomas G. Smith suspected in the Waggoner lynching in the previous June), was given the recruitment job in the Lone Star State, which at the time was considered, with much justification, the home of gunfighters. Canton evidently did some recruitment of cattlemen, however. Rancher George T. Beck was hospitalized in Newcastle, near the South Dakota border, late that winter, and Canton ventured into Wyoming long enough to inform him of the planned raid. Beck later wrote that although he sympathized completely with the cattlemen, he begged Canton to "tell them not to do such a foolish thing, as it would end in disaster."[10]

On April 5, 1892, the day after Canton's bail approval, the cattlemen's army, fifty-two strong, assembled in Cheyenne. Nineteen were ranch owners, managers, and foremen, among them some of Canton's closest friends: Fred Hesse, owner of the 28 Ranch; Charley Ford, manager of the TA; Billy Irvine, of the Converse Cattle Company; Frank Laberteaux, foreman of the Hoe Ranch; and the Canadian brothers John N. and Bob Tisdale (no relation to Texans John A. Tisdale and Martin Allison Tisdale).[11] In addition to the thirteen cattlemen who signed Canton's bond, A. D. Adamson, Richard M. Allen, C. A. Campbell, W. J. Clarke, Fred DeBillier, W. B. Wallace, and Frank Wolcott joined the expedition.

Also on hand were a coterie of range detectives with whom Canton had worked for years: Joe Elliott, Scott ("Quick Shot") Davis, Ben Morrison, and W. H. Tabor. Two others, Mike Shonsey and Phil DuFran, were scouting out the country and would join the expedition later. Tom Smith was back from Texas with twenty mercenaries, unemployed county and federal officers he had found hanging around the federal court at Paris.[12] George Dunning, a gunman recruited by WSGA Secretary Ijams at Silver City, Idaho, joined the ranks; his enlistment later proved to be the first of many blunders to plague the operation. Dunning would later allege that the gunfighters were hired at five dollars a day plus expenses, with the promise of a fifty-dollar bounty for each rustler killed. Six noncombatants accompanied the expedition: three teamsters to drive the wagons, two newsmen—Sam T. Clover of the *Chicago Herald* and Ed Towse of the *Cheyenne Sun*—and a surgeon, Dr. Charles B. Penrose.

In command was Frank E. Wolcott, a fifty-one-year-old New Yorker still called "Major" after achieving that rank in the Union army during the Civil War. Wolcott came to Wyoming in 1870 and two years later was appointed U.S. marshal for the territory. In 1892 he was the manager of the VR Ranch in Converse County. His selection as commander, based on little more than a military title earned thirty years before, was another mistake. Bullheaded and shortsighted, Wolcott had few qualifications as a strategist or a leader of men. He appointed no lieutenants, but Frank Canton, as former chief of the WSGA Detective Bureau, naturally took command of the detective contingent, and Tom Smith assumed leadership of the mercenaries he had recruited.

Late in the afternoon of that Tuesday, April 5, the men loaded their horses, wagons, and supplies on a Fremont, Elkhorn, and Missouri Valley special train at Cheyenne and set out on their expedition. The six-car train would

William ("Billy") Irvine, one of the Johnson County invaders, argued bitterly with Canton and Hesse over strategy. *Author's collection.*

take them 150 miles to Casper, where they would unload and continue north by horseback and wagon. To isolate Buffalo and ensure a surprise incursion, Senator Carey's ranch manager, Ed David, was ahead cutting the telegraph lines into the town.

Only hours into the train trip, Canton and Wolcott clashed. Wolcott and a crew were arranging supplies in the baggage car when Canton entered. Brusquely, Wolcott ordered him out. Canton bristled at the tone, and sharp words were exchanged. "This was the start of a bitter feeling between the two," Billy Irvine said, "which gave us considerable trouble later."[13]

The army arrived at Casper in the early hours of the sixth, unloaded, hitched up their horses, and moved out again before dawn. At a camp on the trail that night Irvine talked earnestly to Wolcott, voicing concern over the Wolcott-Canton discord. The next morning Wolcott "made a very manly speech, resigning command of the expedition for the sake of peace and harmony," Irvine said. "From that time until the night we struck Sheriff Angus and his party, Frank Canton was in command."[14] The way George Dunning remembered it, however, the men were called together and told that thereafter "part of the mob would be in command of Tom Smith, and the rest of them would be in command of Frank Canton." They were "to obey orders and ask no questions."[15]

It was snowing heavily when the main body of invaders, riding ahead of the slower wagons, arrived at the Tisdale brothers' ranch on the evening of

April 7. There they met Mike Shonsey, who reported seeing a bunch of rustlers at the nearby KC and urged an immediate attack.[16] This news triggered a new round of contention as Wolcott and Irvine sided with Shonsey while Canton and Hesse argued for a direct advance on Buffalo as originally planned. Canton, remarkably prescient, pointed out that if a single rustler escaped from the KC and alerted the crowd at Buffalo, the expedition was doomed. Ford, Laberteaux, and Campbell backed this argument, but a majority voted to move on the KC Ranch and wipe out the rustlers there. The change in plans, ensuring a delay of at least a day, lost for the invaders any chance for a surprise strike at Buffalo and was another of the errors in judgment that doomed the expedition.[17]

The invaders moved out from Tisdale's at eleven o'clock on the night of April 8 and rode fourteen miles through a wintry gale to the KC. At dawn they deployed around the cabin, taking up positions in the stable, along the riverbank, and in a draw leading to the river. Shivering from the bitter cold and nervous tension, they watched the cabin for almost two hours. A wagon that Shonsey said had not been there before indicated the arrival of new visitors. The invaders, determined to execute only the guilty, wanted no innocent blood on their hands. They waited.

Only two of the men on the cattlemen's death list, Nate Champion and Nick Ray, were inside the cabin. The others Shonsey had seen the previous day were gone. With Champion and Ray were their visitors, Bill Walker and Ben Jones, out-of-work ranch hands who were trapping game in the area to make it through the winter.

Jones, carrying a bucket to fetch water, came out first. Grabbed as soon as he was out of sight of the cabin, he satisfied his captors of his innocence and told them who remained in the building. When Walker emerged, he was also seized and held with his partner in the stable. Moments later Nick Ray stepped outside, looking about suspiciously. Canton recognized him and passed the word. Ray had taken only a few steps from the cabin when Texas gunman D. E. Booker, alias the Texas Kid, drilled him with a shot. Then rifles on all sides opened up, and Ray, mortally wounded, staggered back and collapsed in the doorway. Nate Champion opened the door and, with bullets snapping all around him, pulled Ray inside.

For an hour the besiegers poured lead into the cabin as Champion returned an occasional shot to let them know he was not dead. Finally a ceasefire was called, and the leaders met to consider options. Deciding to burn Champion out, they sent a detail to the nearby Western Union Beef Company Ranch for a load of hay.

During lulls in the battle the beleaguered Nate Champion scribbled a record of the fight in a pocket notebook. This running commentary as he faced

Nate Champion fought heroically against the invaders and left a classic firsthand account of the battle. *Courtesy Jim Gatchell Memorial Museum, Buffalo, Wyoming.*

death at the hands of his enemies has become a frontier history classic. He wrote:

> Nick is shot but not dead yet. He is awful sick. I must go and wait on him.
>
> It is now about two hours since the first shot. Nick is still alive.
>
> They are still shooting and are all around the house. Boys, there is bullets coming in like hail.
>
> Them fellows is in such shape I can't get at them. They are shooting from the stable and river and back of the house.
>
> Nick is dead. He died about 9 o'clock. I see a smoke down at the stable and I think they have fired it.
>
> I don't think they intend to let me get away this time.[18]

The party that had been sent after hay reported back that none was to be found. Undecided on their next move, the invaders ate lunch and rested. Wolcott called in pickets that had been stationed on the road, another bad mistake.

Champion scribbled on:

> It is now about noon. There is someone at the stable yet. They are throwing a rope at the door and dragging it back. I guess it is to draw me out. I wish that duck would go further so I can get a shot at him. . . .[19]
>
> Boys, I feel pretty lonesome just now. I wish there was someone here with me so we could watch all sides at once. They may fool around until I get a good shot before they leave.

During this period of quiet a capricious Fate dropped, straight into the hands of the cattlemen, the man whose name headed their death list. Jack Flagg left his Red Fork ranch that morning with his seventeen-year-old stepson, Alonzo Taylor, bound for Douglas and the Democratic state convention. Riding a sorrel horse, he came down the road leading to the KC at about 2:30 in the afternoon. Fifty yards ahead of him, young Taylor drove a team hitched to the running gears of a small wagon. The firing had stopped for the moment, and the two were completely oblivious to the drama into which they rode.

The hidden gunmen allowed the wagon and its young driver to pass unchallenged; there was a critical moment of indecision, since the following horseman was not immediately recognized. The rider was almost to the bridge before Charley Ford, stationed with Scott Davis, yelled, "Jack Flagg! Jack Flagg!" and snapped off an errant rifle shot. Failing to live up to his nickname, "Quick Shot" Davis was slow to get the rider in his sights. Flagg spurred his mount and raced for the bridge as other guns belatedly opened up. Young Taylor whipped up his team and clattered over the bridge as Flagg thundered behind with bullets cutting all around. Miraculously, neither was hit, and only one of the wagon team was wounded.

Some of the invaders ran for their horses, picketed some distance away, to take pursuit. The wagon was out of sight over the breast of a hill when Flagg caught up with it. He and Taylor cut the lines to the team, the boy swung up on the uninjured horse, and the two galloped hard toward Buffalo. Seven invaders chased them for a few miles but returned empty-handed.[20]

Allowing Jack Flagg to slip through their hands was another in what was becoming a long string of blunders in this ill-advised and ill-fated expedition. "We were all so mad and chagrined at Flagg's escape that we came near fighting among ourselves," Irvine remembered bitterly.[21]

Champion also did not recognize Flagg. "It is about 3 o'clock now," he was writing. "There was a man in a buckboard and one on horseback just passed. They fired on them as they went by. I don't know if they killed them or not. I seen lots of men come out on horses on the other side of the river and take after them. I shot at a man in the stable just now. Don't know if I got him or not. I must go look out again. It don't look as if there is much show of me getting away. I see twelve or fifteen men. One looks like [name scratched out]. I don't know whether it is or not. I hope they did not catch them fellows that run over the bridge toward Smith's."

The cattlemen were painfully aware that Flagg's escape meant that the element of surprise was lost, for he would surely arouse the countryside. They had no way of knowing that the countryside was already being alerted. Terence ("Coyote") Smith, another of their marked men, had heard the shooting that morning and seen enough from a distance to send him galloping off to sound the alarm. Mobilization for defense was soon under way in Johnson County.

Disagreement over the next course of action again broke out among the invaders. Canton and Hesse argued forcefully for discontinuing the KC siege and striking hard for Buffalo at once, but they were again overruled by Wolcott and the majority, who wanted to finish the job before them. At Wolcott's direction Flagg's abandoned wagon was turned into the instrument of Champion's destruction. Sharpshooters poured heavy fire into the cabin windows to keep Champion down while a crew chopped up pitch-pine posts behind the stables. The posts and straw were piled high enough on the wagon to conceal men walking behind it.

Inside the cabin, Champion scribbled on: "Well, they have just got through shelling the house again like hail. I heard them splitting wood. I guess they are going to fire the house tonight. I think I will make a break when night comes, if alive."

Under cover of a new Winchester barrage, Wolcott and four men pushed the wagon barricade seventy-five yards to the cabin. Champion scrawled: "Shooting again. I think they will fire the house this time."

Wolcott ignited the straw. He and the others ran back to the stable under the cover of smoke. "The house is all fired. Good-bye boys, if I never see you again," Champion wrote and signed his name: "Nathan D. Champion."

When "the king of cattle thieves and the bravest man in Johnson County," as he was called by newspaper reporter Sam Clover, finally ran from the blazing building, with a Winchester rifle in his hand, fifty riflemen were waiting. He went down in a hail of bullets.[22] It was Frank Canton who found the bloodstained notebook in the dead man's pocket, and it was he who reportedly scratched out the name of the man Champion thought he recognized. Many in Johnson County concluded that the name was Canton's own.[23] Another story has it that Canton took Champion's rifle, claiming it belonged to him. This weapon was said to be one of the rifles left at the site of the dawn attempt on Champion's life the previous November.[24]

The invaders pinned a note, "Cattle thieves, beware!" on Champion's bloody vest and left Nick Ray's body to be incinerated in the blazing KC cabin. They turned loose the trappers, Walker and Jones, and prepared to continue their march north. But Champion's brave fight against fearful odds cost the invaders dearly. A full day had been lost, and now the alarm had been sounded by Coyote Smith and Flagg. All that night and the next day horsemen raced across Johnson County alerting settlers, and armed and angry men by the hundreds converged on Buffalo. The cattlemen had lost not only the element of surprise but the war as well.

The invading army reached the TA Ranch, fourteen miles south of Buffalo, in the early-morning hours of Sunday, April 10. There they sustained their first casualty. Texan Jim Dudley, at 225 pounds, was the biggest man in the party, and his horse gave out under his weight. TA manager Charley Ford gave Dudley a gray he said was gentle, but when the big Texan mounted, the horse bucked. Dudley's rifle, hanging by a strap from the saddlehorn, broke loose, struck the ground, and discharged, sending a bullet through his leg. It was a bad wound and needed medical attention. Two TA cowboys started with Dudley by wagon for Fort McKinney but were detained by the aroused citizenry at Buffalo. By the time they finally got the wounded man to the military surgeons at the fort, gangrene had set in. When his leg was amputated, Dudley went into shock and died on the operating table.

From the TA Ranch the expedition pushed on for Buffalo but was met on the road by Jim Craig, one of their supporters, who rode out to warn them against advancing into town. Sam Clover quoted Craig as yelling: "Turn back! Turn back! Everybody in town is aroused. . . . The rustlers are massing from every direction. . . . Get to cover if you value your lives." Again there was disagreement over a course of action. Canton, "morose" ever since his advice had been ignored at the KC, according to Clover, now vehemently argued that they should continue on into town and fight it out there if necessary. Hesse and Smith sided with him.[25]

Canton-haters in Johnson County for years have contended that his insistence on a sustained drive to Buffalo was based on his anxiety regarding the Tisdale murder case and his desire to destroy any incriminating records, but the urgency to get on to Buffalo advocated by both Canton and Hesse could be explained as well by concern for the security of their property.[26] Such concern, as it turned out, was justified. Within days Canton's ranch house was ransacked, and his saddle horse and tack were stolen.[27] Vandals invaded Hesse's house, destroyed furniture and other personal belongings, and shot the piano full of holes. One-Eyed Tex Cherpolloid strutted the streets of Buffalo wearing one of Hesse's expensive store-bought suits.[28]

The arguments of Canton, Hesse, and Smith again failed to convince Wolcott and Irvine. A retreat was ordered, and the invaders fell back on the TA Ranch. Sam Clover said that after this argument, Canton and Hesse would not talk to Wolcott and avoided Irvine. Hesse was so angry, said the newsman, that he would have shot Irvine if they had not been separated.[29] Clover, however, was not with the party long after the return to the TA. Eager to file his sensational story, he rode on into Buffalo. Later that day Phil DuFran, the spy in Buffalo, showed up at the TA with Sam Sutherland. He warned that at least 150 men were mobilized in the town. Robert Foote had "mounted his celebrated black horse and, with his long beard flying to the breeze, dashed up and down the streets calling the citizens to arms."[30] Foote threw open his store, offering guns and ammunition, warm clothing, and food supplies to anyone willing to fight the "whitecaps," as settlers were now calling the invaders.[31]

The buildings at TA headquarters might have been constructed to withstand a siege. The ranch house was built of ten-by-twelve-inch squared logs, and an icehouse and stable were also made of heavy logs capable of stopping a rifle bullet. Major Wolcott was in his glory preparing for defense. Swaggering about on his short legs, he drew on his military knowledge to direct the construction of fortifications. He ordered firing holes drilled in the buildings. On a high knoll that provided an unobstructed view of the surrounding fields, he had trenches dug and ramparts raised to form an outpost fort. Triangular redoubts were built at strategic points. When he was finished the TA was virtually impregnable to rifle fire, and Wolcott was confident nothing short of cannon fire could dislodge them.[32]

Sheriff Red Angus in fact tried to obtain a cannon from the garrison at Fort McKinney but was refused. Angus was deputizing citizens by the hundreds, and by the morning of Monday, April 11, the high ground surrounding the TA was thick with armed and determined men in dug-in emplacements. The day was marked by sporadic long-range rifle fire, but no one was hit on either side. Angus remained in Buffalo receiving new recruits as they arrived from outlying districts. Arapaho Brown, assisted by E. U. Snider, commanded the forces in the field.

That Monday the slow-moving wagons of the invaders were captured by Brown's men. Among the items confiscated were provisions, thousands of rounds of ammunition, two cases of dynamite, and Frank Canton's valise, in which was reportedly found the notorious death list. By this time the besieged cattlemen had lost most of their arrogance. They knew they were in a tight spot and needed help. Their cutting of the telegraph lines now came back to haunt them. A volunteer messenger slipped out that night and rode hard for Gillette, the closest telegraph point, where he wired Governor Amos W. Barber and others, advising them of the precarious situation at the TA.[33]

One of the telegrams went to Moreton Frewen, who had left the Wyoming ranges for India, his native England, and other points but who was in Washington, D.C., at the time. When he received the wire on Tuesday, April 12, Frewen was a luncheon guest at the home of James G. Blaine, secretary of state under President Benjamin Harrison. Frewen still had the telegram thirty years later: "We are held here by the rustlers; can possibly hold them off for three or four days but unless relieved then we shall certainly all hang.

There are twenty of your old friends—can you help us with the president? Teschemacher." Frewen appealed to Blaine, who agreed to bring the matter to the president's attention as quickly as possible.[34]

Governor Barber also acted quickly on receipt of his telegram. He fired off a dispatch to the president:

> An insurrection exists in Johnson County in the state of Wyoming, in the immediate vicinity of Fort McKinney, against the government of said state. . . . Open hostilities exist and large bodies of armed men are engaged in battle. . . . No relief can be afforded by state militia and the civil authorities are wholly unable to afford any relief whatever. United States troops are located at Fort McKinney, which is thirteen miles from the scene of the action, which is known as the TA ranch. I apply to you on behalf of the state of Wyoming to direct the United States troops at Fort McKinney to assist in suppressing this insurrection. Lives of a large number of persons are in imminent danger.[35]

Barber also alerted Senators Carey and Warren to the perilous state of affairs. Together the two Wyoming senators went to see the president, reportedly got him out of bed, and urged immediate action. At 11:05 P.M. President Harrison wired Governor Barber, "I have, in compliance with your call for aid of the United States forces to protect the state of Wyoming against domestic violence, ordered the secretary of war to concentrate a sufficient force at the scene of the disturbance and to co-operate with your authorities."[36]

As historian Helena Huntington Smith has noted, "The rest was like the ending of a B-Grade western motion picture."[37] Colonel J. J. Van Horn, commanding officer at Fort McKinney, received orders "to prevent violence and preserve peace" from Brigadier General John B. Brooke, commanding the Department of the Platte at Omaha. Van Horn called out Troops C, D, and H of the 6th Cavalry and at two o'clock in the morning of Wednesday, April 13, started for the battle site. At his side rode Major Edmond G. Fechet and Captain C. H. Parmelee, Governor Barber's aide-de-camp. It was Parmelee, it will be remembered, who, in his capacity as justice of the peace at Buffalo, had ruled in Canton's favor in the first Tisdale murder hearing.

Meanwhile, Arapaho Brown's besieging army had been busy. Using the running gears of two of the captured invader wagons, they constructed what was called an "Ark of Safety," or "go-devil." Working in a hollow behind a hill, they lashed the wagons together and built a breastwork of eight-inch logs and baled hay six feet high across the front. Up to forty men could be protected from small-arms fire behind this movable barricade while it was pushed forward toward the fortified knoll. Once the go-devil was close enough, bombs fashioned from dynamite sticks taken from the wagons could be lobbed into the fort. In the excitement of the moment, perhaps none of the besiegers took note of how felicitous was the employment of the invaders' own wagons against them, just as the invaders had used rustler Jack Flagg's wagon to finish off his pal Nate Champion.

Throughout Tuesday, the third day of the siege, the two sides exchanged heavy rifle fire, resulting in no severe injuries but many near misses. A bullet clipped a piece from Joe Elliott's hat, another passed through Scott Davis's blanket, and Tom Smith's pipe was shot out of his mouth.[38] A six-teen-year-old boy at the TA was eager to get in on the fighting, Billy Irvine remembered, until a rifle bullet "creased him across the neck just so the blood would ooze out of the wound. [That] quieted the boy, who went and laid in the corner." Irvine added, "It was the last we heard of him."[39] Irvine himself received a painful minor wound when a ricochet struck the bottom of his foot, penetrating his overshoe and boot. It did not break the skin but inflicted a bad bruise.[40] The only serious injury sustained by the whitecaps was another accidental self-inflicted wound. One of the Texans, Alexander Lowther, was crawling to a trench when his six-shooter dropped from his belt and fired. Shot in the stomach, he died at Fort McKinney several days later.

The besieging forces reported no injuries at all. Jumbo McKenzie had his horse shot out from under him.[41] Joe Elliott shot at a man on horseback who "flopped forward in the saddle and rode out of sight." Elliott said he learned later the man was Deputy Sheriff Howard Roles. "He told me that I shot him through the coat, just back of the shoulders. That's one time that I made a bad shot that I was darn glad of it. Howard Roles was a good man."[42]

By Tuesday afternoon Brown's men were inching the go-devil forward over the rough ground toward the TA fort. That night Wolcott proposed a breakout attempt. He wanted to mount up and make a dash through the lines. Irvine, who had backed the major in previous arguments, was against the idea. However, he said testily: "It makes little difference what I think if the move has been decided upon. I am going with you. I am damned sure I don't want to stay here alone."[43] Canton was more sanguine, at least when he wrote about it years later: "There was not a time either in daylight or night but what we could have cut through their lines and come out with our entire party, and we all knew it, but as we had gone to the trouble to build fortifications and they had made the attack on us, we thought we would give them a chance to fight in close quarters if they wanted to do so."[44] As it turned out, a bright moon shone that night, and Wolcott canceled the breakout plan.

In the morning the rustlers prepared for what they believed would be the final crushing blow to the invaders. "During the previous night rifle pits had been dug within 300 yards of the fort and the Go-Devil, or Ark of Safety, was ready for business. The first bomb sent into the enemies camp would have forced some of the men from cover and the sharpshooters in the rifle pits would have sent them to earth. Two hours delay in the arrival of the government troops would have proven, in all probability, fatal to the besieged white caps."[45]

The go-devil was moving forward again at dawn, and both sides were steeling themselves for the climactic battle when the cavalry arrived on the scene in the proverbial nick of time.[46] Colonel Van Horn ordered a cease-fire and held a conference with Red Angus and Arapaho Brown. The rustler leaders said they had no objection to the surrender of the invaders to the army if the invaders were later turned over to the civil authorities for trial. Van Horn reportedly agreed to this provision and, with Major Fechet, Captain Parmelee, Sheriff Angus, and the ubiquitous Sam Clover at his side, rode forward to the fortified outpost with one of his aides flying a white flag of truce. Clover described the confrontation: "Colonel Van Horn and his staff ranged alongside the rampart, inside of which were gathered a dozen of the most grimy yet most determined looking specimens of humanity ever seen. All cast at Sheriff Angus looks of malevolent hatred."[47]

Billy Irvine, one of the men at the fort, described that meeting: "The Colonel said to me: 'Who is in command of this party?' I replied: 'We have no one in command; we are simply an outfit of cattlemen up here trying to protect our property.' He again asked who was in command, plainly showing some temper, and that he did not believe my answer. I replied again, 'We have no one in command, but Major Wolcott is our acting foreman.' 'Very well,' he said, 'I want to see him.'" Wolcott was sent for, and the diminutive major marched to the fort "with as much dignity and assurance as if he had a thousand men." Irvine recalled the exchange between Wolcott and Van Horn with great pleasure. When asked to surrender, "Wolcott replied: 'Colonel Van Horn, to whom do we surrender—to the United States army, or are we to be turned over to the civil authorities of this country? If the former, we will surrender; if the latter, we will NOT surrender.'" According to Irvine, "The Colonel assured him that we would not be turned over to the civil authorities, and he at once surrendered." Sam Clover wrote a similar account, quoting Wolcott as saying, "I will surrender to you, but to that man, (turning to Sheriff Angus) never. I have never seen him before, but I have heard enough of him and rather than give up to him we will die right here."[48]

Canton, who said he was also present during this negotiation, gave a different version. When Van Horn announced he had orders from the president "to arrest all parties on the ground engaged in this combat and to restore order," Canton referred him to Wolcott but said he could speak for the men in the fort. "I told him . . . that we would surrender to the military authorities provided he would arrest this mob who had been firing at us for three days and nights. . . . The officer promised to arrest the leaders of the attacking parties if it were possible for him to do so. We then surrendered to the military authorities with the understanding that we deliver our rifles but retain our side arms. Leaders of the rustlers had all disappeared and I do not think any of them were arrested at that time."[49]

The rustler leaders had not disappeared, of course—in fact one of them, Red Angus, sat astride a horse right beside the colonel—and Van Horn had no intention of arresting them then or later. Contrary to Canton's report, the prisoners were not permitted to keep their six-shooters. Arms secured by the army that day included forty-five rifles, fifty revolvers, and five thousand rounds of ammunition. Forty-six horses were rounded up, and forty-five men were taken into custody, including Lowther, the badly wounded Texan.[50] George Dunning, the Idaho gunman who had never mixed with the others and turned out to be a joker in this deck, hid out in the barn hayloft until everyone had gone and then walked into Buffalo and gave himself up to Sheriff Angus.

Colonel Van Horn's troopers escorted the haggard invaders to Fort McKinney, where they were held under guard in a brick bathhouse. The following day the bullet-riddled body of Nate Champion and the charred remains of Nick Ray were placed on public display in Buffalo. Five hundred people attended the funerals on Friday. On Saturday, April 16, a coroner's jury found that Champion and Ray had been "feloniously killed and murdered" by a list of thirty-nine men, headed by Frank Canton, and "other evil disposed and disreputable persons not to us known." Criminal complaints were filed against the men by Justice of the Peace Reimann. Warrants in hand, Sheriff Angus went to the fort and demanded the prisoners but was refused by Van Horn. Governor Barber had convinced the military that the civil authorities could not guarantee the safety of the prisoners, and he was working to get them out of Johnson County. Wild rumors circulated that a rustler mob was about to attack the fort and remove the whitecaps by force. A newspaper reported that Dudley Champion, the brother of Nate, had confronted Canton at the fort, pulled his six-shooter, and was about to fire when a guard jumped between the two.[51] Joe Elliott described Dud Champion as "a slow-moving, slow-working man" and said he came to Fort McKinney looking for Elliott or Mike Shonsey. "I had no gun," said Elliott, "and if he had killed us there, he could never have been convicted in that country."[52]

On Easter Sunday, April 17, Colonel Van Horn was ordered to remove his charges to Fort Fetterman, near Douglas. They were moved out that day,

The Johnson County invaders awaiting trail. Standing, left to right: Tom Smith, Arthur B. Clarke, J. N. Leslie, Elias W. Whitcomb, D. E. Booker, W. B. Wallace, Charles S. Ford, A. R. Powers, A. D. Adamson, C. A. Campbell, Frank H. Laberteaux, Phil DuFran, Frank Wolcott, W. E. Guthrie, William C. Irvine, David R. Tisdale, Joe Elliott, John N. Tisdale, Scott Davis. Seated, rear, left to right: Frederick O. DeBillier, Ben Morrison, W. J. Clarke, Lafayette H. Parker, Hubert E. Teschemacher, B. C. Schultz. Seated, second row, left to right: W. H. Tabor, J. A. Garrett, W. A. Wilson, J. K. Barling, M. A. McNally, Mike Shonsey, Richard M. Allen, Fred G. S. Hesse, Frank M. Canton. Seated, front, left to right: William Little, Jeff D. Mynett, Robert Barling,, Sam Sutherland, Buck Garrett, George R. Tucker, J. M. Benford, William Armstrong. *Courtesy American Heritage Center, University of Wyoming.*

guarded by three troops of cavalry under the command of Major Fechet. Shortly after leaving the fort, said Joe Elliott, there was a confrontation with a bunch of rustlers who blocked the way. "The soldiers tried to shove them out of the way; they wouldn't move. Major Fechet gave the order, 'Ready arms!,' and 300 carbines flashed out. Those fellows moved!"[53] At Fetterman the prisoners were turned over to the care of two companies of infantry and taken by train to Fort Russell, near Cheyenne.

The departure of the whitecaps brought no calm to Johnson County. On May 3 Henry A. Blair of the Ogallala Land and Cattle Company got an injunction to prevent the planned roundup of the insurgent Northern Wyoming Farmers' and Stock Growers' Association. Writs were issued and served against some thirty county residents by U.S. Marshal Joe Rankin and several deputies.[54] One of those deputies was George Wellman, foreman of Blair's Hoe Ranch, who was specially commissioned by Marshal Rankin in Cheyenne on May 4 to help serve the papers.

One week later Wellman was dead, shot and killed from ambush. This murder strengthened the cattle barons' contention that Johnson County was in a state of anarchy and that their incursion had been necessary and justifiable. Most residents of the county expressed shock at the killing. In a letter to Canton on May 17 Charles Burritt said, "Nothing has occurred that has caused so deep a gloom over the County as [Wellman's] assassination."[55] The killing was blamed on the Red Sash Gang, outlaws led by Charles Taylor, who were taking advantage of the turmoil in the area to raise general hell. Black Henry Smith, Ed Starr, Frank Smith, and Clayton Cruse, all Red Sash Gang members, were thought to have committed the murder but, due to typical investigatory bungling by Sheriff Angus, were never convicted.[56]

Canton and others were convinced that Jack Flagg's Hat Ranch bunch knew a lot more about the Wellman murder than was ever revealed, a belief confirmed to some extent forty-three years later. In 1935 Black Billy Hill returned to Johnson County from Canada, where he had lived for many years, and pointed out a spot on the prairie where George Wellman's pistol had been hidden, buried in a tin can, in 1892.[57]

The invaders' court battle dragged on through the rest of 1892. First-degree murder charges in the deaths of Nate Champion and Reuben Ray were filed against them by Johnson County Prosecutor Alvin Bennett on April 20. The defendants, at Fort Russell, signed a waiver of preliminary examination on May 4, saying they believed "that their persons would be insecure and would be subject to violence which the civil authorities would be unable to prevent" if they were returned to Johnson County. They remained in the custody of the army at Fort Russell until July, when an arrangement was worked out by which they would theoretically be turned over to Johnson County authorities but would in fact remain in the Cheyenne area. In early July the prisoners were taken to Laramie and housed in an unused wing of the state penitentiary. On July 5 they were officially remanded to the custody of Johnson County Deputy Sheriff Roles but remained where they were for change-of-venue hearings before Judge John W. Blake. Per agreement, Judge Blake on July 17 ordered the trials moved to Cheyenne, with arraignment scheduled for August 6.[58]

In Cheyenne, the defendants were quartered in a large auditorium called Keefe Hall but were permitted to come and go as they pleased. Most of them immediately secured arms. On the night of August 3 Canton made a tour of

the city's saloons and at 3:30 in the morning was standing on a corner talking with three men. A pistol belonging to Canton was being examined, according to newspaper accounts, when it fell to the ground or was otherwise
accidentally discharged. A bullet struck Canton at about four inches above
the ankle, penetrating the tibia. He was taken to the Hotel Vendome, where
the wound was treated by a Doctor Grimes and Dr. Amos W. Barber, the
acting governor.[59]

At the arraignment on the sixth Canton was carried into the courtroom
on a stretcher and propped up on pillows. The defendants all entered pleas of
not guilty and were released on their own recognizance after formally signing personal bonds for $20,000 on each of two counts to ensure appearance
at a trial scheduled for August 22. The total bonds posted amounted to
$1,680,000.[60] No one seemed to care when the Texans boarded trains for
home, never to return.

On August 22, the case was continued to the November term of the First
District Court at Cheyenne, with trial set for January 2, 1893. During this
period a bombshell exploded in the form of the published confession of George
Dunning, who had avoided arrest by the army at the TA Ranch and later
walked into Buffalo, where he was taken into custody by Sheriff Angus. In
the county jail, Dunning told of his recruitment as a hired gunman by WSGA
Secretary Ijams and the involvement of some of the state's biggest names in
the invasion plot. Realizing that in Dunning they had a powerful witness
against the cattlemen, the county authorities did not turn him over to the
military to join the other prisoners but spirited him out of the jail at night to
Tom Gardner's ranch. He was kept hidden for months.

In the summer of 1892 A. S. Mercer, a journalist who had previously
been a strong advocate of Republicanism and the cattlemen's cause, switched
political parties. With the zeal of the new convert, he became extreme in his
denunciation of the cattle barons. He encouraged Dunning to write a confession, and he published it in the pages of his *Northwestern Livestock Journal*
in October, just before the elections. Later he wrote and published his ra-
bidly biased account of the Johnson County Cattle War: *The Banditti of the
Plains; or, the Cattlemen's Invasion of Wyoming in 1892 (The Crowning
Infamy of the Ages).*

A storm was raised by the publication of the "Confession of George Dunning," in which major Wyoming political figures, including Governor Barber, Senators Carey and Warren, Judge Blake, and U.S. Marshal Rankin, were
said to have aided and abetted in the invasion. Outraged denials filled the
pages of the press. None of these men ever had to face the charges in court,
but the publication did achieve its desired effect as the Democrats swept the
November elections.

Willis Van Devanter, later a U.S. Supreme Court justice, led the defense in the trials of the invaders and Frank Canton. *Courtesy American Heritage Center, University of Wyoming.*

The trial of the twenty-three remaining defendants in the Champion and Ray murder cases turned farcical. Efforts to impanel a jury went on for more than two weeks. The defense was allowed 12 peremptory challenges for each defendant and the prosecution 6 for each, a total of 414 in all. By January 21, only 11 jurors had been accepted out of 1,064 veniremen examined, and the sheriff had exhausted the rolls of the city's eligible citizens. He asked for additional funds to go out into the countryside after veniremen. Frustrated and running out of money, Prosecutor Bennett moved to dismiss the case. Defense counsel Willis Van Devanter objected, arguing that without a trial, his clients would not be completely exonerated and could be prosecuted again later. Counsel and judge got together and arrived at a solution. To complete the jury, the judge ordered a courtroom spectator to take a seat in the box, and both sides accepted him without a question. Van Devanter asked for a directed verdict of acquittal, which was denied. Bennett then moved for dismissal, Van Devanter entered his objection, which was overruled, and the cases were dismissed. But the trial had officially been held before a jury, and since the double jeopardy rule applied, the defendants could not be retried on the same charges.[61]

Of the millions of words written about the Johnson County Cattle War, perhaps none better summarize the affair than those of the unlettered "Bear George" McClellan, a resident of the area for many years and one of the hunters who had helped Canton capture the Arapaho Indians Beaver and Samuel back in 1885. "My judgment," said McClellan, "is that it was like

Ruby Canton and schoolchildren in Buffalo, Wyoming. Ruby is the tall girl at left. *Courtesy Jim Gatchell Memorial Museum, Buffalo, Wyoming.*

most other human questions: There was cause on both sides. It is true that the cowmen could not secure a conviction in the courts, and that their provocation was great, there is no doubt, but how that could lead a set of sane rational men to think that they could just black list a lot of men in a community and then proceed to go out and exterminate them is more than I could ever figure out."[62]

For Frank Canton, the dismissal of the Champion and Ray murder cases removed one threat to his liberty, but he still faced a murder charge in the John A. Tisdale case. Even as Van Devanter adroitly steered the invaders' cases through the courts, he also brought his skill to bear in Canton's behalf on the Tisdale murder charge. With all the turmoil in Johnson County in the spring of 1892, Canton's case was continued by Judge Blake at the June term of court. In September Van Devanter filed an affidavit for a change of venue, stating that "owing to the excitement and prejudice against him," Canton could not receive a fair trial in Johnson County or in the counties of Sheridan, Crook, Weston, Converse, Natrona, and Albany.[63]

Annie had by this time rejoined her husband in Cheyenne. As the legal maneuvers continued, she and their daughter, Ruby, returned to Buffalo to

Charles H. Burritt, mayor of Buffalo, was a staunch defender of Canton throughout his Wyoming troubles. *Courtesy American Heritage Center, University of Wyoming.*

stay with the Wilkersons. C. M. Lingle, the new publisher and editor of the *Buffalo Bulletin*, noted their return in the October 6 issue of the paper. Three weeks later he said he had "received a pleasant call from Mrs. Canton and Miss Nancy Wilkerson," Annie's sister.[64] No mention was made of Frank or his legal problems. As the time grew near for a trial in the Tisdale murder case, Al Allison and his slain brother's family moved to Buffalo to be available for the court proceedings.[65] Annie Canton and the widow of the man her husband was charged with killing must have met in the streets or shops of the little town. Words spoken between them must have been interesting but were never recorded.

In October Judge Blake heard arguments in the change-of-venue motion. John W. Davidson spoke for the state, and John W. Lacey and Van Devanter represented Canton. Judge Blake sustained the motion and ordered the trial moved to Evanston, Uinta County, in southwestern Wyoming.[66]

On February 24, 1893, Prosecutor Alvin Bennett formally notified C. H. Burritt, counsel for Canton, that the county commissioners, "having regard to the great expense incident to the prosecution of the case in a county as far away as Uinta, and the present financial condition of Johnson County," had voted to dismiss the case. Bennett stated that he would file motion for dismissal and ask that a nolle prosequi be entered.[67] In effect, this notice cleared Canton in the Tisdale murder and lifted his last legal burden in Wyoming. But, like everything else in Canton's stormy history, the absolution was attended with controversy.

Sometime in the three-week period between Bennett's written notice of intent and the formal filing on March 18, Charlie Basch disappeared. In his official motion to dismiss, therefore, Bennett gave as his first reason the absence of the prosecution's chief witness, "without whose testimony a conviction in said cause would be an impossibility." The fact that during the previous year the county expenditures in criminal matters had been heavy and that the expense of another trial would be "a great hardship and burthern" on the taxpayers, "considering the uncertainty of a conviction," now became secondary. Attached to Bennett's motion was an official dismissal request signed by County Commissioners Charles J. Hogerson and A. S. Brock and attested to by the county clerk, none other than O. H. Flagg, who signed with a firm and steady hand but who must have been greatly pained in having to affix his name to a document absolving his enemy Canton.[68]

On Monday, April 3, 1893, Canton's case was called in the Third Judicial District Court at Evanston. Bennett entered his motion to nolle prosequi. But according to the Evanston newspaper: "[Van Devanter] insisted upon going to trial and either have his client acquitted or convicted, well knowing that it would be an acquittal as the state had not the evidence with which to convict. . . . The attorneys consumed considerable time in arguing the motion after which Judge Knight decided that the case should be dismissed without prejudice as the state wished. This leaves the matter open, and if the state should ever be in possession of sufficient evidence to convict there is no bar to prevent them from renewing the prosecution."[69] So Van Devanter, with all his skill, could not obtain complete exoneration, as he had in the Champion and Ray murder cases. The possibility of a reopened case would remain to haunt Canton.

Johnson County spent almost thirty thousand dollars on the invaders' murder cases, and Bennett estimated that another ten thousand would have been required for prosecution of the Tisdale case. Prosecution was thus suspended for the same reason that the cases against the invaders had been dropped: Johnson County was broke.[70] Rustler sympathizers, however, pointed to Basch's disappearance as the real reason. They said Basch, like Bill Walker and Ben Jones, had been spirited away by the cattle barons. Walker claimed that officers in league with the big ranchers had pursued him and Jones into Nebraska, arrested them on spurious warrants, conveyed them all the way to Rhode Island, and kept them secluded in a hotel until the cases against the cattlemen were concluded.[71] Friends of the rustlers now believed the same thing had happened to Basch. An unconfirmed report in a Lusk paper stated, "Basch was escorted out of the country by two officers in the employ of the stockmen, and . . . taken to Kansas City."[72] But it is clear that the decision not to prosecute Canton was made before Basch's disappearance. It is also clear that, despite Bennett's assertion in his March 16, 1892, letter to Amos Barber that new information had surfaced since the original hearing in the Tisdale case, the testimony of Charlie Basch was the only real evidence against Canton.[73]

The argument could be made that Basch fled Wyoming to avoid having to testify. Canton claimed: "[Charlie] was nearly frightened to death by the gang. He is a slow man, not overly bright and of no great mental capacity, and it is believed he was manipulated."[74] Deputy Sheriff Howard Roles saw Basch in Cheyenne just before he disappeared, thought he "acted a little queer," and questioned his sanity.[75] Basch may have feared Canton and his powerful supporters, he may have feared the rustlers, or he may have feared a possible charge of perjury. The question of how and why he left has never been resolved.[76]

Also unresolved is exactly what he saw that December day at Haywood's Gulch. Basch's sworn testimonies at the coroner's inquiry into the death of John A. Tisdale and at the hearing before Justice of the Peace Parmelee were inconsistent and conflicting. Interviews given many years later only added to the confusion.

On April 9, 1935, Basch signed a handwritten statement of his knowledge of the Tisdale murder. He said he saw Canton at the murder site, that he "knew it was Canton and knew his horse well." Canton drew his gun but, recognizing Basch, "put his gun back in his pocket." Basch then added something new. He also saw, he said, "another man standing on the opposite side of his horse about forty rods west of the road." He drew a map showing the relative positions of himself, Canton, the Tisdale wagon, and the other man.[77] A month later Basch was interviewed by J. Elmer Brock, who drew out more details about this mysterious other man:

"You didn't have any idea who that other man was?"
"No."
"Was there any talk at that time in the country that could give you any suspicion of who it might be?"
"Yes—Tom Horn. It was the talk of the country then that it was Tom Horn."
"Was Tom Horn in the country then?"
"Yes."
"You knew him then?"
"Yes, I wasn't well acquainted with him, but I knew him when I seen him."[78]

Basch was eighty-eight when he retold the story to interviewer Ida McPherren in 1938. In this version he made no mention of another man, but for the first time he said he had actually witnessed the murder. "Yes," he said, "I saw Canton fire the shot and saw Tisdale fall back on his load—dead." He said: "[Canton] was hiding in the deepest part of the gulch and when Tisdale approached Canton stepped out in full view of Tisdale and shot him; Tisdale fell back on his load of winter supplies and toys for his children. Canton had not seen me approach and I did not know any one was in the bottom of the gulch until I started down into the ravine. I was on horseback and, of course, Canton saw me immediately upon my appearance on the edge of the gulch, but it had all happened simultaneously—Tisdale reaching bottom of gulch, Canton emerging from cover, and my appearance on horseback at edge of gulch." Basch said: "Up until that moment Frank Canton and I had been close friends. . . . I never believed the things I heard about Canton until I saw with my eyes that he was a scoundrel." When Canton saw him, he pointed his gun but did not fire, said Basch. "He believed that I would keep my mouth shut and that most certainly was my intention when I accidentally came on the scene."[79]

Thus we have five different stories told by Charlie Basch of what he saw that day at Haywood's Gulch. At the coroner's inquest he swore that he saw one man leading a horse but that he recognized neither man nor horse. He testified under oath at the preliminary hearing that although he did not recognize the man, the horse was definitely Fred, Canton's fine animal. In an interview more than forty years later he first told of seeing another man. In a subsequent interview he admitted suspecting this other man might have been Tom Horn. And in a final interview he dropped the second man variant and for the first time stated that he had personally witnessed the murder of Tisdale by Canton.

Which story he would have told on the stand we will never know, but it is little wonder that Van Devanter fought so hard to bring the case to trial. The testimony of Charlie Basch was the core of the case against Canton, and an attorney of Van Devanter's ability would have destroyed the credibility of such a witness before a jury. Had the case gone to trial, it is highly unlikely that Frank Canton, guilty or innocent, would have been convicted.

Whether he was in fact guilty is another question, but after one hundred years of popular writing on the Johnson County Cattle War he has been convicted in the public mind. Based on nothing but the inconsistent accounts of Charlie Basch and the hatred felt by many in Johnson County for their former sheriff, writers have found Canton guilty, not only of Tisdale's murder but also of Ranger Jones's murder, for which absolutely no evidence incriminating him was ever produced. The logical assumption was then made that a man who would cold-bloodedly assassinate two men within a few days must have killed many more the same way. We find Canton characterized as "nothing more than a killer for hire,"[80] who followed "his chosen calling, the killing of marked men for valuable consideration,"[81] leaving "dead men . . . from Wyoming to the Klondike,"[82] a "merciless, congenital, emotionless killer, [who] for pay, murdered eight—very likely ten—men."[83]

The picture painted by these writers was a poor likeness of Frank Canton, given the true history of his life, but the figure they have depicted strongly resembles another character of the period: Tom Horn. Wyoming historians have debated for years whether the notorious western gunman Tom Horn was actually involved in the Johnson County troubles of the early 1890s. Horn was an obscure frontier figure at the time, but a decade later, after a sensational trial for the murder of a fourteen-year-old boy and Horn's subsequent hanging in Cheyenne for that crime, his name became nationally known.

Born in Missouri in 1860, Horn went west and saw service as an army scout and peace officer in Arizona before taking a job as an operative for the Pinkerton National Detective Agency in 1890. By his own account, he did not go to Wyoming until 1894, when he hired on as stock detective for the Swan Land and Cattle Company.[84] But other writers have placed him in Wyoming much earlier and contend that he was in fact directly involved in the Johnson County Cattle War. One biographer had Horn recruiting (in Arizona!) the gunmen for the invasion.[85] Ranch hand Bill Walker claimed that Horn was one of the cattlemen's party at the KC Ranch when Champion and Ray were killed. He could not be mistaken, Walker said, because he remembered Horn from Arizona and the two talked that day of shared experiences on the southwestern cattle ranges.[86] Charlie Siringo, a veteran Pinkerton detective who worked with Horn on several cases, said that Horn "was sent into Wyoming by the Pinkerton National Detective Agency along with a gang of gunmen from the Indian Territory and helped to start the great Johnson County War."[87]

These allegations have not been independently verified, but there is evidence that Horn was in Johnson County in the spring of 1892. Among the deputies that U.S. Marshal Joe Rankin brought in to serve papers on the members of the renegade Johnson County cattle association in May was one Thomas H. Hale. This was in fact Tom Horn, who had used the alias "Tom Hale" while working as a Pinkerton operative in Nevada.[88] George Wellman was ambushed and murdered that month, and Horn, under his true name, was later subpoenaed to appear as a witness in the case against Henry Smith and company.[89] J. Elmer Brock remembered Horn being in the country during this period. He said the gunman was stalking Black Billy Hill but never did shoot him.[90]

And then there is Charlie Basch's story. The allegation that Horn was present at the Tisdale murder scene adds another dimension to the mystery of the Tisdale and Ranger Jones assassinations and Canton's culpability. Canton was accused of murdering for the wealthy cattlemen, but these charges were never proved. Tom Horn, however, was tried, convicted, and hanged for a murder in Wyoming, and by his own admission, the murder was only one of a series he committed for the big ranchers. "Killing men is my specialty. I look at it as a business proposition, and I think I have a corner on the market," Horn told Detective Joe LeFors in a rambling discourse that LeFors elicited and secretly transcribed on January 12, 1902. This damning "confession" led to his conviction and execution.[91]

We know that Tom Horn, a notorious killer for hire, was in the employ of powerful Wyoming cattlemen in the 1890s, that he was in Johnson County about the time of the killings, and that the manner in which Tisdale and Jones were killed (shot down without warning by a hidden rifleman) was fully consistent with his technique. On the other hand, the name of Frank Canton (or Joe Horner), before or after the Jones-Tisdale murders, was never connected with an assassination of this type. Canton undoubtedly knew who committed the crimes. If the testimony of Charlie Basch is to be believed and that of Canton's numerous alibi witnesses rejected, he was at the scene and was no doubt guilty, if only as an accessory. The mystery remains, and will no doubt always remain, unsolved.

Part Three

The Oklahoma Territory Years

KANSAS

Coffeyville

Newkirk
Blackwell
Pawhuska
Nowata

OKLAHOMA
TERRITORY

Pawnee
Ingalls
Skiatook

Perry
Stillwater
Jennings
Lawson
Tulsa

ARK.

Dover
Kingfisher
Guthrie

Checotah

Arapaho
El Reno

INDIAN
TERRITORY

Fort
Smith

Fort Sill

Ardmore

The

OKLAHOMA &
INDIAN TERRITORY

Years

1894-1896

40 Miles

Chapter 7

The Undersheriff, 1894-1895

"This is a strange case."

Governor J. S. Hogg of Texas, July 17, 1894

As his criminal cases proceeded through the courts, Canton's powerful friends found a job for him. Early in 1893 he took a position as superintendent of a packing company on the Missouri River at Nebraska City, south of Omaha. The Nebraska City Packing Company was one of the many enterprises of entrepreneurial businessman Portus B. Weare, who had taken a liking to Canton and who would influence his future greatly.

P. B. Weare was a fifty-one-year-old native of Michigan who, financed by his banker father, had built a fortune in businesses ranging from the exportation to Europe of prairie chickens to commerce in buffalo hides. In the 1880s he established the Weare Land and Live Stock Company, which ran as many as fifty thousand head of cattle in northern Wyoming and eastern Montana. By 1893 he had expanded into grain storage and soon operated sixty-five elevators in Illinois, Iowa, and Nebraska. The packing plant at Nebraska City was established by Weare with the cooperation of his friend J. Sterling Morton, a publisher and horticulturist, longtime resident of the town, dedicated Democrat, and perennial candidate for Congress and the Nebraska statehouse.

Weare's most recent commercial venture was in Alaska Territory. In 1891 he organized the North American Transportation and Trading Company in partnership with former Montana sheriff John J. Healy, who had gone to Alaska in 1882 and established a trading post. Weare and Healy formed their company to challenge the monopoly of the Alaska Commercial Company for the lucrative Yukon River trade. In the spring of 1892 Weare and his son

sailed from Seattle to St. Michael's Island, at the mouth of the Yukon River,
with lumber, materials, and machinery to build a five-hundred-ton river
steamer. Christened the *P. B. Weare,* the boat was completed in time to make
its initial voyage up the river that summer to the Klondike goldfields, then
just developing.[1]

During the early weeks of 1893 Canton traveled between Nebraska City
and Wyoming, making his necessary court appearances, but even before the
last case was decided in April, he was angling for a whole new career under
the guidance of the wily Weare. Weare's enthusiasm for Alaska, that rawest
and most distant of American frontiers, was contagious, and Canton was
infected.

The previous November Grover Cleveland had been elected president for
the second time. Weare saw the presence of a Democrat in the White House
as a rare opportunity. A single U.S. marshal, a man named Orville Porter,
presided over a judicial district comprising the entire Territory of Alaska. If
Cleveland could be persuaded to replace Porter with Frank Canton, a loyal
Democrat, Weare would have a dependable friend in the top law enforcement position in the territory, a condition advantageous to his business ambitions.

For Canton, here was a golden opportunity to leap from obscurity as a
packinghouse manager to prestige as a federal officer, to return to the always
beckoning frontier, and to put thousands of miles between himself and his
many sworn enemies in Wyoming. Backed by Weare, he mounted a campaign to secure the appointment as Alaska marshal. He began calling in his
debts, soliciting the help of the men of power and influence for whom he had
fought and risked his life.

Beginning in February 1893 letters from prominent westerners poured
into the office of president-elect Cleveland, recommending Canton's appointment. Those endorsing Canton formed an impressive list: John A. McShane,
president of the Omaha stockyards and former member of the Nebraska
legislature; George L. Miller, president of the Board of Omaha Park Commissioners; William A. Paxton, Omaha businessman and part-owner of the
Ogallala Land and Cattle Company; George W. Baxter, ex-governor of Wyoming; Francis Warren, U.S. senator and former Wyoming governor; Amos
W. Barber, Wyoming secretary of state; John W. Lacey and Willis Van
Devanter, Canton's attorneys, both former chief justices of Wyoming; T. B.
Hicks, president of the First National Bank of Cheyenne; Henry G. Hay,
cashier of the Stock Growers National Bank of Cheyenne; A. M. Sparhawk,
former sheriff of Fremont County, Wyoming; William H. Parker, former
U.S. attorney for South Dakota; E. S. R. Boughton, organizer of the Frontier
Land and Cattle Company; Henry J. Windsor, Omaha businessman and

Wyoming ranch owner; Dr. J. E. Summers Jr., former surgeon at Fort McKinney; Thomas J. Bouton, editor and publisher; John H. Conrad, Montana businessman and rancher; and St. Clair O'Malley, attorney, rancher, and former Johnson County judge.[2]

Months went by, and no word of an appointment was forthcoming. In January 1894 Canton went to Washington to personally plead his case. He called first on Senator George Shoup of Idaho and presented a letter of introduction from P. B. Weare:

> This will introduce to your kind attention Mr. Frank M. Canton of Johnston [sic] County, Wyo. but now of Nebraska City, Neb. Mr. Canton has an application in for the United States Marshal for Alaska.
>
> I would consider it a great favor if you would give Mr. Canton such aid as you can in getting this appointment. Secretary Morten [sic] personally knows Mr. Canton and recommends him for the position. Mr. Canton has letters from W.A. Paxton of Omaha, Senator Warren of Wyoming and many other of our best Western men.
>
> I am largely interested in Alaska and am anxious that the immense amount of smuggling going on there in whisky and opium should be stopped.[3]

The "Morten" mentioned was J. Sterling Morton, Weare's Nebraska City friend, whom Cleveland had appointed secretary of agriculture. Morton in turn wrote an introductory letter for Canton to Attorney General Richard Olney, who would officially name the new U.S. marshal.[4]

Weare, appealing to the good offices of a third cabinet member on behalf of Canton, wrote Walter Q. Gresham, secretary of state. He reminded him of previous conversations regarding the opening of commerce on the Yukon River. "We are sadly in need in that country of a first class man as United States Marshal," said Weare. He enumerated Canton's qualifications, adding, "I would earnestly request that you use whatever influence you can in this matter to have him appointed, as we need a reliable man and a proper person to hold this position."[5]

Armed with copies of the letters of recommendation to President Cleveland, new letters of support from Chicago Postmaster Washington Hesing and former U.S. Attorney William H. Parker, and petitions in his behalf signed by prominent citizens of Miles City and Chicago, Canton called on Attorney General Olney.[6] It was all for naught. President Cleveland, adhering to a home-rule policy, appointed Alaskan resident Louis Williams as U.S. marshal, and Canton returned to Nebraska City empty-handed. A few months later, without Canton's knowledge, a group of his supporters led by J. Sterling Morton applied for and secured his appointment to the less prestigious position of deputy collector of customs in Alaska. Canton, however, declined the position, saying he did not want to take his family into the wilds of Alaska.[7]

This failure caused Canton to ponder the dark areas of his history. The weight of his legal problems in Wyoming had been lifted, but the stain of his Texas opprobrium remained. The gnawing knowledge that he was still a fugitive from Texas justice was always with him, and he had to wonder if rumors of his past had not somehow reached high levels and thwarted his ambitions. Ever a man of action, he determined to do something to straighten out that past. But while he considered his options, a letter from his old *compadre*, Frank Lake, offered him an opportunity to escape the tiresome work at the packing company and once again pin on a badge in a new frontier.

Frank Lake, one of the few who knew of Joe Horner's transformation into Frank Canton, had left Texas in 1876 for his former Arkansas home. In the mid-1880s he went to Wyoming and filed on land at Canton's request. He later returned to Arkansas and engaged in various businesses until 1890, when he again went to Texas to operate a livery at Vernon. In April 1893 he took a job as clerk of the Otoe Indian subagency in the Cherokee Outlet, Oklahoma Territory. When the Outlet was opened to white settlement in September of that year, he resigned to make the run into the new lands.[8] He located a claim of eighty acres adjoining the infant town of Pawnee and was appointed clerk of the new "Q" County. Other county officers included Register of Deeds Robert Chasteen, a friend of Lake's from Washington County, Arkansas, and Frank Dimon, sheriff.[9]

This new country was infested with outlaws. Members of the infamous Dalton Gang headquartered in the area until October 5, 1892, when they made their celebrated attempt to rob two banks simultaneously in Coffeyville, Kansas, just over the territorial line. Three Dalton brothers and two other gang members were cut down by the aroused citizenry in a hail of gunfire. Of the five bank robbers, only Emmett Dalton survived to receive a prison sentence. In the gunfight, Coffeyville City Marshal Charles T. Connelly and three other townsmen died defending the town.

After the bloody affair at Coffeyville, remnants of the Dalton gang and other outlaws combined to form a new outfit under the leadership of Bill Dalton and Bill Doolin. A rendezvous of the gang was the town of Ingalls, some twenty miles south of Pawnee in adjacent Payne County. On September 1, 1893, a party of federal officers engaged the gang in a vicious firefight at Ingalls. Deputy U.S. Marshals Richard Speed, Lafayette Shadley, and Thomas J. Hueston were killed. All the outlaws escaped except Roy Daugherty, alias "Arkansas Tom" Jones, who was captured, convicted, and sentenced to fifty years in prison.[10]

Five months later the gang struck Pawnee. On the afternoon of Tuesday, January 23, 1894, Bill Doolin, "Tulsa Jack" Blake, and "Bitter Creek" Newcomb held up the Farmers and Citizens Bank. Unable to open the time-locked vault, they scooped up $262 in loose currency, took Cashier C. L. Berry as hostage, and galloped out of town, six-shooters roaring. A hastily organized posse followed and met Berry, released unharmed, but it lost the trail of the bandits.[11]

Four days later the commissioners of Q County drew up a formal resolution for submission to Oklahoma Governor W. C. Renfrow. Recognizing that "the topography of the country and the sparsity of settlement" made the region a "rendezvous for bands of criminals of the most desperate type" who had killed "brave and noble officers in unfortunate combat," and that because of "the peculiar conditions" the U.S. marshal and his deputies had failed to provide the settlers "adequate protection from the invasions of [the] outlaws," the resolution requested the governor "to call upon the United States government for a sufficient force of U.S. cavalry" to assist the sheriff "in the capture, arrest and punishment of the . . . bands of desperadoes . . . notoriously defying the officers of the law and settlers in northeastern Oklahoma."[12]

This desperate request to invoke martial law and introduce military force into the battle against the outlaws was denied, but within a few months a new group of lawmen took charge in Q County, men who would do much to relieve the settlers' apprehension and strike fear into the hearts of the criminals. In April Frank Lake and Frank Dimon agreed to exchange jobs; Dimon would pick up a pen as county clerk while Lake pinned on the badge of county sheriff. Governor Renfrow, who came to Pawnee to calm the settlers' fears, endorsed this unusual arrangement and may even have suggested it after sizing up the men involved.[13]

Even before he took office as sheriff, Lake posted two letters, calling for help and offering deputy appointments. Frank Canton, brooding over his missed opportunity in Alaska, received one; his brother George Horner, cowboying in Knox County, Texas, got the other. Both rode into Pawnee within days. "F.M. Canton of Buffalo, Wyoming, and G.B. Horner of Knox county, Texas, have been sworn in as special deputy sheriffs for Q county," reported the *Pawnee Scout* on May 11, 1894.[14] Not then or later was there any indication in the press that the two men were brothers.[15]

"I recd a letter from Frank Lake of Pawnee Okla. saying that he was appointed sheriff of Pawnee Co. and would like for me to come down and help him run the office," Canton later wrote. "I concluded to visit my old friend at least and look the situation over. I went to Okla. in the Spring of 1894

U.S. Marshal E. D. Nix.
*Courtesy Western History
Collections, University of
Oklahoma.*

[and] decided to again enter the service of the U.S. and the Ter. of Okla. as a field officer to assist in hunting down the Outlaw bands who openly defied the laws of the Country."[16]

With no previous experience as a lawman, Frank Lake needed the skills of the seasoned Canton in the sheriff's office; he quickly elevated his friend from special deputy to undersheriff. Both men also received appointments as deputy U.S. marshals of Oklahoma and Indian Territories. These commissions, issued by U.S. Marshals E. D. Nix of Oklahoma and George Crump of the western district of Arkansas, headquartered at Fort Smith, permitted Lake and Canton to pursue criminals beyond the boundaries of Q County and make arrests across the breadth of the territories.

The immediate concern, however, was the apprehension of local thieves. Canton's first arrest was that of a petty saddle thief, but in May a vigorous campaign against horse thieves was mounted.[17] "Sheriff Lake has been in the saddle for some three weeks and with the assistance of his deputies has returned to their owners seven head of horses and mules," reported the *Pawnee Times-Democrat* of June 1. Undersheriff Canton and a man named J. F. Porter were at El Reno after mules were stolen from Porter's pasture. "They expect to return also with the thief," said the paper. Meanwhile, a report reached Pawnee that a large gang of armed men was moving a herd of eighty stolen horses through the Creek Nation. George Horner, the only officer

Frank Canton, T. A. Henry, and Frank Lake. *Author's collection.*

remaining in town, "in less than an hour's time had a posse of 20 men galloping away toward the location of the herd." At Jennings the posse was
joined by additional reinforcements, but "after spending several days in the
jungles of the Nation, they returned home without any game in the way of
horses or horse thieves."[18]

Within a month the energetic efforts of the sheriff's office to curtail crime
prompted a tribute to Lake from an admiring citizen: "Who caused the horse
and cattle stealing to stop? Frank Lake. Who is it stopped the chicken stealing, house breaking and pilfering at night? Frank Lake. Who caused the
merchants and farmers to sleep sound at night, from Ingalls east to the Creek
line? Frank Lake. Who causes honest people to smile, and thieves to tremble
at the sound of his name? Frank Lake."[19]

While Lake was being lauded, Canton was making plans to finally do
something about that pestiferous Texas fugitive business. He liked Oklahoma and had sent for Annie and Ruby to join him as soon as school was out
for the summer, but the proximity to Texas made him nervous. There was
the haunting fear that he might some day feel the grip of a Texas Ranger on
his arm and find himself on the way back to Huntsville.

In July he ventured into Texas for the first time since fleeing the state
fifteen years before. He went to Amarillo and called on Judge William Buford
Plemons of the 47th District. Judge Plemons, fifty years old and a thrice-

wounded Confederate veteran, was a popular jurist who would be elected to a seat in the Texas legislature later that year. He had been a judge in Clay County, just north of Jack County, Texas, in the 1870s and knew Canton from the Joe Horner days.[20] Canton pleaded his case to Plemons and requested help in petitioning Governor James S. Hogg for a pardon.

There are two stories concerning Canton, Hogg, and their meeting on the pardon appeal. Both are probably apocryphal but interesting nonetheless. According to one, Judge Plemons approached the governor in Canton's behalf but could get no assurance that a pardon would be granted. Said Hogg: "You have got to bring your man in here. By Gatlins, I am not going to pardon him in the bush." Plemons told Canton that if he appeared personally before the governor, he might receive his pardon but that, on the other hand, Hogg might turn him over to prison authorities. It was Canton's decision whether to take that risk. Canton, so the story goes, stuck his six-shooter in his waistband and announced he was going to see the governor. If an attempt was made to return him to prison, he said, Texas would need a new governor in the morning.[21]

Hogg's demand to interview the fugitive personally is central also to the other tale, but in this version Canton took a more subtle approach to that crucial meeting. He had his old friend Burk Burnett, by now wealthy and politically influential, with vast landholdings in both Texas and Indian Territory, invite Hogg to a coyote hunt on one of Burnett's ranges. Canton, without revealing his true identity, presided over the excursion as guide, scout, and master of ceremonies and in the process ingratiated himself with the governor. At the conclusion of the hunt, Hogg shook hands warmly with Canton and extended him an invitation to visit the governor at Austin at any time. Shortly thereafter Hogg was notified that the fugitive Joe Horner was ready to meet with him. An appointment hour was set. Fifteen minutes before that time, Canton walked into the governor's office. Hogg greeted his recent hunting companion cordially, and the two men sat and rehashed their coyote hunt experiences. As the time neared for the Horner appointment and Canton showed no sign of leaving, Hogg stood up, offered his hand, and professed his delight that Canton had stopped by. Canton did not move. He then explained to the startled governor that he was the notorious Joe Horner and that he was there to plead for a pardon.[22]

On July 17, 1894, an extraordinary two-thousand-word plea signed "Joe Horner, alias F.M. Canton" was presented to Governor Hogg. Undoubtedly authored by Judge Plemons, who based it on information supplied by Canton, the entire tone of this document was vastly different from the arrogance of the applicant implied in the foregoing tales. The plea for a pardon began with this ponderous sentence:

With a deep sense of humiliation and prompted only by a duty I feel that I owe to my country, my family and myself, I, Joe Horner, in my proper person do hereby surrender my liberty, my person and all that is sacred and dear to me to your disposal and keeping, and beg to say that I will cheerfully abide whatever disposition you in your opinion think would be right and proper and should you decide to deal gently with me and restore me to my citizenship, which I earnestly pray that you may, I can only pledge you my sacred honor in the name of my maker, that it shall ever be my ambition to so act that you shall never regret having done so, and in this connection, I beg to say, that since the fall of man, and the curse thereafter upon him, sin and crime of various kinds have existed and doubtless will continue to exist to the end, but ere this fall, an all wise and merciful creator, implanted in the human breast certain God-like attributes to be exercised in behalf of the unfortunate.[23]

After a similar verbose discourse on how the virtue of mercy had "inspired poets to write tenderest verses, painters to represent its powers upon canvas, and sculptors to carve its form in marble," the governor was reminded that "it is human to err and to forgive is divine." The petitioner, "without fear of apprehension or a promise of pardon," then submitted what he called "a true history" of his life, which, he said, would "read more like a romance than fact" but which was "nevertheless true."[24]

An untruth, however, appeared in the very first sentence of this recital. The petitioner stated that in January 1877, at the time of the Comanche bank robbery, he was "a young man 23 years old"; actually he was twenty-seven. He pleaded youthful ignorance, saying he "was raised in the country and knew but little of the world and its ways." He was "acting in a reckless spirit" when he, with others, robbed the bank "by force of arms." No mention was made of the charges against him in Jack County or of other crimes he was rumored to have committed.[25]

He described his arrest in San Antonio, his trial, his conviction and sentencing, and his escape from the Bexar County jail. Then, "after roaming over the barren hills of the then unsettled country . . . , crazed by hunger and exposure," realizing that without relief he would die and "driven to desperation" by his situation, he held up a stagecoach and "compelled a passenger thereon to contribute" to his relief. "Then it was," he said, that "justice again rose before" him "like a mountain." He was arrested, tried, convicted, sentenced to another ten years, and conveyed to the Texas State Penitentiary. On August 4, 1879, he again escaped.[26]

However, being a fugitive from the penalty of the law that I had transgressed, I realized it became necessary for me to abandon the

great State of Texas, that I had learned to love so well and I at once
settled in the Rocky Mountains in the Territory of Wyoming, where
I have since resided until recently, when I removed to the County of
Q, Oklahoma, where I now reside.

. . . During my confinement and after the commission of the
two crimes for which I was convicted, I pledged my honor and my
life to so live that the world would be better by my having lived and
I determined to spend the balance of my life in vindicating the law
that I had so unjustly outraged and to my satisfaction I feel that I
have fully redeemed each and all of said pledges, as I don't believe
that there is any man who has done more in the last fifteen years to
suppress lawlessness and enforce the laws of his county than I.[27]

To support this contention, he submitted a thick sheaf of documents, most
of them letters from men of means and influence recommending him for
appointment to federal office but including his certification of election as
sheriff of Johnson County, Wyoming, and his commissions as deputy U.S.
marshal in that state. He cited his service as a member of the Democratic
Central Committee of Wyoming and as a delegate to the National Democratic Convention in 1884. He mentioned his candidacy for the Wyoming
legislature in 1888 and his unsuccessful campaign for appointment as U.S.
marshal in Alaska. He told how he had been appointed deputy U.S. collector
of customs in Alaska but had declined the position because he could not take
his family with him. No reference was made to his two murder indictments
in Wyoming. After his escape, he said, he adopted the name F. M. Canton
and had been known by that name ever since. He recited the various law
enforcement positions he then held. As a husband and father, he appealed to
the governor, also blessed with "a noble and devoted wife [and] loving off-
spring." He stated: "Your Petitioner also has a true and loving helpmate,
[and] a bright and innocent daughter of only nine summers in whose linea-
ments a father's are reproduced. They have been incentives to him to be
worthy of the name husband and father. Most faithfully has he tried to do
this. There needs but one act to bring perfect happiness to this household,
one act to drive away the skeleton of dread from its closets." That act, of
course, was the granting of a full pardon, which would "lift the blight or
curse from those innocent lives now enshrouded in sorrow and dread [so]
that the father, wife and daughter may thank God that mercy as well as
justice reigns."[28]

"This is a strange case," began Governor Hogg's decision, written the
same day. Certain imaginary extenuating factors not appearing in the written appeal but apparently voiced by the petitioner in his interview were accepted and cited by Hogg in his decision. The applicant, wrote Hogg, had
merely "held horses" while his companions robbed the Comanche bank.

Canton called on
Texas Governor
James. S. Hogg with
a plea. *Courtesy
Archives Division,
Texas State Library.*

During the stagecoach robbery, the applicant had appropriated only half of the funds of one passenger, a total of seventy-five dollars, explaining that he needed the money to flee the country. He took the name and address of his "coerced benefactor," promising to return the money and subsequently doing so. The escape from his prison guards was accomplished "by strategem" and without violence. "He now this day surrenders to me and asks pardon," wrote the governor. "His reasons are that he was quite young when he committed the offenses for which he was convicted and that he has in all respects fully reformed." He reviewed Canton's exemplary history, as presented, for the fifteen years since the prison break, duly noting the "many strong endorsements of the highest character showing him to be an upright, honorable citizen and a fearless, trustworthy official."[29]

> He tells me that he has a wife and a little daughter for whom he of course expresses great solicitude. I asked him if his wife knew he was a convict when they were married. This was for the purpose of testing his honor and principles for I felt that if he had married a woman ignorant of his criminal record that he possessed elements of

crime that no pardon could eradicate. Answering me, he frankly stated that before marrying he fully explained his troubles to his affianced and that she cast her lot with him in full light of all the facts and that he married her under his proper name.[30] His daughter, however, is ignorant of all. None of his constituents know of his complications. He seems to have fully escaped the possibility of detection.

Upon the whole I cannot see any good in requiring his further confinement or in having him exposed. No good could result from such course to his innocent daughter [but] great, irreparable damage would be done and a splendid character built up under a cloud of terror would be blemished, and his confiding constituents greatly chagrined. Reform, not punishment alone, is the object of criminal convictions. The applicant has certainly reformed.[31]

Governor Hogg then granted "to said convict Joe Horner a full, unconditional pardon in each case, restoring to him all his rights of citizenship and the right of suffrage."[32]

With a weight removed from his shoulders, a burden that he had borne for fifteen years, Canton could now make a permanent home in Oklahoma. He and Annie made a quick trip to Nebraska City to close their affairs there. They returned to Pawnee within a week, enrolled Ruby in Principal T. D. Harnden's Select School, and settled into their new home.[33]

While undersheriff at Pawnee, Canton was often in conflict with deputy U.S. marshals and their possemen. Since he himself carried two such commissions, this seems odd, but he evidently disapproved of some of Marshal Nix's appointees and harassed them at every opportunity.

His first altercation followed Sheriff Lake's arrest of two suspects on May 19. William McElhaney, alias "the Narrow Gauge Kid," charged with horse stealing in Indian Territory, was quickly turned over to deputies from Fort Smith. The other man, C. V. Bowman, accused of stealing household goods and tools from Indian dwellings within the county, reportedly made a full confession to County Attorney Charles J. Wrightsman and was held for local court action.[34]

But the following week, when all the county officers were off chasing horse thieves, Bowman slipped away from his guard, stole a horse, and escaped. He eluded lawmen for about a month, but late in June two possemen working for Deputy U.S. Marshal Joe Eads of Guthrie nabbed him in the Creek Nation. They brought him to Pawnee, where Canton chained him to other county prisoners.

On June 26 Deputy Marshal Eads arrived with a capias and demanded custody of Bowman. Canton balked, and Wrightsman was called on to resolve the dispute. The county attorney "held that Q County had Bowman in

Anna and Frank Canton and their daughter, Ruby, in about 1894, when they moved to Oklahoma. *Courtesy Jim Gatchell Memorial Museum, Buffalo, Wyoming.*

charge and would hold him until cause was shown, further than had been, why they should give him up." With growing anger, "Eads said he would take him at all hazards, whereupon Canton replied that if he did, it would be after big cartridges were all emptied. Canton then placed a deputy on the inside of the room with the prisoner, shut the door, and stood outside guardian. Eads stated that he would get up a crowd to take Bowman. Canton remarked that he did not need a crowd to hold him."[35]

Neither officer would budge. Finally Canton, losing patience, placed the deputy marshal under arrest. Eads submitted, made bond, and was freed. But he was back a few days later with a court order commanding the sheriff to relinquish custody of Bowman or face contempt-of-court charges. He got his prisoner. The *Pawnee Times-Democrat* complained bitterly about the case and editorialized that Canton was not alone in his disdain for some of the deputy U.S. marshals. "Our people are wholly disgusted with the extreme leniency and favor shown the deputy marshals when guilty of wrong doing. The time has past [sic] for their ill-rule and sway in Oklahoma. Their cussedness under the present status of affairs is past our quiet sufferance."[36] In August, Canton arrested William Nolls, another deputy U.S. marshal, on a warrant charging him with theft of a revolver.[37]

C. V. Bowman, the cause of the Eads-Canton difficulty, proved to be a slippery customer indeed. After beating federal charges against him, he was returned to Pawnee and indicted at the November term of district court. While awaiting trial he escaped again, only to be recaptured by Sheriff Lake a week later after a gunfight in which Lake was "said to have aired Bowman's hat."[38] The elusive Bowman was then jailed at Perry but escaped again in January 1895 and dropped from the purview of the Q County officers.

Another troublesome character at this time was Ben Howell, a reputed "confederate of the Doolin and Dalton gang, [who was] too cowardly to join in their raids."[39] A frequent guest in Sheriff Lake's hoosegow, Howell was indicted at the November 1894 term of district court on charges of burglary, grand larceny, and petit larceny. On the night of November 27 he broke jail with Bowman and an accused horse thief named Warren Hooker. The three stole horses from the nearby Burch livery stable and rode off toward the Creek Nation. Sheriff Lake, with Charles Hook and livery owner J. D. Burch as possemen, recaptured the escapees on December 5 after the gun battle in which Bowman's hat was punctured. Howell was locked up in the Perry jail and escaped again with Bowman a month later. Recaptured in April 1895, he made still another escape attempt before final lodging in the jail at Fort Smith.[40]

But the Shelley brothers were the most dangerous desperadoes with whom Sheriff Lake and Canton dealt during this period. Bill and John Shelley lived in a squatter's cabin in the eastern part of the county near the Arkansas River. Living with them were Bill's wife, Lou, their baby, a small boy said to be Lou's brother, and a huge Newfoundland dog named "Bum." The brothers were arrested in July 1894 after stealing a spring wagon from an Indian. Deputy Sheriffs Bob McCargo and West Wharton tracked the wagon for twenty miles before overtaking the brothers. At the approach of the officers, the Shelleys tried to flee but surrendered when McCargo fired several rifle shots in their direction.[41]

After a few days in jail the Shelleys announced they would plead guilty to the theft of the wagon. While awaiting trial, they caused no trouble and were permitted visits by Lou Shelley. But on the evening of August 15 the brothers overpowered guard Volney Culpepper and escaped.[42]

The county officers kept a close watch on the Shelley cabin, especially after learning that the brothers were "wanted for several vicious murders in other States."[43] But months went by with no sign of the Shelleys. Then, Cook Horton, a Pawnee saloonkeeper and sheriff's deputy, was driving a one-horse buggy when he spotted the brothers on the road to Tulsa. Recognizing them at once, he opened fire with a pistol. The Shelleys returned the fire and, well-mounted on fleet horses, escaped into the dense woods. Horton reported the encounter to Sheriff Lake and said he was certain he had hit one of the brothers in the face.[44]

In January 1895 the officers received a report that a woman with a big Newfoundland dog was living in a heavily wooded area near Checotah, more than one hundred miles southeast of Pawnee in the Creek Nation. On January 27 Sheriff Lake, Undersheriff Canton, and two possemen named A. A. Powe and Enos Willets set out. Lake and Canton were mounted; Powe and Willets drove a hack and supply wagon. At Tulsa the posse was augmented by two more men: Dr. John C. W. Bland, who, according to Canton, "would always get up at midnight if necessary to hunt a horse thief," and Deputy U.S. Marshal Dean Hogan.[45] When the posse reached Checotah late on February 2, City Marshal John H. McCann joined them.[46] A recent snowstorm had blanketed the countryside. Anxious to reach the cabin before dawn, Lake, Canton, Bland, Hogan, and McCann set out on horseback during the night. Powe and Willets followed with their slower vehicles.

At about six o'clock the officers arrived at a small, windowless cabin in a clearing surrounded by heavy timber. It was described by Canton as a "house built of logs with 'chinking' (sticks between the logs plastered with mud), about twelve by twelve feet, a door in the north, and one in the south."[47] Four horses were stabled, a strong indication that the Shelley boys were home. The five lawmen took up positions near the doors, and Lake holloed the building. Recognizing the answering shout as the voice of one of the Shelley brothers, he told them who he was, said that the place was surrounded, and ordered them out. The Shelleys responded with defiance. Canton then told them to send out the woman and children. Lou Shelley, carrying a baby, emerged and ran into the woods, followed by a little boy and the big Newfoundland dog.

Almost immediately the Shelley brothers knocked chinking from between the cabin's logs and opened fire on the officers. John McCann, standing at the south door a few feet from Canton, was struck and fell to the ground. He got back to his feet, and he and Canton emptied their Winchesters into the building, then scurried for the shelter of the trees. "The bullet had hit [McCann] directly over the heart, but had struck his forty-five Colt's revolver that he carried in a shoulder scabbard and glanced off," recalled Canton. "It was a close call."[48] A bullet also struck Dr. Bland in the forearm, inflicting a painful but minor wound.

For most of the day a sniping gunfight continued. The Shelleys seemed well stocked with ammunition and showed no inclination to give up. The frustrated officers suffered in the wet and cold. Finally Canton decided to employ the tactic that had smoked out Nate Champion back in Wyoming. He rode to a neighboring farmhouse and secured a wagon, a load of hay, and three gallons of coal oil. Returning to the battle site, he directed the construction of a go-devil, fitting the wagon with a breastwork of hay held in place by fence rails and rope and saturating the hay with coal oil. Then Powe and Willets, protected by the hay barricade, pushed the contraption up to the cabin while the officers covered them with heavy fire. After some difficulty they shoved the hay against the cabin wall and released the ropes holding it. Throwing more coal oil over the building, they ignited the hay and pulled the wagon free. A bullet from the cabin passed so close to Powe's head, said the *Pawnee Times-Democrat,* that it "knocked his spectacles off. Powe took out his six-shooter and coolly firing a few shots into the crack proceeded on with his work."[49]

The cabin soon was ablaze, and the Shelley brothers came out with their hands raised. One of them could barely walk; he had been shot through both thighs early in the fight. When he was searched for weapons his boots were found to be full of blood. Canton said he then saw why the brothers had not made a break: "John was not able to run, and his brother would not leave him. Just how any man could stand on his feet and fight all day with such bad wounds is more than I can understand, but he collapsed absolutely when it was all over. His brother never had a scratch, although several bullets had passed through his clothes."[50] The face of one of the brothers bore a partly healed scar, which he admitted was a souvenir of the meeting with Cook Horton on the Tulsa road.

The lawmen used snow to extinguish the fire and then entered the cabin. They had poured almost eight hundred rounds into the building during the fight, and "there was hardly a square inch on the inside that had not been struck by bullets," Canton said. In addition to an extensive armory that included four Winchesters, several revolvers, a shotgun, and ammunition for all the weapons, the place was full of stolen goods. There were four new saddles and a large Saratoga trunk packed with unworn men's and women's clothes. The four horses in the stable were also stolen. But Canton had grudging admiration for the thieves. "In all my experience, I have never known outlaws to pull off a gamer fight than the Shelley brothers," he said, perhaps forgetting for the moment Nate Champion's brave fight against greater odds.[51]

With the battle over, Lou Shelley and the children emerged from the woods. The woman, described by Canton as "young and rather good-looking," was greatly distraught, and the officers felt sorry for her.[52] After sending to Checotah for an ambulance and stretcher to move the wounded brother, they allowed her to accompany the prisoners to the town. There they sold the captured weaponry and turned over the proceeds to Mrs. Shelley.

Checotah was on the Missouri, Kansas and Texas Railroad. While Powe and Willets drove the hack and wagon back to Pawnee, Lake and Canton took their prisoners by train to Perry for temporary jailing.[53] Two weeks later they picked up the brothers and conveyed them to Fort Smith to be tried in the court of the famous Judge Isaac C. Parker. The *Pawnee Times-Democrat* praised the sheriff as much for relieving the county of the expense of prosecution as for the capture. Sheriff Lake, it said, had taken them to Fort Smith and would "prosecute them for assault with intent to kill." The paper added: "He will have no trouble in convicting on that charge, as they fought like tigers when captured. Once convicted on that charge they will go to the penitentiary for a longer term than Pawnee county could have sent them and the expense will be on the United States instead of Pawnee county. That's the beauty about it."[54]

The same week that the Shelleys were captured, possemen caught one of the Indian Territory's most notorious outlaws near Nowata. Crawford Goldsby, better known as "Cherokee Bill," was trapped and arrested on January 29, 1895, and taken to Fort Smith, where he was convicted of murder and sentenced to death by "Hanging Judge" Parker. The following July, while awaiting execution, Cherokee Bill somehow obtained a pistol and killed a guard in an unsuccessful escape attempt. An investigation was begun to determine how the weapon had been smuggled into the tightly secured jailhouse. A grand jury found evidence that Lou Shelley had carried the pistol, wrapped in a shawl, into the jail and given it to her husband. Indictments were handed down against Lou, the Shelley brothers, and four other inmates, including the celebrated Henry Starr.[55]

The charges could not be substantiated and were eventually dropped. Cherokee Bill, before his execution on March 17, 1896, said that Ben Howell, the petty thief from Pawnee County, had slipped the gun to him. As a short-termer, serving only a ninety-day sentence, Howell had been made a trustee and granted considerable freedom of the jail grounds. He disappeared about the time of the Cherokee Bill escape attempt. Recaptured, he was not charged in the Cherokee Bill affair but was given an additional six months for walking off.[56]

Meanwhile back in Pawnee the officers were engaging in political wars in addition to chasing outlaws. In August 1894 Frank Lake and Frank Canton were selected as delegates to the Democratic congressional convention at El Reno.[57] Lake received the Democratic nomination for reelection as sheriff at a time when the political tides were running in favor of the Republican Party.

Lake came under criticism from the *Pawnee Republican*, which pointed out that the total bills of the sheriff's office for the quarter exceeded seventeen hundred dollars. "Up to this time there has been no person convicted of any serious offense. There has been one or two fellows convicted of being drunk and possibly carrying concealed weapons, but the horse thieves and other criminals who have committed serious offenses have so far gone unpunished."[58]

The *Pawnee Times-Democrat*, of course, gave him its support. "If Lake isn't elected sheriff of this county the people ought to be stolen blind," proclaimed editor John G. Cash a few days before the election.

The county is presided over by a man of iron nerve. To live in a county with a coward for a sheriff, where every time a desperado or rowdy comes to town he gets drunk and makes the citizens hide out is like living in the wilds of Africa. Lake and his brave deputies allow no such business. No bullies over-ride them and no matter how tough a man may be he must behave or go to jail. Lake would rather be perforated with bullets than allow a man to bluff him or defy the laws which he swore to enforce. He may have his imperfections but he's got the sand. . . . He has a face like a woman and a heart like a tiger.[59]

On November 6 Frank Lake became the first elected sheriff of the county, squeaking out a 4-vote victory out of 1,587 cast in a three-way race.[60] It is difficult to determine if his narrow success on election day was helped or hindered by a fracas that involved Undersheriff Frank Canton and occurred ten days earlier. On October 26 a man answering the description of a Kansas murder suspect was arrested and jailed by Canton, who wired Kansas authorities of the arrest and then left town on business. Returning the next day, he found a telegram from Kansas telling him that he should hold the prisoner, Oscar Rader, "at all hazards" and that officers were on the way. Rader had been released on a habeas corpus, but George Horner had kept his eye on him and told his brother that the man was then in McCool's bunkhouse.

Canton had long been suspicious of Alonzo (Lon) McCool, proprietor of the Lone Star Livery Stable, believing that he marketed stolen horses through his livery operation. "He was an open enemy of the officers of the county, and was especially bitter against me," Canton said. "He never lost an opportunity to warn a criminal if he thought I was hunting him."[61] Canton and George Horner went to the McCool barn and bunkhouse, where they arrested and handcuffed Rader without difficulty. Canton then sat on a wooden keg and read the prisoner the telegram from Kansas. Suddenly McCool, who had been drinking, burst on the scene and began berating the officers.

In his memoirs Canton gave his version of what then happened:

I had taken off my six-shooter and laid my Winchester aside when I first rode in. I had a heavy pocket derringer that I usually carried in my hip pocket when in town. It was a forty-one-caliber Colt. I thought it was a good one, but had never tried it out. . . . [McCool] stepped up close in front of me, and with his left hand slapped me in the face, at the same time dropping his right hand to his hip pocket. In rising from the keg on which I was seated, I pushed him away from me, and at the same time drew my derringer and fired at his head. The bullet struck him in the forehead just over the left eye. He fell on his back, and I supposed from the appearance of the wound that he was shot square through the head.[62]

A physician named Morrow was summoned, and he arrived with Deputy Marshal Joe Eads. Canton, George Horner, Eads, and the doctor carried the wounded man in a blanket to the McCool residence nearby. There Dr. Morrow examined the wound and found that the bullet had not penetrated the skull but had glanced around under the skin and emerged in the back of the head. McCool was unconscious for twelve hours but gradually recovered. Canton said he was so disgusted with the derringer that he threw it away and never carried another.[63]

Canton was arrested, given a preliminary hearing the following Monday, October 29, and absolved of any blame. His testimony at the hearing differed substantially from his autobiographical account. In this version, as reported in the press, his weapon was a double-action revolver, "a self-cocker." When McCool rushed him, Canton attempted to club the man over the head with the pistol, and it "in some way was discharged, the ball striking McCool in the forehead." He had never meant to shoot McCool at all, Canton said, only to strike him with the weapon. The improbability of the claim—that a bullet, accidentally discharged from a pistol being used as a bludgeon, would enter a man's forehead and circle his skull—seemingly did not occur to the authorities. Canton was speedily cleared.[64]

It is interesting, and perhaps significant, that some months later a posseman working for Canton shot a man in the gambling rooms above Cook Horton's saloon and claimed the same excuse. Canton, on a warrant sworn to by his posseman W. S. Harvey, had arrested Herman Proctor for selling whiskey to Indians. That evening Proctor and Harvey met in Horton's poker parlor, and a violent argument ensued. Harvey drew his pistol and attempted, he later said, "to strike Proctor over the head," but the weapon "accidentally discharged" and a bullet hit Proctor in the thigh, breaking the bone.[65]

It appears that Canton distorted the facts of the McCool shooting at the hearing. No evidence was produced to show that McCool was armed, although Canton may have believed he was. At the hearing Canton, aware that McCool might yet die from the wound, may have thought it more prudent to explain an accidental shot while defending himself in a scuffle than a deliberately aimed bullet to the head of an unarmed man. His account written thirty years later, with the threat of a possible murder indictment removed, was probably more accurate. The remarkably similar Harvey-Proctor affair perhaps was less a coincidence than a replay of a previously successful gambit.

Lon McCool had recovered sufficiently from his injury to be back on the streets by November 5 and to vote in the election the following day.[66] But three months later he was confined to his bed, and on February 17, 1895, he died at the age of thirty-six. The press reported the cause of death as erysipelas, which had developed into partial paralysis and hemorrhaging of the lungs.[67] But Canton believed McCool died from the effects of another fight. "I believe he would have finally recovered had he taken good care of himself," said Canton, "but after he got up and commenced feeling better, he started in to beat up a Dutch boy, and got the worst of it badly."[68] McCool left a widow and several small children. One paper said that he "was known by all as kind-hearted and ever ready to accommodate. Had it not been for his weakness at times for strong drink, he would not have had an enemy in the world."[69]

The work of Sheriff Lake and his deputies was consistently praised in the *Pawnee Times-Democrat*. When in February 1895 another Oklahoma paper reported that horse stealing was rampant in Lincoln, Payne, and Pawnee Counties, the *Times-Democrat* rushed to Lake's defense. "Pawnee county has a democratic sheriff that permits no such thieving," it declared. "If there is a horse thief in this country who wants to be brought to the bar of justice, just let him steal a horse from within the borders of this county and that is where he will land."[70]

Undersheriff Canton was particularly aggressive in his law enforcement duties during this period, even to the point of overzealousness. Forty years later a Pawnee old-timer remembered a scare Canton gave him as a boy. He and some other youngsters were driving a team and wagon to Osage City to play baseball. Once out of town, they put the whip to the horses and went careening down the road. They were laughing and having fun when one of them noticed a horseman, Winchester in hand, bearing down on them from behind at full gallop. The frightened boys reined in their team and watched as the mounted man, who proved to be Frank Canton, approached warily. He had been scouting the road for outlaws reported in the vicinity and had mistaken the speeding wagon full of young ballplayers for the gang.[71]

On another occasion Canton incurred the wrath of a man he arrested in error. The two had been passengers on the same hack from Perry to Pawnee, and the man's reticence aroused Canton's suspicions. Inquiry in town disclosed that the stranger's name was Young and that he had set out on foot from Pawnee for his claim at Crystal. Canton had a warrant for the arrest of a man named Felix Young who had once staked a claim at Crystal. Adding two and two, Canton dispatched a pair of deputies to apprehend the man. Found trudging along the road six miles from town, he was arrested and brought back. The man demanded to see County Attorney Wrightsman, whom he had known for several years. Wrightsman identified him as J. P. Young, not Felix, and he was released.

"Mr. Young was about as mad as a man could get," said the *Pawnee Times-Democrat*. "He didn't like the idea of being mistaken for Felix Young and furthermore it was rather tough on a man who had walked six miles on his way home to have to make the same journey again. We are sorry to see innocent men mistaken for criminals, but in a new country where so many outlaws exist this mistake often occurs. A successful officer is a suspicious man."[72]

Canton was particularly on the lookout that spring for a man he wanted badly. John Tregoning, the killer of his friend George Henderson back in Wyoming, escaped from prison in November 1894, and Canton had received a report that he was now in Oklahoma or Indian Territory. On April 7, 1895, Canton wrote William A. Pinkerton, informing him of the report and suggesting that the Pinkerton Detective Agency send an undercover operative to Pawnee to work with him in an effort to track down Tregoning and other notorious outlaws.

Pinkerton answered on the twelfth:

As we have not got the right kind of a man for this rough work out there, I have referred the matter to Supt. McParland at Denver, sending him a copy of your letter. I was greatly pleased to hear from you and did not know of your change of place. . . .

Tom Horn who used to be with our Denver office would be a good man for the place, and I will ask McParland to communicate with him and see if he cannot be got for the service and for the length of time you want him. He is not in our service now. You probably know of him. He is well acquainted all through the western country among cattle rustlers and all that class of men, and is a thorough horseman and plainsman in every sense of the word. I note particularly that you want to get Jack Treganing [sic] who excaped [sic] from the Laramie penitentiary where you sent him for life and that he is down in that country. I should be very glad to hear of his capture.[73]

James McParland, the agency's assistant general supervisor at Denver, wrote Canton the following day:

Yours of the 7th. to Mr. W.A. Pinkerton has been forwarded to me with instructions that if any Operatives at this office who were capable of doing work of this kind were available that I should at once send him forward to you.

You are well aware that it will take a peculiar man to do this work, in fact a man as it were to the Manor born. I have such men at this office but at the present time they are engaged on other operations. In fact I have three that could do this work or that I could detail upon it, but at present they are unavailable and it is impossible for me to say when they would be at liberty. I know of a man although not working for me but I could recommend him as he formerly did work for me. I have not got his address at the present time but he is liable to write me at any time and as soon as he does I will suggest to him the fact that this matter is ready to be taken up and will communicate with you. I can guarantee the man. If he undertakes this matter no better man could be found for the work that you wish to have done. I like you would very much like to get a hold of Tregoning as poor Henderson was an intimate friend of mine.[74]

One of the well-qualified operatives unavailable at the time was the celebrated cowboy-detective Charles A. Siringo. McParland had sent Siringo and Operative W. O. Sayles to Alaska a few weeks before to investigate a large gold theft from a mill near Juneau.[75] Both Pinkerton and McParland had immediately thought of Tom Horn as perfectly fitted for the job in Oklahoma. Horn had left the Pinkerton Agency shortly before and was employed as a stock detective for the Swan Land and Cattle Company of Wyoming.[76]

As it turned out, nothing ever came of Canton's request for Pinkerton involvement in the outlaw war in Oklahoma. And if John Tregoning was in the country, he eluded Canton and other officers. He never was recaptured.

One criminal who plagued officers of the Oklahoma and Indian Territories for years was a "bow-legged, heavily mustached, and droopy-shouldered" cattle thief named Ben Cravens. Born Benjamin Crede Cravens in Orange County, Iowa, in 1864, Cravens was a career criminal, starting as a child.[77] According to the published memoirs of U.S. Marshal E. D. Nix, Frank Canton figured prominently in a dramatic arrest of Cravens during this period.

In May 1894, said Nix, Cravens and a man named William Crittenden stole twenty head of steers from Indians at the Osage Agency. Deputy U.S. Marshals Steve Burke and Will Nix traced the stolen cattle to the pen of a Noble County butcher and arrested Cravens and Crittenden.[78] While being held temporarily in the Perry jail, the two prisoners engineered an escape. Cravens was captured in Caney, Kansas, and returned by Nix and Burke, but he escaped again from the Newkirk jail.

In late June an Indian informant reported that the fugitive was hiding in the home of half-breeds living in the Osage Hills. Frank Lake and Frank Canton joined Nix and Burke in the hunt and, guided by the informant, proceeded by night to the outlaw hideout. Surrounding the house, they waited for light and the appearance of their quarry. But an hour after sunup no one

Prison photos of outlaw Ben Cravens. *Courtesy Western History Collections, University of Oklahoma.*

had stirred from the cabin. Finally, said Marshal Nix, "Deputy Frank Canton, who was noted for his cool daring, walked up to the front door and knocked." A woman's voice responded, and Canton ordered her to open the door. When the woman refused, "Canton gave the flimsy door a hard kick with his heavy boot. The door flew open and there stood Ben Cravens, his forty-five in hand. The audacity of Canton must have surprised the outlaw for he did not offer to shoot before Canton had him covered and had commanded him to surrender. By this time the other deputies were at Canton's side and Cravens was disarmed. Again he was taken to Perry and this time he was placed under such heavy guard that he could not escape. Cravens pleaded guilty and was sentenced to a long term in the federal penitentiary at Leavenworth."[79]

Oklahoma outlaw historian Glenn Shirley placed this incident more than a year later, in August 1895, and added additional details. Canton, he said, got on Cravens's trail after he spotted the outlaw attempting to steal horses near Pawnee. Firing several shots at the fugitive, the officer managed to kill his horse. Canton, Burke, and Will Nix (Lake's participation is not mentioned) trailed Cravens to the hideout in the Osage Hills. Canton burst into the cabin, striking "the door hard, smashing it inward and almost off its hinges." Inside stood Cravens, a pistol in his hand. The outlaw, surprised, did not fire.

Before he could trigger, Canton whacked him across the wrist, sending the revolver skittering into the corner under the bed. "Surrender!" yelled the deputy. Cravens, about to throw up his hands, changed his mind and dived for the gun. Canton leaped after him, whacking him on the jaw. The outlaw grappled the deputy. As they fell to the floor, Canton's head struck the bedpost. He sprawled half-conscious from the blow, and Cravens tried to seize his six-shooter. Steve Burke, racing through the doorway, intercepted the outlaw and bodily hauled him off his victim. Cravens broke loose from Burke and started to leap out the window. But Deputy Nix filled the opening, covering him with his rifle.[80]

Strangely, the Pawnee papers for the 1894–95 period did not record this incident at all. Canton, who might have been expected to recount such a dramatic experience in graphic detail, said only that he "arrested [Cravens] for stealing cattle in the Osage country, took him to Perry, Oklahoma, and delivered him to Deputy United States Marshal Nix, in charge of the Perry jail."[81] Cravens was given only a six-month sentence and by 1896 was back pursuing his criminal career in Oklahoma Territory. He and Canton would cross trails again.

Chapter 8

The Deputy
Marshal, 1896

"Mr. Canton is a shrewd and fearless officer and Mr. Nix made a wise choice when he selected him to perform the detective work."

Pawnee Times-Democrat, May 10, 1895

As the lesser criminals infesting the newly formed Cherokee Outlet counties were systematically rounded up by Sheriff Lake and his deputies, Frank Canton, in his capacity as deputy U.S. marshal, devoted more of his energies to the war on the Dalton-Doolin gang. He would say that he was *"specially* delegated" by Marshal Nix to hunt down the members of this criminal band.[1] An item in the *Pawnee Times-Democrat* of May 10, 1895, lends some credibility to this claim: "On account of this section of Oklahoma being the favorite rendezvous of outlaws, Marshal Nix decided that a good man was needed for special detective work in this region and about the first of last December Deputy Marshal F.M. Canton of this city was appointed for that purpose." In his memoirs, however, E. D. Nix makes no mention of any special assignment given Canton.[2]

After the bloody bank robbery debacle at Coffeyville in 1892 and the Ingalls battle of 1893, leadership of the Dalton gang had devolved on Bill Dalton, the last of the outlaw brothers still active. When Dalton was killed by federal officers near Ardmore, Oklahoma Territory, in June 1894, Bill Doolin assumed the role of outlaw chieftain.[3] Other prominent gang members included George "Red Buck" Waightman; "Cock-eyed Charley" Pierce; William "Tulsa Jack" Blake; George Newcomb, alias "Bitter Creek," alias "Slaughter's Kid"; William F. "Little Bill" Raidler; and Charles "Dynamite Dick" Clifton. The robbery of the Farmers and Citizens Bank of Pawnee in January 1894 was but one of many spectacular crimes attributed to the gang. By 1895 heavy rewards were being offered for the apprehension of the criminals, alive or dead.

Deputy U.S. Marshals Bill
Tilghman and Charles F.
Colcord. *Courtesy Western
History Collections, Univer-
sity of Oklahoma.*

In addition to the highly publicized active gang members, a number of
lesser-known collaborators in Pawnee and Payne Counties provided safe hide-
outs for the gang, fenced their stolen goods, and kept them informed of the
movements of the officers. Foremost among these outlaw supporters and
accessories were the Dunn brothers, who had taken claims south of Pawnee
near the outlaw stronghold of Ingalls. There were five of them: Charles D.
("Dal"), William T. ("Bee" or "Bill"), John E., George E., and Alfred
("Calvin"). Frank Canton would always maintain that, though not directly
participating in the gang's crimes, the Dunns were every bit as dangerous.
Of the gang members, he said, the Dunn brothers "were the worst and the
most vicious and bloodthirsty, but they were very cunning. When the U.S.
government offered rewards for the Dalton-Doolin gang dead or alive, they
made a mistake in not including the Dunns."[4] Another deputy marshal,
Charles F. Colcord, agreed with this assessment. "I believe," he said, "that
the Dunn boys, Dal, John and Bee, were about the worst men that ever infested Oklahoma, or, for that matter, any other country."[5]

Bee Dunn had an interest in a butcher shop operated by G. C. ("Chris")
Bolton in Pawnee. Dunn supplied the meat, which Bolton dispensed over the

counter. Sheriff Lake and Deputy Canton strongly suspected that the beef
was from stolen cattle. In June 1894, Chief of Police Morris Robacker and a
party of Indians from the Osage Nation inspected hides hanging in the Bolton
and Dunn butchering pens and positively identified them as coming from
stolen cattle. Lake and Canton jailed Bolton and an associate named R. C.
Spinning and obtained a warrant for the arrest of Bee Dunn. The *Pawnee
Times-Democrat* expressed surprise and disbelief: "Bee Dunn is out of the
city and has not yet been arrested. It is very probable that our butchers
killed this stock but their friends do not believe for a moment they would be
guilty of purchasing it knowing it to be stolen."[6]

The lawmen had a strong case, and the Dunn brothers knew it. They
became, in Canton's words, "very uneasy and restless" and approached the
officers with a deal: if the prosecution did not go forward, they would help
collar the Doolin gang.[7]

> Sheriff Lake and I then arranged for a conference with Bill Dunn and
> one of his brothers in Pawnee. At this conference we gave the Dunn
> boys to understand plainly that we knew they were members of the
> Dalton gang and had committed many crimes with other members
> of the gang, but that so far as we were personally concerned, we
> would not prosecute them any further and would use our influence
> with United States Marshal Nix to have him promise the same
> thing, provided, however, that they would sign an agreement to the
> following effect: That they would sever all relations with the Dal-
> tons, Doolin, and other outlaws, obey the laws of the country and
> make good citizens, and provided further, that the first time any of
> the Dalton gang came into that part of the country, the Dunn boys
> should immediately bring word to Sheriff Lake and myself of their
> exact location.
>
> We did not ask them to assist us in the capture, nor did we
> expect them to do so. All that we exacted of them was positive
> information as to the time of the arrival of the outlaws, and the place
> they were stopping.
>
> We also agreed with the Dunns that, in the event that we cap-
> tured any or all of the outlaws, we would have United States Mar-
> shal Nix collect the rewards offered for their capture, and turn the
> money all over to the Dunn boys, with the exception of a sufficient
> amount to be paid to Sheriff Lake and myself to cover our actual
> expenses while hunting the outlaws. At that time there was from
> one to three thousand dollars offered for the body of each of the
> "wild bunch," dead or alive.[8]

The brothers accepted the terms with the proviso that Marshal Nix sign
the agreement. Lake, Canton, and the Dunns went to Guthrie, the territorial

capital, and met with Nix. He agreed to the terms, said Canton, and had a formal contract drawn up, which was signed by Nix, Lake, Canton, and the two Dunn brothers.[9]

As a result of the secret agreement, Bee Dunn was not charged in the pending case. His partner, Bolton, was freed on bail, and the case was allowed to languish with a series of continuances. Bolton's reputation was so unsullied that only six weeks later his name was floated as a possible candidate for the sheriff's office at the November election.[10] Months went by, and there were no new developments. Then, in late February 1895, Bee Dunn showed up in Pawnee, his arrival noted in an innocuous news item: "Bee Dunn was up from Ingalls the first of the week looking after his interest in this city."[11] But Dunn's interest in this instance was not Bolton's butcher shop; it was his secret arrangement with the lawmen.

Dunn informed Canton that members of the gang were in the Creek Nation on a horse-stealing expedition. Acting on the tip, Canton, Will Nix, and Steve Burke rode out to scout the area. On February 27 they learned that only the day before, Doolin gang members, driving twenty head of stolen horses, had been attacked by Indians. In the ensuing gunfight the horse of "Dynamite Dick" Clifton was killed, several stolen horses were recovered, and the gang members were scattered. The officers hurried back to Pawnee for reinforcements, but when they returned to the area they found that the outlaws "had taken the precaution to fly to some distant and unknown haunt."[12]

Canton was convinced that the outlaws had been warned by gang sympathizers, and he was incensed at losing his quarry. His remarks to a Pawnee journalist regarding harborers of outlaws carried particular meaning and warning to the Dunn brothers: "Were it not for the numerous friends the gang has at its command, who do everything possible to conceal and protect the outlaws . . . , their capture would be but short work." He said the officers were "determined to vigorously prosecute a number of persons" who were "in the custom of protecting these outlaws." He added, "It is well for persons to understand that the law makes it a very severe offense to harbor criminals."[13]

Canton later admitted that the help provided the gang by the area settlers was accountable in great part to the personality of Bill Doolin himself. He considered Doolin "the squarest and best man" in the gang. "Bill Doolin had always been kind to the poor settlers, often giving them money to buy groceries."[14] Because of this, he said, "it was almost impossible for a party of officers to travel together through that country without being seen by some friends of the outlaws, who would always give the alarm in time for the criminals to escape."[15]

Pawnee County officials in 1897. Sheriff Frank Lake is the bearded man at left. Canton, seated beside him, holds a small dog. *Author's collection.*

So Canton and Lake tried a different tack. In the last week in March they set out together on a still hunt. Well supplied with provisions, they made a night ride to the vicinity of the Dunn settlement and set up camp in a heavily wooded section nearby. They notified the Dunns of their location and told them they intended to remain until the outlaws showed up. They were sure that some of the gang members were bound to show up, since the Dunns were holding a large money stash of George Newcomb's and he would certainly come for his money.[16] Canton knew he and Lake were playing a dangerous game.

> We were taking our life into our hands for we knew that the Dunn boys had no love for us, and that it would be an easy matter for them to lead us into a trap where we would not even have a fighting chance for our lives. But we figured that they would not play the game that way, because if they had us killed, we knew that there would be no money in it for them, and that every officer in the territory would be in the field hunting them down. On the other hand, if they played fair with us, and we succeeded in the capture, they would get a good reward, so we decided that under the circumstances they would do what they had promised.[17]

For a week Canton and Lake waited. Then one of the Dunn boys came with the news that on April 3 a Rock Island train had been held up at Dover in Kingfisher County, some eighty miles west of Pawnee, by gang members later identified as "Bitter Creek" Newcomb, "Cock-eyed Charley" Pierce, "Tulsa Jack" Blake, "Red Buck" Waightman, and "Little Bill" Raidler.[18] In a gunfight with officers, Tulsa Jack had been killed.

"We now expected a report at any time that the outlaws were in the neighborhood," said Canton.[19] He and Lake remained in camp, keeping a close watch, but as days, and then weeks, went by uneventfully, they grew bored. Leaving word with the Dunns where they were going and that they expected to stay the night, the officers on the evening of April 25 rode several miles to the home of George McElroy, a former deputy U.S. marshal. In the morning they found their horses missing from McElroy's corral and spent much of the day locating them. Later they met one of the Dunn boys, who told them that three of the gang—Newcomb, Pierce, and Waightman—had spent the night with Bee Dunn and ridden off early in the morning. He said Bee had attempted to notify the officers but had not been able to find them.

Canton and Lake, already distrustful of the Dunns, were dubious of this story. The coincidence of the outlaws appearing on the very night the officers were absent was not lost on them. Also they suspected the Dunns had something to do with the disappearance of the horses from McElroy's corral. But, untrustworthy as the Dunns were, the brothers remained the officers' best bet to capture the outlaws, and before Canton and Lake broke camp and returned to Pawnee, they reminded the brothers that the special arrangement was still in force.[20]

Within a week the officers learned the full extent of the Dunns' duplicity. The brothers had decided not only to betray their outlaw friends but to double-cross the officers as well. A day or two after Canton and Lake discontinued their still hunt, John Dunn, disguised with a false mustache and long side-whiskers and calling himself "Sam Shaffer, an officer from Texas," appeared in the office of Marshal Nix in Guthrie. He told of the stakeout by Canton and Lake, the overnight stay of the outlaws at Bee Dunn's place, and Bee's unsuccessful efforts to locate the officers. He requested a deputy's appointment so that he could assist in the arrest of the outlaws when they returned to the Dunn place.[21] Whether Nix was taken in by this tale is unclear, but he evidently appointed "Sam Shaffer" a special deputy and gave his blessing to the plan. He did, however, dispatch Deputy Marshals Bill Tilghman and Heck Thomas to follow "Shaffer" and his possemen back to Payne County.[22]

At two o'clock on the morning of May 2 gunfire erupted at the Dunn place. Tilghman and Thomas, camped some distance away, hurried to the scene, where they found the bullet-riddled bodies of Pierce and Newcomb lying outside the house. John, Dal, and Bee Dunn stood over them with guns still hot from firing. The Dunns said the outlaws had been killed resisting arrest. John and Dal Dunn immediately loaded the bodies in a wagon and started for Guthrie, which they reached at two o'clock that afternoon.

The arrival of the Dunns with their grisly cargo caused great excitement in the capital. Acquaintances of the outlaws, officers, and trainmen who had been their victims were called in to make positive identifications. Photographs of the bodies were taken, and curious crowds streamed through the undertaking parlors for three hours to view the remains of the two noted desperadoes.[23]

"The two deputies who brought them in repaired to a private room" with Marshal Nix and a *Guthrie Daily Leader* reporter, where "they gave the details of the taking of the territory's terrors." They said that Pierce and Newcomb had been at the Dunn house earlier on May 1 but had gone to Ingalls for some whiskey. When the two returned, "Shaffer and his men" surrounded the house and, after firing warning shots, killed Pierce in the doorway when he emerged with a rifle and killed Newcomb as he tried to escape through a window.[24] Canton and Lake were notified by telegraph and hurried to Guthrie, where they immediately recognized Dal Dunn and his brother John, or "Sam Shaffer." When he viewed the bodies, Canton pointed to buckshot wounds in the soles of Pierce's feet, indicating that Pierce had been shot while lying down. "It was the general opinion," said Canton, "that they were shot while asleep." He also noted that Pierce appeared to have been dead longer than Newcomb.[25]

Chief Deputy John M. Hale told Canton that Dal Dunn, in a different account, had explained this apparent anomaly. When the outlaws returned from Ingalls, according to this version, the Dunns were hidden in the yard waiting for them. They shot down Pierce and Newcomb without warning, threw their bodies and weapons into a wagon, and covered them with a tarpaulin. John and Dal started off for Guthrie to "claim the reward" while Bee stayed behind "to obliterate all trace of blood in the yard." Somewhere on the road, the Dunns noticed a movement of the tarpaulin covering the bodies. Raising the canvas, Dal found that Newcomb was still alive. A bullet striking his head had inflicted a bloody wound and rendered him unconscious, but had not pierced his skull. Now reviving, "Bitter Creek" weakly tried to raise one of the six-shooters in the wagonbed. Dunn jerked the weapon away as Newcomb pleaded for his life. "As they were just passing a house at the side of the road Dunn did not care to raise an alarm, but struck Bitter Creek a blow with his revolver, and knocked him senseless. As soon as they passed the house Dal Dunn shot the outlaw through the head."[26]

The authorities appeared unconcerned by the inconsistencies in the Dunn brothers' stories and the apparently callous double murder. Everyone just seemed relieved that the desperadoes were gone. Credit for their deaths was spread about liberally. The *Guthrie Daily Leader* lauded Marshal Nix "for putting out of the way these desperadoes. He spent his own money and personally directed the movement of deputies."[27] In relating the story later, Nix himself credited his deputies Tilghman and Thomas, assisted by the Dunns.[28] The *Pawnee Times-Democrat* announced, "The hero of the hour is Sam Shaffer."[29]

But Frank Canton knew that Sam Shaffer, the "Texas officer," was a fictional character, invented and played by John Dunn, and he knew the reason for the charade. As they concocted their treacherous plan, the Dunns had one great fear: the vengeance of the remaining gang members if they learned of the Dunns' betrayal. "Sam Shaffer and his deputies," forever unnamed, were characters invented for the sole purpose of diverting suspicion from the Dunn brothers in the minds of Doolin, Clifton, Waightman, and other gang members still on the loose.

At first, Canton went along with the game while at the same time making sure that his role in the demise of the desperadoes was not forgotten. In an interview with a Pawnee newspaperman he "corrected" portions of "Sam Shaffer's" story as originally published in the *Guthrie Daily Leader* and reprinted in the *Pawnee Times-Democrat*. No mention had been made in that long account of the work of Canton and Lake to bring Pierce and Newcomb to justice. Canton rectified the omission of his own name but failed to include Sheriff Lake in his revision.

The headline read: "TWO MORE BANDITS GONE. KILLING OF BITTER CREEK AND PIERCE. DEPUTY MARSHAL F.M. CANTON DESERVES THE CREDIT FOR THEIR CAPTURE." After explaining that Canton had been selected by Marshal Nix as a "special detective" to hunt down the Doolin gang members, the paper related how Canton had "employed Sam Shaffer and three other good men and placed them in the neighborhood in Payne county" where the Dunn brothers lived.

> The Dunn boys have long been suspected of aiding outlaws and Shaffer and his men had orders to watch their maneuvers, and also to keep Mr. Canton instructed and act under his orders. . . . On May 1st Shaffer found two horses hobbled near Dell [sic] Dunn's and suspected they belonged to outlaws who were secreted nearby. To keep the Dunn boys from rendering the outlaws any assistance Shaffer and his men went to the home of John Dunn and placed him and a brother under arrest, leaving one of the officers to guard them. He then went to Dell Dunn's place and arrested Dell and his brother George and locked them up in a cave.[30]

According to this story, when the outlaws returned, a lively gun battle broke out between Pierce and Newcomb on one side and Shaffer and two of his men on the other. "Bitter Creek fired three shots and then fell dead at the gate riddled with bullets, but before Pierce was killed he had got about half-way across the yard and had emptied both Winchester and pistol." Rewards for the dead outlaws, said the story, totaled over three thousand dollars. "The principal portion of it will be divided among Canton and his four assistants. Mr. Canton is a shrewd and fearless officer and Mr. Nix made a wise choice when he selected him to perform the detective work in this matter. The reward is a pretty good haul but the boys surely deserve it." In another column the paper added, "If we had a few more marshals like F.M. Canton an outlaw famine would soon be upon us, and a revival in trade with undertakers would result in several localities in the territory."[31]

Under the headline "CANTON DESERVED CREDIT," the *Guthrie Daily Leader* reprinted the Pawnee newspaper's story in its entirety, adding: "The above, in the main, is correct. Deputy Canton was the leader of the outfit that killed the outlaws and to him belongs great praise. Mr. Canton is a brave, energetic officer and in company with Sam Shaffer, had been on the trail of the desperadoes for some time."[32]

It was a nice try on Canton's part but failed in its purpose: to get him a share of the reward money. Reportedly he was not even reimbursed his out-of-pocket expenses.[33] When he learned that the Dunns and possibly Bill Tilghman and Heck Thomas had received shares of the rewards, he was irate.

Well aware that he had been duped by the Dunns, Canton felt that the secret agreement was void, and he quickly struck back. On May 9 he arrested Bee Dunn and hauled him before Commissioner Wrightsman on a charge of aiding outlaws. Dunn waived examination and made bond for his appearance at the next term of district court.[34] But the Dunns were now in solid with their new lawmen friends, Tilghman and Thomas, and were riding as possemen with them. At a word from the popular deputies, Marshal Nix arranged to have the charges against Bee dropped.[35]

Bill Tilghman and Heck Thomas, together with Chris Madsen, became the most famous and respected of Oklahoma Territory's outlaw hunters and achieved legendary status as "The Three Guardsmen." Canton never ran afoul of Madsen and always spoke highly of him, but a dislike for Tilghman and Thomas originating with the Dunn brothers affair only intensified over the years. The antipathy was apparently returned in kind; neither officer had a complimentary word for Canton.[36]

The myth of the Texas lawman Sam Shaffer did not hold up, of course. Canton saw to that. He was soon telling everyone in Pawnee County and beyond how the Dunn brothers had double-crossed their outlaw pals. Ru-

Deputy U.S. Marshal Steve Burke
set up a kind of partnership with
Canton in Pawnee. *Courtesy
Western History Collections,
University of Oklahoma.*

mors flew that members of the gang were on their way to kill the traitors
and avenge their fallen henchman. "DUNNS ARE DOOMED," screamed a headline in the *Oklahoma State Capital* only two weeks after the killings of
Pierce and Newcomb. According to this story, the Dunn brothers had murdered the outlaws in their sleep. Fearful of retaliation by other gang members, the Dunns had "barricaded their place, secured a supply of arms and
ammunition, and made their ranch a veritable arsenal." The newspaper related the events of Sunday night, May 12:

> A body of heavily armed men drove up to the Dunn cabin and,
> forming a ring around it, called upon the brothers to come out and
> surrender themselves. . . . When the Dunns, John, Calvin and Will-
> iam, saw the number of those without, they readily realized the
> worthlessness of making a fight and quickly surrendered. The wo-
> men folks tried to dissuade the captors from carrying out their
> purposes but were rudely swept aside. The Dunns were placed upon
> horses and, being told not to make an outcry, were hastily driven off
> toward the mountains. Since then nothing has been heard of the
> band or its captives, and the general opinion is that the Dunns have
> been lynched, as the feeling against them was most bitter. Searching
> parties are out looking for the bodies but as the desperadoes prob-
> ably took the victims to one of their mountain rendezvous the
> prospects of tracing them is very small.[37]

The story, you might say, was exaggerated. The Dunns were not lynched, then or later. The same paper mocked its own story a month later, noting the visit to Guthrie by the Dunn brothers, who had "been shot, killed, hanged and otherwise misused, according to newspaper correspondents." The paper added: "[The Dunns] are as healthy looking corpses as one could wish to see. They are quiet, unassuming gentlemen and have none of the appearances of border desperadoes. They laugh good naturedly at the newspaper notoriety they have achieved, and, as they are law abiding citizens who make a business attending to their own affairs . . . , no harm has been done them by the sensational yarns set afloat."[38]

From the spring of 1895 on, Canton, while retaining his position as undersheriff, devoted little time to county business and concentrated on his work as deputy marshal. His investigations often took him far afield. The *Pawnee Times-Democrat* of June 28 reported that he had returned the previous night "from the Gulf of Mexico where he [had] been several days on official business."[39]

He and Deputy Marshal Steve Burke formed a kind of partnership, setting up an office on the second floor of the county courthouse in Pawnee. They even had a special letterhead printed:

F.M. CANTON   J.S. BURKE

Office of

CANTON & BURKE

Deputy U.S. Marshals[40]

Like Canton, Burke had a weakness for alcohol. Marshal Nix called him "the most unpromising man" Nix had ever commissioned. "His previous record was one of failure, drunkenness, and irresponsibility." Burke had studied law but never practiced. After an unsuccessful attempt at ranching in Texas, he came to Oklahoma in 1889 and worked for an insurance company but was fired for alcoholism. His life in ruins, he found religion and persuaded Nix to give him a chance as a lawman. "He turned out to be one of the best," wrote Nix. "He had the courage of a lion and was an artist with his guns. He gave his body a peculiar side twist when he drew his six-shooter. He called it the 'Fannin County Draw.' It was one of the fastest things I ever saw."[41]

The *Times-Democrat* of May 24, 1895, reporting on a troublesome band of outlaws then operating in Woods County, suggested: "If the people of Woods county want the outlaws wiped out of existence with promptness and dispatch they should secure the services of Canton & Burke of this city who can do the job up in apple pie order. This county with Frank Lake as sheriff and Canton & Burke, deputy marshals, is fast becoming noted as the most moral nook of the territory."[42]

Two young female consorts of the Doolin gang attracted the attention of the officers for a time during the summer of 1895. Fifteen-year-old Annie McDoulet, known as "Cattle Annie," and diminutive sixteen-year-old Jennie Stevens, called "Little Breeches" because of her fondness for men's clothing, were admirers of the desperadoes and acted as spies for them.

According to a Guthrie paper, Jennie Stevens first met Doolin and his long-riders "while sewing up the bullet holes in their clothes after they had come in from a raid." In March 1895 Jennie ran off from her farm home and married a deaf mute named Ben Midkiff but soon "tired of him and went in search of livelier company." She hooked up with a border drifter named Frank Wilson, and the two began selling whiskey in the Osage Nation.[43] On July 3 Canton arrested the couple at Perry and brought them to Pawnee. Wilson was bound over, charged with horse stealing and impersonating an officer, and Jennie was charged with peddling whiskey to Indians.[44] Canton then took them to the jail at Guthrie, where a newspaper noted that Jennie still wore the male attire in which she had been arrested. "She naively remarked on the street as she squirted a stream of tobacco juice at a crack in the sidewalk that she liked men's clothes better than those of her own sex, especially for her business. Her general make-up is that of a gadding girl seeking notoriety."[45]

Released on bond, "Little Breeches" returned to Pawnee County, where she resumed her criminal activities in partnership with "Cattle Annie" McDoulet. "The girls were becoming very troublesome," wrote E. D. Nix, "and it was evident that they were keeping in fairly close touch with the movements of my officers and passing their information along to the outlaws. . . . Wherever they were seen, they were heavily armed with pistols and Winchesters, and it was reported that they were pretty accurate shots."[46]

In August, Sheriff Lake arrested "Little Breeches" again on a county warrant. She was taken to a Pawnee restaurant for supper by a deputy who stood guard at the front door while she ate. After finishing her meal, the pint-sized girl suddenly darted out the back door, leaped on a horse, and galloped out of town. Although all the Pawnee officers were embarrassed by the daring escape performed by a mere slip of a girl, probably no one was more embarrassed than Frank Canton, since it was his horse that Jennie had stolen.[47]

The following day Deputy Marshals Frank Canton, Steve Burke, Morris Zuckerman, and Gant Owens tracked Jennie to a farmhouse where she had holed up with Cattle Annie. As the officers approached, "the women showed fight and several shots were fired before they gave up. Both were in men's clothing when captured." The girls after capture were still bellicose, saying that had they known they were facing only four officers, "they would have fought their way out."[48] On August 26 the girls stood trial at Newkirk. Annie was convicted of the illegal sale of whiskey to Indians. Since she was under legal age, she was committed to reform school at South Framingham, Massachusetts. Jennie, convicted of horse theft, was sentenced to two years at the Massachusetts Reformatory prison at Sherborn.[49]

That summer was a season of embarrassments for Frank Canton. On July 9 while driving a spring wagon with three prisoners to the Guthrie jail, he met with an inglorious and painful accident. After leaving Pawnee he whipped the horses "to a lively gait [and] made a quick turn in the road that caused him to lose his position on the seat and fall out of the spring wagon. In falling, his right foot caught in the brake and twisted his ankle around until it rested against his foot. The prisoners jumped out of the vehicle and released Mr. Canton's foot and tried to straighten his ankle back to its proper position, but the injury was so painful he could hardly endure the operation."[50]

In addition to the pain of his injury, Canton suffered a humiliating ride back to town in the wagon driven by one of his prisoners. He was taken to his home and treated by Doctors Poe and Phillips, who straightened the limb. It was a severe sprain, but no bones were broken. A Guthrie paper inaccurately reported that Canton "had one of his legs broken below the knee and his knee joint dislocated and received other injuries." Acknowledging that Canton was "one of the bravest officers on the force," the paper remarked, "No blame can be attached to anyone, however, as Mr. Canton was doing the driving himself."[51]

He was still hobbling five weeks later when another Guthrie paper noted his first visit to the capital in some time: "Deputy United States Marshal Canton is in the city and manages to get around very nicely with the aid of a cane and a crutch. . . . Deputy Canton is a vigilant and successful officer and has done good work with Steve Burke in the Pawnee district. He will soon be able to use his right leg."[52]

Canton's frequent drinking may have contributed to his wagon accident; it certainly was responsible for the disreputable exhibition in which he and Frank Lake engaged that winter. To all appearances Canton and Lake were the closest of friends. They faced desperate criminals together and seemed to trust and respect each other implicitly. But when they drank too much, a festering wound, twenty years old, opened up. Deep down, Lake still had not forgiven Canton for deserting him in the fight with the bluecoats back at Jacksboro, and Canton, while refusing to admit it, especially to Lake, felt guilty about the episode.

Charles F. Colcord had to deal with Canton's weakness for alcohol. *Courtesy Western History Collections, University of Oklahoma.*

One night the two men became intoxicated in a Pawnee saloon, and the old difficulty came up. A number of deputy marshals were on hand because court was in session, and several tried unsuccessfully to separate the two friends. Finally, Deputy Ike Steel went to J. S. Badger's National Hotel and awakened Charley Colcord, the deputy in charge. "Charley," he said, "you had better get up. Frank Lake and Frank Canton are about to kill each other and nobody can handle them but you." Colcord got up, hurriedly dressed, and went to the saloon with Steel.[53]

In the rear of the building he found a group of men clustered near a large potbellied stove. In a chair near the stove sat Frank Lake, his luxuriant beard spread across his chest and a six-shooter in his hand. Colcord later wrote:

> As I walked in, Frank Canton was standing in front of Lake with his
> left hand on his six-shooter. With his right hand he lighted a match
> against the hot stove and reached out with it to set fire to Lake's
> beard. Someone from behind fanned the match out with his hat.
> Lake said, "Let him alone! Let him alone, I tell you!" I walked up to
> Frank Canton, slapped him on the shoulder and said to him, "Frank,
> come along with me. I have some business for you." He looked at
> me, saluted military fashion and said, "All right, Sir." I took him by
> the arm and led him out of the saloon and on up to where his wife
> and daughter Ruby were living. I knocked at the door and when Mrs.
> Canton opened it I said, "Keep Frank here tonight, don't let him out.
> He is about to get into trouble." As I pushed him in through the
> door I said, "Frank, I want you to be at the Badger Hotel at six in the

morning." And he answered, "All right, Sir." In his thoroughly military mind I was his superior officer, so was able to handle him. The next morning he was at the hotel. I looked up some important papers and had them ready for him to serve and nothing further came of the incident.[54]

At this time Colcord knew nothing of Canton's Texas outlaw history and was mystified by the strange relationship between Lake and Canton. George Horner died at about this time, and Colcord was further perplexed by Canton's reaction to that death. "During all the years I had known Frank I had never seen tears in his eyes," he recalled, "but they were there when Horner died. I suspicioned that there must be some relation between them, for it was entirely unlike Canton—his reaction." Colcord had detected a strong physical resemblance between Canton and Horner. Connecting that fact with Canton's uncharacteristic behavior at George's death, and with hints and rumors he had heard that "Frank Canton" was an alias, Colcord suspected that the two men were brothers. Years later he talked with some old-timers at Jacksboro who confirmed that hunch and also clarified the mystery of the Canton-Lake relationship.[55]

In July 1896 Marshal Nix drastically cut his force of 125 deputies to seventy-five. Those retained were required to post a bond of two thousand dollars, and new job applicants had to "furnish gilt-edged recommendations as to character," the *Pawnee Times-Democrat* reported. "Canton & Burke of this place have both been retained and in a personal letter Mr. Nix commends them very highly for their honesty and integrity. Both these gentlemen are honorable men, shrewd and fearless officers and we are glad Mr. Nix saw fit to continue them on his force."[56]

That summer Canton and Burke supervised the construction of a large new jail to hold U.S. prisoners at Pawnee until they could be taken for trial to Guthrie or Fort Smith. Located behind the courthouse and opposite Badger's Hotel, the new jail, constructed of two-by-fours turned on edge, measured twenty by thirty feet. It contained three cells and was enclosed by a fourteen-foot board fence.[57]

Canton and Burke dissolved their partnership in September. Burke took a new assignment as managing deputy for the courts at Perry, Pawnee, and Newkirk, with Morris Zuckerman as chief deputy. Canton continued "working on his own hook," as the *Times-Democrat* described it. Burke moved to new offices on the second floor of the courthouse, and Canton retained the office they had shared.[58]

U.S. Marshal Nix was coming under increasing criticism from his political enemies, despite his deputies' remarkable record of almost sixty thousand arrests for violations of federal law. His drastic personnel reduction

U.S. Marshal Patrick S. Nagle
delayed the discharge of Deputy
Canton as long as possible. *Courtesy Western History Collections,
University of Oklahoma.*

program of July did not blunt constant charges of financial mismanagement
in the marshal's office during his three-year tenure. A cabinet realignment
by President Cleveland, moving Richard Olney to secretary of state and replacing him with Judson Harmon as attorney general, brought the matter to
a head. Harmon responded to the charges by instituting an investigation of
the U.S. marshal's office at Guthrie. Inspectors from Washington descended
on the territorial capital, reviewed the records, and submitted an unfavor-
able report. Nix was relieved of his duties on January 24, 1896. His replacement as U.S. marshal was Patrick S. Nagle, a lawyer from Kingfisher.[59]

Nagle further reduced the number of Oklahoma field deputies. His report to the attorney general for the first quarter of 1896 listed only forty-
five. The commissions of several of Canton's close associates—Frank Lake,
Steve Burke, Will Nix, Morris Zuckerman, and John M. Hale—were not
renewed. Among those retained were Frank Canton at Pawnee, Morris
Robacker at Pawhuska, Bill Tilghman and Heck Thomas at Guthrie, Chris
Madsen at Fort Sill, and Charley Colcord at Perry. Frank W. Clegg was appointed to assist Canton at Pawnee.[60]

Still pressured by Washington to lower expenses, Nagle in the second
quarter reduced his field deputies to twenty-four. Canton, Robacker, Colcord,
Tilghman, and Thomas survived this deep cut, but Chris Madsen was not
reappointed. Directed to justify the necessity for those deputies retained,
Nagle reported that Robacker and three other officers were Indian police and
were needed to suppress the introduction of liquor on the reservations. Frank

Canton and Charley Colcord were retained to serve the process of the court of the Fourth Judicial District, consisting of Noble, Pawnee, Kay, and Beaver Counties. Interestingly, Bill Tilghman, Heck Thomas, and E. F. Cochran were retained because, said Nagle, these three "made a specialty of pursuing murderers and train robbers."[61]

Members of the old Doolin-Dalton gang had fared badly during the previous year. Tulsa Jack Blake was killed in April 1895 after the Dover train robbery. A few weeks later Pierce and Newcomb were shot to death at the Dunn place. In September Little Bill Raidler was traced to a hideout near Pawhuska and brought down by a blast from Tilghman's shotgun. He survived his numerous wounds, was convicted for his part in the Dover train robbery, and was sentenced to ten years in the federal prison at Columbus, Ohio. In January 1896, Tilghman made a spectacular single-handed arrest of Bill Doolin at a bathhouse in Eureka Springs, Arkansas. The gang leader was brought to Guthrie and held in the federal jail to answer multiple murder and robbery charges. The highly publicized arrest of Doolin probably did more to ensure Bill Tilghman's lasting fame as the foremost lawman of Oklahoma Territory and as one of the greatest officers in the American West than any other accomplishment in his long and eventful career.

Frank Canton resented this acclaim, which he felt should rightfully have been his. He had set as a personal goal the capture of the bandit chief, dead or alive, and there is no doubt he worked hard to achieve that end. Tilghman and Thomas had the advantage of living in Guthrie, the territorial capital and the center of all outlaw-fighting activity. Working directly out of the U.S. marshal's office, they were privy to all new information concerning the outlaws and their movements. As pointed out by Doolin's biographer, Canton may well have "eventually brought Doolin in for the reward money, dead or alive, if given a little more time and if he had not been operating at a disadvantage by competing with the Guthrie marshals, who had the squeeze play on the available informers."[62]

There was also the matter of the Dunn brothers, who Canton always believed were the key to the gang's destruction. Although he detested the Dunns, he had cultivated them in order to get at the prominent gang members. The chicanery of the brothers had cost him a share of the reward money for Charley Pierce and Bitter Creek Newcomb. Then Tilghman and Thomas had compounded what he perceived as an injustice by enlisting the Dunns as possemen and informants to further their own ambitions.

Canton took a jaundiced view of Tilghman's capture of Doolin. In a letter written thirty years later he inferred that the capture was prearranged. He said he and Frank Lake had "made it so hot for [Doolin] that he finally took his wife & slipped out of the country in a covered wagon, a plow & chicken coop tied on the wagon [and] headed for the Ozark Mountains in Ark." The outlaw, he said, was in poor physical condition.

> Bill Doolin had the consumption. He had also been hit in the head with a buck shot in a street fight in Southwest City, Mo. after the bunch had robbed a bank. . . . It was currently rumored at Guthrie that Doolin intended to surrender and stand trial. In a short time Bill Tighlman [sic] came in on the train to Guthrie with Bill Doolin whom he said he had captured at Eureka Springs, Ark. Heck Thomas met them at the depot. Doolin was not shackled nor handcuffed & appeared to be in fine spirits. He was allowed many privileges, in fact Heck Thomas & Tighlman gave Doolin a banquet at Royal Hotel in Guthrie. . . . I am perfectly satisfied and always have been that Bill Doolin surrendered to Bill Tighlman at Eureka Springs.[63]

In March 1896 another gang member bit the dust when Red Buck Waightman was gunned down by officers near Arapaho.[64] Now only one of the major gang members remained on the loose: Charles "Dynamite Dick" Clifton. According to a report the previous October, Clifton had been killed in the hills near Tulsa and his unidentified body buried. Many officers discontinued the search for the outlaw, but Canton had what he believed was reliable information that Clifton was alive and hiding out in Arizona. He was planning a trip west after the outlaw when he was informed that Clifton had robbed and murdered two Mexican sheepherders and disappeared from Arizona.[65]

Dynamite Dick's mother lived at Paul's Valley in the Chickasaw Nation. Alerting informants in Paul's Valley to keep an eye peeled, Canton got a tip in May that Clifton was back in his old stamping grounds. With Deputy Marshal Clarence Young, Canton hurried to the area to find that federal marshals from Paris, Texas, had already arrested Clifton under the name "Dan Wiley," on a charge of introducing whiskey into Indian country. The prisoner, as "Dan Wiley," was sentenced to thirty days in jail by the U.S. commissioner at Paris.

Canton went to Paris and met with U.S. Marshal J. Shelby Williams of the Eastern Judicial District of Texas. He showed Shelby a warrant for the arrest of Clifton, charged with the first-degree murder of Tom Watson in the Osage country, and demanded the prisoner. "When I went to the jail to identify him," said Canton, "Dick had on a very high standing collar, a derby hat, and about four weeks' growth of stubby beard on his face. I sent for a barber and had him shaved, although he protested against this, for he knew what I was looking for. When the hair was shaved off his face and neck a scar the size of a silver half-dollar could be plainly seen on his neck. This scar was caused from cutting a bullet out of his neck, that he had received in a revolver duel in the Osage country with Lafe Shadly [sic] who was killed in the Ingalls fight."[66]

Canton returned Dynamite Dick to Oklahoma, where he had additional warrants sworn out against him for the murders of officers Richard Speed, Lafayette A. Shadley, and Thomas J. Hueston in the Ingalls battle. At Guthrie, Canton was praised for bringing in the last of the gang. "Ever since February, 1894," said a newspaper, "Clifton has been chased by Deputy F.M. Canton, of the Pawnee district, to whom all credit is due for his capture." The outlaw "had been tracked from the Triangle country and back by Deputy Canton."[67]

Bill Doolin reacted strangely to the appearance of his old pal in the Guthrie jail. "When I brought Dynamite Dick into the jail," said Canton, "Bill Doolin's cell was in front of the main entrance, and as he saw the prisoner, he had a look of terror on his face and was very much excited. He asked me if he could speak to the prisoner. I motioned for Dynamite Dick to come up to the cell. The first words that Doolin said to Dynamite were, 'For God's sake, stand pat.' They talked for a few minutes in a whisper, and I could not catch the words. . . . The arrest of Dynamite Dick appeared to worry Doolin. He seemed to be very uneasy for some time."[68]

Canton no doubt hoped to collect the reward for Dynamite Dick, an amount variously given as two thousand or twenty-five hundred dollars, but again he was disappointed.[69] The "uneasiness" Doolin had displayed on seeing Clifton quickly developed into a series of violent fits. Jail authorities provided no medical help for the inmate but did permit him the liberty of the bull pen the entire day "to give him more air and more room to exercise."[70] On July 5, only two weeks after Clifton joined Doolin in the jail, these two dangerous criminals and eleven other inmates broke out and regained their freedom.[71]

Despite prodigious efforts to hunt him down, Dynamite Dick Clifton continued his outlaw career for another year and a half. In a December 1896 gun battle near Blackwell, officers wounded and captured an old outlaw acquaintance of Canton's, Ben Cravens, and killed his partner, whom they believed to be the celebrated Dynamite Dick. Hoping to collect rewards now totaling thirty-five hundred dollars for Clifton, they wired Canton to come and make the identification. Canton took one look at the body and deflated all their hopes by announcing that it was not Clifton.

Charley Colcord was with Canton when he interviewed the badly wounded Cravens. Colcord said the old outlaw was shot through the lung and "had a rag over the hole in his chest." When he coughed, "the rag flew up and blood spurted all over everything near him. Frank Canton then stepped up and said to Cravens, 'Well, they got you.' He replied, 'Hell no, you can't kill me.'"[72]

Canton tried to get Cravens to identify the dead man, but the outlaw refused to assist in any way the man who had arrested him the year before in Pawnee County. The Blackwell officers later learned the dead outlaw was Buck McGregg, alias "Diamond Dick."[73] In November 1897 Deputy Marshals George Lawson and Hess Bussy finally cornered and killed Dynamite Dick Clifton near Checotah, Indian Territory.[74]

Lawmen continued to hunt for Bill Doolin. Bill Tilghman and Heck Thomas, still using the Dunn brothers as informants, also enlisted Tom and Charlie Noble, Lawson blacksmiths and friends of the Dunns. Charlie Noble was courting the Dunn brothers' sixteen-year-old sister, Rose.[75] The Nobles kept an eye on the Lawson home of J. W. Ellsworth, father-in-law of the outlaw; Doolin's wife, Edith, was staying there. In August the spies spotted Doolin making quick visits to see his wife, and they notified Heck Thomas and the Dunns. On the night of August 26 a posse consisting of Heck Thomas, his son Albert, Deputy Marshal Rufe Cannon, Tom and Charlie Noble, and four Dunn brothers waited in hiding for Bill Doolin to emerge from the house. When he came out, leading a horse and carrying a Winchester rifle, Thomas called out to him. Doolin threw up the Winchester and fired in the direction of the voice. He was instantly cut down by a shotgun blast to the chest.[76]

Heck Thomas took personal credit for dispatching Doolin. In a letter written to Bill Tilghman a few days later he said he had used "an old No. 8 shotgun," which he had some trouble getting into operation, but as soon as he "got the shotgun to work, . . . the fight was over."[77] Frank Canton was always dubious of this story but could not provide a consistent alternative version himself. In a letter written in 1925 he suggested that Doolin had been riddled with shotgun pellets after he was already dead.

> I saw the body myself. It was hot summer weather. Doolin had on a clean white undershirt, very thin. The shirt had, I think, 23 buckshot holes. . . . Not a particle of dry blood or any other kind on the body & not even a stain of blood on the undershirt. I called the Doctor's attention to this & I says, what does this mean? He says this means the man was dead before he was shot. The face of the man was the most ghastly sight that I ever saw, even the picture they taken of the dead body in Guthrie showing the naked body from the hip up was a dead giveaway. Bill Dunn used the same shotgun that he murdered Bitter Creek & Pierce with. . . . I suppose Heck Thomas collected the reward on Doolin.[78]

In his published memoirs, Canton said that Doolin was shot by Bill Dunn but in very much the manner described by Heck Thomas. The outlaw, Canton said, got out of a sickbed and "staggered down a lane leading his horse, with his Winchester in his hand. . . . Doolin walked right up to Dunn. As he did so Bill Dunn fired both barrels of a number eight shotgun in the breast."[79] Canton was not alone in his contempt for the Dunns. When Edith Doolin came to Guthrie to claim her husband's body, she was quoted in a newspaper as threatening vengeance against "the Dunn boys" who had been "Bill's friends."[80]

Heck Thomas ultimately collected rewards totaling $1,425 for Doolin. He distributed $106 to each of the four Dunn brothers, further embittering Canton toward both the Dunns and Thomas.[81] After years of chasing members of the Doolin gang, Canton came up empty in the reward department.[82] The continued employment of the Dunns as possemen by Tilghman and Thomas also enraged him, since he never wavered in his conviction that the Dunns were vicious criminals themselves.

Earlier, he had unsuccessfully tried to nail the Dunn brothers on murder charges. On one of his scouts into southern Pawnee County, he stayed overnight at the home of Bruce Miller, a fellow Mason. Miller said that if he and his family could be protected, "he would furnish evidence that would convict three of the Dunn boys for murder." Canton then gave his word as a Mason that he would not repeat what he was told without Miller's consent.[83]

Miller said that he was picking wild plums along the Cimarron River with his wife and daughter one day when three of the Dunn boys approached with the horse and cart of an itinerant peddler. They watched as the Dunns removed the peddler's body from the cart, weighted it with rocks, and threw it into a deep hole in the river. The Millers hid in the bushes until after dark, fearful of the Dunns. He would testify against the Dunns, Miller said, if they were arrested, indicted, and jailed, but he feared for his life and the lives of his family if the brothers learned beforehand that he possessed this incriminating information. Canton later told a reporter:

> He gave me his consent to take this matter up with the county attorney. . . . I realized how serious it was to this old man and his family and promised faithfully to be very careful. . . .
> The grand jury was in session at that time [and] the county attorney concluded to swear the grand jury to absolute secrecy, have them to vote on the indictment so that we could get an order of arrest, but not to report the indictment to the court nor make any record of it until the Dunns were arrested and locked up to protect the Miller family. . . . But before we could arrest them, [the Millers] were all murdered, shot to death in their cabin. Evidently some member of the grand jury had innocently talked of this matter and it had reached the ears of the Dunn Boys. . . . The murder of the Miller family destroyed all the evidence we had against the Dunns for the

murder of the peddler. They were not arrested and the indictment was never reported to the court at Pawnee.[84]

Contemporary records show that in the spring of 1895 Bruce Miller "was assassinated at Ingalls, Oklahoma, shot through the open window of a saloon, by unknown persons, after night."[85] In the fall of that year "'Date' Miller (an elder brother of Bruce and El Miller), with his aged wife and young son, Dorsey, . . . were assassinated after night, in their own home, by persons unknown." The *Pawnee Times-Democrat* of November 1, 1895, mentioned, "Bruce Miller, Dayt Miller and wife had been killed by the members of the mob who are yet at liberty."[86]

Rather than being murders by the Dunns, these killings apparently resulted from an ongoing feud between the Miller clan and a group led by Canton's friends Dr. John Bland and George McElroy. In March 1895 at a trial in Judge Parker's court at Fort Smith, Bland, McElroy, and three others were acquitted of the April 1894 murder of a young German boy at the Miller place. They were retried, however, the following September, charged on two counts of assault with intent to kill and two counts of arson. Convicted, Bland and McElroy were sentenced to twelve years each, and the other three defendants were sentenced to nine years. In 1897 the case was overturned by the U.S. Supreme Court, and the defendants were never retried.[87]

Canton could never bring murder charges against the Dunns, but he still hoped to nail them for cattle theft. In the fall of 1896 he resurrected the old "receiving stolen goods" charge against Chris Bolton and had new warrants issued for Bee Dunn and Amos Pierce, another Dunn confederate, charging them with rustling. "I had received reliable information several times," Canton said, "to the effect that Bill Dunn had sworn that he intended to kill me on sight, and some of my friends advised me to leave the country or he would sure get me. I kept a close watch when traveling over the country and always had one good man with me. An ambush was the only thing that I dreaded."[88]

Bolton's trial was set for the November session of the Fourth Judicial District Court in Pawnee. On the morning of Friday, November 6, Chris Bolton was convicted and sentenced to five years in the federal prison at Lansing, Kansas. An appeal was filed. Judge A. G. C. Bierer set bond at five thousand dollars, and Bolton, unable to find bondsmen for that large amount, was returned to jail.

Some time that day Bee Dunn rode into Pawnee. Canton was notified immediately of the arrival by a friend, but, busy serving court papers, he was not particularly concerned. He had nothing but contempt for Dunn. As he later said: "[I] never expected him to attack me in the open, especially while in town. But this is one time that I had my man sized up wrong."[89]

What Canton did not know was that at the urging of Heck Thomas, U.S. Marshal Pat Nagle had that very day issued Bee Dunn a commission as special deputy marshal. Dunn had taken the oath of office that morning. Emboldened by acquisition of authority that he perceived as placing him on the same level as Canton, he rode hard for Pawnee and a confrontation with his archenemy.[90]

Tension was high in Pawnee that day. Everyone was aware of the Canton-Dunn feud, and news of Bolton's conviction and Bee Dunn's arrival soon spread through town. Dunn positioned himself at the base of a stairway outside Bolton's butcher shop on the west side of the public square, opposite the courthouse. The charge had been set and the fuse was burning. An explosion was imminent. That explosion came in the form of a single pistol shot.

Saloonkeeper Cook Horton was entering his establishment at about 2:30 that afternoon. "I saw Canton on the street and farther down I saw Dunn standing in a stairway," he recalled. "I went on into the saloon for I knew what was going to happen. I had been in there only a short time when I heard a single shot. I knew who had been killed. Canton had killed Dunn for he was faster on the draw."[91]

In his memoirs Canton told the story this way:

> I had a forty-five caliber Colt's revolver which I carried on the right side with the clip over the waist band of my trousers to hold the revolver up. I seldom wore a cartridge belt when on duty in town. I had just stepped out of a restaurant where I had been serving subpoenas, and started to walk up the plank sidewalk in the direction of the courthouse. Ten or twelve men were standing about on the street, the weather was a little chilly, and I had both hands in my trousers' pockets. As I started up the street in a brisk walk, Bill Dunn stepped in front of me. I had not seen him until he spoke.
>
> He says, "Frank Canton, God d—— you, I've got it in for you."[92]
>
> He had his hand on his revolver, but had not drawn it yet. When I glanced at his face I saw murder in his eyes, and I knew that he intended to kill me. I drew my revolver instantly and fired. The bullet struck him almost square in the forehead. As he dropped he pulled his revolver, which fell on the sidewalk near his body. As he lay on his back dying, he was working the trigger finger of his right hand.[93]

In a newspaper interview given twenty-eight years after the event, Canton told it differently. When he and Dunn met, he said, neither spoke a word. For one long moment they locked eyes, and then Dunn went for his gun. It caught in his clothes for a brief second and Canton got off his head shot. "When his gun caught it saved my life," Canton told the reporter. "He had me, but for that. It gave me the advantage. I knew if I got a chance, there was but one shot I could make. . . . Only a few days before I learned at a blacksmith shop that he had a breastplate made of plow steel, with a ridge in the center, and it could turn one of the bullets of those days. If I had shot at his body, I wouldn't have killed him and he would have filled me full of lead before I had known what was happening. It was the closest call I ever had in my life."[94]

Charles Colcord, in town for the session of court, was walking with Canton when the shooting occurred. He later wrote: "[Dunn] reached for his gun without saying a word. But momentarily his gun seemed to hang in his suspenders or his belt, and in that second of delay Frank cut Bee's right eyebrow in two with a bullet. Dunn fell at my feet and Frank said quietly as he turned to me, 'I got him, didn't I?' And that was all that he said about it. I never saw a man die as hard as Dunn did. He would shove out first one leg and then the other, grit his teeth so hard you could hear it from thirty feet away and at the same time he would work the trigger finger on his right hand."[95]

The story that was passed down in the Dunn family was, of course, somewhat different: "Canton was hiding in the space between the meat market and the building next to it, and as Bee came out of the market, Canton stepped in behind Bee and with his gun already drawn and at very close range, said, 'Bee.' When Bee turned, Canton fired, hitting him in the center of his forehead about one-half inch above the brim of his derby hat and killing him instantly."[96]

As word of the shooting spread, tumultuous excitement replaced the quiet tension that had gripped the town. Crowds of shouting men filled the square. Colcord said he arrested Canton on the spot "to protect him from county officers" and escorted him to the courthouse, where Roy Hoffman, assistant district attorney, took Canton and all the witnesses before a grand jury, then in session. "They completely exonerated Canton and complimented him in the highest terms."[97]

According to newspaper accounts and Canton's own version, he walked unescorted to the courthouse and surrendered to Frank Lake, who kept him under guard in the sheriff's office, primarily for his own protection. Rumors quickly spread that other Dunns, bent on avenging Bee, were in or nearing town. Canton later said, "Some of Bill Dunn's brothers were in town when Bill was killed, but they immediately mounted their horses and left the town."[98] Newspaper dispatches from Pawnee the following day, however,

Deputy U.S. Marshals Heck Thomas, left, and Morris Robacker are seated in the front row; two Osage Indian scouts are behind them; and J. H. Havighorst and Assistant U.S. District Attorney Roy Hoffman, right, stand in back. *Courtesy Western History Collections, University of Oklahoma.*

indicated the Dunns arrived Friday night "and threatened to fire the town and kill Canton."[99]

The *Pawnee Times-Democrat,* going to press at the time of the shooting, held up publication long enough to include some details. Dunn, it said, had been "shot in the left temple above the eye, the ball ranging upward." The paper noted: "He fell in his tracks and died without a struggle. His remains were carried into the undertaker's rooms near by and the spot where he fell is marked by the blood and brains that oozed out from the wound." An attempt was made to interview Canton in Lake's office. "He said he had nothing to say until he was called upon the witness stand to testify, only that the act was in self-defense and it all depended upon which man was the quickest with a gun."[100]

Although in later years Canton would tell the story differently, at one time saying that his life had been saved only by the chance catch of Dunn's pistol in his clothes and another time admitting that he had drawn and fired first before Dunn ever pulled his gun, his reputation as a fast-gun artist soared after this incident. As Cook Horton would later say, he did not have to walk out of his saloon to know who had won the gunfight because Canton "was faster on the draw." Veteran cowboy John W. Hunter, witness to the killing, stated flatly, "Frank was the fastest gunman I ever knew."[101]

The shooting was reported in newspapers throughout the territory. Most stories were in the vein of the *Guthrie Daily Leader,* which said, "Deputy F.M. Canton, one of the best officers in the territory, shot and killed Bee Dunn, one of the worst characters in the territory." It was clear that public opinion supported Canton.[102]

Canton was held in protective custody over the weekend. On Monday, November 9, a grand jury, after hearing the evidence in the case, exonerated Canton, finding that he had killed Dunn in self-defense.[103]

Disregarding objections raised by a number of Ingalls citizens, the Dunn family buried Bee in the cemetery there. The night of the burial, someone dumped a pile of fresh hog entrails on the grave, an indication that Frank Canton was not the only one with great contempt for Bee Dunn.[104] Dr. J. H. Pickering of Ingalls noted in his diary: "The feeling in Pawnee is all in favor of Canton. Past reputation is what hurts Dunn. All kinds of reports are afloat in regard to his past life at Ingalls. People are divided on the case. All was looking for Dunn to be killed but expected it to come from some of the remaining outlaws. . . . I think it only a matter of time until more of the Dunn boys are killed or they get Canton."[105]

Publicity resulting from Bee Dunn's killing prompted a letter to a Pawnee resident from a figure out of Canton's past: "Dear Sir: Will you kindly write me and give the particulars of the killing of Bee Dunn by Frank Canton and let me know what the outcome is, or is liable to be, as I am very much interested in the matter. . . . Canton is a fugitive from this state. Yours truly, O.H. Flagg." The *Wyoming State Tribune* in Cheyenne, which had reported in its pages the latest adventure of one of Wyoming's more colorful former residents, published this letter and admonished its author: "Of course everybody in Wyoming knows why 'Jack' Flagg is deeply interested in Frank M. Canton, but his statement that Canton was a fugitive from this state is not justified by the facts and was an unfruitful attempt to injure Canton in Oklahoma, where he holds and fills the important position of deputy United States marshal."[106]

Of course Canton's enemies in Oklahoma and Wyoming would never agree that the killing of Dunn was justified and that Canton had acted in self-defense. Forty years later a man named Oliver Cutter, a butcher shop operator in Worland, Wyoming, and a cousin of the Dunn boys, was quoted in a Wyoming paper as saying, "Canton shot Dunn down in cold blood and . . . he never had a chance."[107]

Bee Dunn was gone, but the other brothers remained, and rumors of their impending vengeance against Canton flew wildly. "There are five [*sic*] more brothers of Bee Dunn," declared the *El Reno News* of November 20. "These threaten to go on the warpath. . . . If they do the territory will have some experienced outlaws. They know all the gangs that ever infested the territory." The *Guthrie Daily Leader* reported in several issues that Bee's brothers were shadowing Canton around that city.[108]

There is no record that the Dunns ever made an attempt on Canton's life, but on the night of November 11, a "masked mob," presumably the Dunns and their supporters, stormed the jail at Pawnee and liberated Chris Bolton, Bee's former partner, and a man named T. A. Shephard, who had also been convicted and sentenced to five years for rustling.[109]

Canton always believed that the best defense is a good offense. Urged on by Canton and Frank Lake, a number of citizens filed cattle theft complaints against John, Dal, and George Dunn, and new warrants were issued for their arrests. At least some of the brothers were still riding as possemen with Heck Thomas. According to Canton:

> They were scouting around over Osage, Pawnee, and Payne Counties heavily armed. Men, women, and children were afraid of them. I finally sent word to Heck Thomas that we held criminal warrants for the Dunn boys, and that I thought that it was his duty as an officer under the Department of Justice to bring these men in and deliver them to the sheriff of Pawnee County. Thomas ignored me absolutely, and did not even treat me with the courtesy to reply to my request. . . . After I had notified him that the Dunn boys were

wanted in Pawnee County, his actions proved to me that he intended to protect them under his authority as a United States Deputy Marshal in defiance of the Territorial laws, so I decided to make him show his hand.[110]

Learning that Thomas and eleven men were camped on the Arkansas River some sixteen miles east of Pawnee, Canton, Lake, and a hand-picked posse of eight experienced men, outfitted with "a good team and light wagon to haul [their] commissary supplies, excellent mounts, and plenty of ammunition," pulled out of Pawnee after dark on a cold winter's night to serve their warrants. At Black Dog Crossing of the Arkansas, they found that the Thomas party had broken camp and headed eastward, toward Skiatook in the Cherokee Nation. For several days the sheriff's posse dogged the trail of Deputy Marshal Thomas and his federal possemen but lost it near the Arkansas. At great risk and discomfort they crossed the partially frozen river in an effort to pick up the trail on the other side, but they found no sign of a large party. Discouraged, they returned to Pawnee.[111]

It is fortunate that these two parties of heavily armed lawmen did not meet. Both sides included determined men who hated to backwater; had the Dunns refused to submit to arrest by the Pawnee officers, a bloody conflict would surely have ensued. Canton said he learned later from "a reliable source" that the Thomas party had been camped in a bend of the Arkansas only a mile away from the camp of the Pawnee posse when they discovered who was following them. "After looking at the river, [they] decided that it was too dangerous to cross with their outfit, and rather than be caught in a trap in the bend of the river, they turned back east and scattered. . . . The Dunn boys left the country and have never been seen in Pawnee County since."[112]

Part Four

The Alaska Years

Canada

Fort Yukon
Circle City
Rampart
Nome
Eagle
St. Michael
Dawson
City

Yukon R.
Tanana R.

Sitka

Dutch
Harbor

The
ALASKA
Years
1897-1899

125 Miles

Chapter 9

The Cheechako, 1897

"The life of a Deputy U.S. Marshal, in this Wild & Wooly West, is
not very pleasant, at the best."

Annie Canton, October 1898

The year 1897 would be a momen-
tous one for Frank Canton. Changes significantly altering his life had actually begun the previous November, the week he shot and killed Bee Dunn.
That was also the week William McKinley, a Republican, defeated Democrat
William Jennings Bryan for the presidency. Turnover in political parties meant
the appointment of a new attorney general and a likely personnel change in
the marshal's office. Pat Nagle's ousting would not have surprised Canton,
nor would he have been shocked if Nagle's replacement, certain to be a Republican, dumped all the Democratic deputies like himself. That was the way
of the political world. But he could not have foreseen the course of action
taken by McKinley's new attorney general, Joseph McKenna, action that
would ultimately lead to criminal indictments against eleven deputy marshals, including himself.

At the general election in November, Dennis T. Flynn, the incumbent
Republican delegate to Congress from Oklahoma, was opposed by James Y.
Callahan, a Fusionist representing both the Democratic and the Populist Parties. At the height of a bitterly contested campaign Charley Colcord was
taking all bets that Callahan would unseat Flynn. William Grimes, chairman
of the Republican Central Committee, offered to bet Colcord that Callahan
would not even win his own county or township. Colcord accepted the challenge. By election day he had almost two thousand dollars riding on Callahan.
Of course Colcord told his deputy friends of the bet, and they all worked
diligently for Flynn's defeat. In November, Callahan was elected by over

eleven hundred votes but carried his county by only four votes and his township by only two or three.[1]

Flynn attributed his defeat to the work of the deputies and swore revenge. Before leaving office, he set in motion a chain of events profoundly affecting the U.S. marshal's service in Oklahoma. On March 26, 1897, T. C. Taylor, a clerk in the attorney general's office, was directed to go to Guthrie and audit the accounts and records of Patrick S. Nagle, U.S. marshal. Taylor arrived in Guthrie on April 3 and began his task.[2]

While Taylor pored over the records at Guthrie, Canton continued his normal duties. His reports for the six-month period of October 1896 through March 1897 show he made thirty-eight arrests for violations of federal law.[3] He also was actively chasing miscreants in his capacity as undersheriff of Pawnee County. In January 1897 he was appointed a special agent of Oklahoma with power to pursue and arrest in Indian Territory one James Henderson, wanted in Pawnee County on charges of grand larceny.[4]

But Canton, painfully aware of the change in the political climate and the probability that his deputy marshal's commission might not be renewed, began some serious introspection. He had been drinking heavily, a vice for which he came under censure from both his wife and his boss, Marshal Nagle. He swore off alcohol again. He was now forty-seven years old, and no longer did a seemingly endless future stretch out ahead of him. He grimly realized that his productive years were diminishing and that financially he had precious little to show for almost two decades of difficult and hazardous work. He began the groundwork to redirect his life.

One of the political changes occurring soon after McKinley's inauguration on March 4, 1897, was the appointment of a Republican governor for Oklahoma. Never missing an opportunity to get close to the powerful, Canton quickly made himself known to the new chief executive, Cassius M. Barnes. On May 20, at Canton's request, Frank M. Thompson, cashier of the Arkansas Valley Bank of Pawnee and an acquaintance of Barnes's, wrote a letter of introduction: "This will introduce my fellow townsman, Mr. Frank M. Canton, Deputy U.S. Marshal for Pawnee County. He visits Guthrie on business and wishes to become acquainted with and pay his respects to the new governor of the territory. Mr. Canton is a worthy citizen and efficient officer, and I bespeak for him your usual cordiality and courtesy."[5]

Before entering a political career, Barnes had served ten years as chief deputy marshal for Judge Isaac Parker's court at Fort Smith.[6] Based on their shared experience, Canton hoped to build a close relationship with the governor, a relationship that might lead to a territorial appointment if his job as a federal officer was lost.

As he looked for new avenues of opportunity, Canton read with heightened interest the press reports of fabulous gold strikes on the Yukon River of Alaska, the frontier that had attracted him four years before. Like thousands of others, he developed a virulent case of Klondike fever. He went to Chicago and conferred with his old friend P. B. Weare, who, through his North American Transportation and Trading (NAT&T) Company, was heavily involved in Alaskan enterprise and still wielded considerable political influence. Canton knew that with the change in the national political picture, the appointment as U.S. marshal in Alaska, his onetime ambition, was not in the cards. But, lowering his sights, he was now willing to accept a deputy's position to help pay for a trip to the new El Dorado. P. B. Weare wrote to U.S. Marshal Louis L. Williams at Sitka, Alaska, on May 20, urging the appointment of a deputy marshal who could be relied on to look out for the interests of the NAT&T Company in the Alaskan interior and recommending Frank Canton for the job.[7]

There was an urgency in Canton's efforts to find a new job. By late May it was evident that the investigation of the marshal's office at Guthrie by Special Examiner T. C. Taylor would have severe repercussions. Taylor had focused on the accounts of eleven deputies, of whom Canton was one. He began extensive interviews of the deputies and the defendants they had arrested, challenging every reported expense. The eleven men under scrutiny were called to the Guthrie office and required to justify all their expenses for the previous two quarters. On June 10 Canton signed sworn statements that his accounts for the periods were correct in all particulars with exceptions enumerated. Those exceptions filled eleven typewritten legal-sized sheets. By his own admission he had "padded" the accounts, charging for mileage that he never traveled, for prisoners' meals that he never provided, and for possemen who did not accompany him. Marshal Nagle forwarded Canton's sworn statements, together with those of the other deputies, to Washington on June 18.[8]

Six days later T. C. Taylor submitted a twenty-eight-page report to Attorney General McKenna. Among other suggestions for improvement of the marshal's office at Guthrie, he recommended reducing the number of field deputies to twelve. He further recommended, "On account of the evidence of so many fraudulent charges . . . , action on the accounts of [the eleven deputies] for the December quarter, 1896 and March quarter, 1897 be suspended . . . and that the deputies be dismissed from the service."[9]

At the end of June, Marshal Nagle revoked the commissions of eight deputies but retained four who were under fire: Frank Canton, Charlie Colcord, Ike Steel, and Harry Callahan. On July 27 he received a telegram directing him to dismiss them all. He wired back the same day: "I revoked the commissions of eight of the parties last quarter, Canton quite a few days ago.

Will notify Colcord, Steel and Callahan of your message and revoke their commission."[10]

Later Nagle explained in a letter why he had delayed revocation of four commissions. Colcord and Steel, he said, were men of honesty and integrity, and he did not believe they entered fraudulent claims. His investigation of Callahan was incomplete. "In reference to Canton," he said, "I will say that I allowed him to remain on the force for the reason that he had been a good officer for more than twenty years, and like Steel was always called upon when any dangerous work was to be done. Outside of what he admitted in his statement, his work has always been first class, so far as I know. He had at one time drank to excess but about six months ago stopped entirely and I felt like helping him all I could."[11]

Investigator T. C. Taylor later alleged that he was terrorized at this time by Frank Canton and "found it necessary to take several armed men with him to protect him from Canton who threatened to waylay him and take his papers away from him." Taylor said he was warned by Bird S. McGuire, later Oklahoma delegate to Congress, "never to meet Canton alone."[12]

U.S. Marshal Williams at Sitka, meanwhile, had received P. B. Weare's letter urging Canton's appointment as a deputy in Alaska. Totally unaware of the storm brewing in the U.S. marshal's office in Oklahoma Territory, Williams looked favorably on the proposal. He acknowledged Weare's letter on June 21 and said that he had "also received other endorsements as to the Ability, Integrity and Diligence of Mr. Canton." He added: "Relying upon your personal acquaintance with Mr. Canton I am satisfied that he is a fit man for the place and as soon as Congress makes provision for the appointment of a deputy at Circle City, I will take pleasure in giving him the position."[13]

That was all Weare and Canton wanted to hear, and they moved fast. On July 2 Weare wrote Williams:

> Our understanding in Washington was that the Sundry Civil Bill made an appropriation [for] an additional three Deputy U.S. Marshals, and a Commissioner has already gone forward under this bill and appropriation.
>
> Our ship sails from Seattle Wash. July 25th for Circle City, and another about the 20 of August and we would be pleased if you could see your way clear to appoint Mr. Frank M. Canton, and let him go up on the ship sailing the 25th of this month. This can only be done by your forwarding the papers to him care of our office in Seattle, Wash. and also sending a dispatch to the nearest point reached by wire that you have appointed him, so that we may order him out of Oklahoma and be in time for the ship sailing the 25th of this month. . . .

Portus B. Weare finally arranged an appointment for Canton in Alaska. *Author's collection.*

Under orders from Washington, we have had a Notary appointed, who goes in on the ship sailing the 25th of this month and he will swear in the Commissioner, and he can also swear in your Deputy, if you like, otherwise we will have Mr. Canton come to Sitka and be sworn in by you, and come back and take our ship that sails in August.[14]

Canton also wrote Williams, accepting appointment as deputy marshal at Circle City. However, Weare's ambitious plan was rushing things a bit too much for the workings of federal bureaucracy and the efficiency of the 1897 mail service. There was simply not enough time for a July 2 letter to reach Williams and have him react as requested before a July 25 sailing from Seattle. Canton also had to close his affairs in Pawnee, make provisions for his wife and daughter during his absence, go to Seattle, and purchase the necessary supplies for a lengthy sojourn in the Arctic.[15] The July 25 sailing date was not met, but Weare booked Canton on a ship leaving Seattle, bound for St. Michael, on August 8.

Although Canton's appointment as deputy marshal in Alaska was not yet official, Weare put him on the company payroll. Weare wrote S. L. Moore, general freight agent of the Northern Pacific Railroad in St. Paul, on July 28: "This will introduce you to Mr. F.M. Canton, who is on his way to Alaska in the employ of this company. Kindly furnish him transportation from St. Paul to Seattle, Washington, as usual, and oblige."[16]

Canton bid Annie and Ruby good-bye at the Perry depot on July 30. They would go to Buffalo to remain with the Wilkersons while he was away. Part of his NAT&T Company salary was to be forwarded to Annie in Buffalo.[17]

It happened that two of Canton's acquaintances from Guthrie, both former lawmen, had contracted the Klondike fever and were going to Alaska at the same time. The three Oklahomans quickly joined forces. Frank G. Kress was a former deputy U.S. marshal who was being grubstaked by a group of Oklahomans. William W. Painter, who had also served as a deputy marshal and as sheriff of Logan County, was going on his own.[18] Canton saved these men considerable expense when, through P. B. Weare, he wangled passes for them covering the ocean passage from Seattle to St. Michael and for the riverboat trip up the Yukon. "The fare this way is $200 and 10 cents per pound for all baggage," Kress wrote in a letter to his family. "We got free transportation for ourselves and baggage, which left us more money to use, so we bought a great supply of clothing."[19] They purchased "footware of different kinds, woolen stockings and heavy underwear, arctic socks lined with lambs' wool, and several pairs of strong buckskin moccasins." In addition, said Canton, "We bought all kinds of tools that a pioneer would need in placer mining, building cabins, etc." Acting on the advice of an old sourdough, Canton bought a "Yukon stove," which would become invaluable in the northern country.[20]

About nine o'clock on the evening of August 5, 1897, the Oklahomans left Seattle on board the *Cleveland,* a steamer chartered by the North American Transportation and Trading Company, on a three-thousand-mile voyage to St. Michael. An aged vessel with a reputation for ill fortune after several mishaps along the South American coast, the *Cleveland* was 165 feet long and 24 feet wide. Originally designed for freight, it had been converted to passenger use. Cabins accommodated only about 40 of the 164 passengers on board; the rest were crammed into the forward hold. "You would be surprised at the class of people en route for Alaska," Kress wrote. "Instead of the rough class of men we expected to meet, it is entirely different. Nearly all are gentlemen of refinement, a good many professional men, such as doctors, lawyers, etc. There are five ladies on board." A few days out at sea, someone took a survey of the passengers. Canton, Kress, and Painter were the only Oklahomans. Others came from twenty-two different states and territories and four foreign countries. There were three from the District of Columbia. Of those who would divulge their political inclination, there were 73 Republicans, 27 Democrats, 11 Silver Republicans, 3 Gold Democrats, 3 Populists, and 1 Prohibitionist.[21]

Among the passengers were Captain Patrick H. Ray and First Lieutenant Wilds P. Richardson, U.S. Army officers under orders to recommend sites for military posts on the upper Yukon. Captain Ray was an experienced Alaska hand, having seen army service at Point Barrow in the 1880s. Canton and

The Steamship *Cleveland* leaves Seattle for Alaska. *Courtesy Special Collections Division, University of Washington Libraries, negative number Wilse 245.*

Richardson had known each other previously at Fort McKinney when Canton was sheriff of Johnson County.[22]

After a two-day stopover at Dutch Harbor for coal, the *Cleveland* continued on to St. Michael on the Alaskan mainland. There Canton wrote Frank Lake:

> Dear Frank: We left Seattle Aug. 5; had a long trip over the North Pacific Ocean and Behring [sic] Sea. We start up the Yukon River today on the steamer John J. Healy, 2,000 miles. I don't know whether we will make it through or not; we may be snowed in. All recent reports from the Upper Yukon are to the effect that there is plenty of gold up there but no provisions, and that the people are bound to starve up there this winter. Three of us are taking 2,800 pounds of provisions; will have a good dog team when I get up there, good guns and plenty of ammunition. As there is moose, cariboo [sic] and deer, I don't think I will starve. Remember me kindly to all the boys and tell them not to start up here until next spring, then to be well fixed for money and provisions. Will write you if I can get a

letter out this winter. I would give anything if I could only hear
from my wife and little girl. I hope they got off from Pawnee all
right. I may not get to hear from them this winter; this is the
hardest part of it all with me.[23]

St. Michael was full of prospectors awaiting passage back to the States. As
Canton noted, they reported a scarcity of provisions and a real possibility of
starvation in the Yukon mining camps once the river froze. The Yukon was
expected to begin freezing within a month, and time was short. Refusal of
the NAT&T to allow passengers to take more than 150 pounds of luggage on
their riverboats complicated the situation. Agents of the company assured
Canton that there was plenty of food at Circle City but would not guarantee
that their steamboat could make the ascent of the river to the town before
the freeze. Faced with the problem of getting upriver with their 2,800 pounds
of provisions, Canton and his partners split up. Frank Kress went ahead on
August 28 aboard the *John J. Healy*, while Canton and Painter remained
behind with most of the supplies. Together with sixty others in the same
predicament, Canton and Painter organized a limited stock company and
purchased a small stern-wheeler from a nearby Jesuit mission. They christened the boat *St. Michael* and loaded it with forty-five tons of provisions.
Two river-wise Eskimos were employed as guides. "Manned entirely by
amateurs who knew nothing about steamboating—a lawyer, a doctor, several clerks, some salesmen, and one lone tramp printer," volunteer stockholders who made up in nerve and audacity what they lacked in nautical
skill, the *St. Michael* set out with its cargo across eighty miles of open water
to the mouth of the Yukon and began the long journey up the river toward
Circle City.[24]

Canton and Painter followed a week later in the *P.B. Weare*, an NAT&T
Company riverboat. The river was running high and strong, and the *Weare*
struggled against the current. Progress was slow. Just above the mouth of
the Tanana River, slush ice was encountered. "This meant that our hopes for
reaching Circle City or Dawson that fall had gone glimmering," recalled
Canton. "The next thing to do was to find some side stream in which we
could anchor our boat and get into winter quarters as quickly as possible."[25]

They overtook the *St. Michael* and its cargo of life-sustaining provisions
at a point about eight hundred miles upriver and still some five hundred
miles below Circle City. On the recommendation of their Eskimo guides,
they decided to winter at the mouth of Big Minook Creek, fifty miles up-
stream, where a small settlement, called Rampart City, had been established.
There they were greeted by Frank Kress, who excitedly told them that he
had dropped off the *John J. Healy* after learning that rich gold strikes had
been made on nearby Little Minook Creek. Many others had deserted upriver

Cheechakos constructing a cabin at Rampart City in 1897. Note the caches mounted on stilts. *Courtesy VF-Rampart Collection, accession number 64–92–719N, Archives, Alaska and Polar Regions Department, University of Alaska, Fairbanks.*

boats, and even stampeders from Circle City and Dawson had joined the rush to Rampart. Kress said he had already filed for a lot in the little town, which was filling up fast.[26]

The unofficial mayor of Rampart was Al Mayo, a veteran of twenty-four Alaskan winters, who, with his Indian wife and children, ran a trading post on the site. Within weeks the town's population grew to almost one thousand, and prices skyrocketed. Tiny cabins sold for eight hundred dollars and prime town lots brought twelve hundred.[27] Canton refused an offer of one hundred dollars for the "Yukon stove" he had purchased in Seattle for five dollars.[28]

Most of the stockholders in the *St. Michael,* including Canton, chose to unload their provisions and dig in for the winter at Rampart. But a stubborn few insisted on continuing up the river in the battered stern-wheeler. They bought out the shares of those who remained and, despite two boiler explosions and a fire, finally reached Circle City.[29]

On September 17 Frank Kress, for consideration of one dollar, assigned two-thirds ownership in his town lot to Canton and Painter.[30] The partners

The cabin built by Canton, Bill Painter, and Frank Kress at Rampart. Rex
Beach would later live here, as would Wyatt Earp and his wife. *Courtesy
Yukon Archives, Ernest Pasley Collection, Whitehorse, Yukon, Canada.*

put up a fourteen-by-eighteen-foot cabin constructed of spruce poles chinked
with the thick, spongy "reindeer moss" that covered the ground. They made
a door from the pine boxes in which their goods had been shipped. A white
flour sack covered the single window. A stovepipe fashioned from empty
tomato cans was attached to Canton's sheet-iron "Yukon stove," which provided heat and served as a cooking facility. After the wet moss froze, the
cabin became so airtight that they had to add a ventilator to the roof for
fresh air. After the erection of a cache, a storeroom built on poles eight feet
above the ground as protection against wild animals and roving sled dogs,
Canton could claim they had "the most comfortable quarters in the camp."[31]

Canton wrote Attorney General McKenna, reporting that he was iced in
at Minook Creek and could not report to Circle City to assume his duties as
deputy marshal until the next spring. "I knew I would not have much official work to do in the Minook Creek District," he later said, "so I planned to
put in the winter prospecting for gold."[32]

He had no way of knowing, but in fact his appointment had never gone
through. On August 3, shortly after Louis Williams promised to make that
appointment, he was replaced as U.S. marshal for the district of Alaska by

James M. Shoup, the brother of U.S. Senator George Shoup of Idaho. On August 21, while Canton was on his way to Alaska, Marshal Shoup wrote Portus Weare in Chicago, informing him that he had appointed a man named J. J. Rutledge as deputy at Circle City. A disappointed Weare answered on September 16:

> It seems to be a series of unfortunate matters in the effort to get Frank M. Canton appointed as Marshal with headquarters at Circle City. Our Agent in Washington wires us that he had seen your brother [Senator George Shoup] and that you would appoint Canton. Williams also wrote us that he would appoint him. Canton was here and said that he had written Williams that he would take the place, and I personally wrote Williams and asked him to appoint Canton, sending the papers to Seattle. I then ordered Canton in on one of our boats and he went forward and is at present at Circle City.
> ... If it is possible I hope you can see your way clear to appoint him. We have a large amount of property in the country and want law and order and we know Canton can keep it.[33]

In faraway Rampart, Canton was unaware of this exchange. Caught up in the gold rush excitement, he was busily acquiring mining claims. On September 18 he purchased rights to Gold Placer Mining Claim No. 10 on Alder Creek from James R. Austin for the sum of one hundred dollars. Two days later, for a like amount, he bought rights to another claim of Austin's, Placer Mining Claim No. 13 on Julia Creek.[34] After completion of the cabin, he had time to prospect his own claims. In October he recorded two claims on Russian Creek and another on Alder Creek. In November he recorded two more, one on Little Minook and the other on Hunter Creek. In December he also recorded another lot in town.[35]

On November 26 Canton wrote a fourteen-hundred-word letter to his wife in Buffalo, describing life in Rampart and his growing disillusionment with the entire venture. It was evident he sorely missed his family: "I think the last letter I wrote you was sent down the river from here Sept. 20 to connect with the ocean steamer at St. Michael's. I do hope you received it and all the others I wrote you.... You don't know how badly I want to hear from you. Just think! I haven't heard a word from you since I left you at the depot at Perry on the 30th of July.... The evenings are so awfully long here; I put in many lonesome hours sitting in my cabin in the dim light, thinking of home.... If I ever get home I think I will appreciate it and be satisfied to remain there for the rest of my days."[36]

He had staked six placer claims on different creeks in the district, and some of the claims were "fair prospects," he said. Minook Creek offered the best chance for a rich strike; a few days previously one Minook Creek claim had yielded an eight-ounce nugget valued at $136. His health was good; he was "almost well of the catarrh," but working the claims was slow and arduous labor. The ground, frozen solid to bedrock, had to be burned over with hot wood fires before any dirt could be shoveled out. Snow was three feet deep on the ground, and temperatures, normally thirty-five degrees below zero at night, sometimes reached seventy or eighty below.

Prices were steep: "bacon forty-five cents per pound; coffee and tea one dollar; salt twenty cents; coal oil fifteen dollars per case." It would "cost a man twelve hundred dollars a year at least" just for the essentials of life, he said, so he would have "to make plenty of money to even stay." He thought Rampart City was a good camp, but there was no post office. A man had been employed to take letters by dogsled to the nearest post office at Circle City and to bring mail back. The man was paid one dollar a letter each way. "It will probably take him sixty days to make the trip, if he ever gets back," Canton said ruefully.

"This is different from any country I was ever in in my life," he said, "and if I were to write you a full description of life on the Yukon it would take more paper than I have with me. . . . I frankly admit that if I had known the conditions here and the hardships that one has to endure, I would not have come. . . . If I had a friend who wanted to come, I would say decidedly DO NOT COME, for mining purposes at any rate."

As for his future, Canton said that if his claims turned out well he probably could sell them "at good figures," but if not, then the camp would "be dead" and the claims would "be worth nothing." In the event of a Rampart bust, he intended to try somewhere else in the summer. "I came to this country to make some money," he said stubbornly. "I intend to do it if there is any earthly show. . . . I am here and here I am going to stay until I do something or demonstrate thoroughly that there is nothing in it. . . . I have not been here long enough to form an idea as to what I will do in the future nor what there is in this country. . . . If I do not strike anything here I think I shall go up to Dawson in the spring on the first boat. . . . There will be no chance to get any claims, but there may be something else which I can get into."

It is noteworthy that there is no mention in this long letter of a deputy marshal appointment. Nor is there a reference to any service he might be expected to render Weare's NAT&T Company in return for the salary he had been promised. Although he said that since leaving home his only mail had been a letter from Ed Desmond, a Pawnee friend, by late November he must have gotten a word-of-mouth report from Circle City of Marshal Shoup's August appointment of J. J. Rutledge to the deputy post. From this letter it would appear that Canton had given up entirely on his hope of a deputy's commission, which in turn was Weare's justification for putting him on salary and paying his expenses to Alaska. Strangely, however, he shared none of this with Annie.

Nor did he tell her of a disastrous overland stampede in which he and his partners participated shortly after their arrival at Rampart, a trip in which one of their party died and Canton and the others narrowly escaped death. He described the incident in great detail some years later.[37] In the fall, before the first snow, a party of moose hunters came into Rampart with a handful of coarse gold they said they had found at the head of Big Minook Creek, some twenty-five miles away. A general stampede ensued. A group of "cheechakos" (Arctic tenderfeet) made up of Canton, Frank Kress, Bill Painter, two young fellows named Tucker and Powers, and a pair of Chicago men, each carrying a seventy-five-pound backpack, set out for Big Minook through very rugged country. It began to rain, and the second day the rain turned to snow. Estimating that they were within five miles of their goal, they made a cache of their packs and most of their provisions and pushed on.

By the morning of the third day they still had not reached their destination, but now snow covered the ground three feet deep and the streams they had waded were over the banks and roaring through the gorges. Tucker and Powers had dropped behind and were missing. To Canton and the others, all thought of gold on the Big Minook was forgotten; it was now a question of whether they could get back to Rampart alive. "I have had many close calls in my life," Canton said, "but I felt that this was the most serious proposition that I had ever been up against."[38]

They started back, making slow progress through the deep snow in their cumbersome gum boots. The swollen streams, now impossible to wade, were their toughest obstacles. Frank Kress, who had worked in logging camps in Minnesota and Michigan and was the best woodsman in the party, showed them a way. At the first stream he took his trail ax and felled a spruce tree across the gorge, thus providing a precarious bridge to crawl over "like a coon," as Canton put it. By this slow and arduous means the five made their way back toward Rampart. Bill Painter, who, Canton said, "was about seventy years old and had been a remarkably vigorous man," began to play out. "I think he was the gamest man that I ever met, but the terrible hardships and exposure that we had passed through for several days were too much for him, although he was too game to admit it. Finally he dropped behind."[39]

Canton, no youngster himself and painfully aware of every one of his forty-eight years, was the first to notice that his friend was missing. Calling to the others to make camp, he went back for Painter. He found him exhausted and asleep on the trail. When Canton aroused him, Painter said that he was all in and could go no farther. Canton tried to get Painter's adrenaline going.

William W. Painter accompanied
Canton on the great adventure in
the North. *Courtesy Western
History Collections, University
of Oklahoma.*

I insulted him, cursed him, and abused him until he got to his feet.
Then he tried to brain me with his trail axe. I expected this and
dodged the blow that he aimed at my head. He said that he was a
better man than I was, and could walk me to death, and if I did not
believe it, to follow him. This was what I had wanted him to do and I
followed him. When we had walked about halfway to camp he sank
down in the snow. . . . He said that he could go no farther and
begged me to leave him. . . . He asked me to forgive him for striking
at me with his axe, and to take a message to his family in Oklahoma.
I told him that I had no idea of leaving him and that I intended to get
him in. He was a larger man than I am, but I got him on my shoulders and carried him into camp.[40]

As the men rested and warmed themselves, Powers, one of the two who
had been missing for three days, staggered in. Frostbitten and almost fam-
ished, he told how he and his partner, Tucker, had become lost and almost
died of exposure. When Tucker could not go on, Powers left him, seeking
help, and by sheer luck struck the trail of the rest of the party. He estimated
that Tucker was about three miles on his back trail. Canton and Frank Kress
took what little food remained and started back for Tucker as the others proceeded to the cache, which held more food and blankets. Canton and Kress
found Tucker, but he had been dead for several hours. They covered the body
with logs and branches and returned to their party. Canton said that after
drying out and eating a hot meal at the cache site, he slept for ten hours

Rex Beach and Canton were close in Alaska and renewed their friendship many years later. *Courtesy Lomen Family Collection, accession number 72–71–44N, Archives, Alaska and Polar Regions Department, University of Alaska, Fairbanks.*

straight. The next day they met a relief party from Rampart with sledges and dog teams and learned that two other Cheechakos had died on the stampede to Big Minook.

Canton said it took him a week to get the soreness out of his limbs.

> It was the hardest trip that I ever made in my life. To think of it now that it is all over, it seems to be a hideous nightmare. I thought I knew how to travel in the mountains, or anywhere else, and take care of myself, but this trip taught me a lesson that I shall never forget, and one that was worth a great deal to me during my stay in Alaska. I have traveled a great deal since, through the wilds of Alaska, by dog teams, and rivers, over the ice in winter, and in all kinds of boats over the water in summer, but I never suffered with cold and hunger as I did on my first trip in the stampede up Minook Creek.[41]

Shortly after this trip Frank Kress had a falling-out with Canton and Painter and moved out of the cabin. He left to return to the States on one of the first boats out the next spring and is not mentioned again in Canton's account.

It was during this winter that Canton met and befriended Rex Beach, a twenty-year-old college student from Michigan who had dropped his books and joined the mad rush to the Klondike. Together with Robert W. Service and Jack London, Beach was destined to achieve worldwide fame for capturing in words the romance of the great Klondike gold rush. In the winter of

1897–98 he looked and acted older than his years; Canton described him as "a handsome young fellow about twenty-four or twenty-five years of age . .., a husky chap with plenty of backbone and nerve." Canton added, "I think he could stand up under a pack on the trail as long as any man that I ever met, and he was as good as the best on snowshoes."[42]

Beach, who spent two winters at Rampart City, described the town as it appeared at this time:

> There we were, some fifteen hundred souls, and twelve saloon
> keepers, all dumped out on the bank of the Yukon to shift for our-
> selves in a region unmapped and unexplored. It was late autumn,
> none of us newcomers had ever spent a winter in the Arctic, grub
> was scarce, there was not enough stoves to go around. Not one in ten
> of us knew how to toss a flapjack or tear a foot rag. Gold had been
> discovered, to be sure, but we could only guess what it looked like in
> the native state. There were no roads nor trails, every valley was a
> no man's land, every rushing river was a highway to adventure and
> every gulch was filled to the brim with a purple haze of mystery.[43]

Chapter 10

The Sourdough, 1898-1899

"Frank Canton [was] one of the most incredible figures in the Wild West. Rancher, stockman's detective, deputy U.S. marshal, bounty hunter and killer, he left dead men and legends from Wyoming to the Klondike."

James D. Horan, *The Authentic Wild West: The Outlaws*

As 1898 dawned, James M. Shoup, U.S. marshal for the District of Alaska, learned that, contrary to a belief he had held for five months, he still had no deputy in the upper Yukon area. J. J. Rutledge, the man he had appointed the previous August, had proceeded to the Klondike by the Chilkoot Trail, reaching the Canadian boomtown of Dawson City in late September. Lured by the gold fever, he decided to spend the winter right there. In a letter written from Dawson on September 28, 1897, he told Shoup that with the approach of winter, it was too dangerous to attempt a trip downriver to Circle City and that he would remain where he was. He then had the temerity to ask Shoup to see that his wife received his deputy's salary while he wintered at Dawson.[1]

Marshal Shoup, who did not receive the letter until January 1898, was not amused by this effrontery. He immediately fired Rutledge and reported the dismissal to Attorney General McKenna.[2] He dug out P. B. Weare's correspondence, with its strong endorsements for the appointment of Frank M. Canton, said to be then at Circle City. Three weeks later Shoup wrote Canton at Circle City, notifying him of his appointment as deputy marshal at a salary of $750 a year, payable monthly. He also wrote Weare, informing him of Canton's appointment. He requested Weare's signature as a bondsman for Canton, in the amount of $10,000. Weare received and answered this letter on March 3: "We have signed the [bond] today . . . and have sent it by one of our men going to Circle City and it will probably reach Mr. Canton early in May."[3]

Canton, oblivious to all this, was still looking for gold. In late March, with Bill Painter and Rex Beach, he set out on a one-hundred-mile trek over the mountains to the upper reaches of the Tanana River where Indians had reported finding gold nuggets. More experienced in Alaskan travel by this time, they were well equipped with a good sled and dog team, plenty of food, the "Yukon stove," and a small tent. Canton located a claim on Quail Creek on the first of April and another on a stream they named "Quartz Creek," in the Troublesome River Mining District.[4]

This trip was marked by a wild sled ride in which he and Beach slid down a mountain slope and almost sailed off a precipice into space and a one-thousand-foot drop to the canyon below. Topping a ridge above timberline, they had found a snow-covered trail extending before them for a mile. Young, devil-may-care Beach challenged Canton to ride the sled down the hill with him. Canton accepted, and in moments they had unhitched the dogs, turned then over to Painter, and were in the sled—Beach in front, Canton behind—plummeting downhill. "The slope was getting steeper," Canton recalled, "and the sled was gaining momentum so fast each second that I could scarcely get my breath. I am sure that the swiftest express train that I ever traveled on was slow compared with the gait we were going. The fine snow almost blinded us, but as Beach was in front I was better protected from the flying snow, and in glancing over his shoulder I noticed that our sled had changed its course, and was heading straight for the precipice over the canyon on the right." Canton yelled for Beach to jump as he rolled off. After "about a dozen somersaults," he found his feet just in time to see Beach and the sled disappear into a snowbank below. Beach, seeing the danger, had shifted his weight sufficiently to turn the sled. Riding the edge of the precipice, he "struck the soft snowdrift below with such terrific force that the sled made a tunnel into the snow about thirty feet." Beach crawled out, uninjured, after what Canton thought was truly a "miraculous escape from death."[5]

Soon after this Canton learned of his appointment and performed his first duty as an officer in Alaska. A steamboat officially named the *Seattle No. 1*, but called also the *Walrus* and the *Mukluk*, had wintered near the mouth of the Koyukuk River, a hundred miles below Rampart. A party of stampeders led by W. D. Wood, mayor of Seattle, had built the boat the previous August at St. Michael for the trip up the Yukon. They had got only as far as the Koyukuk when the ice caught them. Among the 150 gold-mad stampeders on the boat were a number of dangerous, violent men. Wood, who had formed the party in San Francisco and chartered a ship for the trip to St. Michael, had almost been lynched on the San Francisco docks by some of the company when he tried to leave twenty-five tons of their personal

The stern-wheeler *Seattle No. 1* was commandeered by ruffians until Canton arrived. *Courtesy Yukon Archives, MacBride Museum Collection, Whitehorse, Yukon, Canada.*

baggage behind to make more room for the cargo of foodstuffs and goods he was taking to the northern country to sell.[6]

Stampeders from the *Seattle No. 1* and the *May West,* another ice-locked riverboat, wintered in a jerry-built village on an island at the mouth of the Koyukuk. This tent town was named "Woodworth" after Mayor Wood and Captain Worth of the *May West,* but soon the inhabitants, disgruntled because they had not reached the goldfields, were calling the place "Suckerville." Meetings were held, and Wood, threatened with physical violence, was forced to sell his goods at Seattle prices, thereby losing the enormous profits he had expected to reap at Dawson. He finally struck out on foot for St. Michael and a ship home, financially wounded but fortunate to have escaped with his life.[7]

With Wood gone, a gang of toughs under the leadership of a man calling himself Tom Barkley took control of Suckerville and seized the *Seattle No. 1* and its remaining cargo. The steamboat captain, hearing that a lawman was at Rampart, came upriver and asked Canton to return with him and restore order until the ice broke up and the boat could proceed upriver. "I realized this was a big job for one man to tackle," Canton said. But, being "the only United States officer on the Yukon for eighteen hundred miles," he set out with the captain.[8]

Arriving at the camp, he boarded the riverboat and found three tough-looking, pistol-packing men playing cards in the captain's cabin. When they wanted to know who he was and the nature of his business, he announced that he was "Frank Canton, Deputy United States Marshal of Alaska," and that his business was to take charge of the boat and all its contents. The leader, a big fellow who looked vaguely familiar to Canton and answered to the name Tom Barkley, spoke up: "I guess you are out of your latitude. There is no law in this country except what we make ourselves." Having been "dumped out" far from the goldfields, they had lost opportunities for rich strikes in the Klondike. To recover damages, they had seized the boat and its contents. He concluded with a threat to kill anyone who interfered with them.

Canton then jerked his pistol and disarmed the three men. "I lined them up against the wall," he said, "and told them that I felt like shooting the whole bunch and would like to do so, but that the ground was frozen so hard that it would be a mighty cold job to dig a grave and would still be colder to cut a hole in the ice and throw them into the river. But I told them in language which I think they understood that I intended to enforce the law so long as I remained in camp and that this was the last time that I would ever let them off. . . . Then I opened the door, and ordered them to file out leaving their guns on the inside."

The next morning Canton hoisted an American flag over the steamer as notice that law had come to Suckerville. He posted handwritten broadsides calling for a mass meeting, at which he announced that he represented "the Department of Justice of the United States Government" and that anyone found in possession of stolen goods would be arrested and prosecuted. He called for volunteers to assist him and swore in twenty special deputies.

When, a few days later, he was informed that Barkley and his two pals had valuable furs taken from the steamboat, he and five deputies raided their cabin. Canton found a number of fine skins, which the captain and his purser said they had purchased from Eskimos. Canton arrested the three men and called a miners' court. "I summoned a jury of twelve men, appointed one man to defend, and one to prosecute the prisoners, and sat as a trial judge myself. . . . The defendants were all found guilty. Barkley was fined one thousand dollars, the other two were fined five hundred dollars each, and the furs were ordered returned to the owner. As I had no place to confine the prisoners and I knew they could not escape from the island until the ice broke up, I released them on their recognizance."

About this time Canton remembered why the face of the man called Tom Barkley was familiar to him: he had seen it in circulars for a fugitive from Idaho wanted on multiple murder charges. As he recalled, there was a large reward offered for his capture. Hungry for that reward, Canton planned to arrest Barkley when the ice broke, take him up to Dawson on the *Seattle No. 1*, and turn him over to the Canadian North-West Mounted Police for return to the States. Knowing that he was dealing with a dangerous man, he kept a sharp eye on Barkley, but one night as Canton was boarding the boat, a bullet crashed into the door, missing his head by inches. The shot was so close that his face was cut by splinters. Grabbing his Winchester, he followed tracks leading from the bushes where the shot had been fired directly to the Barkley cabin. "My first impulse was to shoot him on sight," said Canton, "but I wanted the reward offered for his capture, for I felt I was entitled to it, and I still did not think that Barkley suspected that I knew his past record. I thought that the best way to handle the matter was not to make the arrest until the steamer was ready to start. From that moment I never let him get out of my sight in the daytime, and I had a friend watching his cabin at night with instructions to shoot him if he attempted to leave the island." From this surveillance Canton learned that Barkley and the wife of the ship's clerk were carrying on a clandestine affair at night. He kept this information to himself.

It was now May and the river ice was beginning to break up, an awesome sight that Canton described vividly: "Without any warning the ice began to move—miles of it, slowly at first, but in less than twenty minutes the noise of acres of thick ice, bursting and jamming, sounded like the explosion of thousands of tons of dynamite. Large pieces of ice the size of an acre of land and ten feet thick would shoot out of the water onto the land and uproot big trees. Icebergs were coming down the river turning end over end." Canton watched from the deck of the riverboat as Suckerville was inundated. "Water was three to five feet deep in the cabins, and running all over the island. Thick blocks of ice were floating down the swift current smashing cabins and trees in their path. Men and women were all fighting for their lives in the ice-cold water. . . . Some of them climbed trees for safety. We were having a hard fight ourselves to keep the heavy ice from damaging the steamer."

In the midst of this chaos Tom Barkley and one of his friends appeared alongside the steamboat on some logs they had lashed together. Barkley

The ice breakup in the Yukon River, described so graphically by Canton.
Courtesy Anchorage Museum of History and Art.

shouted up to Canton, pointing to a half-submerged cabin on the flooded
island. The ship's clerk and his wife were on the roof of the cabin, calling for
help. Barkley wanted the steamer's lifeboat to attempt to rescue the beleaguered couple.

> I told him that he could have the lifeboat, and gave him a long pole
> with a spear and ice hook on one end for his partner to fight the ice
> flow. I believed that Barkley would do all he could to save the woman at
> least. They headed the lifeboat for the whirlpool of ice, and shot out
> into the boiling rapids. It looked like certain death. They had about
> one chance in a thousand to steer their boat through the swift cur-
> rent and get out of the ice floe. . . . At times the boat appeared to be
> on top of an ice cake, and at other times a block of ice would be
> under it throwing the boat clear out of the water. But the men held
> on, fighting for life.

Somehow they reached the cabin and took the clerk and his wife off. As
they pulled for higher ground, the cabin toppled over and was swept away in
the swift current. The heroism of the two rescuers deeply impressed Canton, who called it "the most splendid exhibition of nerve" that he had ever

witnessed. He was so impressed, he said, that shortly after the ice went out he gave up thought of the reward money and let Barkley escape downriver in the lifeboat.

In a letter written sixteen years later, Canton admitted that the Suckerville episode was "the hardest job" he had "ever tackled." Barkley, he said, "was one of the toughest men in that country." Canton added: "He came near getting me. However, I took the conceit out of him. . . . I let $3500.00 slip thru my hands when I turned him loose and sent him down the Yukon River. I did it more to get him away from this little woman and keep her husband from finding out anything about her than for any other reason. However, the heroic act of saving this woman and her husband in the surging waters and ice of the Yukon River certainly made me admire the courage of the fellow. It was a brave act."[9] One historian has pointed out that Canton's motives in letting Barkley go, "an uncharacteristic gesture of sentimentality," may have been more than a little pragmatic. "He was still a long way from Circle City, where there was no jail capable of holding a desperate man, and much further from Idaho, where the reward might have been withdrawn. Getting rid of Barkley made sense."[10]

Having witnessed the breakup of the ice in the Yukon River, Canton, by Alaskan tradition, shed his "cheechako" label and became a "sourdough." Like everyone else in Suckerville, he was eager to move on to the Klondike. In his memoirs he recalled that he went upriver on the *Seattle No. 1* but that the boat was so badly damaged by the ice that extensive repairs were required. It would be two more weeks before it was fit to load passengers and steam to Dawson, where it finally docked at three A.M. on June 25, 1898. The disembarking passengers were a sorry sight in their ragged clothing patched with flour sacks. "It had taken them three hundred and fourteen days to reach the Klondike by the all-water route, and those who had any funds instantly booked return passage home."[11]

Canton had left Suckerville earlier with Captain Worth on the *May West.* He stopped at Rampart long enough to collect Bill Painter and his belongings and to sell their cabin to Rex Beach. "I remember very well the cabin you and Captain Painter built at Rampart City," Beach wrote Canton many years later, "and I remember especially the fact that you used a lot of logs that had been burnt over and some parts of that cabin were about like the inside of the fire box of a boiler."[12]

That cabin housed another famous western lawman the following winter. Wyatt Earp and his wife, Josie, came up the Yukon in September 1898 on the riverboat *Governor Pingree* and, like Canton the year before, were stopped by the ice at Rampart. They rented Canton's old cabin from Beach at one hundred dollars a month and felt themselves fortunate.[13]

The *May West*, with Canton and Painter aboard, was the first boat up the river to Dawson in 1898. *Courtesy Yukon Archives, Vancouver Public Library Collection, Whitehorse, Yukon, Canada.*

Canton and Painter continued on the *May West* to Fort Yukon, Circle City, and finally Dawson City, which they reached on June 8.[14] In his memoirs Canton wrote: "When I reached Dawson I struck the hardest town that I had ever seen. . . . It was a wild, picturesque, lawless mining camp. The like had never been known and never will be seen again. It was a picture of blood and glittering gold dust, starvation and death."[15] However, as pointed out by a Klondike scholar, this assessment of Dawson is far from accurate: "The truth is that, thanks to the presence of the Mounted Police, not a single murder took place in Dawson City in 1898, and very little major theft."[16] The years had evidently warped Canton's memory on this point. He himself lauded Dawson for its order and tranquillity in a newspaper interview that summer: "Frank Canton, United States deputy marshal in Circle City, and in former years an officer of the peace in many of the largest camps of the West, has said that nothing he has ever seen approached Dawson as a model mining camp. Accustomed as he has been to dealing with the roughest class of criminals, his commendation of Dawson as a law-abiding town has great weight."[17]

In Dawson, Canton informed the agents of the NAT&T Company of his arrival. Missing no bets, he also made an appearance at the NAT&T Company's chief competitor, the Alaska Commercial Company, and on June

Canton took the riverboat *Portus B. Weare* down the Yukon, guarding the gold belonging to the man for whom the boat was named. *Courtesy Yukon Archives, Martha Louis Black Collection, Whitehorse, Yukon, Canada.*

23 secured a letter addressed to all agents and captains of the company and signed by J. P. Hansen, assistant superintendent: "Bearer, Mr. Frank M. Canton, is the U.S. marshal of the Yukon District. I have entered into arrangements with Mr. Canton, entitling him to such service as you in your respective positions, may render him. Please extend such to him with the customary courtesy of our company."[18]

The NAT&T Company had an immediate job for Canton, the type of assignment that Portus Weare had had in mind when he had lobbied for the deputy marshal appointment. Over the winter the company had accumulated a large amount of gold (one million dollars, according to Canton) and wanted to send this downriver on the *Portus B. Weare* to St. Michael for transshipment to the States. Canton's services were required to guard this treasure. The gold, in buckskin sacks valued at twenty-five hundred dollars each, was packed in reinforced wooden boxes, locked and sealed. The boxes were so heavy that twelve men were required to carry one of them on board. Canton engaged Bill Painter and three other men as guards to assist him.[19]

The voyage down the Yukon was uneventful except for the death of a man named Paul Dinslee from typhoid fever. Dinslee had been at Suckerville and assisted Canton in his difficulties with the Tom Barkley crowd. He was also a fellow Mason. When he died, Canton had Captain T. D. Mariner put in to shore and, together with twenty-eight other Masons, presided over burial and Masonic rites for Dinslee. It was, Canton believed, the first such funeral ever held on the Yukon River.[20]

Canton took seriously his duties as a Mason. At Dawson he helped bury a Mason named Frank Hertz. He boxed up the man's belongings and shipped them with a letter to the family in Berwick, Pennsylvania. William Hertz, a brother, wrote Canton a letter of gratitude. "Money cannot repay the kindness you have shown my brother," he said. "I only hope I may be able to repay some of the kindness some day. I am not a Mason but shall certainly try to be one as soon as possible."[21]

At St. Michael the gold was transferred to the ocean vessel *Roanoke*. Bill Painter, who had had his fill of the northern country, went on to San Francisco as a guard for the treasure and from there continued on to Oklahoma. He wrote Canton from Guthrie on August 5: "Frank Cress [*sic*], a would be friend of yours, has been mis-representing a great many things about you as well as myself. He has written to friends here that you were drunk in Alaska the most of the time, and God knows the most of the time we were in Alaska together, there was no whiskey nearer than 400 or 500 miles." Painter had exchanged letters with Annie Canton and said she was "wonderfully pleased to hear" that her husband would "make some money in Alaska" and that his health was better in Alaska than it had been when he left the States. Painter hoped that Canton would be able to dispose of their property at a fair price and that he could "return home in September in good health."[22]

If Canton planned on leaving Alaska that summer, he reconsidered. He returned to Circle City, where on July 10, U.S. Commissioner John E. Crane officially swore him in as deputy marshal.[23] At Circle he moved into a cabin that also served as an office. Adjoining this place was a large cabin, which he refurbished for use as a jail at a cost of $192.75, but this building was hardly escape proof and required a guard twenty-four hours a day when prisoners were confined there.[24]

As the only commissioned peace officer in the interior of Alaska, Canton worked closely with the Canadian North-West Mounted Police, who maintained strict law and order across the border in Yukon Territory.

> When outlaws escaped from the Canadian authorities and drifted down to the American side, I usually picked them up and held them at Circle City until the Canadian officers came after them, which they always did promptly. The N.W.M.P. would then return the same compliment to me by holding criminals who had escaped from the American side until I could get them down to Circle City. We dispensed with all red tape relative to requisitions and simply worked together in the interest of good government, and for the

Circle City, where Canton took up his duties as deputy U.S. Marshal. *Courtesy Yukon Archives, Martha Louis Black Collection, Whitehorse, Yukon,, Canada.*

protection of honest citizens on both sides of the line. The result was that we rid the country of some very bad men.[25]

This convenient arrangement may have been practiced during the early days of Canton's tenure, but later correspondence between Canton and Superintendent Samuel B. Steele of the Mounties, stationed at Dawson, indicates that normal extradition proceedings were followed. In a letter to Steele on March 28, 1899, Canton stated that he had warrants for the arrest of one M. S. Denahen, captain of the steamer *Sovereign*. Denahen was wanted for grand larceny at Juneau, and Canton believed he was then at Dawson in the company of a woman named Nebbie, alias the Blue Jay. "Please arrest and hold him at all hazards," Canton asked. "Notify me and this Gov. will stand all expenses. We want this man by all means. He will have to be held in your territory for extradition papers which I will obtain as quick as possible."[26]

Throughout that summer Canton worked alone on the upper Yukon, performing what he modestly called "a man's job." But in the fall, when a steamer appeared at Circle City with Captain Wilds P. Richardson, newly promoted, and a force of four hundred U.S. Army troops, it was, Canton said, "the most pleasant sight" that he had witnessed since landing in Alaska. "For I knew that I now had the backing of 'Uncle Sam' in reality, and could discharge the duties of my office without having to take my life in my hands every minute of the time. . . . The presence of these troops stationed at Circle City had a wholesome effect on the lawless element along the Yukon River, and when I needed any assistance in making arrests the commanding officer would always furnish me a sufficient number of troops to assist me, which took a great burden off my shoulders, and I found it much better than having to play a 'lone hand.'"[27]

Wilds Richardson established a military police patrol under a Corporal Delaney at Circle City; the patrol was of great help to the deputy marshal on several occasions. One such case was the attempted robbery of a saloon on December 24, 1898. At about 3:30 in the morning Joseph Morenzy was alone in his establishment when he was confronted by two masked men. "One of them called Morenzy's attention to the fact that he had a pistol by pointing [it] at his head." The robber demanded the keys to a large trunk containing miners' money held for safekeeping. Morenzy grappled with one of the robbers, dislodging his mask, and recognized him as a man named Breckinridge. In the struggle Morenzy was struck in the head by three pistol bullets. Miraculously, none of the wounds were fatal. The bandits fled with $650.[28]

Canton, with the help of Corporal Delaney's military police, arrested Breckinridge and several other suspects. The others were later released for lack of evidence, but Breckinridge was held on charges of assault and robbery with a dangerous weapon. Commissioner Crane set bail at five thousand dollars, and Breckinridge was remanded to the custody of Deputy Marshal Canton for trial at Sitka.[29] It would be six months before the prisoner could be taken by boat to Sitka, however, as Canton explained in a letter to his boss, Marshal Shoup, and this presented a real problem. He reported that because of "the serious charge and the desperate character of this man," Canton had "turned him over to the military authority for safe keeping on account of having no suitable jail . . . and the expense of keeping him here until next summer."[30]

Canton and Crane openly expressed their appreciation for the help of the military in the Breckinridge case, running the following notice in the Circle City newspaper: "U.S. Marshal Canton and Judge Crane wish to publicly thank Captain Richardson for his personal help and Corporal Delaney . . . for activeness and perseverance in following up the clews of the case."[31] But privately Canton was troubled by the role of army troops in enforcing civilian law. He and Captain Richardson differed on the issue and debated it in a friendly fashion. Richardson claimed that the creation of a military district for northern Alaska by Congress empowered the army to make civilian arrests. On January 2, 1899, Canton wrote Marshal Shoup, setting forth his views and requesting clarification:

> I desire to ask you a few questions in regard to the authority of the military forces in this country. Capt. Richardson . . . holds that he can arrest citizens for having committed any offense against the U.S. or civil law and has made a number of arrests among citizens for minor offenses in his own responsibility. In my past experience for sixteen years as Dept. U.S. Marshal I have never known the military authority to be vested with that power where there was no military reservation or where martial law had not been declared. I hold that the civil law is supreme in time of peace and that the military authority have no legal right to arrest citizens unless it be in cases where the marshal, after having first made an effort to arrest parties by due process of law, finds that he is unable to succeed. He can then call upon the military authority for assistance. It is then their duty to [honor] his request. As all warrants issued from any court in this Territory [are] directed to the U.S. marshal, I hold that you are the executive officer of your district and responsible for all arrests made in the territory by virtue of writs issued from any court. Do you not think I am right[?][32]

Knowing that the marshal's answer would take months to receive, Canton declared that he would hold firm to that stand until officially overruled by his superior. He said he did "not desire to clash with the military," that he and Richardson were "the best of friends," and that he wanted "to work with them in harmony," but that he felt duty-bound "to maintain the authority" of the marshal's office. "While the military authority may be able to make some assistance in case of emergency," he concluded, "I claim that the civil authority is fully capable to cope with the element in this country and to enforce the civil law."[33]

An even more pressing problem for Canton during this period was the matter of finances. In his year-end report to Shoup he complained, "On account of the outrageous prices we are compelled to pay for provisions here it is impossible to board prisoners for anything like the amount allowed by the Dept. of Justice." He had tried to board prisoners at three dollars a day but could find no takers. "They charge $1.00 & up for meals here even at lunch counters," he said. Repairs and alterations to the jail had been necessary to keep his prisoners from freezing, but guards were required day and night. "The wages of a common laborer in this country is $10.00 per day," he said. "It is impossible for me to employ a guard for less than $6.00 per day. I am

aware this is more than the Department allows in other Districts, but feel
confident that when they understand the situation and realize the cost of
doing business in this country, they will reimburse me for the extra expense
until a suitable jail can be provided. . . . It has been a hardship on me to
discharge the duties of the office as I have had no funds at my command and
have been compelled to borrow money to meet expenses."[34]

Three months later Canton still had received no reimbursement from
Shoup, and a note of desperation and anger is evident in his letter to the
marshal written on March 28:

> The long looked for mail from the outside came in here on the 22nd
> inst. I was very much disappointed not hearing from you as this was
> the first mail we have had this winter.[35] I certainly expected to hear
> from you; there are no funds here to meet the expenses of running
> this office, and I have had to put up everything myself.
>   Now I want to say this to you: I wrote and mailed my accounts
> to you from here about Jany 2nd, '99 & never have had any returns.
> I need some money very bad and wish you would send in some
> funds at once. I have 7 or eight prisoners on my hands endighted
> [sic] to appear for trial at Sitka & no money to do business with.
> This makes it very embarrassing for me.[36]

Canton's reports and a few surviving contemporary newspapers provide
fragmentary insights into Canton's activities that second long winter in the
North. On December 22, 1898, the Circle City Hook and Ladder Company
held a Firemen's Smoker at the Grand Opera House. Captain Richardson
was the guest of honor, and Frank Canton, Fire Commissioner, was called on
for remarks. After the 125 in attendance ate dinner, a three-round "sparring
exhibition" between two amateur lightweights was held, followed by a wres-
tling match featuring Foreman Clark and Alphabet Conroy.[37]

Circle City experienced a major fire on January 14 when the Alaska Commercial Company storehouse burned to the ground. Army personnel and
crews from two ice-locked steamers pitched in to help the fire company confine the conflagration to the single building. The burning storehouse was
directly opposite Commissioner Crane's cabin, and Mrs. Crane provided hot
coffee and food for the fire fighters while the commissioner himself brought
out a bucket of whiskey and a dipper.[38]

Earlier that month Commissioner Crane issued some twenty arrest warrants for thieves who had stolen a quantity of liquor from the U.S. custom-
house at Fort Yukon. On January 3, armed with the warrants and accompanied
by an Indian guide and several deputized guards, Canton left for Fort Yukon,
eighty miles downriver, by dogsled. On January 15 he was back with a number of prisoners and witnesses. At hearings in Crane's court, passengers

Stephen MacPhee, William S. Hill, and William Jones of the steamer *Victorian*, ice-bound at Fort Yukon, were charged with the liquor theft, bound over for trial at Sitka, and sent to Canton's jail.[39]

A man named John Montgomery drifted into Circle during the winter and began a campaign of cabin burglary. But, according to the *Yukon Press*, he did not take into account Frank Canton, "a certain blue-eyed, solitary man with hair slightly tinged with grey, who sat in his little cabin and ruminated on the evil ways of just such characters as Mr. Montgomery." Apprehended by Canton in February, Montgomery was convicted on two counts of robbery in the commissioner's court and sentenced to six months in each case. Montgomery later escaped the flimsy jail, and Canton alerted camps up and down the river to be on the watch for him. On April 17, 1899, he was nabbed at Eagle City, and Special Deputies George Tyler and A. F. Burton returned him to Circle.[40]

The *Yukon Press* of February 15, 1899, carried a notice that George F. Bemis, Circle City watchmaker and jeweler, had a limited number of snow glasses left in stock. "Now is the time to get a pair before it is too late," the paper advised. Smoked glasses were essential items for travel in the Arctic, where snow-reflected sunlight made snow blindness a constant danger.[41]

Late that winter Canton, with several other men and two dog teams, made another trip to Fort Yukon after fugitives. Each man wore smoked glasses when they left, but Canton mislaid his at a camp on the return trip. "I knew that it would be dangerous to attempt to make the trip without some protection for my eyes," he said, "so I decided that I would try the Esquimo plan, which was to use burnt charcoal and make a black mark under each eye. . . . However, this plan did not work in my case. In the afternoon of the first day on the trail my eyes began to itch and burn. The sensation was most unpleasant. The next day I was much worse, but kept on my feet the best I could. On the afternoon of the third day I began to suffer intensely. I felt as though needles were piercing my eyeballs, and I could see nothing. My men put me on one of the sleds and on the fourth day we reached Circle City."[42]

Canton remained in his cabin in almost total darkness for two weeks. His vision gradually returned, but an army doctor advised him to leave Alaska as soon as possible and go back to the States, where he could get proper treatment. As related in his memoirs, this is what prompted him to tender his resignation as deputy marshal in the summer of 1899 and leave Alaska.[43]

What actually happened was a great deal different. The Oklahoma expense-padding affair, which he thought was buried in the past, returned to haunt him. Investigator T. C. Taylor had filed his report to the attorney general in June 1897. The deputies under fire were dismissed, but the case was not allowed to die. Urged on by fellow Republican Dennis Flynn, still smarting from his defeat in the 1896 campaign, Attorney General McKenna pressed criminal charges against the former deputies for submitting fraudulent accounts. In March 1898 a federal grand jury in Guthrie, after hearing testimony from Taylor and F. B. Crossthwaite of the U.S. Treasury Department, who had conducted his own investigation, handed down indictments against eleven former deputies, including Frank Canton, who was indicted on sixteen counts.[44]

At the November 1898 term of the district court in Guthrie five former deputies were convicted and fined. In the elections held that month Dennis Flynn was returned to office, reducing the pressure to press the prosecution, but the U.S. attorney's office kept the cases open on the federal court docket.[45]

In October 1898 Annie Canton wrote a stirring defense of her husband and the others accused and sent a copy to P. B. Weare in Chicago. The only basis for the investigation was Flynn's bitterness after his defeat for office in November 1896, she contended. Flynn "swore then he would get even with all the Deputies for the part they took in the campaign." She charged that Taylor's investigation focused on statements of notorious whiskey peddlers, stock thieves, and deadbeats generally—men the deputies had arrested and convicted. Taylor, she said, "would also take the Deputy in a room and have him make a statement, where, when, and under what circumstances he made certain arrests . . . months after [they were] made, . . . a splendid test of one's memory."[46]

She said that the deputies were told that if restitution was made for any overcharges, no criminal prosecutions would result. "All being poor men and not able to fight a civil law suit or desiring the notoriety of a criminal prosecution," the deputies believed the promises and "left with the Marshal money enough . . . to pay all claims the Marshal might have against them, pending settlement with the Department." The accounts of the indicted deputies—all of whom, significantly, were "active in the fight against Flynn"— had been settled with Nagle, she said.

Annie explained the difficulty a deputy faced in conforming to Justice Department rules regarding expenses. Instructions from the marshal's office often contradicted the departmental rules, she said. A deputy, while searching for one man, often ran across and arrested another for whom he had a warrant. In this event, instructions from the marshal's office were to charge all expenses to the second man's account. This, she said, "was a technical violation of the law." Distances between points were established "as the crow would fly" rather than being based on the actual mileage by available road. No allowance was made for a deputy having to go miles out of his way to find a bridge when the streams were high and unfordable. These "ironclad" rules made a deputy "feel like he had traveled more miles than he

U.S. Marshal James M. Shoup
hired and fired Frank Canton
without once seeing the deputy.
*Courtesy Anchorage Museum of
History and Art.*

could get paid for, and the temptation [was] placed before him to pad a little."
She alleged that all of the so-called abuses were known and condoned by the
marshal. "The life of a Deputy U.S. Marshal, in this Wild & Wooly West,"
she concluded, "is not very pleasant, at the best, and the Government is not
very generous with them."

On October 28, 1898, Weare forwarded Annie's statement to Marshal
Shoup at Sitka, saying that it had "to do with some vicious prosecution made
against F.M. Canton down in Oklahoma." He added, "I send it to you more
as a memorandum, so that, if you have already been advised by the Department of the situation, that this will show you that an effort is being made to
hurt Canton's character."[47]

Shoup, waiting for direction from Washington, did not respond to this
letter for more than three months. In early February 1899 he received that
direction, an order dated January 17 from the attorney general's office to
terminate Canton's commission. On February 6 Shoup wrote Canton:

> I have been advised by the Honorable Attorney General that in
> March 1898 [*sic*] the United States Marshal for the District of Okla-
> homa was directed to remove you from office and enjoined against
> further employing you in any capacity, and that subsequent to that
> time you were indicted for rendering false accounts to the Govern-
> ment in the capacity of deputy United States marshal. These are
> matters of record in the Department of Justice, and as the order
> referred to has not been revoked, the directions given to the marshal

234   THE ALASKA YEARS

of the district of Oklahoma should apply to all other United States
Marshals. You are, therefore, hereby notified that you are removed
as Deputy United States Marshal for the District of Alaska, and you
are directed to deliver to the United States Commissioner at Circle
City all property in your possession belonging to the Government of
the United States.[48]

On the same day Shoup wrote the attorney general, acknowledging the
directive and confirming Canton's dismissal.[49] He also wrote Commissioner
Crane, directing him to take responsibility for any government property in
Canton's possession. Crane was also to employ a jail guard at a cost "not
exceeding ($6.00) six dollars per day," until a new deputy marshal was as-
signed to Circle City.[50]

Three days later Shoup finally responded to Weare's October letter, saying that he was "very much grieved" to learn of Canton's indictment and
that, based on Weare's assurance that "Canton was all right and that the
prosecution was vicious," he had originally "decided not to remove him until the matter was investigated." But new instructions from Washington now
gave him no alternative, and he had removed Canton from office. "I regret
very much," he said, "that I did not know of this when you asked me to
appoint Canton, and before you sent him to the Yukon. Had I known of this,
of course, I would not have appointed him under any circumstances, but I
know that you will regret it as much as I."[51]

Shoup's letter of dismissal was not received by Canton for almost foi
months. Canton's anger and outrage is evident in his response of May 24:

Yours under date of Feb. 6 at hand by private messenger of P.B.
Weare's communications to the NAT&T Co. I wrote you fully in
answer to your letter in 1897 in regard to the Oklahoma business. It
surprises me that after so long a time the Atty General should take
action in a case of this kind, especaly [sic] after I had been assigned
to this isolated country and after having been thoroughly advised
that there would [be] no trouble come in any way as far as the
Oklahoma matters were conserned [sic]. I, of course, accept your
letter of dismissal, but I accept it under protest until such time as I
can have an opportunity to appear personally before the Oklahoma
courts and the Atty General and represent my case in person.[52]

It took weeks for Canton to close his affairs at Circle City and dispose of
his property. He tried to sell his claims, but buyers were scarce and he still
held title to many claims when he left Alaska. The summer was waning as
he boarded a riverboat for the journey down the Yukon to St. Michael and
Cape Nome. At Nome he took passage on the *Cleveland*, the same steamship that had brought him to Alaska two years before. The voyage was marked

by a severe storm in the Bering Sea; it lasted thirty-six hours and blew the *Cleveland* some four hundred miles off course. The coal supply was exhausted, Canton said, and to keep the steam engines going, the crew burned two thousand bushels of wheat stored in the holds for ballast. When the wheat ran out, those on board cannibalized the ship, ripping out every combustible item to make steam. "We cut down every mast and cabin on the upper deck and tore out all wooden lining on the inside of the big steamer, and all plank floors were burned," Canton said. The *Cleveland* finally drifted into Dutch Harbor, the coaling station in the Aleutians, for refueling. The remainder of the voyage to Seattle was uneventful.[53]

The bright sunlight on the water brought a recurrence of Canton's eye problem. He "suffered considerably" during the voyage but improved rapidly after reaching Seattle.[54]

Part Five

The State of Oklahoma Years

Blackwell•

•Fairfax

Afton•
Grove•

Enid• Redrock •
Perry•

•Pawnee

Jay•

Stillwater•

•Tulsa
•Sapulpa

Guthrie •

Stroud•

•Chandler

• Muskogee

Edmond•
Oklahoma City •

•Henryetta

•Shawnee

Sentinel•
Hobart•

Norman•

Anadarko •

Cache
Snyder• •

•McAlester

•Fort Sill

• Ada

Frederick

•Lawton

Texowa

•Walters

•Ardmore

Durant•

The

OKLAHOMA

Years

1900-1927

35 Miles

Chapter 11

The Bounty Hunter, 1900-1906

"With the help of Frank Canton, who . . . was a fearless officer . . . , we either captured or run the outlaws out of Comanche County."

Rufe LeFors, *Facts As I Remember Them*

Canton wrote Marshal Shoup on September 28, 1899, from Seattle regarding settlement of his accounts. Shoup responded within a week, directing his letter to his former deputy at Buffalo. It is clear from this letter and later correspondence that because of the long delays in receiving funds from the U.S. government, Canton's activities as deputy marshal at Circle City had been financed by P. B. Weare and the NAT&T Company. Accompanying Shoup's letter was a statement of Canton's account for the last two quarters of 1897 and the first quarter of 1898. Canton was asked to sign the statement before a notary and return it, signifying his approval. "I will pay Mr. Weare the amount he advanced to you from any moneys coming to you from the Government in excess of the orders previously given to you," Shoup said.[1]

Because of bureaucratic bungling by government functionaries, the involvement of the NAT&T Company, and the cloud hanging over him in Oklahoma, Canton's accounts were badly entangled. Many months would pass before he received most of the salary and fees due him. Back in March, at the time of his dismissal, the chief of the Division of Accounts, in a memo to Henry Rechtin, disbursing clerk in the Department of Justice, had recommended that Canton's salary be withheld, "in view of the fact that he fled the jurisdiction of Oklahoma and did not stand his trial."[2] Later Rechtin took the matter to the attorney general, who approved payment.[3] Canton's salary and fees for the period July 1, 1898, to January 31, 1899, a total of $439.60, were eventually paid.[4]

In October 1899 Rechtin prepared a check covering salary and fees for the months of February and March 1899 and a voucher to cover the eleven days in April before Canton's official termination date. He mailed these documents, however, to Circle City, Alaska. When Canton, then at Buffalo, learned of this blunder, he was understandably irate. It was winter, and he knew full well that it would take the better part of a year for that check to make its tortuous way to the high Yukon country and back. He wrote Rechtin, demanding a duplicate check. That bureaucrat, citing the proper section of the *Revised U.S. Statutes,* answered: "Duplicate checks can only be issued after the expiration of six months from the date of issue of the original check and the furnishing of a bond of indemnity. If the original check does not turn up before April 7, 1900, and you will so advise me then, I will send you instructions to enable you to make application for a duplicate check."[5]

Canton was also having trouble clearing his accounts with Marshal Shoup. In October 1899 a Department of Justice examiner went over the records and "said that if he were the Marshal he would not pay the accounts of F.M. Canton as deputy marshal in Alaska, for the reason that Canton was indebted to the Government in another district." Shoup explained to the attorney general that the account for the feeding of prisoners was in Canton's name but that "the supplies were furnished by the North American Transportation and Trading Co." and the company was still unpaid. Canton was due $460.45 for fees and expenses, but he had authorized the payment to the NAT&T Company and guards. Shoup asked the attorney general if there was "any reason why the accounts of F.M. Canton should not be paid the same as those of any other deputy marshal." On November 21 the attorney general's office approved payment, but it was several months into the year 1900 before there was a final resolution of Canton's accounts.[6]

For Canton the Alaskan episode had been a financial bust. As a prospector, he had failed to strike it rich, and he had little to show monetarily for his service as an officer in the northern country. But the Alaska experience had been a great adventure, and adventure was what drove the man. Riding the cars of the Northern Pacific to a reunion with his family at Buffalo, he must have thought long and hard about his past and his future. His great ambition, appointment as a U.S. marshal, was impossible with Republicans in control of the White House. He could not even obtain a deputy's commission as long as criminal charges remained pending against him in the Guthrie court, and he was discredited in the Justice Department. In spite of his difficulties with the U.S. Marshal Service, he loved the work and hoped to get back into it at a more propitious time in the future. As he pondered other career alternatives, he knew that the excitement and the challenge of law enforcement were now so deeply in his blood that he could not seriously consider any other profession.

Buffalo, Wyoming, as it looked when Canton returned in 1899. *Courtesy American Heritage Center, University of Wyoming.*

The return to Buffalo would be memorable; he had not seen his wife and daughter for more than two years, and it was now over seven years since his abrupt departure from town during the tumultuous days of the Johnson County Cattle War. As he left the train at Sheridan for the final leg of his long journey, the stagecoach ride into Buffalo, he found Annie waiting on the station platform. She had come to warn him that his enemies were preparing a warm greeting for him in Buffalo. Word of his return was all over Johnson County, spread by what was still known as the "rustler gravevine."

Martin Tisdale, the oldest son of John A. Tisdale, was now twelve years old and employed as a horse wrangler by two of Canton's old foes, Tom Gardner and Lew Webb. Young Martin had been only four when his father was killed. By the time he was nine he was working for Gardner and Webb and being reminded almost daily that the man who had murdered his dad was Frank Canton. When news came that Canton was coming back to Buffalo, Gardner and Webb told Martin that he had a job to do. They gave him a pistol and explicit instructions. He should be waiting at the stage station in Buffalo when Canton's coach arrived. He was to have the pistol stuck in his waistband behind his back. He was to approach Canton when he stepped off the coach and say the following: "Are you Frank Canton? You murdered my

Martin Tisdale was twelve years
old when he waited with a gun
for Canton's return. *Courtesy
Tom Tisdale.*

father." Then he was to pull the gun and shoot Canton. Gardner and Webb
would be hidden nearby with pistols to be sure that the job was finished.

Fred Hesse, who had returned to Buffalo after the war, got wind of the
assassination plot and told Annie, who hurried to Sheridan to meet the train
and warn her husband. To avoid meeting young Tisdale, Canton stopped the
stagecoach as it approached Buffalo, got off, and walked on into town. Gardner,
Webb, and Martin Tisdale returned to their ranch, and the confrontation
never occurred.[7]

Canton's return to Buffalo was undoubtedly fraught with tension. With
so many of his enemies in and around Buffalo, the possibility of sudden
gunplay was ever present. The strain took its toll, and Canton began drink-
ing heavily again. This led to an explosive situation, recalled by J. Elmer
Brock. Will Foster had long been associated with the rustler element of
Johnson County; his name had appeared on the published blacklist of the
Wyoming Stock Growers Association as early as 1885. He particularly aroused
Canton's ire when he rode Canton's prize horse, Fred, while Canton was
under arrest following the invasion. Brock recalled nothing unusual about
Foster except that he seemed never to laugh and was always on the alert;
anyone approaching his camp at night invariably found him awake.

Canton and Foster had a violent encounter in the Occidental Bar. Canton
had been drinking heavily when Foster entered. Brock, who witnessed the
episode, recalled:

Canton spied him and asked him to take a drink. Foster said, "No, I won't drink with you."

Canton said, "Do you know that I followed you eighty miles in Oklahoma to kill you when you were down there?"

Foster said, "Yes, I know that."

"Well," he said, "Do you know I came up here once to kill you?"

And Foster said, "Yes, I know that. You poisoned my dog but you never got to me."

Canton said, "No, I didn't then, but I'm going to kill you now!" And he reached for his gun.

Well, with a man like Canton that didn't just mean perhaps. So Foster drew his gun and being younger and quicker, instead of shooting Canton, he had a little of the edge, he hit him over the head with his six shooter, and he hit him so hard his gun flew out of his hand. Canton, instead of finishing drawing his gun and killing Foster was going to kill him with his own gun. When he stooped down to pick it up Foster grabbed him and pushed him back from over the gun and picked the gun up and beat him until I suppose he imagined he had beat him to death. Most everybody wanted him to around Buffalo in those days. But Canton didn't die, although they said it took about 60 stitches to patch up his old head.[8]

Brock said he was also present when Canton returned to the streets after recuperating from the beating and ran into Foster. Canton stepped out onto the sidewalk in front of the Myers Hotel and saw Foster walking toward him. "I was across the street," said Brock, "and I was so jittery I didn't want to run away and I didn't want to look, so I sat there and watched. And Foster walked by Canton within three feet of him. He never turned his head and he never changed his gait. He walked on up the street as if Canton had been nothing but a post. I think that took a little bit more cold blooded nerve than I ever was privileged to witness before. After Foster had passed some distance, Canton turned around and went back inside the building."[9]

The hatred felt by many in Johnson County toward Frank Canton did not extend to his family or in-laws. Annie and Ruby were well received in Buffalo, and the Wilkersons, although staunch defenders of Canton, were never harassed or criticized because of the relationship. Percy Wilkerson, Annie's brother, was a saddler, and an exceptionally good one. Many cowboys of the area who despised Frank Canton, cowboys like Martin Tisdale, rode on Wilkerson saddles and bragged of their quality.[10]

At Buffalo, Canton and his wife resided in a boardinghouse owned and operated by Annie's mother, Julia Wilkerson.[11] The Wilkersons other daughter, Nancy, also lived there. Ruby lived next door with Percy Wilkerson, his

Buffalo schoolgirls' flag drill team in front of the Johnson County courthouse in September 1899. Ruby Canton is fourth from the left, front row.
The occasion was not to mark the return of Frank Canton but to welcome
home soldiers from the Spanish-American War. *Courtesy Jim Gatchell
Memorial Museum, Buffalo, Wyoming.*

wife, Maggie, and Hannah Duke, a servant. Nine days after the Cantons and
the Wilkersons celebrated Ruby's fourteenth birthday on December 9, 1899,
a son was born to Percy and Maggie Wilkerson.[12]

Annie, with the help of Ruby, who was developing into a beautiful, self-
sufficient young girl, had opened a restaurant in Buffalo to augment the
meager funds Canton provided during his absence in Alaska.[13] For many
months this little restaurant provided the Cantons their only source of income. Despite the difference in ages, thirty-two-year-old Annie, her sister,
Nancy, nineteen years old in 1899, and Ruby were very close. Together they
entered into church work and activities of local women's organizations and
were popular with the ladies of Buffalo.

During this period in Buffalo, Frank Canton decided to become a professional bounty hunter, stalking wanted fugitives for the reward money on
their heads. He was motivated not only by his need for money, an old problem, but also by the hope that he could reestablish himself in the U.S. Marshal Service by pulling off a noteworthy capture. Despite his recent unhappy
experience with the Justice Department, his ambition to some day be appointed to a U.S. marshal's post remained.

Sunday morning gathering at Buffalo in 1902. Ruby Canton, wearing dark hat, is sitting on right porch rail. Her aunt, Nancy Wilkerson Stevens, is standing second from the right on the porch. *Courtesy Johnson County Library, Buffalo, Wyoming.*

The papers were still full of accounts of the search for bandits who had held up a Union Pacific train at Wilcox, Wyoming, on June 2, 1899. After stopping the train, the robbers exploded dynamite under the car containing the express safe, blowing the car apart. Another charge, set off under the safe, broke it open but destroyed most of the bonds and currency inside. During their escape the bandits shot and killed Sheriff Joe Hazen of Converse County.

The robbery was attributed to six members of an outlaw gang the newspapers were calling "The Wild Bunch," headquartered in the Hole-in-the-Wall country of Johnson County.[14] On June 10, 1899, the Union Pacific Railroad and Pacific Express Companies jointly posted rewards of two thousand dollars per head for the bandits, dead or alive. The U.S. government added one thousand dollars per head to the bounty, bringing the total reward money offered to eighteen thousand dollars, an enormous amount of money at the turn of the century. Despite an intensive manhunt throughout the summer, no arrests had been made when Canton arrived in Buffalo in early October.

Believing Canton was still in Alaska, J. C. Fraser, the new superintendent of the Denver office of the Pinkerton Detective Agency, wrote him there on October 18. The agency had learned from Frank Lake and Arthur Sparhawk, a former Wyoming sheriff and stock detective, of Canton's employment as a deputy U.S. marshal in Alaska. Fraser said that he "would like to keep in communication."[15]

The letter went to Juneau and was forwarded to Canton in Buffalo. He responded, explaining that he was no longer a federal officer, nor was he in Alaska, but adding that he was interested in the rewards offered for the Wilcox train robbers. He asked for a clarification of the identity of the suspects and whether the Pinkertons would pay his expenses if he undertook a personal hunt for them. Canton's letter was referred to William A. Pinkerton, company head, who sent it on to James McParland, assistant general superintendent of the Western Division of the agency.

McParland wrote Canton in November that his letter had been referred to him by "Mr. Dickinson," a frequently used alias of William Pinkerton.

> The facts are that nobody has been indicted for this hold-up, but it is a "dead cinch" that the Roberts brothers, Geo. Curry and very possibly "Butch" Cassidy are the main movers, if not the entire outfit, that held up the train.
>
> They can easily be identified not only by the train men but by parties who saw them after the robbery and before and after the killing of Sheriff Hazen. Their names are not given in the circulars, nor did the officials deem it wise to issue warrants or file information against them until they were located. The reward as offered in the circular still holds good and any person locating one or all of these men would have no trouble, in my opinion, in obtaining the reward and I don't know of any person I would sooner see lift this reward than yourself.
>
> If you should succeed in locating these men, even if we had to go and get County Officials to assist us to make the arrest, you would be entitled to this reward. I hope that you will do the best you can on this matter and that you will be successful.
>
> At the same time I am not in a position to offer any other inducements to you other than what is offered in the circular. At the same time if I can be of any assistance to you and if you want anything run down that you are not able to get after yourself, let me know and if there is anything to it you will get due credit.

McParland closed by reminding Canton to "treat this letter confidential so that nobody will know that we are interested in this matter."[16]

Since the Pinkertons would not finance Canton's expedition after the robbers, Canton tried the railroad company. The day he received McParland's letter he wrote to his old friend T. Jeff Carr, now employed as a detective by the Union Pacific. Carr replied on December 12, commiserating over Canton's Alaskan disappointments: "Am sorry you did not yet make a good strike up there and hope your claims may yet prove rich. You must have had some rough experiences there. The U.S. ought to pay a deputy in that frozen zone good salary, but I presume they don't." As for the Wilcox bandits, he said that he had had little part in the hunt because an ulcerated foot had incapacitated him. "I went as far as Casper in a special caboose & engine, and got poor Joe Hazen to leave Douglas & go to Casper and he got killed a day or two afterward, for which I was very sorry." Carr believed that "Curry and the 2 Roberts Bros." were in the gang but thought that six or more were involved in the robbery. He said that the rewards were still offered but that no warrants had ever been issued. "I wish you could get on the trail of them & get them," Carr said, "but I guess the R.R. would not pay the expenses." He thought that "Tom Hale or Horn" and two other detectives had been looking for the robbers for some time.[17] The railroad company had "many detectives applying to go out hunting if the R.R. [would] pay well for their time." It was unlikely, in Carr's opinion, that the company would agree to any up-front funding but would "trust to their own detectives and the large reward" to bring the criminals to ground. "Where is Harve Ray, I wonder," Carr remarked almost as an aside. "He is in the biz or was up there a year or more ago."[18] Carr assured Canton that he would let him know if an opening developed. Well aware of the unquenched embers of the Johnson County Cattle War and the stir that Canton's return must have made, Carr asked, only partly in jest: "Ain't you afraid of your scalp there; how do[es] the gang take it? Jack Flagg & Co."[19]

Early in January 1900 Canton found an outlaw informer who agreed to lead him to "Flat Nose George" Curry, one of the suspects in the Wilcox robbery, for a share of the reward money. On January 8 and 9, 1900, Canton wrote William Pinkerton, detailing a plan he had devised to waylay Curry and kill or capture him. He asked again for the Pinkerton Company's help in arranging expense money for the venture and suggested that if funds could not be advanced to him as an independent investigator, he would be interested in taking employment as an operative for the detective agency.

The letter was turned over to McParland, who threw cold water on the Curry ambush idea. "I think it is useless to submit this proposition," he replied. Circulars announcing the rewards had been broadcast by the Union

Pacific, he said, and the company would not commit to anything additional, "as they would think a person that would not take their word . . . , would not do any work if he got what he demanded before giving any information. . . . If this party you speak of can locate George Curry, that is, give such information that will lead to his arrest, he will be entitled to the $3,000.00 reward, but the Company and ourselves would prefer the taking of George Curry alive."[20]

McParland said he was sure the railroad would reimburse Canton for his expenses if Curry was tracked down. "But I think," he said, "if the party that claims to know where he is intended to give him up the incentive of the reward would induce him to do so without further preliminaries." The man could not "be beat out of the reward as any court in the United States would decide in his favor" and the railroad "would not attempt to contest it." The Pinkerton man assured Canton: "If you would get the man to give up George Curry you would be well rewarded yourself," but he reminded Canton that the Union Pacific had already "laid out a lot of money" chasing down blind alleys and pursuing false leads from purported informants. "I do not place you on the list with the other parties that made these propositions," he hastily added, "as I am thoroughly satisfied you are honest in the matter." He said he was sorry to hear that Canton had not been fully paid by "Uncle Sam, but he is slow pay." Unfortunately, there were no job openings in the agency, and he could not help Canton in that regard.[21]

In a letter to McParland on January 30 Canton indicated he intended to pursue the plan to get George Curry with his informant despite the rebuffs he had received. "I hope your scheme will be successful," McParland replied, "not only on account of rounding up these people, but for your own self. If the other party deals fairly with you and your [sic] successful, you will have a nice piece of money." After passing along some confidential intelligence that the agency had gathered on George Curry and other outlaws in the gang, McParland reminded Canton: "This information is strictly for yourself and for your guidance and will help you in case you have got to act. You needn't say where you got [it] . . ., just give whatever story you see fit."[22]

Frustrated in his attempts to get financing from the Pinkertons or the Union Pacific, Canton turned to his brother John Wesley, who had prospered in his Texas ranching operation and had acquired some capital. Wes was interested in the venture but was not prepared to simply turn funds over to his brother. In December he came personally to Buffalo with his wife, Ann, and rented a house. When Canton went out after Curry, Wes went with him.[23] Canton's manhunt focused on George Curry because he alone of all the Wilcox robbery suspects had remained in the region; Butch Cassidy, Harvey Logan, and the others had fled to New Mexico. Curry had resumed his cattle-rustling activities in the northern country, and Canton was "working" another rustler to get him to betray the fugitive. His search centered on Montana, but the wily outlaw kept on the move and ranged that winter and spring into Wyoming and Utah. How close Canton and Wes Horner came to apprehending the notorious outlaw is not known, but their hunt ended abruptly when Flat Nose George Curry was shot and killed by a sheriff's posse on April 17, 1900, near Castle Gate, Utah.[24]

Now that the long shot of a big payoff in rewards had fizzled and overtures to the Pinkertons for a job had been rejected, Canton was still in bad financial shape, and the future looked bleak. He was indebted to friends who had advanced him money, and their requests for repayment were becoming increasingly pointed. A man named Anderson who had loaned Canton money in Alaska sent a newsy letter from Dawson City in December 1899, in which he remarked, almost as an afterthought, that he would appreciate receiving "the small indebtedness."[25] When he had not heard from Canton three months later he wrote again: "You know I let you have that money when you were in great need of a few dollars. Kindly let me hear from you."[26] Canton had borrowed fifty dollars from J. H. Havighorst of Guthrie, Oklahoma, and the money had not been repaid in September 1900.[27] These debts bothered him considerably. The man had many faults, but even his severest critics never accused him of being a deadbeat or one who welshed on loans.

When census taker Ira Buell enumerated the residents of the Wilkerson homes in Buffalo on June 1 and 2, 1900, he wrote "none given" under the occupation column for Frank Canton. Canton was not in Buffalo that summer. In later years he would say that he was in China as "chief packer" with a detachment of the U.S. Army sent as part of an international military relief force at the time of the Boxer Rebellion. He told this fable to reporters, who repeated it in feature stories on his career, and it has become part of his legend.[28] His autobiography, however, contains no mention of his participation in a Chinese military adventure, nor do the records in the National Archives.[29]

Actually Canton returned to Alaska that summer to dispose of claims he held there. He was back in Seattle by September. The trip was successful, and he brought some money back with him. Within a month he was negotiating with a friend in Stephens County in southern Oklahoma for the purchase of some property there.[30] This transaction never came about, but clearly Canton at this time was planning on a return to Oklahoma.

He was in Buffalo during the fall, and a figure from the Johnson County Cattle War accused him of murdering an old enemy that winter. "The regulators," Bill Walker told his biographer, "put the burr on E.U. Snyder and Arapaho Brown. . . . They never managed to catch up with Snyder, but they finally got poor old Arapaho. The neighbors claim that the old squawman was attacked by Frank Canton and Bill McCann while eating his supper at his homestead near Buffalo—that he was shot to death, his body thrown across his woodpile and burned to a crisp."[31]

This fiction has added to Canton's notoriety in Wyoming as a red-handed killer, but it is unfounded. Andrew S. ("Arapaho") Brown was murdered at his Powder River ranch on January 22, 1901, and his body was burned, but no mystery surrounded the slaying. His killers, C. E. Hollibaugh and Eric ("Kid") Bunten, were quickly arrested. They confessed to the murder, and within two months they were tried, convicted, sentenced to life terms, and imprisoned. Neither Canton nor anyone named "Bill McCann" was suspected of involvement in the crime.[32]

By January 1901, Canton had already left Wyoming and was back in Pawnee renewing friendships with Frank Lake, Cook Horton, Charles J. Wrightsman, and others. As with his original move to Pawnee in 1894, he came to Oklahoma with heavy disreputable baggage. In 1894 it had been his outlaw record in Texas; in 1901 it was the open indictment at Guthrie for defrauding the government. Calling on friends in positions of power had worked in 1894; Canton saw no reason why it should not work again. He visited Horace Speed, longtime U.S. attorney for Oklahoma with whom he had often worked, and asked him to look into the case. Since the indictments had originated with the Justice Department, Speed said he could not take the responsibility of dismissing without an order from the attorney general.[33]

On April 10 Canton wrote Willis Van Devanter, now assistant U.S. attorney general in the Roosevelt administration. He sketched out his record as a deputy marshal from 1894 until 1897, saying he had resigned "to accept a similar position up in Alaska." After the Taylor investigation, his accounts had been disallowed by about two hundred dollars. "I made this good," he claimed, "by paying the Marshal the amount in full for all disallowances, and was told that the matter was settled." Notification by Marshal Shoup that he was discharged because of an indictment in Oklahoma for "excessive mileage or something of that kind" came as a great surprise and disappointment, he said. "I have no doubt but that I would have been appointed Chief Marshal of the New District at Cape Nome, Alaska, as my services as Deputy on the Ucon [sic] River had been very satisfactory; but this ruined my prospects for advancement, and placed me under a cloud with the Department. I returned here [Pawnee] about two months ago. I have never seen the indictment against me, nor had the papers served on me. I am anxious to have the case dismissed and cleared from the Docket so that it will not necessarily bar me from holding a position under the Department of Justice." Canton said that during his many years as an officer his accounts had never been questioned. "I have no doubt but that the Agent, Mr. Taylor, did what he thought was his duty in making his report, but if I could have met him in the Marshal's office at Guthrie, O.T., before his departure and have gone over my accounts with him, I think that I could have made a satisfactory explanation to him," he said.[34]

Canton asked Van Devanter to intercede with the attorney general and urge him to either dismiss the case or permit U.S. Attorney Horace Speed to "use his own judgment." The latter option would have been fine with Canton, since Speed had already promised he would quash the case if given the authority. "It will be very gratifying to me to get this matter cleared up," Canton said, "and I assure you that what you do for me in this case will never be forgotten." He said that if he could "get this matter settled," he would send for his wife and daughter in Buffalo, Wyoming, to join him. "I have entirely quit drinking," he assured Van Devanter, "and am in very good health."[35]

The indictment was still not dropped after this exchange, but U.S. Attorney Speed assured Canton that the Justice Department had no plans to press the case and that he should just forget about it. "Mr. Speed," said Canton, "after a careful examination of the matter, advised me that my record was clear, and that he was ready and willing at all times to endorse me for an appointment in this class of service."[36]

Despite Speed's endorsement, Canton was not appointed deputy by William D. Fossett, now U.S. marshal in Guthrie. The old fraud charge may have played less of a part in this rejection than old-fashioned politics: Fossett was a Republican, and Canton was still a staunch Democrat. But Canton knew that political winds changed. He stayed on in Oklahoma, where he had many friends and, since the departure of the Dunns, no deadly enemies, as in Wyoming. Bee Dunn's old butcher shop partner, Chris Bolton, had resolved all his legal problems and was running a saloon in Pawnee, but Bolton was no gunman and did not represent a threat. Canton noted ruefully that Bolton was prospering and that in April he announced plans to build a large new hotel on the square.[37] Canton took a job as a deputy under newly elected Sheriff John Chrismon of Pawnee County and bided his time.

One of his old outlaw adversaries exploded into the news again in March 1901. Canton had last seen Ben Cravens, badly wounded and under arrest, at Blackwell in December 1896. Cravens survived and received a twenty-year sentence in the penitentiary at Lansing, Kansas. In November 1900 he escaped and made his way to familiar haunts in the Otoe Indian Reservation. There he teamed up with another ex-convict named Albert Welty, alias Charles Thomas, and launched a new crime spree.[38]

On March 18, 1901, Cravens and Welty, the latter dressed as a woman in sunbonnet and Mother Hubbard, held up a store in Redrock, shot and killed a man named Alvin Bateman, and escaped in a wagon with a small amount of money.[39] In the Pawnee County sheriff's office, Canton received a call from Redrock over the newly installed telephone system, notifying him of the crime. He immediately set out for the fords of the Arkansas River to intercept the criminals, who were expected to make for the Osage Reservation.[40] The outlaws, fleeing in a driving rainstorm, overturned their wagon. Enraged, Cravens shotgunned Welty in the face, took the horses, and left his partner for dead. Welty did not die, however, but walked to a farmhouse, where pursuing officers found him. He was later arrested, tried, convicted of the murder of Bateman, and given a life sentence.[41]

Cravens, meanwhile, did not head for the Osage Reservation as Canton anticipated but rode hard in the direction of Pawnee. Jean Branson, an officer from Perry, cut the outlaw's trail and followed him to the farm of Isom Cunningham a few miles out of town. Branson hurried to Pawnee, and soon a posse led by Sheriff Chrismon surrounded the Cunningham house. Cravens made his escape "in a perfect hailstorm of bullets" after a fierce gun battle in which Deputy Sheriff Tom Johnson was mortally wounded.[42] "The rapidity with which he worked his artillery was such that the firing made a continuous sheet of flame," said Deputy Sheriff Jack Murray. After emptying his rifle, the outlaw fell to the ground and reloaded and then got up again and emptied it and then unloaded his revolver with equal rapidity." Murray thought Cravens was "the rapidest shot he ever saw."[43]

Frank Canton, miles away watching the crossings of the Arkansas, took no part in this gunfight. In the following months he certainly looked for Cravens, by now the territory's most wanted outlaw. Rewards for Cravens's capture increased from one thousand dollars to a mouth-watering ten thousand dollars.[44] But after the fight at Pawnee, Cravens disappeared from Oklahoma, and Canton did not see him again until January 1912. The outlaw served a stretch in the penitentiary at Jefferson City, Missouri, under the name Charles Maust. He was recognized as Cravens and, on his release in 1911, taken by deputy marshals to Guthrie and tried in federal court for the murder of Bateman. The defendant adamantly maintained that he was Charles Maust, but Canton and others identified him positively in court as Ben Cravens, the noted bandit and murderer. Cravens was convicted and sentenced to a life term at Leavenworth federal prison. He was paroled in 1947 and died three years later.[45]

Ben Cravens was one of the last of the old-time desperadoes to terrorize Pawnee County and the surrounding area. The country was growing up, and most of the hard characters who had challenged lawmen like Canton during its early years had died, been imprisoned, or drifted on. Canton's remaining months as an officer at Pawnee were mundane and lacking in the excitement on which he thrived. In early May, for example, he collared three hog thieves, charged with larceny of eighty head of pigs.[46]

He did make one notable arrest that spring, following the dim trail of a man named C. E. Stanton, alias Hicks, wanted on charges of horse and cattle stealing, obtaining money under false pretenses, and forgery. Canton left Pawnee on April 29, stopping in Guthrie long enough to visit his old friend Bill Painter.[47] He then followed Stanton and his wife by train through western Texas and New Mexico and back to the Chickasaw country, southeast of Ardmore, where he made the arrest. The *Pawnee Times-Democrat*, reporting the capture, said that Canton "added to his reputation as a detective" and that "the only clue [he] had to follow in tracing the fugitive" was Mrs. Stanton's unusual pet, "a small prairie dog in a bird cage."[48]

The conversation with Bill Painter at Guthrie had concerned more than Klondike reminiscences. Painter was angling for appointment as sheriff of one of the new counties to be carved out of surplus lands of the Kiowa-Comanche and Wichita-Caddo Indian tribes. This region of southern Oklahoma, bordering the Red River and covering forty-six hundred square miles, was to be opened to settlement in the summer of 1901. The land was divided into Comanche, Kiowa, and Caddo Counties, with county seat townsites to be named Lawton, Hobart, and Anadarko respectively.[49]

Painter, a good Republican and a former sheriff, had the inside track with Governor William M. Jenkins for appointment as sheriff of one of the new counties. When that appointment came, he said, there would be a position for Canton as deputy. Canton, bored and restless at Pawnee, was interested.

To avoid the confusion and violence that previous land rushes had generated, officials decided that rights to purchase land at $1.75 per acre would be determined by lottery. Of 150,000 registrants, only 13,000 were lucky winners in the drawings, but when the lands were opened on August 6, 1901, more than 160,000 people rushed into the new country.[50]

Bill Painter was appointed sheriff of Comanche County, with headquarters at Lawton. Canton joined him there and once again found himself in the raw frontier environment he loved. Lawton mushroomed around a central intersection of Main Street and "Goo-Goo Avenue," the latter named after a line in a popular song, "When you make dem goo-goo eyes at me!" By November eighty-six saloons could be counted, one for every hundred residents. Like all boomtowns, Lawton attracted many hard cases and criminal types.[51] "When this country opened up for settlement," said Canton, "many of the loose criminal element drifted into Lawton and the town grew from a small village to a camp of more than ten thousand people in a week, and some of the toughest men in the Southwest were there—whiskey peddlers,

County and city officers pose in Lawton, Comanche County, Oklahoma. Sheriff W. W. Painter is at the far left, and Heck Thomas, chief of police, is fifth from left. *Courtesy Western History Collections, University of Oklahoma.*

'three card monte men,' the 'big mit' man—and every kind of gambling fraternity was in operation in shacks and tents day and night. They also had the 'stick up' man, and the midnight murderer who was ready if necessary to cut a man's throat for twenty-five dollars."[52]

County officers took their oaths of office on a lot set aside in the middle of town for a courthouse square. A covered wagon on the southwest corner of the square served as a temporary courthouse. Sheriff Painter and his deputies chained their first prisoners to a heavy wagon wheel. One burly prisoner walked off and was later recaptured on Cache Creek, still carrying the wheel.[53]

At the first municipal elections, Attorney Leslie P. Ross was elected mayor and veteran lawman Heck Thomas chief of police. Among Thomas's appointees to the police force was Rufe LeFors, brother of Joe LeFors, the cowboy, stock detective, and lawman Canton had known in Wyoming. Thomas and

LeFors also served with Canton as sheriff's deputies. Thomas retained his deputy U.S. marshal's commission and during this period held police authority at three levels of government: municipal, county, and federal. Rufe LeFors had little use for Sheriff Painter, who, he said "was after all the money he could get out of the office for the short time he was to hold the office." LeFors added: "If a criminal was arrested by his deputies, he would get all the money out of him and his friends and let him get away. He had one or two deputies that I believed to be honest." One of these was Frank Canton, for whom LeFors had high regard.[54]

In Comanche County, Canton pulled off a notable arrest arising from a feud between James D. Furber, a former deputy marshal, and a one-armed saloonkeeper named Marion Sneed, "a member of a family of petty criminals," as he was described in a newspaper account. Furber had a drinking problem and, when drunk, was heard to threaten Sneed's life. Sneed, in turn, told people he would put out Furber's light. On September 6, 1902, in the rear of a grocery store in Texowa, a small Comanche County town on the Texas-Oklahoma border, Sneed did just that.[55] Sneed claimed that Furber had gotten drunk in his saloon, had shot out all the lights, and had run off Deputy Sheriff Donahue, who investigated the disturbance. Furber and Sneed then crossed the street to the grocery. Sneed said that when he asked for a match, Furber responded that he was a match for anyone, pulled his pistol, and fired at him. Sneed then drew his weapon and poured six bullets into the former officer. County Attorney S. M. Cunningham accepted the findings of a Texowa coroner's jury that the killing was in self-defense and did not press the case with the Lawton grand jury.[56]

Jim Furber had been a friend of Frank Canton's, who perhaps could relate to Furber's weakness for alcohol. Canton went to Texowa, asked questions, and examined the physical evidence at the scene. His investigation convinced him that Furber had been deliberately murdered by Sneed, who had a reputation as a man-killer. On learning that the county attorney did not intend to seek an indictment, "the Canton temper flashed." He told Cunningham in clear language what he thought of Cunningham and his office and then "persuaded" the attorney to reverse himself and seek a murder indictment. A warrant was issued, but Sneed had disappeared. Canton spread the word to his lawman friends to keep an eye out for the one-armed man. In November, Sneed was arrested on a minor charge in Houston, and Canton was notified. He obtained an extradition requisition and set out after the man. After some difficulty getting the requisition honored at the office of Texas Governor Joseph D. Sayers in Austin, Canton arrived in Houston and took charge of the prisoner. He returned him to Comanche County and was a key witness at the trial before District Judge James E. Gillette. After an hour of deliberation, the jury found Sneed guilty of first-degree manslaughter, and Judge Gillette sentenced him to eight years in prison.[57]

Canton and Sheriff Painter remained good friends despite their opposing political affiliations. But friendship did not prevent Canton from blocking Painter's machinations when the November elections neared. A heated fight between Democrat William Cross and Republican Bird S. McGuire for the Oklahoma congressional delegate seat developed that fall. Of course Painter supported McGuire and, as Canton told it in later years, took illegal steps to ensure his election.

"I found out that Captain Painter was planning to vote 500 Comanche Indians at the last minute and so set about to try to put one over on him," recalled Canton. Knowing that his pal Burk Burnett, a staunch Democrat, and Quanah Parker, the famous Comanche chief, had a long-standing friendship, Canton wrote Burnett explaining the situation and asking for a letter to Parker "telling him not to let his Indians vote." Canton asked Burnett to send the letter to him so that he could personally present it to Quanah Parker. "The letter came," said Canton, "and I rode out to the reservation. Parker was a well educated Indian and could talk English but he had one of his two daughters read the letter to him." Burnett warned Parker in his letter that if the Comanches voted, "they would certainly get in bad with the government at Washington, for they had no legal right to vote." Canton added: "He further told Parker that if they did vote the government would take all of his wives away from him but one, would make his people pay taxes and work the roads. Parker listened to the letter and then he rose and wrapped his blanket about him. He said in a stately manner, 'Captain Painter, he good friend, he want Comanche vote republican. Indian agent, he good friend, he want Comanche vote republican. But Burk Burnett he best friend. He say you his friend. Then you Quanah's friend. Comanches no vote tomorrow from this reservation.'" Canton said that on election day he "saw Quanah Parker driving over the country herding in all stray Indians and not an Indian vote was cast that day."[58]

In relating how he also thwarted a Republican plan to vote 150 blacks at Cache, Canton revealed his inherent racism: "I went to Cache [election day] morning and stationed myself in a prominent place, told the election judges that every black man who voted would be challenged and put in irons, and had men with six shooters and Winchesters station[ed] around town in prominent places. . . . When the train pulled into Cache there were wooly heads sticking from every window. . . . When the train pulled out the 150 negroes pulled out with it. . . . The loss of 650 votes in one sweep was too much for the republican party to withstand so they went down to defeat."[59]

Bill Painter chose not to run for another term at the first Comanche County election that November. Democrat C. C. Hammonds easily defeated Republican U. Humphrey for sheriff. Hammonds discharged most of Painter's deputies but retained Frank Canton.[60]

In February 1903, Canton made a difficult arrest when he collared a horse thief named Roy Stevens. He traced the man to the home of Stevens's brother-in-law, R. E. Miller, a merchant in the village of Walters. Miller met Canton at the door and told him that Stevens had departed the territory. When Canton said he intended to search the house, Miller objected strenuously and refused the officer entrance. "Canton said he'd go if he had to kick the door open." He forced his way in and Miller struck at him. Canton grabbed the man, pinioned his arms, wrestled him outside, and struggled to handcuff him. All the time he was being harassed by Miller's wife, who "got into the game and did a turn at scratching." Canton finally subdued and shackled Miller. He then searched the house. In a large closet he found a pile of old clothes and rags. "Canton began rummaging in these when he came on to a shoe. Following this up he came to a man's leg and then body and finally drew out the man he was after." He arrested Stevens and charged Miller with being an accessory and with resisting an officer.[61]

Canton's wife and daughter remained in Buffalo during the two years he spent in Pawnee and Comanche Counties. It had been agreed that Ruby would finish high school there while Frank tried to get established in some kind of permanent job in Oklahoma. Annie no longer had the restaurant, but she solicited seamstress work and sold women's ready-to-wear clothing. She ran an advertisement in the pages of the *Buffalo Bulletin*: "Mrs. F.M. Canton has taken the agency for Chas. A. Stevens & Bro. of Chicago, one of the largest manufacturers of ladies' tailor made suits, cloaks, dress skirts and all kinds of waists, and she has a fine line of samples of all kinds of goods to choose from. This firm is first class in every way and guarantees everything turned out by them. Anyone wanting anything in this line will do well to call on Mrs. Canton. She is also prepared to do all kinds of plain sewing."[62]

At times Canton failed to write his family regularly, and for this neglect he was chastised in a letter from his teen-aged daughter:

Dear Papa,

Mama and I have both written to you but have had no answer. It has been two weeks at the least since we have heard from you. Here Mama is working every day until she is just sick but still no letter comes.

If you want her to be sick in bed just keep on as you have been doing, never writing or letting us know about you. Worring [sic] so is what is going to make Mama sick.

Ruby Canton, practicing with one of her father's pistols. *Courtesy Johnson County Library, Buffalo, Wyoming.*

What have you been doing for the past month[?]

We have not heard anything of you for so long that it will be news to us if it is a month old to you.

I am going to school now and find it very nice, a great deal more so than I expected. Nancy has been a way [sic] having a good time up in Sheridan.

I must close now to get ready for Sunday School. Let me hear from you soon.

Your Daughter

Ruby Canton[63]

Despite his negligence, Canton missed Annie and Ruby and wanted the family back together again. He had always been torn between his deep affection for his family and his love of the excitement of the trail and the chase. In September he would be fifty-four years old, no longer a young man. For most of the time since he had left for Alaska six years before, he and his family had been separated. It was unfair to them and unfair to himself. He knew he had to find a position more stable and permanent than that of a boomtown deputy sheriff.

He consulted with Burk Burnett, his friend of almost thirty years, who had extensive cattle interests in the Osage Nation and was an officer in the Cattle Raisers Association of Texas. Through Burnett's influence, Canton on June 15, 1903, was appointed cattle inspector for the organization, with responsibility for criminal work relating to Texas cattle ranging in the Osage Nation, north of Pawnee County.[64] He sent for his family[65] and moved into a house at Fairfax, a tiny community just north of the Arkansas River.[66] The family was reunited and he had a steady income, but he was back doing the same kind of work he had done in Wyoming twenty years before.

That work meant the apprehension and conviction of cattle thieves, and with characteristic energy and determination Canton set about the task. He soon broke up a gang led by a man named Tom Jordan, a rustler and suspected bank robber. The *Pawnee Times-Democrat* reported that Canton captured two suspects, Clark Hawkins and Elmer Schooley, and took them to Pawnee, where they were charged with selling stolen cattle. The ringleader, Tom Jordan, was hiding out, said the paper, but Canton was on his trail and had "evidence of a startling nature which [would] go far toward breaking up a lot of systematic wholesale stealing in this country."[67]

Canton got his man. Jordan was arrested, convicted of cattle theft, and sentenced to four and a half years in prison. "Members of the Texas Cattle Raisers Association have reason to feel proud of Frank Canton," said the paper.

> From Mr. Canton we learn that Tom Jordan has been under suspicion for some time, and while everything pointed to Jordan's guilt, his tracks were so well covered as to make detection and conviction almost impossible. But Canton never gives up when he is sure he is on the right track and he just kept pegging away until a chain of evidence was woven around Jordan that could not be broken down. While Tom is "game," he is quick to see the uselessness of going up against court and jury with such an array of facts against him as Mr. Canton possessed, so he weakened and entered a plea of guilty on three counts. It is a big victory for Canton and will do much toward breaking up the cattle stealing in the Osage country.[68]

When Canton learned late in 1905 that Osage Indian agent Frank Frantz was to be appointed governor of Oklahoma by President Theodore Roosevelt, he began another campaign for commission as a federal officer. The day before Frantz was inaugurated on January 16, 1906, Canton wrote him a three-page letter, reviewing Canton's experience as an officer and requesting Frantz's help in securing appointment as chief deputy in charge of fieldwork in Oklahoma. He asked for a letter of endorsement addressed to President Roosevelt. Referring to the unresolved issue of his account difficulties, he now blamed

John M. Hale, chief clerk under Marshal Nagel: "Hale . . . informed me that certain items in my accounts had been disallowed by the Department of Justice. These items I promptly paid to the Guthrie office. My claims for services were made out under the direction of Mr. Hale and were approved by him before they were forwarded to Washington. I had no knowledge of any discrepancies or disallowances in my reports until the date of final settlement with the Guthrie office, immediately prior to my departure for duty in Alaska. The errors, if any were made, were entirely due to Chief Clerk Hale's misinstructions."[69] Canton did not shoot for the top job, the U.S. marshal post that he had always coveted, because he knew a replacement for incumbent Marshal William D. Fossett had already been chosen by the president himself.

Ironically, Canton's old friend Burk Burnett inadvertently played an important part in the events leading to Roosevelt's decision. In April 1905 Roosevelt was the guest of honor at a wolf hunt that Burnett and his cousin Sloan Simpson hosted on the Burnett range near Frederick in southwestern Oklahoma. Burnett, like Canton, was a lifelong Democrat and not in the president's political camp. But his cousin Sloan, son of the cattle king and banker John N. Simpson, was so captivated by Roosevelt after meeting him at a cattlemen's convention in Miles City, Montana, and later at Harvard, that he joined the Republican Party. When war broke out with Spain, young Simpson enlisted in Roosevelt's Rough Riders and served in Cuba. In 1904 he was a delegate at the Chicago Republican convention that nominated Roosevelt for reelection. It was Sloan who suggested the wolf hunt, which featured the extraordinary feats of John R. Abernathy, known locally as "Catch-'em-alive Jack," who caught wolves and coyotes with his bare hands. Roosevelt was delighted by Abernathy's exhibition and the companionship of frontier characters, like crusty old Burk Burnett and Quanah Parker, who took part in the hunt. At Roosevelt's personal request, the wolf-catcher in 1905 was appointed a deputy under Fossett and early the following year replaced Fossett as marshal.[70]

Abernathy named Chris Madsen as his chief deputy in charge of fieldwork, but Canton's campaign to secure a deputy's commission continued. On March 24, 1906, John T. Lytle, secretary of the Cattle Raisers Association of Texas, wrote a letter to "whom it may concern," reporting that the Executive Committee of the association on March 22 had passed a resolution recommending their inspector, F. M. Canton, "a first class detective," as "eminently qualified in every respect to fill any position of trust with the United States Government, especially that of Deputy United States Marshal in Oklahoma Territory."[71]

When Governor Frantz went to Washington in April, William F. Smith, a

The wolf hunt arranged for President Theodore Roosevelt on Burk Burnett's range. Jack Abernathy, center, holds a captured wolf. Quanah Parker kneels in front of Captain Bill McDonald of the Texas Rangers. Burk Burnett, in suit and tie, stands between Abernathy and Roosevelt. *Courtesy Western History Collections, University of Oklahoma.*

member of the Executive Committee of the Cattle Raisers Association of Texas, wrote him there suggesting that Frantz take the opportunity to clear up the old charges against Canton in the office of the attorney general. "From what I can learn," said Smith, "these charges are all wrong and should be removed. Our Association are [sic] anxious that they should be removed... . Mr. Canton is a good officer and needs the appointment as Deputy U.S. Marshal to help him in the discharge of his office in making the arrest of thieves. Any assistance you can give Canton in that line will be appreciated."[72]

Frantz called at the Department of Justice, where he presented Canton's January 15 letter and other endorsements and said that he "should be pleased if Mr. Canton's record could be cleared up in order that the Marshal of Oklahoma could appoint him as one of his deputies."[73] On April 17 Glenn E. Husted of the Department of Justice wrote Assistant U.S. Attorney General Charles W. Russell and reported on the governor's visit. Husted said he had examined the nine-year-old files and discussed the case with T. C. Taylor, who told him that there were "many other things" concerning Canton that did not appear in his report. Taylor "was reliably informed that Canton had robbed a bank in Texas and found it necessary to change his name upon coming to Oklahoma." Husted added: "Mr. Taylor says Canton was known as a bad man and had killed a number of people or made threats against [them]; that he found it necessary to take several armed men with him to protect him from Canton who threatened to waylay him and take his papers away from him. Mr. Taylor says he has also been informed, and he thinks by Mr. McGuire,[74] that Canton has since made threats against him, and he thinks Mr. McGuire advised him never to meet Canton alone." In spite of all this, Husted said, Taylor harbored "no ill-will against Mr. Canton" and felt that "perhaps he may have reformed."[75]

Russell responded two days later: "You had better talk fully and frankly with Gov. Frantz and send for Mr. Taylor to take part in the interview."

> As to the charge about Canton's accounts I should be disposed to be easily convinced that Canton had changed since 1896, if there was nothing else against him, and if he is known to be very efficient in the performance of the work, as his reference to running down the Dalton gang of train robbers suggests.
>
> Even his threats against Mr. Taylor which I suppose occurred about ten years ago might be overlooked in view of their ambiguity and probable emptiness.
>
> We might undertake to do something in the way of running down the "many other things," including bank robberies of which Mr. Taylor spoke, so far as this can be done without any particular expense.[76]

The problem was apparently never resolved in Washington, but Marshal Jack Abernathy, who claimed to have caught over a thousand wolves and coyotes with his bare hands, was not intimidated by nit-picking bureaucrats. Late in 1906 he went ahead and awarded Canton a deputy's appointment.

Abernathy may have wanted Canton for a single job—to assist in the arrest of Jim Miller, probably the deadliest killer the Southwest ever knew. James Brown Miller, murderer for hire, was believed to be responsible for the deaths of dozens of men in Texas and Oklahoma. On August 1, 1906, Deputy U.S. Marshal Ben Collins was ambushed and shotgunned to death near his home in Emet, Indian Territory, and evidence pointed to Miller as the assassin. The suspect was traced to the home of his sister in Hobart, Oklahoma. Marshal Abernathy, Deputy Marshal Canton, and two Kiowa County deputy sheriffs—John Harris and Jesse Morris—closed in on the house on the morning of December 4. They sent in a friend of Miller's to tell him that the house was surrounded and that the officers demanded his surrender. Miller, pistol in hand, met him in the doorway, but after a look at the determined officers armed with Winchesters, he quietly submitted to arrest. Abernathy and Canton took their notorious prisoner to Guthrie and jailed him. Miller was free on bail in the Collins slaying case when, after another murder, a mob lynched him at Ada, Oklahoma, on April 19, 1909.[77]

Canton's final service as a deputy U.S. marshal did not last long; his appointment was soon canceled on orders from the attorney general's office in Washington.[78] But any disappointment Canton may have felt was short-lived. Momentous changes were unfolding in Oklahoma, changes that would drastically alter the course of Canton's life and make his loss of a federal deputy's commission a trifling affair.

Chapter 12

The General,
1907-1916

"This is not the first instance where General Canton's presence has avoided bloodshed and riot. In his official capacity he represents the strong arm of the law and does his duty and obeys orders without argument or delay."

Newspaper clipping in Canton scrapbook

Proponents of Oklahoma statehood began their campaign soon after the formation of the territorial government in 1890. A convention calling for statehood was held in Oklahoma City as early as December 1891. For years action was delayed as arguments raged over whether Oklahoma Territory and Indian Territory should remain separate or should be combined as a state. In Congress, advocates of statehood for the twin western territories of New Mexico and Arizona further complicated the issue. Finally, on June 16, 1906, President Roosevelt signed the Hamilton Statehood Bill making it possible for Oklahoma Territory and Indian Territory to combine and enter the Union as the forty-sixth state.[1]

From this point on, events moved fast. On November 4 an election was held for selection of delegates to a state constitutional convention. This body completed its work in July 1907. An election to ratify the constitution and install state officials was scheduled for September 17. Nominees for governor of the new state were the incumbent territorial governor, Republican Frank Frantz, and Democrat Charles N. Haskell.[2] Born in Ohio forty-five years before, Haskell had taught school before being admitted to the bar in that state. In 1900 he came to Oklahoma and settled in Muskogee, where he became active in the struggle for statehood and was a leading delegate at the constitutional convention.[3]

Frank Canton attached himself to the political future of Charles Haskell.

Thomas H. Owen, a son of Pickett Owen, for whom Canton had worked as an orderly during the Civil War, was Haskell's campaign manager and introduced the two men. During the campaign Canton was Haskell's constant companion and self-appointed bodyguard. "Wherever Haskell went, there also went Canton, whether the trip was by rail, team or automobile," a newspaper reported. Although Haskell was "forced to stand a great amount of joking from his friends because of the fact that he had such a body guard on his campaign trips," a bond of friendship developed between the two men during the summer and fall of 1907. According to the news account, Canton, "known as one of the most accurate shots in the west," was "extremely modest and silent, [shunning] notoriety through the press." The paper added, "His deeds and battles would never become known were it left for him to do the telling."[4] But certainly Canton was not so "modest and silent" that he would not take advantage of the opportunity to ingratiate himself with Haskell and impress the gubernatorial candidate with his ability and accomplishments. That he was hugely successful soon became apparent.

On September 17, 1907, the constitution was ratified, and Charles Haskell was elected governor. During the two months between the election and the presidential proclamation that officially made Oklahoma a state, Canton reinforced his rapport with Haskell. His perseverance paid off handsomely; even before November 16, the day chosen by President Roosevelt for the official proclamation, Haskell announced that he intended to appoint Canton to the position of adjutant general of the new state.

The news was met with some surprise but with generally favorable editorial response. Typical was the comment of the   Acknowledging that the appointment of "one of the best known officers in the two territories [was] being greeted with satisfaction," the paper reported that a number of candidates had sought the office "and it was freely predicted until recently that the plum would go to an Indian Territory man."[5] A Lawton paper said that Canton owed "his success to his record as a fighter and stayer, both physically and politically.." The writer noted, "There is a familiar saying among his friends: 'Canton's always there.'" He had a gun, said the paper, that he called "his 'trusty,' each notch in the handle standing for a life snuffed out in the pursuance of official duty." The paper added, "Canton is without doubt one of the most fearless officers in the west, cool headed and courageous."[6]

A correspondent for the   emphasized Canton's age and experience: "He was a sheriff in Wyoming before men now married and with families were born. That doesn't mean that Canton is anything like a hundred years old. It means simply that he has crowded into his life about six or seven times the experience that would come to other men in the same time. . . . In every way his appearance suggests his reputation and the kind of life he has led."[7] A

Fort Worth paper said that Canton's appointment "came as a decided surprise. He himself was surprised, for the position had been unsolicited." After
rhapsodizing over the career of a son of Texas who "was born not far from
Fort Worth [ ], received his early training in the Lone Star State, and still
[had] many relatives and well-wishers here," the paper described him as
"one of the West's picturesque characters."

> Rugged from many years service on the open plains, blunt and plain
> as the result of great honesty in all his dealings, big-hearted and
> philanthropic from meeting and overcoming uncommon obstacles,
> he is a type that is seldom met with nowadays. He is getting old—
> perhaps he is nearly 60, but in his eye still lingers that spirit that
> upon provocation will flare up with undiminished fire. There re-
> mains the same undaunted courage in his breast that once led him
> fearlessly against the outlaws of Wyoming. His bravery, like rare old
> wine, has been mellowed with age, and Oklahoma will have in Frank
> Canton a worthy adjutant general.[8]

Secretary H. E. Crowley of the Cattle Raisers Association of Texas wrote
a glowing congratulatory letter to Canton on November 11:

> Nothing pleases me more than to hear of the promotion of any of
> our boys who have been connected with the Association, and espe-
> cially in cases like this of yours—where I know that merit has
> brought about the promotion. I beg to congratulate you on this
> splendid manifestation of appreciation of your ability as an officer
> and a man, and while the Association regrets exceedingly to lose you
> . . . , we rejoice to see you called up higher—and we know that while
> you leave us to accept a great field of usefulness we can still number
> you as our friend. Your place with the Association will be hard
> indeed to fill, and I state unhesitatingly that we cannot hope to
> procure one for your place who will give such universal satisfaction
> as you have done.[9]

Roosevelt's proclamation of Oklahoma statehood on November 16 was
telegraphed to those waiting in Guthrie. When the wire was received, Dr.
Hugh Scott, secretary to outgoing Governor Frantz, stepped to a gallery
overlooking the street and fired a six-shooter into the air as a signal to the
crowds waiting below that Oklahoma was now officially a state in the Union.
There was rejoicing and celebration as the inauguration ceremony for Governor Haskell proceeded, highlighted by a two-mile-long parade through
Guthrie.

The first act of Governor Haskell after taking the oath of office was the
appointment of Frank M. Canton as adjutant general. With a stroke of the
gubernatorial pen, the man who had never served a day in any military

Crowd gathered at Guthrie on November 16, 1907, for declaration of Oklahoma statehood and the inauguration of Governor Haskell. *Courtesy Western History Collections, University of Oklahoma.*

force became commander of the former Oklahoma Territorial Militia, now the Oklahoma National Guard, with the rank of brigadier general. "I had never had a great deal of military training," Canton later wrote in a classic understatement, but he said he "knew in a general way what the duties of the Adjutant General were." He moved his family to Guthrie and set about his new duties with verve.[10]

Although Canton had no personal military experience, he had been around army officers and installations a great deal of his life. He had known and worked with army officers, from the Union army headquarters at Springfield, Missouri, during the Civil War to the army outposts of Alaska during the Klondike gold rush. At forts in Texas, Wyoming, and Oklahoma he had undoubtedly learned much about the workings of the military, although his statement that he "had never had a great deal of military training" led one Canton scholar to scoff: "His military experience was limited to shooting soldiers at Jacksboro."

Frank Canton, looking very proud,
in his new general's uniform.
*Courtesy American Heritage
Center, University of Wyoming.*

But even detractors had to admit that he certainly looked the part. Spare
of frame and ramrod straight, with his angular, craggy face, his square chin,
and a mustache trimmed in the English military style, he was still a handsome man and looked every inch the soldier. A news release from Guthrie
described him as "about six feet tall, slender, and made mostly of sand."

> He is about fifty years old [ ]. He has searching grayish blue eyes,
> strong, resolute jaws, and a thin, angular face. His small mustache,
> streaked with gray, usually is closely trimmed. He is a silent man
> and this adds to the grip his appearance makes upon the observer.
> Probably a better shot with revolver or rifle cannot be found in
> Oklahoma. He can shoot more accurately with a high pressure rifle
> at a distance of hundreds of yards than many good shots can at fifty
> yards. Canton has carried and slept with guns all his life. They have
> been his constant companions, and most of the time they have been
> his only source of safety.[12]

Before his official appointment, Canton spent several days with General
Alva J. Niles, the territorial adjutant general whom he was replacing. Together they went over the duties of the office, which Canton later enumerated:

> The Adjutant General was recognized by the War Department as
> head of the Military Department of the state with the rank of briga-
> dier general and subservient to the governor only. Of course the

governor was commander-in-chief, but his duties as chief executive were so numerous that he had no time to give to the Military Department. The Adjutant General was also President of the Examining Board for the commission and promotion of all officers and was held responsible by the War Department and by the governor of the state for the efficiency of the entire Military Department of the state. Under the military law the Adjutant General was also ex officio quartermaster general, paymaster general, surgeon general, and chief of ordnance. During my administration I was president of the Military Examining Board relative to the efficiency of officers for commissions and promotion.[13]

The man who helped Canton most in his new position was an old friend who probably should have received the appointment as adjutant general. Roy V. Hoffman was assistant U.S. district attorney at Pawnee in 1895 when Canton was a federal officer there, and the two had worked closely together on a number of cases. Born in Neosho County, Kansas, on June 13, 1869, Hoffman was educated at Kansas Normal School at Fort Scott. His parents moved to the Sac and Fox Agency in 1889, and after studying law and being admitted to the bar, he joined them in Oklahoma. In 1893 he established a morning newspaper, the   an organ for the Democratic Party, which he later sold to Leslie G. Niblack, who continued its publication for many years. Hoffman practiced law in Guthrie, served as assistant district attorney at Pawnee, and was private secretary to Governor Wm. C. Renfrow. When the Spanish-American War broke out in 1898, he enlisted in the Oklahoma Battalion of the First Territorial Volunteer Infantry and received a captain's commission. He remained in the territorial militia after the war and was made a colonel in 1900. At the September 1907 election that installed Haskell as governor, Hoffman, at the age of thirty-eight, ran for one of the two new U.S. Senate seats but was defeated by Thomas P. Gore. It was Colonel Hoffman who organized the impressive parade in Guthrie on statehood day.[14]

Although by reason of his military experience Hoffman was better qualified for the job of adjutant general, his political ambitions and relative youth may have prompted Governor Haskell to pass him over for Canton. Hoffman drew on his knowledge of the existing officer personnel to help Canton form his staff. The recommendations were submitted jointly by Canton and Hoffman and were accepted and announced by Governor Haskell. Several members of the former territorial militia were named to the general staff: Canton's predecessor, Brigadier General Alva J. Niles, who was made paymaster general; Major F. H. Racer, surgeon general; Captain A. L. Edginton, who was put in charge of ordnance and promoted to major; and Lieutenants John Davis, O. J. Perren, and Walter S. Ferguson, who were promoted to the rank of captain. New officers were Harry W. Pentecost, who was made in-

spector general with the rank of colonel, W. T. Hutchings, named judge ad-
vocate general and commissioned a major, and staff members Charles
McFarren, with a rank of lieutenant colonel, and a Mr. Stone of Oklahoma
City, who received a captain's commission.[15]

Following the experience of the Spanish-American War, in which the nation found that it had neither a well-prepared U.S. Army nor adequately
trained National Guard units to meet an emergency, a bill was passed in
Congress in 1903 to provide arms, ammunition, and equipment to National
Guard units. If called into federal service, National Guardsmen were to receive per diem pay equal to regular army personnel. Equipment and funds
were to be provided only if the Guard met certain standards of efficiency
established by the War Department and monitored by U.S. inspectors. Ap-
propriations for armory rent, construction of rifle ranges, and pay and sub-
sistence for troops called out by the governor to maintain the peace were to
be provided by the state legislature.

Adjutant General Canton soon discovered that the militia he commanded
did not meet the minimum federal requirements. "The National Guard of
Oklahoma at that time consisted of one regiment of infantry," he recalled.
"At least there was supposed to be a regiment, but I found that it was only a
skeleton organization of about six hundred poorly equipped men with Roy
V. Hoffman as Colonel. . . . After looking over the situation of the guard
from every angle, I realized that I had a man-sized job on my hands to build
up the organization to a twelve-company regiment and meet the standard of
efficiency required by the Secretary of War."[16]

His first challenge was to steer a bill through the Oklahoma legislature
for basic maintenance and training of the Guard. After six months of work
lobbying members of the first Oklahoma legislature, Canton was rewarded
with a National Guard Maintenance Bill, which was passed by the narrow
margin of two votes on May 22, 1908. It provided for a National Guard
Organization formed around a regiment of 945 men, supported by a company of engineers, a hospital corps unit, and a signal corps unit. A reserve
militia was also authorized, which could be speedily mobilized in case of
national need. Units were required to assemble for drill and instruction a
minimum of twenty-four times a year and for at least one annual inspection. All officers and men were required to attend an annual muster, which
was not to exceed ten days in length. During their participation in the annual encampment, the volunteers were to be paid by the U.S. government at
the same rate as federal troops. For a private, this amounted to fifty cents a
day. A State Military Board, created to act as an advisory body for the governor, was also empowered to prepare and promulgate rules and regulations
governing the Guard. Canton, as adjutant general, headed this board, which

also included the regimental troop commander, Colonel Hoffman, and the judge advocate, Major Hutchings.[17]

The measure did not give Canton everything he wanted—he had planned for two regiments, one in each of the former territories—but it gave him a base from which to work. For instance, a provision of the law set penalties for any employer who refused to allow a guardsman to attend camp. Canton claimed credit for a later supplement to the law: "The officers and men . . . often found when they returned from camp that they had lost their job with their civilian employer. . . . I finally had the legislature to enact a law to the effect that if any employer should discharge an employee on account of military duty, that he was liable to a heavy fine."[18] "I decided from the beginning," Canton wrote in his memoirs, "that the only way to build up and maintain an efficient Guard was to keep politics out of the organization and I enforced this rule to the letter during my tour of duty as Adjutant General."[19]

He may have maintained a politics-free National Guard, but of course it was necessary for him to wade through the political quagmires to achieve the benefits he desired for the organization. The guardsman were required to attend training sessions twice a month, but no provision had been made by the legislature to cover their expenses. Canton felt this was an intolerable situation and lobbied members of the legislature for relief. A group in the legislature characterized by Canton as "socialists and pacifists" put "politics above patriotism" and blocked the effort. They were led by John A. Simpson, "a militant voice of agriculture" who was later president of the Farmers' Union. Strongest support for Canton and the Guard came from William A. Durant, a Choctaw leader. To Canton's great alarm, Simpson introduced a bill during the fifth legislature to abolish the National Guard entirely. Durant, who was chairman of the House Appropriation Committee, succeeded in quashing the measure.[20] "In spite of the opposition to the Military Dept.," Canton wrote, "I finally succeeded in recruiting the regiment up to its full peace strength and with the Auxiliary Corps Field Hospital, Signal Corps, Engineer Corps, Medical Infirmary and two troops of cavalry, I had about 1400 well equipped and well trained officers and men in the National Guard."[21]

In the summer of 1908 the Oklahoma National Guard held its first annual encampment at Fort Riley, Kansas. The commanding general was not in attendance the first few days, however, because he had taken the Guard's rifle team to Camp Perry, Ohio, for the national sharpshooting competition. One of the features of the meet was a revolver shooting match between the commanders attending. Canton proved that age had not diminished his skill with a pistol: he walked away with first prize, hitting the bull's eye with every shot at twenty-five yards and racking up such large scores at fifty

The general, in all his finery,
preparing to attend the presidential inauguration of William Howard Taft in 1909.
*Courtesy Western History
Collections, University of
Oklahoma.*

yards and seventy-five yards that he easily defeated all his opponents.[22]

At Kansas City on the return trip Canton ate a lobster dinner and became
seriously ill with ptomaine poisoning. For forty-nine hours his condition
was critical. He was still weak when he arrived in Oklahoma City, but after
conferring with the governor, he left for Fort Riley, Kansas, and the Guard
encampment.[23]

Any doubts Canton may have harbored as to the exalted status he now
enjoyed as adjutant general were dispelled in February 1909, when he was
invited to officiate at the inaugural parade for newly elected President William Howard Taft. U.S. Army Major General J. Franklin Bell, chairman of
the Committee on Military Organizations and grand marshal of the parade,
wrote Canton on February 20: "I hereby tender you an appointment as Aide-
de-Camp on my staff for the occasion of the Inauguration of the President,
March 4, 1909. . . . I shall be much gratified if you can find it convenient and
agreeable to send an acceptance, which I should regard as an expression of
your willingness to undertake on Inauguration Day any appropriate duty
assigned you."[24]

Attired in a newly tailored dress uniform aglitter with brass buttons and gold braid and epaulets, his waist encircled with a sash, white gloves on his hands, and a sabre at his side, General Canton attended the inauguration accompanied by Annie, equally resplendent in the latest finery. Staunch Democrat Canton no doubt enjoyed even more the presidential inaugurations of Woodrow Wilson in 1913 and 1917, to which he and Annie were also invited.[25]

Canton must have cast an envious eye at his counterpart in Texas, Adjutant General W. H. Maybre, who commanded not only the Texas National Guard but also the storied Texas Rangers. Canton knew he was better prepared by his experience to head a force of civilian peace officers like the Rangers than a regiment of uniformed military men. Oklahoma had no state police force, but Canton tried very hard to remedy that lack.

In January 1909, with the help of Representative Martin L. Turner of Murray County, he had Bill 113 introduced into the legislature for consideration. It called for the establishment of a state police department patterned after the Texas Rangers, the Arizona Rangers, and the New Mexico Mounted Police. Sixteen professional peace officers were to be appointed and paid $100 a month and expenses. Their chief, reporting to the adjutant general, was to receive $150 and expenses monthly. The measure, endorsed by the Oklahoma Sheriffs' Association, proposed that each officer "was to be a conservator of the peace throughout the state and [was to] have power to serve criminal and civil process in any county in the state and authority to make arrests, but was to be governed by the law regulating sheriffs in the discharge of similar duties." The bill was favorably reported out of committees of both houses of the legislature, and its passage seemed ensured. But proposed amendments stalled it on the floor, and Bill 113 died when the legislature adjourned.[26] Canton was disappointed. The militia, he said, was at the governor's disposal "in local troubles and public disasters, in cases of riots and unlawful assemblies," but its members were "not trained for police and detective work." However, his arguments did not persuade members of the legislature, and he never found another sponsor for his bill.[27]

The first test of the state's military forces came in the spring of 1909. Statehood had not brought universal rejoicing in the eastern half of the new state. Many Indian and black residents of what had been the Indian Territory preferred life under the former tribal governments, which had been wiped out and replaced by the white man's government.

Trouble had begun the previous year. In early July 1908, disgruntled Creek Indians and black supporters gathered at a place called the Old Hickory Stomp Grounds, located several miles from Henryetta in Okmulgee County. Rumors spread that Indians led by a charismatic Creek named Chitto Harjo, or

"Crazy Snake," and blacks led by Abe Grayson, half Creek and half black, were arming themselves to expel all whites from the district. On July 8 Okmulgee County Sheriff W. E. Robertson and Sheriff William L. ("Dock") Odom of McIntosh County drove out to the Hickory Grounds in a buggy to talk to Harjo. The Indian refused to speak with them, however, and thirty or more armed Snake followers surrounded the buggy and demanded they leave. The officers retreated to Henryetta. The following night a group of Indians slipped into town, set fire to several buildings, and openly bragged they intended to burn Henryetta to the ground. Terrified whites fled the area. Sheriffs Odom and Robertson appealed to the governor for military protection.[28]

After only eight months of statehood, with a poorly equipped National Guard still in reorganization, Haskell was reluctant to dispatch troops. He sent General Canton to Henryetta to survey the problem and make a recommendation. Canton, confident of his negotiating ability with Indians, went to the Hickory Grounds alone and unarmed and met with Crazy Snake. Canton told the Creek that his armed group "must be disbanded, as under the state laws no one had a right to carry arms except officers. . . . After the adjutant general had promised him protection all arms were laid down and his forces disbanded. That finished the Snake 'uprising' of [that] year."[29]

But the following spring the followers of Crazy Snake and Grayson gathered again at the Hickory Grounds. To feed those assembled, raids were made on nearby farms for provisions. One settler's entire year's supply of smoked pork was stolen. His complaint to Sheriff Odom began the chain of events that came to be called "The Smoked Meat Rebellion."

On the night of March 24, 1909, a posse of fourteen men rode to the Hickory Grounds and concealed themselves in the underbrush around the encampment. At dawn they were discovered, and a two-hour gun battle ensued in which one posseman was killed and four others were wounded. Three Snakes died and twelve were wounded before the defenders surrendered. Forty prisoners were taken, all blacks except five Creeks and one renegade white. None of the insurgent leaders were found.

On March 27 the clerk of the district court at Eufaula issued a warrant for Crazy Snake. A party of six men, led by Sheriff Odom's twenty-two-year-old son, Deputy Sheriff Herman Odom, set out to make the arrest. When another gunfight broke out at Harjo's home, Herman Odom and Ed Baum, city marshal of Checotah, were killed. The other officers retreated, leaving their dead companions.

This new violence inflamed passions throughout the area, and armed men for miles around converged on Checotah to join in what they now saw as all-out war. Sheriff Odom telephoned Governor Haskell with an urgent appeal for state troops. The governor's office released a statement to the press: "Upon the telephoned request tonight of Sheriff Odom of McIntosh County, Governor Haskell directed Adjutant General Frank M. Canton to assume charge of the situation, and to order all the necessary Militia to the scene of today's battle between the officers and the Creek Indians."[30]

Actually, the governor circumvented his adjutant general, notifying Colonel Roy Hoffman of the situation by telegram at one in the morning. "I was directed forthwith to take such of our forces as I deemed necessary and proceed immediately to the scene, [to take] the offenders into custody and deliver them to the proper civil authorities," Hoffman said in an interview years later. "This was the substance of the telegram, the official copy being on file with the adjutant general, I suppose."[31]

Hoffman telephoned his subordinates around the state, and by the next day companies from Muskogee, Oklahoma City, Chandler, Durant, and Shawnee, as well as a hospital corps unit from Oklahoma City, were boarding trains bound for Henryetta. In all, 175 enlisted men and 25 officers under Hoffman's command converged on Okmulgee County.[32]

Canton, miffed that the governor had ordered out the Guard without conferring with him, remained in Guthrie throughout the operation, keeping in telephone contact with Hoffman and downplaying the affair in statements to the press, which had sensationalized the story in banner headlines across the state. Although he did not directly criticize the governor's decision to call out the troops, Canton left the impression that perhaps there had been an overreaction. He said in an interview on March 30:

> I am rather of the opinion that some wild newspaper writer has worked off a small sized riot as an Indian war or race war. The only element of danger lies in the fact that sensational writers have caused the excitement and some one may have to do something to keep up the show. It is unfortunate that the affair was so greatly magnified. From my reports there have been but two men killed since the trouble started and those were officers who seem to have had extremely poor judgment. The reports sent out at first to the effect that officers had killed three was without foundation. We have had entirely too much magnifying regarding this trouble and unless writers confine themselves to facts, it is possible they may be requested to leave the country.[33]

Hoffman's troops and local posses rounded up about 150 followers of Crazy Snake without further loss of life but failed to capture the leaders. On April 1 the guardsmen struck their tents and returned to their homes. Canton's displeasure with the governor's handling of the affair was exacerbated when Haskell called on Bill Tilghman to undertake a one-man hunt for Chitto Harjo, who was wounded during the fighting but then vanished. Tilghman

Governor Charles N. Haskell and the staff officers of the Oklahoma
National Guard. General Frank Canton sits between the governor's wife
and Colonel Roy Hoffman. *Courtesy Western History Collections, University of Oklahoma.*

The general and his staff at National Guard exercises at Camp Frank
Canton, 1909. *Courtesy Western History Collections, University of
Oklahoma.*

spent four weeks searching for Crazy Snake, who had been indicted for murder in McIntosh County, but returned empty-handed.[34] The failure of the noted man hunter, according to one account, could be explained only by Tilghman's preoccupation "with trying to dig up some dirt on his rival, Frank Canton."[35]

The National Guard's summer encampment that year was near Chandler at a new site christened "Camp Frank Canton." When Haskell came to review the troops, the adjutant general had an opportunity to dress up in his formal uniform again and, surrounded by his staff, sit for photographs with the governor and his wife.

The following spring Canton, still smarting from Haskell's handling of the Crazy Snake affair and further depressed by a lingering serious illness plaguing his daughter, Ruby, drank too much and lost his temper with the governor. It almost cost him the job for which he had worked a lifetime. "The band incident," as the press tagged the affair, began in April 1910, when Bird McGuire, the Republican representative to Congress, came to Guthrie to kick off his congressional campaign. Lieutenant A. C. Garrison, leader of the Guard's regimental band, called out his musicians in full uniform to play for a function sponsored by McGuire and Guthrie Republicans. According to Garrison, this was not unusual: the band had played for a number of nonmilitary affairs, and it gave the band members an opportunity to pick up a few dollars.[36]

Canton, however, "in an irate mood" and still carrying a grudge against McGuire, the man he blamed for helping prevent his appointment as deputy U.S. marshal four years earlier, heard of the arrangement and sent for Garrison. Canton fumed that he was "damn tired of having the band appear on so many political occasions," and he denied permission for the musicians to perform. Garrison then said he would have the members go home, remove their uniforms, and return in civilian clothes for the concert. At this, Canton exploded, saying that this was insubordination and that if Garrison carried out his intention, a resignation would be demanded. The band leader went ahead with his plan, and the regimental band, in civilian clothes and with borrowed instruments, played for the Republican gathering. "I have nothing but the highest admiration and respect for General Canton, personally," Garrison later told a reporter, "but I did not think that this order was fair to the boys."[37]

When Governor Haskell became aware of the difficulty, he penned a note to McGuire: "It came to my knowledge within the last five minutes, for the first time, that the military band was out in citizens' clothes at your meeting, and by my orders. I certainly had no knowledge of the matter at all. I am glad the band is out and should have directed them to appear in uniform had any suggestion been made to me, or my attention in any way called to the matter."[38]

Canton had been drinking when he learned of Haskell's letter at about eleven o'clock on the night of April 8. Enraged, he stormed to the Royal Hotel, where Haskell had rooms, and confronted the governor on a stairway landing. "I want you to understand that you cannot countermand my orders, and, by God, sir, if you do, you will pay for it!" witnesses quoted him as shouting.[39] Canton then "proceeded to tell [Haskell] some truths his ears [had] long deserved; told them, too, in language much more forcible than eloquent."[40] The proprietor of the hotel, J. M. Brooks, and several bystanders rushed between the state officials. Brooks removed a revolver from Canton's pocket, and a report quickly spread that the adjutant general had pulled a gun on the governor. Canton was hustled out and taken to the rooming house where he boarded with Annie and Ruby.[41]

According to one newspaper account, Haskell was "panic stricken" and requested protection from the city police.[42] Bert Wolverton, "one of the bulkiest members of the police force," patrolled the vicinity of the Royal Hotel for the rest of the night. Other officers kept Canton under surveillance and watched him leave his rooming house and go to his offices near the police station, where presumably he rearmed himself. He walked in the direction of the Royal Hotel but, perhaps daunted by the sight of Officer Wolverton, did not attempt to enter. He then returned to his home.[43]

When interviewed by reporters the next day, Haskell said Canton would be asked to resign. He would not comment on the argument or the reported gun-pulling by his adjutant general other than to say, "Isn't drunkenness enough reason for accepting his resignation?" Canton, eager to present his version of the controversy, was more garrulous with newsmen: "I went to the governor's apartments to talk things over and he started a row. He told me to go to a warmer climate. I did not try to draw my revolver, as reported, although I carry such a weapon as part of my duties. Far from trying to injure the governor, I have saved him several times from being hurt." According to this dispatch, Canton was expected to be arrested and charged with disturbing the peace and carrying concealed weapons.[44]

By the time Haskell and Canton met later that day, tempers had cooled and bruised egos healed. The governor issued a public statement that he "probably would not accept the resignation of Adjutant General Frank M. Canton, tendered him earlier in the day. . . . The governor gave as the chief reason for being magnanimous the critical illness of General Canton's daughter and the further fact that the old soldier had given him bodily protection in by gone days."[45]

Although Canton's behavior had been outrageous, Haskell genuinely liked and admired the man and did not want to humiliate him. Within a few months there would be another election, and Haskell had already decided not to seek a second term as governor. Haskell chose to let Canton remain in his position for those months and let the next governor deal with him. And so the affair blew over. Canton's resignation was not accepted, and he was not arrested by the municipal authorities.

A special election had been called for on June 11, 1910, to determine a permanent state capital. Guthrie, Oklahoma City, and Shawnee were competing for the honor. In Tulsa on election day, Haskell studied the late returns and decided that Oklahoma City would come out on top in the vote. He telegraphed his secretary in Guthrie to take the state seal to Oklahoma City at once, and he chartered a special train to that city for himself. Arriving on June 12 in time for breakfast, he took a room in a hotel and personally lettered a sign, "Governor's Office," which he affixed to the door. The election ballots were still being counted when Oklahomans learned that their state capital had been moved overnight. Although the vote was decisive—3 to 1 for Oklahoma City over Guthrie, with Shawnee running a distant third—businessmen and promoters at Guthrie were shocked and dismayed at the turn of events. They contested the election in the courts and delayed movement of all state governmental offices for several months. When some of them physically tried to prevent the removal of the state records, Haskell called on the National Guard. Canton moved in with troops and maintained order during the transferal.[46]

The Democratic primaries were held in August 1910. Lee Cruce, a lawyer and banker from Ardmore, became the party's candidate for governor. His Republican opponent was J. W. McNeal of Sentinel. Canton worked especially hard for the election of the Democratic candidate that year, for McNeal was vice-president of the First National Bank of Sentinel and the bank's president was Alva J. Niles, former adjutant general. If McNeal was elected, there was little doubt that Niles would be reappointed and Canton would be out of a job. At the general election on November 8, Cruce won handily and became the second governor of Oklahoma.[47]

Lee Cruce was born on July 8, 1863, at Marion, Kentucky. He received legal training at Vanderbilt University and in the law offices of two older brothers, both attorneys, at Marion. He was admitted to the bar in 1888 and three years later joined his brothers at Ardmore in the Chickasaw Nation, where they engaged in banking and the law. In 1903 Cruce became president of the Ardmore National Bank. When he married the beautifully named Chickie LeFlore, a member of a prominent family in the Chickasaw and Choctaw affairs, he became an intermarried citizen of the Chickasaw Nation, a status that aided him in his political career.[48]

Governor Lee Cruce used General
Canton and the National Guard to
enforce Oklahoma laws. *Courtesy
Western History Collections,
University of Oklahoma.*

Long before the election results were known, Canton had opened a campaign to secure reappointment by the new governor. With Cruce he followed his usual strategy, ingratiating himself personally and soliciting endorsements from prominent friends. Even before Cruce took office on January 8, 1911, he was receiving messages lauding the incumbent adjutant general. Charles F. Colcord, Canton's old lawman pal who had become one of the state's wealthiest men when he struck oil in the famous Glenn Pool, wrote the new governor recommending Canton's reappointment. He said that Canton, with whom he had worked for many years, was "one of the bravest and best officers" he knew.[49]

Charles J. Wrightsman, another wealthy oilman, also urged Canton's reappointment. Wrightsman, former county attorney and U.S. commissioner at Pawnee, said he had known Canton intimately since 1894 and had worked closely with him when Pawnee and Payne Counties were "infested with the worst element of outlaws and desperate characters." Canton, "absolutely fearless," was largely responsible for "bringing to an end such reign of terror." His "personality, character and officership" were of the highest order. "No man has greater personal courage, and probably none now living is possessed of a vaster range of experience in dealing with the lawless elements of society than friend Canton." Wrightsman stressed Canton's loyalty to his friends and superiors and said that his reappointment would "gratify a host of his friends throughout the State." He added that he would not endorse Canton if he "believed that [Canton] had in his veins any of the virus of Haskellism or the bombast of military dress parade."[50]

Thomas H. Doyle, judge of the Criminal Court of Appeals, wrote that he had known Canton for eighteen years. Canton had "proved himself to be in every respect a first class official." Doyle added: "His efficiency and splendid record in his present position is unquestioned. He has always been an active working democrat, and is thoroughly identified with the democratic party in this part of the State, and in my opinion has the unanimous endorsement of his party here. I know he is honorable, upright, conscientious, capable, and well worthy of the trust imposed by this position. In fact I do not believe a better man could be found for the position than General Canton." Doyle reminded Cruce that during the campaign, Canton had been "active and untiring in his labors" on behalf of the governor-elect. "It is my sincere hope and wish that you will find it agreeable to appoint General Canton to his present position," he said.[51]

After the embarrassing altercation between Governor Haskell and his adjutant general, Cruce had doubts regarding Canton's stability and sobriety. He allowed Canton to continue with official duties, but he made no announcement of an appointment for six months. It was a difficult period for Canton, who wanted the reappointment very badly and tried to assure the new governor there would be no repetition of the notorious "band incident." When Cruce finally announced the reappointment in June, Canton wrote an obsequious letter of acceptance and appreciation:

> I have the honor to acknowledge receipt of my commission as Adjutant General of the State.
>
> I want to thank you sincerely for the honor you have conferred upon me, and to assure you I shall do everything in my power to prove to you that I am worthy of the trust and confidence that you have placed in me.
>
> I have held a number of honorable positions in the past, but I have never had a commission tendered me before that I have appreciated so thoroughly and felt so proud of as I do of this one. My short acquaintance with you has been of the most pleasant nature, and when in consultation with you I feel that I am talking to a friend and an honorable, conscientious man. It will be a pleasure to me, and I assure you that I consider it an honor to be in a position where I can assist you to make a success of your administration.[52]

Cruce was an activist governor with strong views on law enforcement. Having no state police force at his command, he frequently called on Canton to enforce the statutes and maintain order during his administration. An early opportunity was presented by the Oklahoma City streetcar strike in the spring of 1911. When nonunion conductors were dragged from their cars and beaten by strikers, indignant businessmen led by Charley Colcord asked the governor to intervene. Cruce said that he could not call out the Guard unless the local authorities had exhausted all means to bring order, but the governor sent Canton to see if he could help. Colcord told his old friend that the mayor and the sheriff could not or would not bring the situation under control, so he wanted to organize an armed force from city clubs to do the job. "Frank Canton told me to go ahead," Colcord said, "that I could handle it, and he would be within three feet of me all the way through. . . . And he stuck to his word—he was with me continuously through the whole affair."[53] Cruce authorized Canton to activate three companies of militia and have them on alert, but they were never called in. Colcord and his civilians calmed the situation and got the streetcars running.[54]

Governor Cruce wanted stricter enforcement of laws concerning prohibition, gambling, prizefighting, and breaking of the Sabbath, enforcement that he felt had been neglected during the Haskell regime. Statewide prohibition had been adopted as an amendment to the new constitution in the election of 1907; the other offenses were carryovers from Oklahoma Territory legislation. Although his attorney general, Charles West, advised that the National Guard should be employed only to enforce civil law when assistance was requested by local officials or when there was reason to believe local officers were unwilling or unable to enforce the law, Governor Cruce called out the troops on many occasions during his term, and Adjutant General Canton was kept busy.[55]

At least four times Cruce resorted to the Guard to suppress prizefighting. The first was on the Fourth of July, 1911, when a bout was scheduled between two aspirants for Jack Johnson's heavyweight title. Broadsides were distributed throughout the state announcing the fight, between Carl Morris and Jim Flynn, to be held near Tulsa. The match drew national attention, and sportsmen converged on the area. Tulsa boosters and businessmen welcomed the event, but church leaders protested to the governor. On July 3 Cruce wrote Canton, ordering him to move "in secrecy" and see that the fight did "not occur in Tulsa or any other portion of Oklahoma." Canton did his job well. He went to Tulsa, met in private with the promoters, and persuaded them to cancel their plans. The fight never took place in Oklahoma.[56]

Acting on the governor's orders in February 1913, the adjutant general led a squad of guardsmen into the Oklahoma City auditorium to prevent a prizefight. The crowd, which included several members of the state legislature, were awaiting the start of the bout when Canton marched in and stationed his troops around the ring. He climbed through the ropes and addressed the crowd. "This contest tonight positively cannot take place," he said. The crowd filed out quietly.[57]

A month later Canton and ten guardsmen appeared at Sapulpa, where a fight was scheduled between Carl Morris and Con Comiskey. This time Canton tried a different approach. He did not absolutely ban the match but announced that if either of the contestants "really knew anything scientific about the boxing game, they would be given a chance to show it. On the other hand, if their knowledge of the game extended only to those rudiments which deal with pummeling, it would be best for them not to start at all." The two battlers agreed to present a "scientific boxing exhibition," but within a minute and a half of the first bell, Comiskey was on the floor with two teeth missing. As Canton entered the ring to stop the fight, Morris departed from the other side. "The general had two or three of those present examine Comiskey and it was found that in addition to the two teeth, he had lost some blood. The fight was then declared off. The general ordered the crowd to disperse, which they did, very orderly." Carl Morris did not reappear "until after General Canton left town."[58]

On another occasion, Canton was ordered to Tulsa to prevent the Shaughnessy-Roman prizefight. The promoters had boasted that nothing would stop the bout, but when they learned that Canton had called out Company A of the National Guard and had issued each of his militiamen forty rounds of ammunition, they quickly canceled the fight.[59]

Responding to complaints of local ministers, Cruce even called on Canton to stop a "roping contest" at McAlester in October 1914. The rodeo had been going on for three days when Canton arrived. Seven men were already injured, and nine steers were so badly hurt that three of them had to be killed. When the clergymen learned that the promoters planned to extend the affair through Sunday, they protested that it would be "an open violation of the Sabbath." Canton's arrival brought a sudden end to the "roping contest."[60]

The most dramatic incident involving Cruce's use of the Oklahoma National Guard to suppress what was considered sinful behavior occurred in April 1914 at Tulsa. Although the governor had previously announced that he would use all force at his disposal, including troops, to prevent racetrack gambling in the state, horse-racing promoters at Tulsa led by R. J. Allison went ahead with plans for a spring racetrack event complete with betting. Cruce notified Judge L. M. Poe of Tulsa to be prepared for legal action and on April 11 sent Canton to the scene with orders to pressure the civil authorities to stop the proceedings. "After two days conference with the County Attorney, Sheriff and other officers, I gave it up," Canton said. "District Judge L.M. Poe was the only officer in the city who tried to enforce the law, but he was alone and powerless. The County Attorney left Tulsa; the city was full of gamblers and race horses from Juarez, Mexico, Arizona,

General Canton with his troops at the Tulsa Fairgrounds to prevent horse races. A group of racing touts are gathered behind him. *Courtesy American Heritage Center, University of Wyoming.*

Jamestown, Va. and other points. I saw that they were fully determined to openly defy the governor and the laws of the State."[61]

Races were held on Monday, April 13, and, after observing the open betting, Canton requested Judge Poe to issue an injunction to stop the racing. Allison and his partners ignored the court order and proceeded with their Tuesday races. Canton wired Cruce: "Injunction issued against Tulsa County Fair association and Tulsa Jockey club yesterday. Hand bookmaking and open gambling on the races was carried on today and the betting was heavier than yesterday except that the books were made from hand instead of booths. Betting both in grandstand and pit below. In my opinion only method to prevent open and defiant violations as here indicated is to place Tulsa fair grounds under martial law and place militia in control to see that the law is not violated."[62]

The governor immediately wired Canton to stop the gambling and authorized use of whatever militia forces Canton deemed necessary to carry out this order. "Gamblers and law violators shall not long flaunt their vice in the face of the decent citizenship of Oklahoma," he said, describing the issue as "a contest between order and anarchy, between good and evil." Cruce followed his wire with a written executive order declaring the Tulsa fairgrounds under martial law. "It was to meet just such exigencies as this that the state militia was organized," he said, "and so long as it is used to protect society and enforce the law, it should have and will have the support and encouragement of every law-abiding citizen in the state."[63]

Company A of the National Guard was headquartered at Tulsa, but Canton, not wanting to get local citizen-soldiers involved in the squabble, did not call this unit up. He brought in Company E from Pawnee and Company B from Chandler by train and placed them under the direct command of Major Winfield Scott. The combined force of one hundred men pitched camp during the night in the center of the fairgrounds. When the racing enthusiasts and gamblers assembled at the track on Wednesday, Canton read the governor's proclamation. "The races are over," he declared.[64]

R. J. Allison appeared with an order issued by Superior Court Judge M. A. Breakenridge restraining Canton from using troops to stop the races. General Canton brushed it aside. "I pay no attention to court orders," he said, "Governor Cruce is my commander." Canton's troops cleared the stands of all spectators except reporters and track employees. Allison, stubborn to the last, sent five horses to the post for the first race. When the horses broke out of the gate, a squad of militiamen lined up along the fence fired a volley over the heads of the jockeys. Canton announced that if another race started, his orders were to "shoot to kill." That concluded the race meet at Tulsa.[65]

"This is not a Fair," wrote Guard Captain Gus Hadwiger to a newspaper the next day, "but simply a congregation of gamblers and toughs who seem to be working under the orders of one J.B. Allison [ ], who, I am informed, is a man of questionable character and who has been repeatedly prosecuted for violation of the liquor law in this state."[66]

Promoter Allison complained bitterly in the papers about the high-handed treatment he and his friends had received. He hinted that blood would be shed if the races were not allowed to continue. Wild rumors spread that the sheriff would lead five hundred deputies to the track the next day to confront the militia and force continuation of the races, but the reports were unfounded.[67] Allison did challenge the governor in the courts, however. He brought suit against Governor Cruce, General Canton, and Major Scott, claiming damages of $39,290. At a trial held in Oklahoma City in June 1915, a jury exonerated the defendants and assessed court costs against the plaintiff.[68]

During the Cruce administration Canton and the Guard were involved in several serious conflicts over county jurisdiction. The first was a battle over short-lived Swanson County. Born on August 13, 1910, when Governor Haskell issued a proclamation that its inhabitants had met the requirements for a new county, Swanson died on June 27, 1911, when the state supreme court ruled in favor of adjoining Kiowa and Comanche Counties, which had contested its creation.

While the legal fight raged, a court-appointed receiver attempted to remove the records from Snyder, the Swanson County seat, but was repulsed by angry citizens. A judge authorized the Kiowa County sheriff to arrest the Snyder officials for contempt of court, but after an incursion into Swanson the sheriff reported, "There couldn't be enough men mustered in Kiowa County to take the officials in custody [and] a strong army would be necessary to enforce the order of the court."[69] County Attorney J. A. Fain of Comanche County went to the capital to seek assistance. He described the situation in Swanson County as near-anarchy and pleaded for state militia. Governor Cruce refused the request for troops but sent General Canton to investigate. After talking with the Swanson County officials, Canton reported that there was no threat of anarchy and that the residents would abide by the decision of the court in the suit still pending. The adjutant general's visit had a calming effect, but two years passed and further threats of military intervention were required before the dissolution of Swanson County was completed and the contested districts were assimilated by Kiowa and Comanche Counties.[70]

The Delaware County fight of 1912 also threatened to burst into warfare. At the time of statehood in 1907, the town of Grove, in extreme northern Delaware County, was declared the county seat, but residents to the south agitated for a more central location. Three years later ten acres almost in the county's exact geographical center were deeded to the county by Jay Washbourne. Boosters circulated a petition to move the county seat to Jay, a new town named after the benefactor, and built a two-story courthouse on the site. The petition received the requisite number of signatures, and voters approved the move at an election. The commissioners at Grove refused to release the county records, however, charging that the petition was fraudulent and that the hastily constructed Jay courthouse was unsafe. The quarrel went to the state supreme court, which ruled in favor of Jay. On December 11, 1911, Governor Cruce proclaimed Jay the seat of Delaware County, but the commissioners at Grove continued to defy the state government, securing a court order to prevent the transfer of the county records.

Meanwhile, Bill Creekmore, called by Canton "the King of the bootleggers in Oklahoma," quietly purchased 240 acres adjoining the Washbourne holdings and platted a town he called "New Jay."[71] He erected a large two-story concrete building and deeded it over to the county. The commissioners at Grove moved the county records into the new building and declared New Jay the county seat.[72] Governor Cruce, furious at the maneuver, issued orders to Canton on January 3, 1912, to go to Delaware County "at the earliest possible moment" and to enforce the designation of Jay as the county seat. He was directed to use military force only if "absolutely necessary."[73]

Canton alerted Company A at Tulsa to stand ready and, accompanied only by Sergeant Major H. A. Randall, went himself to the scene of trouble. He took the train to Afton, where he transferred to a mail hack for the twenty-mile ride to Grove, which he reached at noon on January 4. There he held a "spirited meeting" with the county officials. Although Canton threatened use of military force, the commissioners stubbornly refused to move the records. Sensing that the officials were looking for a face-saving "out," Canton suggested a compromise. He would move the records himself, but if anyone interfered, he would call in the Guard. The commissioners grudgingly agreed to this plan.[74]

Canton, Randall, and the commissioners climbed into a two-horse surrey and drove the twelve miles to Jay. Their appearance "caused some little stir" as the surrey passed through both Jay and New Jay. Canton noted that armed guards stood watch at each of the courthouses. "The sheriff of Delaware county has imported professional gun men from adjoining towns and some from out of the state to assist him," an Oklahoma newspaper reported. "These men, it is said, have been sent into Jay at the instance of the townsite promoters of the proposed New Jay."[75]

Canton and Randall took lodgings in a private home for the night. At about ten o'clock they heard gunfire and rushed out to find that some of the jittery courthouse guards had begun shooting blindly through the woods separating the two towns. The two forces were a half mile apart and no one was hit, but the rest of the night was tense, with both sides expecting an attack at any moment. During that long night the telephone lines were cut, and Canton had no way of calling the militia for assistance.[76]

In the midst of a sudden snowstorm the next morning Canton assembled a corps of Jay citizens to move the records. He found that they had some tough gunmen of their own. "It was a rather dramatic scene," a newspaper reported, "when Gen. Canton met the notorious Sam Boney, the Indian gun man [and] partisan of old Jay. . . . It was noticed that each looked straight into the eyes of the other. 'Sam,' said the general, 'I am glad to meet you. I have heard much about you and they tell me you are a bad Indian.' 'No,' said Boney, 'I am no bad Indian.'"[77]

With Canton at the head, the "old Jay" forces set out with wagons and teams to get the county records. When confronted by Sheriff Bud Thomason and his guards, Canton "took occasion to reprimand Sheriff Thomason for permitting his men to open fire on the evening before, and spoke as one having authority." Thomason stood aside, and the records were moved with no violence.[78]

Later that day Canton returned to Grove, where he received a telegram from Justice John B. Turner of the Oklahoma Supreme Court advising him that he was restrained from moving the Delaware County records. If he had already moved them, read the telegram, he was to move them back. Said Canton:

> I disregarded the order from the Supreme Court, returned to Oklahoma City and reported my tour of duty to the Governor. In a short time I was cited for contempt by the Supreme Court. I appeared before the court and answered to the charge. My answer was: That the Supreme Court had no jurisdiction over me in this case. I claimed that if they wanted to get service on me, they should have served notice on the Governor, my Commander-in-Chief, and let him countermand his order to me, if he desired to do so, otherwise, as a Military Officer, I would have been liable for court martial and a dishonorable discharge for disobedience of orders of my Superior Officer. Judge Robert L. Williams wrote the opinion in this case and held that I was not in contempt of court.[79]

Canton's actions in the Delaware County dispute were widely acclaimed in papers throughout the state. "There is considerable credit due General Canton in advising with the two factions there and for his assistance in bringing about an amicable settlement of the trouble," one paper noted.[80] "This is not the first instance where General Canton's presence has avoided bloodshed and riot," said another. "In his official capacity he represents the strong arm of the law and does his duty and obeys orders without argument or delay."[81] Still another lauded him as a diplomat:

> If the state of Oklahoma should ever find occasion to establish a diplomatic service, Adjutant General Frank M. Canton has demonstrated his right to be placed at its head. Although his office is one of war his greatest achievements have been in the way of peace.
>
> His latest diplomatic triumph is the settlement of the difficulties at Jay, where both sides were reported to be oiling up their squirrel rifles for a real old-fashioned court house war. But Canton appears on the scene, says a few soothing words, and the trouble is all over.
>
> With Canton to settle all of the troubles which may arise in the state, there is no need to maintain a militia establishment in Oklahoma at all. Whenever the militia is demanded, the governor simply sends General Canton to the scene of war and his presence is as effective as a whole regiment of infantry, with a few Gatling guns thrown in for good measure.[82]

During the flap over Canton's defiance of the state supreme court, one paper reported, with tongue in cheek: "Rumor has it that if the Supreme

Governor Robert Williams, the third Oklahoma chief executive to appoint Canton adjutant general. *Courtesy Western History Collections, University of Oklahoma.*

Court of this state sees fit to reprimand Adjutant General Canton for following Governor Lee Cruce's instructions in the Jay county seat case, that arrangements have been made whereby the various members of that august body will draw straws to see who delivers such reprimand in person. The task will be such an agreeable one, on account of General Canton's affability, that they all seek the honor."[83]

While praise was being heaped on the head of Canton, Governor Lee Cruce was having serious political problems. In the legislative race of 1912 many of Cruce's political opponents were elected, resulting in a hostile House of Representatives. Claiming a mandate to "clean house," that body in 1913 embarked on a wide-ranging investigation of Cruce appointees and departments. Adjutant General Canton was one of the few officials and the National Guard one of the few state institutions spared. Three impeachments came out of these investigations. There were other near-misses, including the governor, who escaped impeachment by a single committee vote.[84]

Cruce did not seek a second term in 1914, and the race for the Democratic candidate for governor attracted many contestants, including Al Jennings, a former outlaw and convict. Robert L. Williams, the man who wrote the decision holding that Canton was not in contempt of court in the Jay case, resigned as chief justice of the Oklahoma Supreme Court to enter the campaign. Williams won in a close primary election, and in the November balloting he was elected with less than 40 percent of the votes in a three-way race. He took office on January 11, 1915.[85]

Robert Lee Williams was an Alabaman, born near Brundidge on December 20, 1868. He studied for the ministry, was licensed as a Methodist preacher, and rode the religious circuit in Texas for two years. He later taught school and studied law. He followed the legal profession in Oklahoma and Indian Territories after the land openings. The prominence he gained from his leadership at the constitutional convention of 1906 led to a seat on the state supreme court. Although he had never attended law school, he was elected twice to the highest judicial office in the state.[86]

Two days before he turned over the reins of government to Williams, Lee Cruce wrote Canton, thanking him for his help over the previous four years:

> I would feel that I had failed miserably as Governor of this State if I did not give to you some lasting expression of my appreciation of your friendship, your loyalty and your splendid work. I have met many men in my time in many walks of life, but I never found one yet who is truer to his friend than you are. Your efforts to uphold my hands have been commendable and have met with uniform success.
>
> I thank you for it all, and now as the administration closes, and we each go our separate way, I shall remember with gratitude the splendid aid you have been to me, and I trust that many years of useful service to the people may be vouchsafed to you by that kindly Providence who over-rules and guides us all.[87]

Some observers believed Canton, now sixty-six, would retire at the end of Cruce's term and go his "separate way" as Cruce hinted in his letter. Some newspapers jumped to that conclusion; the *St. Louis Republican* in a December 12, 1914, dispatch from Fairfax, Oklahoma, said that the adjutant general was "about to retire from active public life and return to his home in the now civilized Osage country."[88]

Canton, however, was not yet ready to walk away from the job he so dearly loved. As was his custom, he again carried on a private campaign for office, soliciting friends to write the new governor urging his reappointment. Typical was a letter from C. R. Gilmore to Governor-Elect Williams:

> You will shortly be called upon to name an Adjutant General and in this connection I wish to appeal to you as a citizen of the State and officer of the Guard to appoint a man of experience and integrity. Such I consider General F.M. Canton. For the last six years we have been associated [and] he has not wavered in performing the mission entrusted to his care. I wish particularly to refer to our association at two prize fights and a race meet. . . . I know that great inducements were offered General Canton to permit the Comiskey-Morris fight to proceed and to permit another fight at Sapulpa to begin against

the orders of the Governor. Baser considerations were offered him, tempting an appetite he has manfully lived down, but without effect. Also his actions at the Tulsa race meet last spring were above reproach and strictly in keeping with his line of duty as I saw it. Under very trying circumstances, when it seemed certain human life would be lost, by his firmness and bravery he cleared the grand-stands and grounds of a large crowd of people—many vicious—without a serious personal encounter.[89]

Canton received his reappointment and in January 1915 began his eighth year as adjutant general under his third governor. The year was to bring five diverse emergencies requiring the use of the National Guard. The first of these was reminiscent of Oklahoma's former outlaw days. On March 27 seven horsemen rode into the town of Stroud and held up two banks simultaneously. Aroused citizens grabbed guns and fought the outlaws. Two bandits were hit and captured as the others galloped out of town. One of the wounded robbers turned out to be the leader, Henry Starr, a criminal who had plagued Oklahoma since the early 1890s. Sheriff George Arnold and County Attorney Streeter Speakman of Lincoln County rushed to Stroud and organized posses to chase the robbers. In response to Speakman's telephone request for militia to help in the search, Canton issued verbal authorization to Captain Harry B. Gilstrap of Company B at Chandler. Within twenty minutes Gilstrap and ten militiamen, armed with rifles and several hundred rounds of ammunition, entrained for Stroud. There they joined sheriff's deputies in a sweep of the surrounding countryside. Two days later they returned, exhausted and empty-handed.[90] "The effort we put forth was unsuccessful, but we have the satisfaction of knowing that we did all we could do and without the part taken by members of the militia, the pursuit would have been far less effective," Gilstrap reported to Canton, adding that he believed the robbers escaped into "the jungles of Creek country."[91]

Canton called out Guard units the following month to protect spectators at an Oklahoma City automobile race. Fearing that death or injury to race fans might result from the "daredevil driving," Major Winfield Scott led 8 officers and 115 enlisted men to the track, where thousands had congregated. Guardsmen kept spectators twenty feet back from the racing lanes and maintained order in the stands. The event went off smoothly.[92]

Labor troubles at Enid claimed the Guard's attention in May. The Industrial Workers of the World (IWW) labor union targeted farm workers in the Oklahoma wheat country that spring, and agitation by its organizers led to a series of disturbances and the arrest of four IWW members. On May 31 angry mobs formed on the streets of Enid, demanding the release of the men. A nervous Sheriff E. Hume of Garfield County wired Canton for assistance. Canton activated Company K at Enid under Company Commander Ralph R. Jarboe, who issued arms and ammunition to his three officers and twenty-nine enlisted men and marched them to the aid of the sheriff. After much discussion, a compromise was reached between the mob leaders and the authorities: the four union organizers would be released on their promise to leave town and the mob would disperse peaceably. The Guard's prompt response had again defused a potentially explosive situation and prevented bloodshed.[93]

A prizefight promotion at Tulsa in the fall of 1915 involved the Guard in a far less dangerous operation. Old warhorse Carl Morris was matched against Tony Ross for a bout on October 1. Clergymen again called on the state to prevent what they viewed as an exhibition of barbarism. Canton no longer involving himself personally in these matters, since straitlaced Lee Cruce, unbending enforcer of the state's laws, was no longer his boss. Canton delegated Lieutenant Albert R. Harris to handle it. "The fight was conducted in a very orderly manner," Harris reported, "until the fourth round when Carl Morris knocked down Tony Ross with a foul blow. Whereupon the referee stopped the fight without instruction from me."[94]

When a policeman was killed in Muskogee on Christmas Day and officers arrested and charged two black men with the crime, racial tensions threatened to explode. Angry white mobs formed outside the jail, and local officials called for the militia. On Canton's order, Captain J. L. DeGroot hurried to the jail with thirteen members of Company F. They stood on the steps of the building with loaded rifles at the ready, facing a crowd of more than a thousand. DeGroot requested fire trucks, but when they arrived, the firemen refused to turn their hoses on the crowd. Mob members succeeded in smashing a jail side door from its hinges before they were repelled at gunpoint. Tensions were heightened even further when about seventy-five armed black men attempted to reach the jail by way of an alley but were driven back by guardsmen. Two hardware stores were broken into and weapons and ammunition stolen. Additional militiamen continued to arrive from outlying districts to reinforce the guardians of the jail. At about midnight, guards slipped the two prisoners into an automobile at the rear of the jail and sped out of town. But racial tensions remained high, and rioting was feared. Adjutant General Canton himself showed up the next day to take personal command of the troops, which remained in Muskogee for two days, until passions cooled.[95]

The year 1916 was momentous for Frank Canton and the Oklahoma National Guard. Although President Woodrow Wilson campaigned for reelection that year with the slogan "He Kept Us Out of War," it became increasingly apparent in Washington that the United States would soon be drawn into the European conflict, then in its third year. The nation's military forces had to be modernized and expanded. Military men advocated the mobilization of the existing National Guard units of the various states as a stopgap measure while the U.S. Army was being strengthened.

A stimulus to this strategy was provided on March 9, 1916, when the forces of a Mexican bandit and revolutionary named Francisco ("Pancho") Villa crossed the border and attacked the American town of Columbus, New Mexico. Congress quickly enacted the National Defense Act of 1916, which authorized expanded funding for the National Guard and greater federal control over the units.

With the direction the military arm of the state was taking, Governor Williams saw no role for an anachronism like Frank Canton. He promoted Canton to major general and asked for his resignation, to become effective July 1. Canton accepted the decision gracefully. He realized that the Oklahoma National Guard was about to be federalized and would come under the command of career military men. Without any military experience or training, he had for nine years headed the state's military force, improved its capability, and employed it to the satisfaction of three governors. But the governors were civilians, with no more military background than he possessed. U.S. Army brass would be something else entirely. What he had accomplished was remarkable, but Canton knew it was time to move on.

Fast-moving events made Canton's last month in office hectic. On June 3 the National Defense Act was passed by Congress and signed into law by President Wilson. Only sixteen days later Wilson called the entire National Guard of the United States into federal service. The Oklahoma Guard was ordered to mobilize quickly for deployment to the Mexican border in support of General John J. Pershing's punitive expedition against Pancho Villa.

Directed to prepare a central mobilization site, Canton arranged with Oklahoma City officials for use of the state fairgrounds. Men from around the state began assembling at what was called "Camp Bob Williams." The regular army approved the use of the fairgrounds as a temporary measure but urged the establishment of a permanent mobilization camp. Winfield Scott, now a lieutenant colonel, selected a site near McAlester. Before Canton could move, Secretary of War Newton D. Baker ordered him to transfer the Guard to the old Camp Frank Canton training grounds at Chandler. But a team of army inspectors, touring that location, found hogpens on the rifle ranges and privies close to the water supply. They declared it unsuitable and countermanded the order. Canton, confused and angered by the conflicting directives, ordered mobilization plans suspended until the regular army made

Canton, just before retirement as adjutant general. *Courtesy Western History Collections,
University of Oklahoma.*

up its collective mind. The Guard was eventually mustered at Fort Sill, the
logical choice from the beginning. There Colonel Roy Hoffman attempted
to whip the unit into shape during a few weeks of intensive drill.

On July 1, 1916, Frank Canton retired. Nineteen days later the Oklahoma National Guard left for Texas and its first operation as a unit of the
U.S. Army.[96]

Chapter 13

The Legend

"Canton is extremely modest and silent and shuns notoriety through the press and his deeds and battles would never become known were it left for him to do the telling."

Newspaper clipping in Canton scrapbook

The Cantons had moved to Oklahoma City from Guthrie when the capital was changed in 1910. After Frank's retirement they moved in with their daughter, Ruby, now thirty years old, unmarried, and living alone in a modest home at 400 East 4th Street in Edmond.

After graduation from Buffalo High School in 1903, Ruby had spent a year at the Chicago College of Music studying under the world renowned Swiss composer Rudolf Ganz. Rejoining her parents in Oklahoma, she was offered a position as head of the music department at Oklahoma A&M College but chose to continue her education, majoring in library science. In July 1908 Governor Haskell appointed her librarian at Central Normal School (later Central State Teachers College) at Edmond, a position she held for the next two decades. She was reportedly the first person to teach library science in Oklahoma. She continued advanced studies in later years at the University of Chicago, Columbia University, the University of Pittsburgh, and Carnegie Tech.[1]

Despite the prominence of his position as adjutant general of the state—the celebrity, the fine uniforms, the travel, the attendance at functions of national importance, and the opportunity to socialize with presidents and governors—Frank Canton had not benefited financially from his years in the office. The job was poorly paid, and there was no pension.[2] Still needing an income, he went back to work for the Cattle Raisers Association of Texas.

In 1917 he also took a brief shot at the oil business, then in its ascendancy in Oklahoma. Hoping to trade on the prestige of his name, a group of oil field developers, incorporated as the Wyandotte Oil Company, made him a vice-president. There were glowing newspaper accounts that the company's exploratory wells on leased land near Tulsa were successful and that Canton was prospering. Said one: "It is hardly to be expected that General Canton would be connected with the losing end of any proposition he tackled and his present business shows conclusively that he has added another 'notch to his gun.'"[3] Another paper concluded, "General Canton's latter years are being recompensed in fitting fashion."[4] But the oil venture was not the success news accounts suggested. Canton was soon out of the business, with little financial gain.

At the age of sixty-seven, he was still vigorous. In addition to work for the cattlemen's association and oil speculation, he found time and energy for what he viewed as a vital patriotic pursuit. In 1917 poor tenant farmers in eastern Oklahoma, led by socialists and anarchists, mounted an uprising against the newly passed conscription law in what became known as the "Green Corn Rebellion." On August 3 they were routed by a "brush patrol" of about seventy well-armed citizen patriots on the banks of the Canadian River. Canton hurried to the scene to assist in the arrest of some 450 antiwar militants during the following week. Of the protesters, 184 were subsequently indicted, and about 75 received prison terms.[5] Frank Lake, now in the real estate business in Sequoyah County, wrote Canton that month, saying he was sorry he had not joined him in the roundup of draft resisters. "I have no patience, whatever, with [this] class of citizenship," said Lake. "Nothing short of the firing squad should be considered, and the sooner they are disposed of, the better it will be for the country."[6]

He was also in attendance when the Cattle Raisers Association of Texas held its forty-first annual convention at Fort Worth in 1917. At the closing session, all those who had been present at the first meeting of the association at Graham, Texas, on February 15, 1877, were asked to come forward and take seats of honor on the stage. Nine elderly men, including some of the most successful and respected cattlemen of Texas, responded. One of the nine was Frank Canton, who accepted the applause of the audience and had his picture taken with the pioneer cattlemen after the meeting.[7]

This was probably the low point of Canton's dissimulation of his life. He never attended that initial cattlemen's meeting in Graham. While those early ranchers were meeting in February 1877 to discuss how to deal with the rampant outlawry plaguing the district, Joe Horner, one of the outlaws, was in jail awaiting trial for bank robbery. Forty years later that same man, now calling himself Frank Canton, had the effrontery to pose with the pioneers and accept the approbation of the membership. How many of those old-timers were aware of Canton's history and remembered him as the outlaw

Pioneer Texas cattlemen meeting in Fort Worth in 1917. Left to right: W.
B. Slaughter, Burk Burnett, D. B. Gardner, Frank Canton, J. H. Graham,
and L. T. Clark. Only Canton did not belong in this picture. *Courtesy
Texas and Southwestern Cattle Raisers Foundation.*

Joe Horner is not known, but Burk Burnett, another of the nine on stage,
certainly knew that Canton did not belong with the others.

Canton was not a member of the association in 1917, nor had he ever
been, but he was welcomed to association functions and was provided a job
as field inspector in Oklahoma. Two years later, at the annual meeting in
Dallas, the association passed a resolution honoring Inspectors Canton, Eli
Moore, and T. J. Poston and made them honorary members for life.[8]

"Despite his years, Canton is apparently as active and vigorous as ever," a
Sapulpa paper reported in noting Inspector Canton's appearance in town to
assist in the prosecution of suspected cattle thief Floyd Katon. "Straight as
an arrow he walked into the court room this morning wearing his army
overcoat."[9]

"This work isn't like that of the old days," Canton was quoted in another
newspaper article, several years later. "I don't go to the hills and the sticks,
the caves and the canyons and underbrush like I did as a young man. My
duties are to assist the county attorney in prosecutions after our field men
and sheriffs have rounded up the men charged with cattle stealing." The
article went on to extol Canton, "as courageous a man thirty years ago as

Frank Canton, the legend. *Courtesy Jack DeMattos.*

ever rode the plains, [whose] intuition, perception and judgment were not excelled by any other law enforcer of the West." Desperadoes felt his "uncanny power" in Wyoming, Montana, New Mexico, Colorado, Oklahoma, and in Texas, where "he taught the arts of man-catching" to the Rangers. "And now he is old and never rides a horse any more or straps a revolver on his hip. But the stern look of the unafraid frontiersman is still on his face. Unlike the commonality of old men, he lives in the present. Much of the past he was glad to forget."[10]

Not the least of the many errors in this story was the suggestion that Canton wanted to forget the past. On the contrary, he was working very hard to remember and record his experiences. He had long believed that the history of his life should be preserved, that the adventures he had experienced would fascinate younger Americans. Seeing the growing popularity of western novels and motion pictures in the years following the turn of the century, he hoped that perhaps his life story had commercial value as well. Long before his retirement as adjutant general, he had begun work on an autobiography.

Evidence of that work had appeared a dozen years before. The July 6, 1904, issue of *Breeders Gazette,* a western cattlemen's publication, contained an article entitled "Gratitude Twenty Dollars Bought: A True Story of the Capture of a Famous Cattle Thief." It concerned the capture of Teton Jackson and was ostensibly written by "G. B. Gooddell," a Wyoming cattleman, about his "old friend," identified only as "Frank C." However, Gorham B. Goodell, a member of the Wyoming Stock Growers Association and a longtime friend of Canton's, probably did not author the piece. More likely it was written by Canton himself and published under the misspelled name of "Gooddell."[11] After his retirement Canton submitted the article to the *Cattleman*, a monthly magazine of the Texas and Southwestern Cattle Raisers Association, and it appeared in the issue of March 1917, without reference to a previous publication. The article was incorporated almost entirely word for word, with a change from third to first person, in Canton's autobiography.[12]

In 1906 a story entitled "The Capture of Samuel and Beaver: A Tale of the Arapahoes" appeared in *Breeders Gazette*, and this time the author was given as F. M. Canton.[13] The piece also found its way into the pages of the *Cattleman* in 1918.[14] With minor revisions, it eventually became an entire chapter in Canton's autobiography.[15]

Sometime after these initial attempts at autobiography—the year 1908 has been suggested—Canton began to write his story in full, or at least as fully as he ever intended to write it.[16] He wrote with soft pencil in a series of school tablets over a long period of time. His deteriorating penmanship is mute testimony to his advancing years and the arthritis that gnarled his fingers. The title page read:

MEMORIES OF THE BORDER
By General Frank M. Canton
Adjutant General, Oklahoma National Guard
Cowboy, Ranger, Sheriff and Marshall [sic]

On page one he promised, "What I shall write in this life story will be the plain uncolored truth." Much of what he wrote was true, of course, but not all of it was plain, and whitewash colored large sections.[17]

Even as he penned his life story, Canton, with typical duplicity, denied doing so. "I have been asked a great many times by different writers to allow them to write a history of my life," he said in a 1913 letter, "but I have always refused . . . , altho I have no doubt that I could write a true history of my life which would be very interesting reading to the public, and especially to Western men of my age who would remember a great many incidents that I have been thru, but I don't care enough for notoriety for that sort of thing."[18]

As he labored over his composition, he contacted friends he thought might help him in the marketing of the work. Rex Beach, who had become a successful author, immediately came to mind. In January 1910 he wrote Beach in New York, asking if Beach was indeed the man Canton had known in the Arctic. "Yes, I am the man wanted," Beach answered in May. "I am the Rex Beach who wintered with you at Rampart City, Alaska, and I have often thought of the trips we made together and of the rich claims we staked together (almost)."[19] The two maintained a sporadic correspondence for the remainder of Canton's life.

In early 1915 Canton told Beach of his writing efforts and suggested the author might want to complete the book on Canton's life. "I am much interested in your letter . . . regarding the writing of a book of your experiences and motion pictures made therefrom," Beach answered. He had never written biography, he said, because fiction was easier and more profitable. In addition, magazine contracts had him "bound hand and foot." There were "lots of men who could and would" write down Canton's "stories," but "biographical books do not sell well." He encouraged Canton to explore the motion picture possibility. "I believe you could make good money from a motion picture of your experiences. . . . Neither you nor your friends should be called upon to finance such an enterprise, and I think some company can be found which will make the picture at its own expense, featuring the incidents in your career. In that event you would be relieved from all financial burdens and receive a royalty upon the selling price of the film. This is by all means the most satisfactory way to go about it." Beach said that he knew both Will Irwin, the writer, and Al Jennings, the Oklahoma outlaw, who had collaborated on a book and motion picture depicting Jennings's experiences and that he would try to find out how successful they were.[20] "I think," he said, "the proposition is a good one and will make some more inquiries among motion picture people about the possibilities in it."[21]

On February 13 Canton sent Beach copies of the two magazine articles he had published on his Wyoming experiences. Beach acknowledged receipt and said that he expected to see "Mr. Selig of the Selig Polyscope Company" soon. He would "take up the motion picture matter with him personally." Meanwhile he would try to find someone to handle Canton's literary material.[22]

Nothing came of Beach's efforts at that time, but his inquiries sparked the interest of a man named T. O. Warfield, a writer, promoter, and owner of the Warfield Advertising Company of Omaha, Nebraska. Warfield tried to involve Major Gordon W. Lillie of Pawnee, Oklahoma, in the Canton venture. Lillie was a western showman who, as "Pawnee Bill," had competed successfully against his rival, "Buffalo Bill" Cody, and was well-known nationally. Warfield wanted Pawnee Bill's name associated with any Canton project.

"I have been thinking very seriously about the Frank Canton story, which we discussed when I was in Pawnee," he wrote Lillie in April 1916. He doubted that Beach would or should author the book, since Beach had no experience with factual material, which was more difficult to write. "Rex Beach's name on such a story would be a big asset," he said, "but I believe that your name signed to it would get the thing over almost as easily. Rex Beach is known for fiction stuff only. You are known as one of the most and perhaps *the most* typical representative of the Wild West that is left. I do not mean to scorn Mr. Canton's experiences by that remark, but I do mean that you are more widely known as such than he. Your signature to the story would carry some weight of authority which I am pretty sure Mr. Beach's name would not, with all due respect to him." Warfield offered to ghostwrite the Canton story and market the finished product with Pawnee Bill as author. "I have been writing for a living most of my life," he said, "and I believe I can do justice to putting Mr. Canton's life into story form. Then, by signing your name to the story, I am quite certain that *The Saturday Evening Post* would take it on, provided the bloody part of it were softened to accord with the present public taste."[23]

His confidence in an acceptance by the *Saturday Evening Post* was based on two factors:

First, they created a bad impression through playing up Jennings as a hero, when as a matter of fact, Jennings is pretty widely known as a tin horn desperado; I think they should be willing from a sense of justice alone, if for no other reason, to give the side of the story that was in support of the law to offset the story of Jennings' outlawry which was played up as heroic and ridiculed the law and the officers.

Second, Hearst's Magazine is about to spring the autobiography of Colonel Cody, which I think will be largely faked up, for most of Cody's stories have been faked up; but nevertheless will be made intensely interesting.

It has been my observation that when one magazine starts a big serial like this, other magazines try to offset any prestige or public favor by running a competing class of stuff.

My idea would be to write the story so that it could be divided up into a series of at least twelve coordinated but different episodes for installment purposes, and then to have the story follow in book form. This is almost the invariable rule of the best sellers nowadays for publishers are able to size up the possibilities of a book from its reception in installment story form.

I do not know that there would be much to the moving picture end of it, because Wild West stuff is pretty dead nowadays and also the censorship on blood and thunder films is pretty strict.

Warfield proposed an equal division of proceeds from a magazine sale between Canton, Lillie, and himself. As for "by-product profits," Canton would hold reprint rights and receive all returns from book sales, whereas Lillie and Warfield would retain motion picture rights and divide any profits from that source. Warfield said that if Lillie and Canton agreed with his proposal, he would come to Oklahoma and spend the necessary time "to get the facts of the story and to acquire a sufficient sense of local color and atmosphere to properly carry it through."[24]

Nothing came of Warfield's proposal. The offer was ideal for Pawnee Bill— he stood to gain financially by contributing nothing other than his name— but Canton balked. Although he was willing to employ the services of a professional writer, he saw no reason to share any monetary rewards deriving from his life experiences with a third party simply for the use of a name. He kept the Warfield option open, however, and continued to correspond with the Omaha promoter. In December, Warfield reported that he had contacted *Hearst's Magazine* and that they were "at least sufficiently interested in the story to submit the proposition to all of their publications, [but] that on account of other material, they could not use it." Warfield still hoped to be of further service to Canton in getting his "remarkable story" published.[25]

Meanwhile, Canton tried other approaches. He wrote his old friend Charles Wrightsman, now living in New York City, the home of Rex Beach, and suggested that Wrightsman call on Beach and discuss the Canton book. Wrightsman turned Canton's letter over to Hy. R. Wohlers, a Broadway agent. Wohlers wrote Canton that he had approached *Collier's Weekly* regarding the book and that the editors wanted to see the manuscript.[26]

When Canton answered that he was still working on it, Wohlers responded: "You may be sure that I shall be glad to give attentive consideration to the matter of placing your autobiography after it has been prepared." Noting that "an advance copy [would] help considerably," he said he hoped "to cut away a lot of red tape," which was usual with magazines, so that it would "get early attention."[27]

During this period Canton was also corresponding with men out of his past. In the spring of 1913 he wrote Tom Irvine, the Montana sheriff who had helped lead him into a career in law enforcement. Irvine answered on March 12, filling Canton in on his life since they had worked together and asking for an account of Canton's experiences during those years.[28]

In a 1914 letter to his army friend Wilds Richardson, Canton said he was considering a trip to Alaska in the summer of the following year. Richardson, now a colonel stationed at Valdez, wrote that Canton would find a trip down the Yukon River very interesting. "The country [is] much changed from what it was when you and I spent two years together there," he said.[29] Canton never made the Alaskan trip.

In 1919 Canton published an article entitled "The Wyoming Cattle War" in the *Cattleman*.[30] It was drawn almost entirely from his manuscript and later appeared as chapter 4, "The Johnson County War," in his book. He later authored another piece, "Reminiscences of a Veteran Officer," in which he discussed early rustling activities in Texas and the formation of the cattlemen's association, repeating once again the falsehood that he had been one of the founders of the organization in 1877.[31]

Burk Burnett died at Fort Worth on June 26, 1922. Together with many other old-timers, Canton attended the funeral of the wealthy Texas pioneer. "Captain Burnett appreciated his friends more than any other man I know," he told a newsman. If he thought Burnett's appreciation might extend to a personal bequest, Canton was disappointed. Burnett left some money to relatives and longtime employees, but the bulk of his estate, estimated at between six and fifteen million dollars, went to Anne Burnett, a granddaughter.[32]

The following year two Texas cattle inspectors died in a sensational shooting reminiscent of the violent Old West. On Easter Sunday, April 1, 1923, Dave Allison and H. L. Roberson were shot and killed in Seminole, Texas, by two suspected rustlers the inspectors were investigating. Tom Ross and Milt Good, the gunmen, were quickly apprehended and indicted for murder. Outraged cattlemen's association members spared no expense in the prosecution of the killers. Canton had known Allison and Roberson well and also was acquainted with Tom Ross by reputation, for under his original name of Hill Loftis, Ross had ridden the outlaw trail with elements of the Doolin gang back in 1895.

The murdered men had long histories as lawmen in the Southwest and were widely known and respected. Canton was one of a horde of cowmen and law officers on hand at Lubbock for the month-long trial. Many friends of Good and Ross also were in attendance. The excitement gripping the town stirred the blood of old warhorse Frank Canton. Tad Moses, an officer of the cattlemen's association, said that Canton, suspecting he had only a few more years to live, remarked more than once that he wished the Ross and Good crowd would start something, since "he would not mind going out in a blaze of gun fire against such as they were."[33]

While the jury was out, Canton and stock inspector Ed Davis waited impatiently in the lobby of the Merrill Hotel. A man came in from the courthouse, took a seat beside Canton, and made a remark about the jury. Canton, who was becoming increasingly hard of hearing, spun around and asked, "What did you say about the jury?" As he did so, a pistol dropped from his right hip pocket.

The man glanced at the weapon. "You dropped your gun," he said. Canton cupped his ear with a hand. "What did you say about a jury?"

"You dropped your gun!" shouted the other man.

"That's all right, I have another one," Canton snapped. "Now, what did you say about a jury?"[34]

Ross and Good were convicted and sentenced to fifty-five and fifty-one years, respectively.[35] After the trial Canton rode partway home in an auto-

mobile with Tad Moses, who uncorked a bottle of tequila for the trip. "Stimu-
lated by the tequila, he talked incessantly about his past," Moses recalled.
He went into detail about his early days in Texas when he was Joe Horner.
Of course the shootout with the black soldiers at Jacksboro was prominent in
this recital. He admitted that he was "young and inclined to 'too 'em up' a
little" when he visited Jacksboro, but he added that the black troops killed
his partner and, aware of Horner's reputation as a troublemaker, "knew they
had to kill Horner or Horner would kill as many of them as he could." He
said he killed "two or three" soldiers before having his horse shot out from
under him in the street and eventually making his escape.[36]

The tequila worked its magic and Canton even talked about the Comanche
bank robbery, a subject he had assiduously avoided for many years. He spun
a tale of pure romance, worthy of an Owen Wister story. He had not been
with a gang at Comanche at all but had been alone, and he had gone there to
visit a girl. Although "the young lady bore a good reputation and was a
daughter of prominent people," Horner was intimate with her. One night he
climbed in the window of her room, intending to leave before daybreak, but
the sun was well up when the lovers awoke, and he stayed in the girl's room
until nightfall. It happened to be the day of the bank robbery. Horner was
arrested, could not prove an alibi because he would not implicate the girl,
and was convicted on circumstantial evidence.[37] Of course, had there been
any truth to this yarn, it would have made a wonderful chapter for Canton's
manuscript, but the outlaw career of Joe Horner never appeared in that work.

In 1925 Fred Sutton, an Oklahoma old-timer who had known legendary
western lawmen Bat Masterson, Bill Tilghman, and others, corresponded
with Canton. Sutton was gathering material for a book on the gunfighters
of the Old West and asked Canton about his experiences. On August 7 and 8
Canton answered with two long letters, laboriously scrawling the words in a
hand cramped with arthritis and rheumatism. He wrote of the Daltons and
the Dunns and of Tilghman and Thomas, giving his version of those controversial days of the 1890s. He had written an autobiography in which he had
"only touched on the 'high spots,'" he said. "But what I have written is
absolutely true, & can be verified by the records in each country where I
have served as an officer. . . . I feel that this life story should be published as
a matter of history, but I am not able financially to pay for the publication. A
great many writers have requested me to give them stories from my own
experience for their benefit, but none of them have offered to pay me anything for doing so. I can write a story of the old west that no other living
man can duplicate & tell the truth, for the men who could have done so, are
dead. I knew them all."[38]

Canton completed his manuscript, but he was never to see it published,

Canton's body lying in state in the Oklahoma capitol with an honor guard
and a large photograph of the general displayed. *Courtesy American
Heritage Center, University of Wyoming.*

nor did the motion picture possibilities ever work out. By 1925 he was aging
noticeably. He had lost almost all his hair and was now losing his hearing.
Perhaps as a lingering effect of the snow blindness he had suffered twenty
years before, his eyes were becoming very sensitive to light, and he had to
wear dark glasses most of the time.[39]

His infirmities forced his retirement as cattle inspector, and the Texas
cattlemen's association awarded him a small pension.[40] He and Annie continued to live very simply in the home of their daughter. Ruby, who never
married, helped support them on her librarian salary.

In the summer of 1925 Ruby vacationed with the Wilkersons at Buffalo
and wrote to "Papa Dear," giving news of the family and the town. "Uncle
Perce" was suffering from rheumatism and had sought relief at the hot
springs, just as Canton had many years before. "There is lots of talk here
about oil in the Billy Creek field just six miles south of our old ranch," she
said. "Everyone seems to think that oil is there altho no wells have been
brought in yet. The man who owns our place told me that the ranch is outside of what is called the oil structure. We went out past the ranch the other

night and it doesn't look very well—not kept up well. . . . Everyone here asks about you and would love to see you and Mama too. I am feeling fine. Worlds of love to you both."[41]

Canton became increasingly feeble. On September 1, 1927, he was confined to his bed, and a doctor was summoned. After examining the old man, Dr. S. N. Stone told Annie that Canton had cancer and his remaining days were few. On September 15 the little family quietly celebrated Canton's seventy-eighth birthday. Twelve days later he was dead.[42]

The body was taken to Oklahoma City on Wednesday, September 28. There, fitted out in the general's dress uniform, it lay in state in the capitol building on the morning of September 29. Removal to Fairlawn Cemetery was made at two o'clock in the afternoon, and Canton was interred with full Masonic and military rites. Active pallbearers were high-ranking officers of the Oklahoma National Guard: Major Charles B. Keller and Colonels Elta H. Jayne, R. S. McClain, Floyd J. Bolend, Earl Patterson, and William S. Key.[43]

Honorary pallbearers and funeral attendees included other members of the military and many high-ranking civilian state officials, past, current, and future, as well as frontier veterans who had known and worked with Canton in territorial days. Former Governor Lee Cruce was there, as were Graves Leeper, secretary of state; R. A. Sneed, state treasurer and later secretary of state; A. S. J. Shaw, state auditor and later candidate for governor; Carl Rice, chairman of the board of affairs; and Thomas H. Doyle, then serving as judge of the criminal court of appeals. Academia was represented by Professors J. B. Amos of the University of Oklahoma and Otto W. Jeffries of Edmond Teachers College. Oklahoma National Guard officers paying their respects included Adjutant General Charles Barrett, Colonel Colin Valentine, and Major F. B. Patterson. Among former frontier lawmen who had ridden with Canton in the old days were Charles F. Colcord, Wylie Haynes, and Buck Garrett. There were other Old West veterans: Zack Mulhall, pioneer rancher and showman; Fred Sutton, frontier old-timer and chronicler of western gunfighters; George W. Spencer, an Oklahoma boomer of 1889; Harry W. Clegern, an early-day real-estate promoter; and Dr. Curtiss Day, a pioneer physician. Canton's nephews Glenn and Clyde Burnett, the sons of Tillman and Minnie Belle (Horner) Burnett, came from Texas for the funeral.

The flag-draped coffin was carried to the grave site by the uniformed National Guard officers. Frederick Bailey delivered a Christian Scientist reading, followed by Miss Vivian Cooter, of the First Church Christ Scientist, who sang, accompanied by Mrs. E. L. Fulton. After the final Masonic rites, a firing squad from Company A of the 179th Infantry saluted the fallen gen-

Mourners at Canton's burial. *Courtesy American Heritage Center, University of Wyoming.*

Pallbearers with Canton's casket. *Courtesy American Heritage Center, University of Wyoming.*

eral with a rifle volley. The flag was then removed from the casket, folded in the time-honored solemn military style, and presented to Annie and Ruby.[44]

Canton was eulogized in the Oklahoma press. Editor A. D. Dailey doubted if, in "the history of the United States," there was "a more active, a more useful, a more colorful life, as a peace officer, than that of General Frank M. Canton," who worked with peace and diplomacy where possible but who "was a man of great determination and courage and a terror to outlaws" and who "did more to establish law and order in Oklahoma, in Jackson county [sic], Wyoming, and in Alaska, than any other man." Dailey added: "Nature endowed him with a kindly disposition, and no man could desire a better friend or companion. He was greatly beloved in Oklahoma . . . and I doubt if any man in this state had more friends than General Frank M. Canton.[45]

Another editor wrote, "The man who died at Edmond Tuesday was literally born to the role he filled with such success." During fifty years of service, he confronted dangers few men ever faced: "Canton knew exactly what to do and exactly how to do it. He thought straight, he saw straight, and hence was able to shoot straight. He was able to think straight because he knew nothing of the distracting influences of fear. Probably he died without ever knowing what fear really is. His nerves were as quiet as the finest tempered steel, and for that reason he could think of nothing but his target, see it clearly, and shoot directly into its heart. . . . The states that spread their acres from the Mississippi out towards the sunset owe a mighty debt to Frank Canton and his kind."[46]

The editor of the *Cattleman* said that Texas had produced "no more lovable a character" or more fearless or "conscientious champion of law and order than Frank M. Canton. If he ever knew fear, even his most intimate friends could see no trace of it. Throughout his eventful life as a cowboy, soldier, and frontier officer there was none of the swagger or overbearing disposition authority to wear a gun gives to many a man."[47]

Adjutant General Charles F. Barrett wrote that Canton "was a man of unusual personality and the central figure in many lurid and exciting incidents of early day and western frontier life. Without embellishment and freed from the record doubtful and chimerical exploits attributed to him by sensation mongers, his career was a most colorful and adventurous one." He was, said Barrett, "always on the side of the law and an inveterate foe" of the lawless. "He was the ideal frontier peace officer; tireless in pursuit, and personally brave and courageous to a fault. . . . General Canton was a firm and loyal friend, an implacable and fearless foe. He was a capable and upright officer and an efficient and worthy public servant, and if I were delegated to write his epitaph, I would put down in the language of that West of which he was a part: 'HERE LIES A MAN.'"[48]

The unpretentious gravestone of Frank M. Canton. *Author's collection.*

Afterword

"Uncle Joe [was] a brave, honorable and respectable citizen."
Mrs. R. L. Askew
"Too bad he didn't hang."
Anonymous Buffalo reader

Annie Canton had barely adjusted to the death of her husband of more than four decades when tragedy struck again. The summer after Canton's death, Ruby became very ill, and doctors found a malignancy. Annie took her daughter to a St. Louis hospital for treatment, but Ruby's condition worsened rapidly. On July 18, 1928, she died at the age of forty-two. Annie brought the body back to Oklahoma and buried it beside the grave of Frank.

Ruby had been well liked and highly respected at Central State College, where she had worked for twenty years. A special book collection at the college was designated the Ruby Canton Library, and a stained-glass window was dedicated to her memory in the chapel of the school.[1]

Alone now in the Edmond home, Annie pored over her husband's handwritten manuscript and the clippings and memorabilia of his eventful career. There was a wealth of material about his later life, especially his career as adjutant general, but little concerning his early years. Knowing next to nothing of his life as Joe Horner, she wrote three of his surviving siblings in Texas, asking for information. Two of Canton's sisters, eighty-year-old Mary Jane Sams and sixty-eight-year-old Minnie Belle Burnett, responded in December 1927, relating what they knew of the Horner family history. John Wesley Horner, at eighty-four, could not write a letter, but a daughter interviewed him and passed along his recollections.

Annie had a sense of history and was a member of the Oklahoma Historical Society. Knowing that her husband's remarkable story should be preserved for posterity, she contacted the University of Oklahoma at Norman and arranged to deposit his manuscript and papers in the newly formed Frank Phillips Collection at the university library.

Professor Edward Everett Dale, a native of Texas who in his youth had cowboyed in some of the same areas as had Canton a generation earlier, was head of the university history department and was custodian of the Frank Phillips Collection.[2] After reading the five thick tablets containing Canton's autobiography, he agreed that the story should be published. Dale had the manuscript typed, corrected the spelling and syntax, divided it into chapters, and incorporated the magazine articles Canton had previously published. He wrote a short preface describing how the manuscript came to his notice and an introduction extolling the role of the frontier lawman in the development of the great West and the contribution of Canton, "one of the most picturesque and efficient of the veteran peace officers," in that development. Professor Dale touched lightly on the author's early history, mentioning that his real name was not Frank Canton and that "in his youth he became involved in a difficulty that caused him to leave his Texas home and disappear into the farther depths of the American wilderness." Many years later, "this early difficulty was adjusted and Mr. Canton absolved from all blame in connection with it." His real name did not matter, said Dale, for it was as Frank M. Canton that his memory was "honored, not only in Oklahoma, but throughout all that wide region reaching from the Mexican Border to Cape Nome, and from the Mississippi River to the Rockies and far beyond."[3]

Dale wisely allowed Canton to tell his own tale, making few editorial changes. The work, often defensive in tone, was replete with falsehoods of commission and omission. It was uneven, extensively detailed in areas of relative insignificance and chary of information in more important matters. But on the whole the writing was surprisingly good. "Canton must have been largely self-educated, but his style has about it a stark beauty which reminds the reader of Conrad," Professor Dale thought.[4] The book was so well written, in fact, that at least one historian has suggested that it was ghostwritten.[5] Dale, however, had the good sense not to tamper with Canton's words, which reveal much about the man, his views and attitudes, and the exciting times in which he lived. Dale chose to omit Canton's account of his years as adjutant general but summarized them in an editor's conclusion: "The story of these achievements could be written from the letters, clippings, and other material among his private papers, but it has not seemed wise to do so. His life story is his own story, and he has told simply and well of its most interesting and picturesque phases."[6]

Professor Dale changed the title of the manuscript from "Memories of the Border" to "Frontier Trails" and placed it with the Houghton Mifflin Company, which published it in 1930 as one of their Riverside Press editions. The book was 237 pages and sold for three dollars. Reviews were favorable. The introductory paragraph in the foreword, in which Canton distilled his fifty-year experience as an officer, was described by one reviewer as "one of the best summaries ever written."[7] The *Boston Transcript* said it was "brimming with hair-raising adventure and combats" and was "a valuable addition to Americana."[8] The *New York Herald-Tribune* said there was "never a more perfect example of a man of action than Canton, [who] neither apologizes or explains. In parts his book is as bald as a bill of lading, but in other parts it achieves a stark and simple beauty and a genuine suspense."[9]

When Charles Colcord learned that Canton's book was to be published, he wrote Dale, offering to pay fifty dollars for the first copy off the press. A Houghton Mifflin editor found the request "very amusing" and forwarded a copy and a statement that it was the first. Dale presented the volume to Colcord and gave the fifty dollars to Annie Canton.[10]

A Hollywood literary agent contacted Dale, saying he believed he could sell the book for production as a motion picture, but nothing came of the venture. Because of the Great Depression, motion-picture producers "had virtually stopped buying anything," Dale was informed.[11] Annie, pleased that her husband's story had at last been presented to a national audience, continued to perpetuate the myth that Canton was the prototype for the fictional western characters of Owen Wister and Rex Beach. Still holding the mistaken belief that Canton was born in Virginia, she told a reporter in 1938 that it was "generally conceded" that Canton had "inspired Wister to write his novel with a Virginian as the hero." She added: "My husband spent much time with Mr. Wister, giving him the framework on which 'the Virginian' was based. The writer always said he drew the central character around my husband."[12]

She also firmly believed that Rex Beach drew on the character of her husband in creating the fictional heroes of his novels, but Beach never admitted to that. In a letter to Canton, he indicated that the fictional town of "Flambeau" in his novel *The Barrier* was actually Rampart. The characters and incidents were fictitious, he said, although he admitted, "Some of the people in the story were suggested to me by men I met there, as for instance, Lieut. Bell, Al Mayo, and others." He did not identify Canton as a model for any of his fictional creations, although certain of the man's mannerisms or speech patterns may well have been incorporated into Beach's characters.[13]

Frontier Trails, with a new introduction by Edward Everett Dale, was republished by the University of Oklahoma Press in 1966 as one of their Western Frontier Library editions. In the thirty-six years since the first publication, editor Dale had learned a little more about the author. New information had surfaced, he said, to show that Canton had never been a Texas Ranger, as Dale had stated in his earlier introduction.[14] Noting that Canton "left blank the period of his life from about 1871 to 1878," Dale said he had investigated and learned that "Frank Canton's real name was Joe Horner and that he had lived in Texas for some years on the 'wrong side of the law' as a fugitive from justice."[15]

Dale may have known more about the suppressed early life of the author than he chose to include when he wrote his first introduction back in 1930. Annie Canton was still living then, and Dale was careful not to write anything that would embarrass her or diminish the acclaim she wanted for the memory of her husband. But by 1966 the last of the Cantons was gone.

Canton's small pension from the Cattle Raisers Association of Texas stopped with his death. Annie had no income and, after Ruby died, no means of support at all. In December 1928 she moved to Oklahoma City, hoping to find work at the university or the state historical society. "I have sold my house," she wrote Professor Dale, "and am packing up and will later be in Oklahoma City, and will be ready to take any place which might be open or need a house-mother. I will let you know where I am and if you have any place in mind, please think of me."[16]

Annie remained active in the Christian Science Church, the Eastern Star (an order of members of Freemasonry and their female relatives), and the Oklahoma Historical Society. When the historical society opened a large new building in Oklahoma City in 1930, she was appointed the official visitor's guide and held this position for fifteen years, until failing health forced her retirement.[17]

Her scant savings were soon exhausted, and she spent her last years in a Masonic Home at Guthrie. On June 15, 1946, she broke her hip in a fall and required constant attendance by a nurse for nine months. Thereafter she was confined to a bed or chair. A woman came in to take care of her and keep up the apartment. "Life has been *very* hard the last ten years," she wrote in 1947. She had "a very nice large room" with her own pictures, radio, and writing desk and was comfortable. But she added: "All the patients on this (5th) floor are dumb, blind, or in wheel chairs and it is not as pleasant as it might be. . . . It is hard to sit here as I do so much of the time by myself. I do have so many friends that are kind and good to me, but it is lonesome."[18]

Annie died on September 3, 1948, at the age of eighty-one. Her body was taken to Oklahoma City and interred near the graves of Frank and Ruby in Fairlawn Cemetery.[19]

The controversy surrounding the life of Frank Canton did not subside with the publication of his autobiography. The book reinforced the views of his admirers, but his critics found it mendacious and self-justifying. Opinions, pro and con, only hardened with the passage of years.

After the appearance of a 1971 magazine article recounting some of the criminal history of the Texas desperado Joe Horner, and his later metamorphosis as the noted lawman Frank Canton, a niece of Canton's wrote author William B. Secrest, objecting to the piece. Mrs. R. L. Askew of Graham, Texas, a daughter of John Wesley Horner, was eighty-five years old, her brother was ninety, and she had two cousins about her age. "We are all proud of the Horner name," she said. She deplored the representation of her "dear uncle" as a criminal. "He certainly *was not* a Bank Robber, thief or a murderer," she adamantly declared, attributing these vicious tales to writers who "probably had a grudge against him because he was trying to rid the country of the outlaws." She admitted that her "Uncle Joe" had run into "trouble over at Jacksboro with some Negro soldiers in 1874 or 1875 and had to shoot his way out in self-defense," but she said that "to keep from having any more trouble he simply got on his horse and rode out of Texas." She objected strongly to the author's assertion that Horner "high-tailed it" to Wyoming. "Uncle Joe [was] a brave, honorable and respectable citizen." She said that he made a splendid record as an officer, and she referred Secrest to *Frontier Trails*, which was "all truth." Canton's niece requested that the author write another article correcting "the bad things" he had written about Joe Horner.[20]

A diametrically opposed view of Canton can be found in the copy of *Frontier Trails* on the shelves of the Johnson County Library in Buffalo, Wyoming. A reader inserted his own critique in penciled marginal notes in the volume. Passages are underlined with terse comments: "Not true! Lies! False!" In block capital letters is the accusation: "LIAR, THIEF, MURDERER." Canton had closed his chapter on the Johnson County Cattle War by commenting that he was broken financially by the affair. The anonymous critic responded, "Too bad he didn't hang." A terse summation is made on an endsheet: "This book is such a Pack of lies—I hope very few people ever read it! I'm sorry I did."

And so, in memory as in life, Joe Horner, alias Frank Canton, a hard man in a hard time, remains one of the most controversial figures of the turbulent frontier era. Like the milieu that produced him, his life was complex, often contradictory, but forever fascinating.

Notes

The Frank M. Canton Collection in the Western History Collections of the University of Oklahoma at Norman (CC–WHC), containing Canton's manuscript, scrapbooks, letters, clippings, documents, photographs, and memorabilia, was donated by his widow after his death and is a rich lode of information about the man's life. Also valuable is the Frank Canton Collection at the American Heritage Center at the University of Wyoming at Laramie (CC–AHC), consisting primarily of articles and newspaper items presented by his sister-in-law, Mrs. A. W. Stevens of Buffalo, Wyoming. The General Records of the Department of Justice (GRDJ) provide much information regarding Canton's service as a federal officer. Court records, newspaper files, and other archival material consulted are listed below and in the bibliography.

Introduction

1. *Daily Oklahoman*, September 28, 1927; *New York Times*, September 28, 1927.
2. Thrapp, *Encyclopedia of Frontier Biography* 1:222.
3. Frink, *Cow Country Cavalcade*, 89; Hutchins, "The Jekyll-Hyde Gunman."
4. Kittrell, introduction to Mercer, *The Banditti of the Plains*, xxxiv–xlvi.
5. Drago, *The Great Range Wars*, 262.
6. Prassel, *The Western Peace Officer*, 145–46.
7. Horan, *The Authentic Wild West*, 233.
8. Rex Beach to Anna Canton, November 30, 1928, CC-WHC, Box 1, Folder 34.
9. Tad Moses to Edward Burnett, March 12, 1937, CC-AHC.

Chapter 1. The Cowboy, 1849–1873

1. The boys were William, Sam, John, Richard, and Ben. The daughter's name has been lost to history. The family history is derived from letters written to Canton's widow after his death. Mary Jane Sams, Canton's sister, in a letter dated December 14, 1927, provided details, although she said it was difficult because the old family

Bible had been lost (CC-WHC, Box 1, Folder 47). Other information is contained in an undated letter from Minnie Belle Burnett, another sister (CC-WHC, Box 1, Folder 47), in a letter from Ethel Horner, a niece, dated February 15, 1928 (CC-WHC, Box 1, Folder 47), and in additional details reported by Ethel after interviewing her father, John Wesley Horner (CC-WHC, Box 2, Folder 12).

2. Horner's first wife apparently came from a well-to-do Ohio family. "I am sure their people were prominent as one Auntie visited us in Indiana & took Sister Jennie back to Cincinnati on a visit & Jennie thot [sic] they were wonderful & houses grand," Mary Jane Sams remembered in 1927. "Sister Eliza was the brightest of the seven sisters. . . . [She] was poring over books (& our father kept a fine library) & best of all she had such a wonderful memory. Jennie was beautiful & such a lovely figure. Moved like a princess & was inclined to a little vanity" (Mary Jane Sams to Anna Canton, December 14, 1927.

3. Minnie Belle Burnett to Anna Canton.

4. Mary Jane Sams to Anna Canton, December 14, 1927. In addition to the cited letters, the Horner family history is reconstructed from official records: U.S. Census, Henry County, Indiana, 1850; Benton County, Arkansas, 1860; Denton County, Texas, 1870; and Young County, Texas, 1880; Texas State Penitentiary, Huntsville, Records for Joe Horner; Oklahoma State Department of Health, Certificate of Death, Frank Melvin Canton.

5. Mary Jane Sams to Anna Canton, December 14, 1927.

6. Confederate Records, Military Service Branch (NNMS), National Archives. To be accepted, Horner lied about his age, saying that he was only forty-three. Clark's Regiment of Recruits later became the Seventh Regiment of the Missouri Cavalry.

7. Crouch, *A History of Young County,* 223–24.

8. Ethel Horner to Anna Canton, February 15, 1928.

9. Minnie Belle Burnett to Anna Canton.

10. "Alton's Disaster in War between States," undated clipping from the *Alton Telegraph,* Hayner Public Library, Alton, Illinois.

11. Minnie Belle Burnett to Anna Canton.

12. "Life of Frank Canton Rivals Fiction for Thrills," undated clipping from an Oklahoma paper in CC-AHC; Ethel Horner to Anna Canton, February 15, 1928.

13. "Life of Frank Canton Rivals Fiction for Thrills." John Wesley Horner recalled in 1927 that Joe "fell in with an immigrant train" headed for California and "drove a team for them," but Horner made no mention of the deadly fight or of a second trip (Ethel Horner to Anna Canton, February 15, 1928).

14. Crouch, *A History of Young County,* 223.

15. Ibid.; Ethel Horner to Anna Canton, February 15, 1928.

16. Minnie Belle married Tillman H. Burnett, one year younger than Burk, in 1884 and had four children. Kate and Phoenix M. Burnett, six years Burk's junior, were wed in 1881 and had three children (U.S. Census, Knox County, Texas, 1900).

17. Ibid.; Mari Sandoz, *The Cattlemen,* 46–47. Kit Carter was the son-in-law of the celebrated Indian fighter Lawrence Sullivan ("Sull") Ross, who in 1859 was appointed by Sam Houston to raise a company of Rangers to protect the frontier settlements against Indians. Ross was credited with the rescue of the long-sought Comanche captive Cynthia Ann Parker, in 1860. He later was a brigadier general in

the Confederate army and sheriff of McLennan County. In 1886 he was elected governor of Texas (Douthitt, *Romance and Dim Trails*, 31; Webb, *Handbook of Texas* 2:506–7).

18. The Congress of the Republic of Texas had originally authorized the organization of companies of volunteer minutemen as protection against Indian attacks in 1841. Volunteers were unpaid but were exempted from the poll tax, the tax on a saddle horse, and road repair duties. In 1861 the Texas state legislature enacted a law allowing every frontier county to raise one or more companies of minutemen (Webb, *Handbook of Texas* 2:214).

19. According to family tradition, both Joe and John Wesley Horner served as Texas Rangers (Ethel Horner to Anna Canton, February 15, 1928, and Crouch, *A History of Young County*, 223). Joe Horner himself wrote in a 1913 letter that he joined the Texas Rangers at eighteen years of age and "served five years during the Indian days" (Frank Canton to Job Ingram, November 5, 1913, CC-WHC, Box 1, Folder 55). There is no record, however, of Joe Horner, John Wesley Horner, or Kit Carter in the Ranger files at the Texas State Archives (Frances T. Ingmire, Texas Ranger Service Records, 1847–1900, 6 vols.; Donaly E. Brice to the author, October 26, 1992).

20. In newspaper interviews and his memoirs Horner consistently placed the year of this drive as 1869 (Canton, *Frontier Trails*, 3; "Early State History Told," undated, unidentified clipping, CC-WHC, Box 2, Folder 18; "Blazing the Cattle Trails," reprinted in the *Kerrville Mountain Sun*, November 5, 1925, and the *Edmond Enterprise*, November 12, 1925; "Famous Trail Was Blazed by Jesse Chisholm, Says Canton," *Wichita Daily Times*, November 22, 1925). But other accounts differ. The year has been given as 1867 (Douglas, *Cattle Kings of Texas*, 350; Webb, *Handbook of Texas* 1:253), and 1870 (Hinton, *History of the Cattlemen of Texas*, 77). In the foreword to his memoirs (*Frontier Trails*, xix), Horner says that he was seventeen when he went on this drive, which would have made the year 1867, but his descriptions of incidents on the trail and the state of development of the towns indicate that the year was 1868. *Frontier Trails* was published in two editions, 1930 and 1966. All citations will be to the 1966 edition unless otherwise specified.

21. Huckabay, *Ninety-Four Years in Jack County*, 121–22.

22. Canton, *Frontier Trails*, 4.

23. Ibid., 6.

24. "Early State History Told." Horner gave this account of the cattle drive in an interview in the 1920s. He repeated the story of the drive again in at least two feature newspaper articles: "Blazing the Cattle Trails," and "Famous Trail Was Blazed by Jesse Chisholm." These accounts are generally consistent but contain a few minor discrepancies when compared with the story as it later appeared in his published autobiography. For example, in the later work the number of beeves demanded by the Indians had doubled to one hundred (Canton, *Frontier Trails*, 8).

25. Canton, *Frontier Trails*, 8.

26. Huckabay, *Ninety-Four Years in Jack County*, 122.

27. Canton, *Frontier Trails*, 9–10.

28. The two night herders showed up the next day. One was still mounted, providing the crew with a total of three mounts to continue the drive. The horse of the other herder had broken a leg during the stampede and was left behind ("Famous

Trail Was Blazed by Jesse Chisholm"). As Douglas related the tale, each of the Burnett hands retained a mount, but the men had to walk during the day so that the ponies could be kept fresh for emergencies (*Cattle Kings of Texas,* 350).

29. "Early State History Told."

30. The wild Texas cattle were very dangerous to a man afoot, often charging with their long horns lowered. When cattle were to be driven through the streets of a town, cowboys rode ahead, warning everyone to get inside. In Abilene a woman ignored this warning and was tossed on the horns of a steer into the herd and was trampled to death (Streeter, *Prairie Trails and Cow Towns,* 60).

31. Canton, *Frontier Trails,* 11.

32. Ibid., 12; "Famous Trail Was Blazed by Jesse Chisholm."

33. Miner, *Wichita,* 32, 48; Dykstra, *The Cattle Towns,* 47.

34. Canton, *Frontier Trails,* 12. Slaughter is said to have sold his herd of eight hundred head at Abilene for $32,000 (Hunter, "Colonel C. C. Slaughter," 436). Since the average Texas steer brought only thirty dollars at Abilene in 1868, Slaughter's cattle must have been of exceptionally high quality. This herd of eight hundred was probably the one mentioned by Joseph McCoy as a "very choice selection" of "the many fine herds of cattle that arrived in Abilene in the spring of 1868" (McCoy, *Historic Sketches of the Cattle Trade,* 215).

35. Canton, *Frontier Trails,* 12; "Famous Trail Was Blazed by Jesse Chisholm"; Hinton, *History of the Cattlemen of Texas,* 80.

36. The first auction of Texas longhorns at Abilene was held on July 22, 1868; as reported in the *Junction City Weekly Union,* "Large sized work cattle averaged thirty dollars per head, 2-year olds ten dollars per head" (quoted in McCoy, *Historic Sketches of the Cattle Trade,* 245).

37. Dykstra, *The Cattle Towns,* 98.

38. Henry, *Conquering Our Great American Plains,* 61–62.

39. "Famous Trail Was Blazed by Jesse Chisholm."

40. Canton, *Frontier Trails,* 12. The Snyder brothers, Dudley H. and J. W., brought some of the first cattle into Nebraska (Yost, *The Call of the Range,* 44).

41. In his recitation of this story quoted in the *Wichita Daily Times,* Horner said that two men accompanied him on this search ("Famous Trail Was Blazed by Jesse Chisholm"); in his memoirs, he said there were three (*Frontier Trails,* 13).

42. Horner gave this name as Sam Tate in his autobiography (*Frontier Trails,* 15).

43. "Famous Trail Was Blazed by Jesse Chisholm." In his autobiography, Horner said that he had cautioned Tate "never to carry more than five cartridges in the cylinder of his revolver, so that the hammer would always rest on an empty chamber," but the advice went unheeded until this accident, which "taught him a lesson" (*Frontier Trails,* 16). The lesson was evidently lost on Horner himself; twenty-four years later, in a similar sixgun-dropping incident, he would be struck by a bullet-- the only gunshot wound he would receive in a long, violence-filled career.

44. Canton, *Frontier Trails,* 16–17; "Famous Trail Was Blazed by Jesse Chisholm." In both of these accounts, Horner includes a story of a massacre of "about eighty or one hundred" Pawnee men, women, and children by Sioux warriors at a place nearby he called Moran Canyon. This had happened, he said, only a few days before and was described in graphic detail by the soldiers from Fort McPherson who had helped bury the dead Pawnees. His account sounds very much like a description of the

Battle of Massacre Canyon, in which a Sioux war party surprised a Pawnee buffalo-hunting party, killed an official total of sixty-nine men, women, and children, wounded eleven severely, and captured eleven others. This action occurred on August 5, 1873, however, five years later (Potomac Corral of the Westerners, *Great Western Indian Fights*, 185–88). Horner no doubt heard of the massacre from Indian friends on the Pawnee reservation in Oklahoma many years afterward and incorporated the story into his account for dramatic effect.

45. Brown, *Hear That Lonesome Whistle Blow*, 71, 94; Canton, *Frontier Trails*, 19.

46. "Famous Trail Was Blazed by Jesse Chisholm."

47. Canton to Ingram, November 5, 1913.

48. The town was originally called Lost Creek, then Mesquiteville, and then Jacksborough in 1858 when it became the county seat. In 1899 the name was officially changed to Jacksboro, which for clarity it will be called in this work (Webb, *Handbook of Texas* 1:900).

49. Hamilton, *Sentinel of the Southern Plains*, 92.

50. Ibid.

51. Ibid., 91.

52. Horner made the claim in a 1913 letter (Frank M. Canton to Cecil H. Smith, May 28, 1913, cc-whc, Box 2, Folder 4) and in *Frontier Trails*, 24. It was repeated in Thrapp, *Encyclopedia of Frontier Biography* 1:221, and Hutchins, "The Jekyll-Hyde Gunman," 4. The protection of the Indians by the military is recounted in Hamilton, *Sentinel of the Southern Plains*, 92, and Capps, *The Warren Wagontrain Raid*, 168. Horner identified the Jack County sheriff as Lee Crutchfield, but Michael McMillan was sheriff in July 1871; Lee Crutchfield did not assume office until 1874 (Tise, *Texas County Sheriffs*, 277; Capps, *The Warren Wagontrain Raid*, 166).

53. This name sometimes appears as "Cotman" (e.g., Strong, *My Frontier Days*, 77; Huckabay, *Ninety-Four Years in Jack County*, 149). It also has been spelled "Cotner" (Horton, *History of Jack County*, 147) and "Catman" (Crouch, *A History of Young County*, 223). The name is recorded as "Cotnam" in the court records of Jack County and is so spelled here. See *State of Texas v. Joe Horner*: Number 332.

54. Crouch, *A History of Young County*, 223.

55. Horton, *History of Jack County*, 147.

56. This undated statement was written on the stationery of Sheriff C. C. Hammonds of Comanche County, Oklahoma, when Horner was a deputy there in 1903 (cc-whc, Box 2, Folder 23).

57. Ibid.

58. Ibid. In a November 18, 1912, letter to J. C. Lindsey, the brother of James P. Lindsey, Horner said that the horses lost to the Indians that night on Dillingham Prairie numbered fifteen, not ten, and that they belonged to him (cc-whc, Box 1, Folder 59).

59. Ibid. Horner said that his brother's earlier claim was rejected: "[He] has never received anything yet, and I don't believe he ever will."

60. Ibid.

61. DeArment, "'Hurricane Bill' Martin," 40.

62. Haley, *The Buffalo War*, 44.

Chapter 2. The Outlaw, 1874–1879

1. Webb, *Handbook of Texas* 1:900.
2. Horton, *History of Jack County*, 119.
3. McConnell, "Five Years a Cavalryman," November 1933, 76–77.
4. Strong, *My Frontier Days*, 18.
5. Ibid., 80.
6. Ibid.
7. Horton, *History of Jack County*, 120.
8. Huckabay, *Ninety-Four Years in Jack County*, 143–44.'
9. Tise, *Texas County Sheriffs*, 277; Horton, *History of Jack County*, 108.
10. Johnson, identified as one of the Horner-Cotnam gang, is misnamed "Bally" in Strong, *My Frontier Days*, 42. His John Kinney gang association is noted in Gibson, *The Life and Death of Colonel Albert Jennings Fountain*, 113, 123.
11. Strong, *My Frontier Days*, 42–43.
12. Ibid., 17.
13. Ibid., 42.
14. Ibid., 43.
15. Ibid., 44–45.
16. Ibid., 45.
17. Ibid., 79.
18. Ibid., 78–80.
19. Statement of Henry Strong to Honorable J. R. Fleming, *State of Texas v. Joe M. Horner, George Horner and Wageman alias Redding*: Number 384.
20. *State of Texas v. Joe Horner*: Number 327.
21. *State of Texas v. Joe Horner*: Numbers 332, 335.
22. "Uncle Sam Forced Buffalo Hunters to Become Cattle Rustlers, Canton Asserts," undated, unidentified clipping, CC-WHC, Box 2, Folder 15; "Famous Trail Was Blazed by Jesse Chisholm"; Canton, *Frontier Trails*, 25.
23. *State of Texas v. Joe Horner*: Numbers 327, 332, 335.
24. Strong, *My Frontier Days*, 18; Horton, *History of Jack County*, 66.
25. Horton, *History of Jack County*, 66–71.
26. Hamilton, *Sentinel of the Southern Plains*, 60–62; Webb, *Handbook of Texas* 1:915.
27. Hamilton, *Sentinel of the Southern Plains*, 138; Horton, *History of Jack County*, 76. Horton erroneously placed this incident in 1874 and said two soldiers were killed.
28. Canton, "Reminiscences of a Veteran Officer," 23.
29. Leckie, *The Buffalo Soldiers*, 79.
30. McIntire, *Early Days in Texas*, 53.
31. McConnell, "Five Years a Cavalryman."
32. Horton, *History of Jack County*, 120.
33. Carter, *The Old Sergeant's Story*, 95–96.
34. *Portrait and Biographical Record of Oklahoma*, 50–51.
35. Horton, *History of Jack County*, 121.
36. Ibid. Over the years the number of buffalo soldiers killed in the fight in-

creased, in the memory of some Texas old-timers, to as many as five (Frank Kell to J. Elmer Brock, September 10, 1936).

37. Forty-one years later Thomas Horton visited Horner in his Oklahoma City office and asked how that bullet missed his knees. "I guess I had my knees in my pockets," Horner replied (Horton, *History of Jack County*, 121–22).

38. Ibid. Horton's account of Joe Horner's battle with the troopers agrees in basic details with that related in a 1928 letter to Mrs. Frank Canton and written by Ethel Horner after interviewing her father, John Wesley Horner, cc-whc, Box 2, Folder 12.

39. Records of the Adjutant General, RG 94, National Archives. Incredibly, of the seventy-one enlisted men of the Tenth Cavalry at Fort Richardson in October 1874, fully twenty-seven were "taken sick or wounded during the month."

40. *Frontier Echo*, February 22, 1878.

41. Records of the Adjutant General, RG 94, National Archives.

42. Ethel Horner to Anna Canton, February 15, 1928.

43. Mrs. R. L. Askew to William B. Secrest, January 24, 1972, and William B. Secrest to the author, July 13, 1992.

44. Horner gave this account to Tad Moses, who repeated it in a March 12, 1937, letter to Edward Burnett (cc-ahc).

45. *State of Texas v. Joe Horner*: Number 332.

46. *State of Texas v. Joseph Horner*: Number 361.

47. Crouch, *A History of Young County*, 224.

48. Huckabay, *Ninety-Four Years in Jack County*, 142.

49. McConnell, "Five Years a Cavalryman."

50. *State of Texas v. Joe Horner*: Numbers 415, 416.

51. *Frontier Echo*, September 18, 1875; *San Antonio Daily Express*, September 16, 1875. Escaping with Horner were J. Foughs and George Conn, charged with horse stealing, suspected burglar James Potts, and suspected hog thief William Wales. These four went east as Horner rode west. George Conn (or "William Corn" as the name was sometimes reported), a black man, was killed a month later at Fort Griffin by Shackelford County Sheriff Henry C. Jacobs (*Frontier Echo*, October 16, 1875).

52. *San Antonio Daily Express*, September 16, 1875.

53. Floyd Shock to Frank M. Canton, September 29, 1915 (cc-whc, Box 2, Folder 3). Shock remembered the time of this incident as "the spring of '75," but after forty years he might have been wrong as to season.

54. *Houston Daily Telegraph*, February 4, 1876.

55. *San Antonio Daily Express*, February 4, 1876.

56. D. W. Roberts, Lt., Commanding Co. D, Frontier Battalion, to Major John B. Jones, Commanding Battalion, February 16, 1876 (Adjutant General's Files [A.G.F.], Archives Division, Texas State Library, Austin).

57. Frink, *Cow Country Cavalcade*, 139; Smith, *The War on Powder River*, 120.

58. Campbell, "Pioneer Peace Officers," manuscript in T. A. Campbell Collection.

59. From an undated *New York Sun* clipping (Canton File, Tisdale Collection).

60. Strong, *My Frontier Days*, 82.

61. The *San Antonio Daily Express* of February 4, 1876, erroneously reported

that nine men took part in the robbery. Strong, *My Frontier Days*, 81–82; Statement of Fred Bader, September 1878, *State of Texas v. Joe M. Horner, George Horner and Wageman alias Redding*: Number 384. For some reason Strong never mentioned George Horner in his book.

62. *San Antonio Daily Express*, February 4, 1876.

63. Strong, *My Frontier Days*, 83.

64. *San Antonio Daily Express*, February 4, 1876.

65. Ibid.

66. Ibid., March 14, 1876.

67. *State of Texas v. Joe M. Horner, George Horner and Wageman alias Redding*: Number 384.

68. *Frontier Echo*, February 11, 1876; March 10, 1876.

69. *State of Texas v. Joe Horner*: Number 327; Lelia Vene Cozart, District Clerk, Jack County, Texas, to the author, January 29, 1992.

70. *State of Texas v. Joe M. Horner, George Horner and Wageman alias Redding*: Number 384; *State of Texas v. W. Z. Redding, A. H. Murchison, T. R. Redding*: Number 388.

71. *A List of Fugitives from Justice* (1878), 14, 70, 77; *A List of Fugitives from Justice* (1886), 85. To a capias for Redding issued by Comanche County in April 1877, Sheriff Jonathan J. Bozarth of Llano County appended: "When last heard from he was on the clear fork of the Brazos river with a herd of cattle, or the head of the Colorado River. Supposed to be passing from one place to the other and on a sharp look out. We have papers here for him and would like to get hold of him" (*State of Texas v. Joe M. Horner, George Horner and Wageman alias Redding*: Number 384).

72. *Galveston Daily News*, February 29, 1876.

73. *San Antonio Daily Herald*, March 2, 1876.

74. Strong, *My Frontier Days*, 78; P. W. Reynolds to J. R. Webb, March 8, 1947 (J. R. Webb Papers, Research Center, Hardin-Simmons University); *Frontier Echo*, April 14, 1876; *Fort Worth Democrat*, April 22, 1876.

75. The *San Antonio Daily Express* reported, "The indictment in this case measured fourteen feet of foolscap" (March 16, 1877). Henry Strong said the indictment "was eleven feet long in old handwriting" (Strong, *My Frontier Days*, 83). Listed were eleven hundred-dollar bills, eleven fifty-dollar bills, twenty-two twenty-dollar bills, eleven ten-dollar bills, and thirteen five-dollar bills, totaling $2,165. Stolen also was $3,155 in unknown bills. The total theft was $5,320 (*State of Texas v. Joe M. Horner, George Horner and Wageman alias Redding*: Number 384).

76. *San Antonio Daily Express*, March 16, 1877; *State of Texas v. Joe M. Horner, George Horner and Wageman alias Redding*: Number 384.

77. John Wesley Hardin, Bill Taylor, George Gladden, John Ringo, Mannen Clements, Jeff Ake, Brown Bowen, Samuel Pipes, and Albert Herndon of the Sam Bass gang, and Ham White, the premier stage robber of America, all were ensconced in the Austin jail during this period (Reed and Tate, *The Tenderfoot Bandits*, 217; Hardin, *Life of John Wesley Hardin*, 126; Raymond, *Captain Lee Hall of Texas*, 131–32; Parsons and Parsons, *Bowen and Hardin*, 64–67; Dugan, *Knight of the Road*, 22–24).

78. *State of Texas v. Joe M. Horner, George Horner and Wageman alias Redding*: Number 384. J. R. Fleming, with R. G. Armstrong, was a major owner of the H.R. Martin bank of Comanche.

79. Ibid.

80. *San Antonio Daily Express*, April 3, 1877. "Joe Horner has now made his second escape from prison since he was arrested for robbing the Comanche bank," the paper noted on another page. No report of an earlier escape attempt from the Bat Cave has been found; perhaps the reference was to Horner's escape from the Jack County jail.

81. Ibid., April 6, 1877.

82. Ibid., April 18, 1877; *State of Texas v. Joe Horner*: Number 368.

83. *San Antonio Daily Express*, April 20, 1877.

84. Patterson later was foreman on the jury that convicted Horner of breaking telegraph wires. The following year he was elected to the first of two terms as sheriff of Uvalde County (*State of Texas v. Joe Horner*: Number 374; Tise, *Texas County Sheriffs*, 503).

85. *San Antonio Daily Express*, April 21, 1877. Jim Jones escaped across the border but was arrested by Mexican authorities less than a month later. On May 14 Lieutenants Lee Hall and John B. Armstrong and Sergeant A. L. Parrott of the Texas Rangers brought him back from Piedras Negras. Jones, under indictment in Maverick County for horse stealing, was identified by John Melifont as one of the stage robbers. He joined thirty-two other fugitives, including the infamous John King Fisher, rounded up by Hall and his Rangers in a sweep of the outlaw-infested country around Eagle Pass (Raymond, *Captain Lee Hall of Texas*, 86–88; *San Antonio Daily Express*, May 15, 1877; May 22, 1877; May 25, 1877).

86. *State of Texas v. Joe Horner*: Number 368.

87. *State of Texas v. Joe Horner*: Number 374.

88. *San Antonio Daily Express*, May 1, 1877.

89. *State of Texas v. Joe Horner*: Number 374.

90. *San Antonio Daily Express*, May 2, 3, 9, 1877.

91. Texas State Penitentiaries, "Description of Convict When Received: Joe Horner, No. 5920, May 5, 1877"; Billy M. Birmingham, Texas Department of Corrections, to the author, November 18, 1992. This was probably the last time Horner ever gave anyone his correct age and birthplace.

92. Walker, *Penology for Profit*, 16, 52.

93. Ibid., 43.

94. Ibid., 20.

95. Hardin, *Life of John Wesley Hardin*, 129–31.

96. Walker, *Penology for Profit*, 66.

97. Apparently the thought was alive in his old haunts as well. On July 27, 1877, only twelve weeks after his imprisonment, the *San Antonio Daily Express* printed a story that he had escaped from Huntsville. Then, in March 1878, the Jacksboro paper reported that he had escaped and had been seen in Graham. Editor Robson was dubious, noting that Sheriff Crutchfield had not been informed of an escape by Horner. "If it was true," said Robson, "every telegraph wire in the State would be red hot carrying the news" (*Frontier Echo*, March 15, 1878).

98. Walker, *Penology for Profit*, 52.

99. Ibid., 56.

100. Ibid., 51.

101. Hanson, *Powder River Country*, 226: "Joe Horner's sister was married into one of the most prominent families in Texas. . . . He was supposed to have escaped from jail with the help of a girl or her family. Some say the jailer's daughter became enamored with him and helped him escape."

102. *List of Fugitives from Justice* (1886).

Chapter 3. The Sheriff, 1880–1886

1. Oklahoma State Department of Health, Bureau of Vital Statistics, Oklahoma City: Certificate of Death, Frank Melvin Canton.

2. Canton, *Frontier Trails*, 26.

3. The correct title of the cattlemen's organization was the Wyoming Stock Growers Association (<sc>WSGA).

4. Canton, *Frontier Trails*, 28.

5. Bailey, "Wyoming Stock Inspectors." Neither the "indemnity bonds" file nor the "appointments as deputy" file in the Thomas H. Irvine Papers at the Montana Historical Society Library contain reference to Canton's service as a deputy under Irvine.

6. Gooddell, "Gratitude Twenty Dollars Bought," 129; Burnett, "Frank Canton, the Sheriff"; Bard, *Horse Wrangler*, 4. Floyd Bard, the son of Charles Warren Bard, erroneously placed this time as the spring of 1877.

7. Hill, "Buffalo," 129–30.

8. Gooddell, "Gratitude Twenty Dollars Bought." Canton may have written this description himself (see chapter 13), but it probably was very accurate.

9. <sc>WSGA Letters 1:100, quoted in Bailey, "Wyoming Stock Inspectors," 13.

10. Ibid., 12.

11. Canton, *Frontier Trails*, 34.

12. Canton to Sturgis, November 11, 1881, quoted in Bailey, "Wyoming Stock Inspectors," 14.

13. Burnett, "Frank Canton, the Sheriff."

14. <sc>WSGA letter file, July–December 1882, quoted in Bailey, "Wyoming Stock Inspectors," 66.

15. Canton, *Frontier Trails*, 34.

16. Stock Brand Certification No. 144, Local History Collection, Johnson County Library, Buffalo, Wyoming.

17. Johnson County, Wyoming, Commissioners' Books, entry for March 15, 1882.

18. Bailey, "Wyoming Stock Inspectors," 71. Certification of Canton's election was not issued until July 1883. A copy is in the Texas State Archives, Austin.

19. Quoted in Burroughs, *Guardian of the Grasslands*, 154.

20. Johnson County, Wyoming, Commissioners' Books, April 2, July 3, 1883.

21. Ibid., February 1, April 5, November 12, 1883.

22. *Laramie Boomerang*, February 19, 1884.

23. Bard, *Horse Wrangler*, 5.

24. Canton, *Frontier Trails*, 35.

25. Rietz, "Johnson County," 7–8.

26. McDermott was U.S. marshal for Wyoming from August 1894 until July 1898 (Robert R. Ernst, Consultant to U.S. Marshal's Service, to the author, August 20, 1992); White, *Index of U.S. Marshals*, 58. He was sheriff of Converse County from 1901 until 1905 (Heritage Book Committee, *Pages from Converse County's Past*, 729).

27. Burnett, "Frank Canton, the Sheriff"; *Laramie Daily Sentinel*, August 18, 1883.

28. Johnson County, Wyoming, Assessment Rolls, 1883, Wyoming State Archives, Cheyenne.

29. Bancroft, "Interview with Sheriff Frank M. Canton."

30. *Cheyenne Daily Leader*, February 2, 1884. A commission issued by the Wyoming governor was required to extradite fugitives from other states and territories. Many of these were issued for Canton's deputies, but he was personally commissioned as state agent for extradition purposes on eight occasions from October 24, 1884, until August 26, 1887 (Canton File, Tisdale Collection).

31. *Big Horn Sentinel*, November 29, 1884. The <sc>WSGA blacklist is reproduced in Hall, *Documents of Wyoming Heritage*.

32. Canton, *Frontier Trails*, 36.

33. Frye, *Atlas of Wyoming Outlaws*, 81.

34. Canton, *Frontier Trails*, 36.

35. *Buffalo Bulletin*, April 9, 30, 1891.

36. Bancroft, "Interview with Sheriff Frank M. Canton." A prison built at Laramie in 1872 served as a federal penitentiary until Wyoming statehood in 1890, when it became the Wyoming State Penitentiary. During Canton's term as sheriff, Wyoming contracted to house its convicted felons in various facilities, including local county jails, the Detroit House of Corrections in Michigan, and the Illinois State Prison at Joliet (Frye, *Atlas of Wyoming Outlaws*, 241–303).

37. *Big Horn Sentinel*, December 13, 1884, and January 10, 1885; Frye, *Atlas of Wyoming Outlaws*, 281. The name is given as Harry "Anable" in the *Sentinel* and as "Arable" in the prison records.

38. Frye, *Atlas of Wyoming Outlaws*, 275–87.

39. *Big Horn Sentinel*, October 18, 1884; November 8, 1884.

40. McLaird, "Ranching in the Big Horns," 181; Wright, "Necrology."

41. *Big Horn Sentinel*, January 24, 1885. Marriage license of Frank M. Canton and Anna May Wilkerson (Wyoming State Archives, Cheyenne). This document is an early example of Canton's misrepresentation of his age, which is shown as thirty. He turned thirty-five the previous September.

42. *Big Horn Sentinel*, January 24, 1885.

43. Johnson County, Wyoming, Assessment Rolls, 1884.

44. *Big Horn Sentinel*, February 28, 1885.

45. Ibid.

46. The story of the Bill Booth case is taken from issues of the *Big Horn Sentinel*, April 11, 1885, through March 6, 1886; Bancroft, "Interview with Sheriff Frank

M. Canton"; "The Canyon Secret," unidentified clipping, CC-AHC; Myers, *Buffalo's First Century*; Hill, "Buffalo," 139–40; Frye, *Atlas of Wyoming Outlaws*, 305–6; Canton, *Frontier Trails*, 43–48.

47. Frank M. Canton file, CC-AHC.

48. Bancroft, "Interview with Sheriff Frank M. Canton."

49. Ibid.

50. *Big Horn Sentinel*, December 6, 1885.

51. Ibid., January 2, 1886.

52. Ibid., December 26, 1885.

53. Johnson County, Wyoming, Commissioners' Books, July 7, 1886.

54. *Big Horn Sentinel*, February 6, 1886. J. Elmer Brock wrote in a letter to Russell Thorp on March 26, 1935: "I found a bill for the repair of three sets of shackles which Booth . . . had cut up with pen points. Later on I found the bill from the blacksmith who made a special set of shackles for this man, as well as an item in the bill for riveting them on him" (quoted in Burroughs, *Guardian of the Grasslands*, 154).

55. *Big Horn Sentinel*, February 27, 1886.

56. There were eleven legal hangings carried out in Wyoming counties between 1871 and 1903. The first was in April 1871 at Cheyenne. Canton's execution of Bill Booth in March 1886 was the fifth. The famous hanging of Tom Horn in Cheyenne in November 1903 was the last (Frye, *Atlas of Wyoming Outlaws*, 303–10).

57. A copy of this commission is in the Gatchell Museum, Buffalo, Wyoming.

58. Grayce Miller, "Frank Canton Most Colorful and Feared of All Wyoming Sheriffs," *Buffalo Bulletin*, August 21, 1958.

59. *Big Horn Sentinel*, March 6, 1886.

60. Ibid. Bills totaling $383.18 were submitted to cover the costs of Booth's execution: F. M. Canton (expenses), $141.25; T. Webber (lumber for scaffold), $58.31; Ben Cool (moving scaffold), $10.00; C. J. Hogerson (building scaffold), $129.59; C. W. Hine & Co. (lumber for scaffold), $44.03. The county commissioners authorized payment on April 7, 1886 (Johnson County, Wyoming, Commissioners' Books).

61. Bancroft, "Interview with Sheriff Frank M. Canton"; Cummins, *Jim Cummins' Book*, 71; Hanna, *An Old-Timer's Story of the Old Wild West*, 63; *Buffalo Bulletin*, July 2, 1959.

62. Details of the capture of Teton Jackson are from several undated and unidentified clippings in CC-WHC, Box 2, Folder 15; *Big Horn Sentinel*, October 17, 31, 1885; W. F. Hosford to C. W. Wright, quoted in Bailey, "Wyoming Stock Inspectors," 141–43; Canton, *Frontier Trails*, 36–42; Burt, *Powder River*, 309–10; DeArment, "Teton Jackson."

63. Burt, *Powder River*, 309–10. Burt owned a ranch in Teton Jackson's country and got this story from Chris Gross, whom he knew in later years.

64. Canton, *Frontier Trails*, 39–40.

65. Ibid., 41.

66. Ibid., 42. Canton said that Utah had offered rewards totaling $3,500 for Jackson, dead or alive (*Frontier Trails*, 37), but later said that he received from Idaho a reward of unspecified amount, which he shared equally with his two deputies (ibid., 42). The *Cheyenne Daily Leader* of October 22, 1885, reported, "Sheriff Canton

and his deputies secured some $1,500 dollars in rewards by the capture of Jackson and the recovery of the mares."

67. Undated clipping from a Blackfoot paper in cc-whc, Box 2, Folder 15.

68. *Big Horn Sentinel*, December 6, 1885. A coroner's jury found the shooting of Stevens "entirely justified" (ibid.), but two and a half years later Gross was indicted and tried for murder. He was "honorably acquitted, the evidence in the case showing conclusively that the shot that killed `Red Cloud' was fired in self-defense" (*Big Horn Sentinel*, July 7, 1888).

69. Burnett, "Frank Canton, the Sheriff."

70. Bancroft, "Interview with Sheriff Frank M. Canton"; *Big Horn Sentinel*, December 6 and 19, 1885, January 2 and 9, 1886; Frye, *Atlas of Wyoming Outlaws*, 284. Canton brought a civil suit against the deranged man, Orin Cook, and it still was unresolved seven years later when Canton left Johnson County (*Buffalo Bulletin*, November 10, 1892).

71. Canton, "The Capture of Samuel and Beaver"; Canton, *Frontier Trails*, 49–73. The article in *Breeders Gazette* included photographs of Canton, Sharp Nose, Black Coal, Washakie, and Mollie.

72. Bailey, "Wyoming Stock Inspectors," 94. The Frontier Land and Cattle Company paid McClellan and Glass $2.50 a day for the period from August 13 to 30. Canton paid them the same and billed the <sc>WSGA. He was reimbursed $133.00 for the expedition expenses. Canton misspelled Bear George's name "McClennan."

73. Canton, *Frontier Trails*, 57–58.

74. Ibid., 60–61.

75. Ibid., 63.

76. Ibid., 65–66. Canton never mentions him, but the celebrated scout Frank Grouard was dispatched by the post commander at Fort McKinney to help settle Canton's dispute with the Arapaho (Murray, *Military Posts in the Powder River Country*, 155–56).

77. Canton, *Frontier Trails*, 69.

78. Ibid., 72.

79. Ibid., 73; *Big Horn Sentinel*, December 11, 1886; Frye, *Atlas of Wyoming Outlaws*, 284. A correspondent for the *Cheyenne Daily Sun* saw the Indians when they arrived in Rawlins on their way home and said they now spoke English and "appeared to be well supplied with currency." In prison, one had learned the trade of shoemaker, and the other had learned furniture polishing. They gave their names as Frank Gilgonang and James Harnescap.

80. *Big Horn Sentinel*, January 2, February 13, March 20, July 17, 1886; Johnson County, Wyoming, Commissioners' Books, July 8, 1886; Frye, *Atlas of Wyoming Outlaws*, 285.

81. Bancroft, "Interview with Sheriff Frank M. Canton."

82. Bancroft, *History of the Pacific States*, 792.

83. McPherren, "Charles Basch."

84. Annie M. Canton to J. Elmer Brock, August 31, 1947, quoted in Hanson, *Powder River Country*, 224–25. The following month Frank Canton stopped at the Brock place again on his way to Buffalo with his prisoner Teton Jackson (ibid., 223).

85. Ibid.; *Big Horn Sentinel*, December 12, 1885.

86. Johnson County, Wyoming, Assessment Rolls, 1885. The lots were numbers 1 through 3 in block 3.

87. *Big Horn Sentinel,* December 19, 1885.

88. Ibid., January 2, 1886.

89. Canton File, Tisdale Collection. In 1885 the sheriff of Navarro County, Texas, of which Corsicana was the seat, was J. L. Walton, not "Wallace" (Tise, *Texas County Sheriffs,* 389). The 1886 Texas fugitive list showed Alf Rushing wanted in Navarro County for "theft of a beef." He was described as a "cow man," thirty years old, six feet and two inches tall, with red hair, and was "last heard of in Montana."

90. *Big Horn Sentinel,* March 6, 1886.

91. Ibid., March 27, 1886.

92. Johnson County, Wyoming, Commissioners' Books, April 7, 1886; *Big Horn Sentinel,* April 17, 1886.

93. *Cheyenne Daily Sun,* April 27, 1892.

94. LeFors, *Wyoming Peace Officer,* 52.

95. *Big Horn Sentinel,* August 28, 1886.

96. Ibid., July 3, December 25, 1886.

97. Ibid., May 15, 1886; Woods, *British Gentlemen in the Wild West,* 127. Canton may have felt indebted to Chapman, who had given him "material assistance" in the arrest of Samuel and Beaver the year before (*Buffalo Echo,* quoted in the *Laramie Daily Sentinel,* September 19, 1885).

98. Flannery, *John Hunton's Diary* 6:114.

99. *Big Horn Sentinel,* May 15, 1886. Before coming to Wyoming, Chapman had worked for the DHS outfit in Montana. A DHS cowboy named John Barrows remembered him as "a unique character . . . , an able cowman and a good rider [whose] distinguishing characteristic was his dare-deviltry. He was utterly lawless, a happy-go-lucky, unreliable friend, and an enemy to be feared. No small boy carried a chip more constantly on his shoulder than did Roach Chapman, the boss of our outfit" (Barrows, *U-Bet,* 136).

100. *Big Horn Sentinel,* May 29, 1886.

101. Ibid., June 28, July 17, August 14, 1886.

102. Ibid., September 11, 18, 1886.

103. Ibid., September 25, 1886; Canton, *Frontier Trails,* 42. Jackson was recaptured in 1888 and returned to prison. Pardoned in 1892, he lived for a number of years quietly on a small ranch in Fremont County, Wyoming, and died in the county home at Lander in 1927 (DeArment, "Teton Jackson").

104. *Big Horn Sentinel,* July 31, 1886. Jim Enochs was later elected sheriff of Sheridan County (Bard, *Horse Wrangler,* 46).

105. *Big Horn Sentinel,* September 4, 11, 1886.

106. Canton was generous to Snider in his autobiography, describing him as "a good man and a big-hearted fellow, [although] not sufficiently aggressive to make good as a Western sheriff" (*Frontier Trails,* 78). But Snider was aggressive enough to shoot twice at a Crow Indian for the crime of leaving a gate open, and Sheriff Canton had arrested him for it (Murray, *Military Posts in the Powder River Country,* 151).

107. *Big Horn Sentinel,* October 2, November 6, 13, 1886.

108. Ibid., November 13, 1886.

Chapter 4. The Detective, 1887–1890

1. Canton, *Frontier Trails,* 77.

2. Johnson County, Wyoming, Commissioners' Books, 1887.

3. Frye, *Atlas of Wyoming Outlaws,* 272–301.

4. Quoted in Bailey, "Wyoming Stock Inspectors," 135.

5. From a Cheyenne newspaper quoted in Flannery, *John Hunton's Diary* 6:107.

6. <sc>WSGA minutes quoted in Burroughs, *Guardian of the Grassland,* 148.

7. Ibid., 151.

8. Ibid., 151–52.

9. Copy of appointment dated November 3, 1886, is in *Ex parte Horner,* July 17, 1894, Governor's Pardon Papers.

10. Burroughs, *Guardian of the Grassland,* 152.

11. Ibid.; Bailey, "Wyoming Stock Inspectors," 135–36.

12. Bailey, "Wyoming Stock Inspectors," 60.

13. *Sundance Gazette,* April 29, 1887.

14. *Big Horn Sentinel,* April 23, 1887; *Sundance Gazette,* April 29, 1887

15. *Big Horn Sentinel,* September 3, 1887.

16. *Sundance Gazette,* September 16, 1887; *Big Horn Sentinel,* September 24, 1887; Frye, *Atlas of Wyoming Outlaws,* 271, 289.

17. Quoted in Bailey, "Wyoming Stock Inspectors," 95.

18. Ibid., 95–97.

19. Burroughs, *Guardian of the Grassland,* 129, 134.

20. Ibid., 130.

21. Smith, *The War on Powder River,* 59.

22. Ibid., 116–17.

23. Burroughs, *Guardian of the Grassland,* 130.

24. Kittrell, introduction to Mercer, *The Banditti of the Plains,* xxvi.

25. Bailey, "Wyoming Stock Inspectors," 146; copy of appointment as stock inspector, dated May 26, 1888, is in *Ex parte Horner,* July 17, 1894, Governor's Pardon Papers. Strangely Canton, in his published memoirs, never mentioned his service as detective chief for the <sc>WSGA.

26. F. M. Canton to Thomas H. Irvine, May 18, 1888, Thomas H. Irvine Papers.

27. Annie M. Canton to J. Elmer Brock, August 31, 1947, quoted in Hanson, *Powder River Country,* 224–25; *Big Horn Sentinel,* September 8, 22, 1888.

28. *Big Horn Sentinel,* November 10, 1888.

29. Thrapp, *Encyclopedia of Frontier Biography* 1:27.

30. David, *Malcolm Campbell, Sheriff,* 69.

31. Quoted in Smith, *The War on Powder River,* 119. Rancher W. E. Guthrie, who would ride with Canton in the famous "cattlemen's invasion" of Johnson County in April 1892, said, "The sheriff [Angus] and his deputies were well known outlaws" (Guthrie, "The Johnson County Invasion; or, The Wyoming Rustler War").

32. *Big Horn Sentinel,* January 12, 19, February 16, March 23, April 20, 1889. Rheumatism plagued many men who often slept out on the ground in the northern country. Nate Champion, a Texan destined to play a prominent role in Canton's life, also was bedridden with the ailment. He was helpless when two friends took him to

NOTES TO PAGES 83–90

a desolate spot at the Bighorn Hot Springs, covered him with hot mud, and departed. Champion thought he had been left to die. But later, when the friends returned and removed the mud, he felt better. The treatment was continued until he could walk again (Walker, *Stories of Early Days in Wyoming*, 103).

33. LeFors, *Wyoming Peace Officer*, 57; Canton, *Frontier Trails*, 79. Both Canton and LeFors spelled the name "Haywood," but it appeared as "Heywood" in newspaper advertisements.

34. LeFors, *Wyoming Peace Officer*, 57–58.

35. Ibid., 58.

36. *Big Horn Sentinel*, July 27, 1889.

37. Smith, *The War on Powder River*, viii.

38. F. M. Canton to Thomas B. Adams, March 17, 1887, quoted in Burroughs, *Guardian of the Grassland*, 159.

39. Author interviews with Tom Tisdale, June 21 and July 28, 1992; *Cheyenne Daily Sun*, April 27, 1892.

40. The cases against the six defendants appeared in Criminal Appearance Docket No. 1, District Court, Johnson County, as numbers 168 and 172 through 178 inclusive (Smith, *The War on Powder River*, 118–19); *Big Horn Sentinel*, July 6, 13, 1889.

41. "The Wyoming Cattle War," *Frank Leslie's Weekly*, June 2, 1892; Smith, *The War on Powder River*, 117.

42. Smith, *The War on Powder River*, 121. Ellen Watson was called "Cattle Kate" in the contemporary press, but this was apparently a deliberate attempt to confuse Watson with a notorious trollop named "Cattle Kate" Maxwell in order to blacken her character (Hufsmith, *The Wyoming Lunching of Cattle Kate*, 43–44).

43. Clay, *My Life on the Range*, 164–65; Mokler, *History of Natrona County*, 275.

44. *Buffalo Bulletin*, October 23, 1890, July 2, August 13, 20, 1891; Undated, unidentified clipping, cc-whc, Box 2, Folder 14; Mokler, *History of Natrona County*, 274–75; Frye, *Atlas of Wyoming Outlaws*, 121.

45. Smith, *The War on Powder River*, 148–49. A strong case has been made that Elliott and Smith lynched Waggoner and that the third man was a nonparticipating prisoner named Burns, whom Elliott was conveying from the Buffalo jail (Hawthorne, "Conflict and Conspiracy," 12–17).

46. Johnson County, Wyoming, Assessment Rolls, 1889. The two new town lots were numbers 16 and 17 in block 3.

47. Tanner, "The Disposal of the Public Domain in Johnson County," 64–65. Canton abandoned the property after the events of 1892 and paid no more taxes. On May 28, 1898, Sarah E. Webber was granted a sheriff's deed and took possession.

48. Johnson County, Wyoming, Assessment Rolls, 1890. Among Canton's assets were "private libraries" valued at $55.

49. Burnett, "Frank Canton, the Sheriff."

50. Ibid. The land was valued at ten dollars per acre irrigated and five dollars for grazing.

51. Quoted in Bailey, "Wyoming Stock Inspectors," 117.

52. Copy of appointment dated November 12, 1890, is in *Ex parte Horner*, July

17, 1894, Governor's Pardon Papers. The *Buffalo Bulletin* announced the appointment in its issue of December 11, 1890.

53. Frye, *Atlas of Wyoming Outlaws,* 116; Pointer, *In Search of Butch Cassidy,* 60–62.

54. From an interview with T. Jeff Carr about Canton in the *Cheyenne Tribune,* December 5, 1907.

55. *Cheyenne Daily Leader,* quoted in the *Buffalo Bulletin,* April 9, 1891.

56. *Buffalo Bulletin,* April 30, 1891; *Laramie Boomerang,* September 22, 1891; *Cheyenne Tribune,* December 5, 1907. In 1900, Brown was transferred to an insane asylum at Washington, D.C. Parker was pardoned on Christmas Day, 1897, by President William McKinley and later rode with the gang of his brother, Butch Cassidy (Frye, *Atlas of Wyoming Outlaws,* 259; Baker, *The Wild Bunch at Robbers Roost,* 110).

57. Wister to his mother, June 26, 1891, quoted in Wister, *Owen Wister Out West,* 116.

58. Watson, *The Real Virginian*; Payne, *Owen Wister,* 314. Payne contends that the character of the Virginian was based primarily on a Wyoming cowboy named George B. West (ibid., 203).

59. Wister to his mother, June 25, 1891, quoted in Wister, *Owen Wister Out West,* 115.

60. Wister to his mother, June 26, 1891, quoted in ibid., 117–18.

61. *Buffalo Bulletin,* July 2, 1891.

62. Ibid., July 9, 1891.

63. Ibid.

64. Ibid., August 20, September 10, 17, 1891.

65. David, *Malcolm Campbell, Sheriff,* 127.

66. *Buffalo Bulletin,* August 11, 1892; author interview with Tom Tisdale, July 28, 1992. Some of the press, and some officers perhaps, confused Champion with an outlaw named Charles Taylor, who operated in Johnson County at this time. A story in the *Chicago Blade* of March 12, 1892, and reprinted in the *Buffalo Bulletin* on March 31, 1892, was headed "FOUR BAD MEN" and told of "unhung scoundrels" Nat [sic] Champion, Lee West [sic, Lou Webb], Al Allison, and Jack Flagg. Champion, it said, came from Texas under the name Charles Taylor. "His true name is as yet unknown in Colorado or Wyoming."

67. *Buffalo Bulletin,* December 17, 1891.

68. Ibid. According to a story passed down in the Tisdale family, Champion later suspected Gilbertson was in on the plot to kill him (author interview with Tom Tisdale, July 28, 1992).

69. *Buffalo Bulletin,* February 4, 1892.

70. Although all other contemporary and later accounts give Ray's first name as "Nick," it is recorded as "Reuben" in the information filed against those accused of killing him (*State of Wyoming v. Frank M. Canton et al.:* Number 379).

71. Quoted in Penrose, *The Rustler Business,* 21. See also the *Chicago Herald,* April 19, 1892; David, *Malcolm Campbell, Sheriff,* 122.

72. Smith, *The War on Powder River,* 159. According to the Tisdale family story, one of Shonsey's arms was bandaged, indicating that he too had been hit by one of

Champion's bullets. Champion did not kill Shonsey on the spot because he did not blame the gunmen as much as he did those that hired them (author interview with Tom Tisdale, July 28, 1992).

73. Author interview with Tom Tisdale, July 28, 1992; Hanson, *Powder River Country*, 259–60.

74. As to Canton's involvement, it is significant that Jack Flagg, his bitter enemy, in a series of articles running the following spring in the *Buffalo Bulletin*, did not name him as one of those assaulting Champion. Flagg said that six men were in the party, but he identified only Elliott and Shonsey (Flagg, *A Review of the Cattle Business*, 60–62). The "confession" of George Dunning, one of the Johnson County invaders, was first published in A. S. Mercer's *Northwestern Livestock Journal* in October 1892. It named Canton, Elliott, Tom Smith, and Fred Coates as the men who attacked Champion, and it alleged that the <sc>WSGA had offered $1,500 for each rustler killed (issue of October 15, 1892, reprinted as an appendix to Mercer, *The Banditti of the Plains*, 172–73). Charley Ford, manager of the TA Ranch, twenty miles south of Buffalo, has also been named as one of the party (March 1978 interview with B. H. Turk, former sheriff of Johnson County, in Local History Collection, Johnson County Library, Buffalo).

Chapter 5. The Accused, 1891

1. *Buffalo Bulletin*, November 26, 1891.

2. Ibid.

3. B. H. Turk interview.

4. Smith, *The War on Powder River*, 120; Burroughs, *Guardian of the Grassland*, 73.

5. Frink, *Cow Country Cavalcade*, 139.

6. Smith, *The War on Powder River*, 120.

7. Smith, *The War on Powder River*, 161.

8. Woods, *British Gentlemen in the Wild West*, 124.

9. *Cheyenne Daily Sun*, reprinted in *Buffalo Bulletin*, December 17, 1891.

10. This story apparently first appeared in Flagg's *A Review of the Cattle Business*, published in eleven installments in the spring of 1892. It was repeated in Mercer's polemic, *The Banditti of the Plains* (26), and has appeared in virtually every pro-rustler account since.

11. *Buffalo Echo*, December 12, 1891; Bard, *Horse Wrangler*, 40.

12. *Buffalo Echo*, December 12, 1891.

13. Statement of Charles F. Basch taken at Sheridan, Wyoming, April 9, 1935, CC-AHC. The *Cheyenne Daily Leader* of March 8, 1893, reported Freeman as exclaiming, "Then Canton has killed him."

14. Statement of Charles F. Basch, April 9, 1935.

15. "Testimony of Charles Franklin Bash [*sic*], May 11, 1935," recorded by J. Elmer Brock, Tisdale Collection.

16. Smith, *The War on Powder River*, 166.

17. From the testimony of Basch at the hearing before Justice of the Peace Carroll

H. Parmelee, December 8, 1891, and reported in *Buffalo Bulletin*, December 10, 1891, and *Buffalo Echo*, December 12, 1891.

18. Recorded by J. Elmer Brock, May 11, 1935, Tisdale Collection.

19. *Buffalo Echo*, December 5, 1891. Floyd Bard remembered the name of the man who discovered Jones's body as Jim Ricker (Bard, *Horse Wrangler*, 42).

20. *Buffalo Bulletin*, December 10, 1891.

21. Flagg, *A Review of the Cattle Business*, 67.

22. Canton, *Frontier Trails*, 84.

23. *Buffalo Echo*, December 12, 1891.

24. Unidentified, undated clipping, CC-WHC, Box 2, Folder 15.

25. The *Buffalo Bulletin* issue of December 10 and the *Buffalo Echo* of December 12 were devoted almost exclusively to the hearing. The testimony covered four full columns over three pages.

26. *Buffalo Echo*, December 12, 1891.

27. Ibid.

28. Flagg, *A Review of the Cattle Business*, 68.

29. *Buffalo Echo*, December 12, 1891.

30. Ibid.

31. Ibid.

32. Author interview with Tom Tisdale, July 28, 1992; April 13, 1892, clipping from a Cheyenne paper in CC-WHC, Canton Scrapbook.

33. H. S. Elliott to F. M. Canton, December 16, 1891, CC-WHC, Box 1, Folder 2.

34. *Buffalo Bulletin*, December 24, 1891; Canton, *Frontier Trails*, 85; Smith, *The War on Powder River*, 175.

35. Canton, *Frontier Trails*, 85–87; Fred Hesse afterward related essentially this same story (Smith, *The War on Powder River*, 175).

36. *Sheridan Enterprise*, January 2, 1892, quoting the *Cheyenne Daily Leader*.

37. *Buffalo Bulletin*, February 4, 1892. The issue of December 24, 1891, however, contained only the simple announcement: "F.M. Canton and F.G.S. Hesse left for the east on Thursday last."

38. Canton, *Frontier Trails*, 87.

39. *Cheyenne Daily Sun*, December 25, 1891; *Sheridan Enterprise*, January 2, 1892, quoting the *Cheyenne Daily Leader*; undated, unidentified clipping, CC-WHC, Box 2, Folder 15.

40. *Buffalo Bulletin*, December 31, 1891.

41. *Cheyenne Daily Leader*, December 8, 1891.

42. *Cheyenne Daily Sun*, December 25, 1891.

43. Rollinson, *Wyoming Cattle Trails*, 282.

44. Baber, *The Longest Rope*, 111.

45. John C. Thompson, "In Old Wyoming," *Wyoming State Tribune*, December 22, 1941.

46. Illinois State Board of Health, Cook County, Certificate of Death, Helen Canton; *Buffalo Bulletin*, January 28, 1892; Canton, *Frontier Trails*, 87.

47. *Buffalo Bulletin*, December 10, 1891; *Buffalo Echo*, December 12, 1891.

48. Hope, "Joe Elliott's Story," 154–55.

49. Ibid.; *Buffalo Bulletin*, February 11, March 10, 1892.

50. *Buffalo Bulletin,* March 31, 1892.

51. Although in later years a rumor was prevalent in Buffalo that "the real reason for the invasion was to secure and destroy the records in the courthouse of that town that incriminated Frank Canton in the murder of Tisdale" (Agnes Wright Spring note in CC-AHC), it is clear that the cattlemen's decision to raid the county was made *before* the murder of Tisdale.

52. *State of Wyoming, Plaintiff, v. Frank M. Canton, Defendant, Information Charging the Said Defendant with the Murder of John A. Tisdale,* District Court Journal No. 3, Johnson County, Wyoming; *Buffalo Bulletin,* March 14, 1892.

53. The letters of Judge Blake and County Attorney Bennett were printed in full under the headline "<sc>TWO REMARKABLE DOCUMENTS" in the *Buffalo Bulletin,* March 24, 1892.

54. Ibid.

55. Ibid.

56. Canton bondsmen in the invading army were Hubert E. Teschemacher, William C. Irvine, Fred Hesse, Lafayette H. Parker, A. R. Powers, Elias W. Whitcomb, Arthur B. Clarke, John N. Tisdale, David R. Tisdale, Charles S. Ford, Henry W. Davis, William E. Guthrie, and Frank H. Laberteaux. In addition to those named, other bondsmen were George P. Bissell and Ralph M. Friend (*State of Wyoming v. Frank M. Canton:* Number 21). John N. and David R. Tisdale, brothers, were not related to John A. Tisdale, the murder victim.

Chapter 6. The Warrior, 1892–1893

1. Stuart, *Pioneering in Montana,* 194–209; Thrapp, *Encyclopedia of Frontier Biography* 3:1380.

2. Millions of words have been written about the "cattlemen's invasion." It received national attention in the contemporary press. The guns had hardly cooled when Jack Flagg, the most literate of the rustlers, authored a history of the war. Entitled *A Review of the Cattle Business in Johnson County, Wyoming, since 1882, and the Causes that Led to the Recent Invasion,* it ran serially in the *Buffalo Bulletin* from May 5 to July 14, 1892. This treatise did not make much impact beyond the immediate area, nor did "The Confession of George Dunning," which was published in A. S. Mercer's *Northwestern Livestock Journal* in October 1892. But Mercer's 1894 book, *The Banditti of the Plains; or, The Cattlemen's Invasion of Wyoming in 1892,* with the hyperbolic subtitle *The Crowning Infamy of the Ages,* drawn in large part from the writings of Flagg and Dunning, eventually found wide readership and is the basis for most of what has been written about the invasion since. Virtually all of the secondary accounts of the Johnson County Cattle War have followed Flagg and Mercer in excoriating the cattlemen as greedy and murderous plunderers. It was thirty-six years before a general audience had an opportunity to read an opposing view. With the publication of *Frontier Trails,* Frank Canton's memoirs, in 1930, the cause of the invaders was defended by one of them. Two years later additional support for the cattlemen's view appeared in Robert B. David's *Malcolm Campbell, Sheriff.* A defense of the invaders written in 1914, *The Rustler*

Business, by Dr. Charles B. Penrose, who accompanied the expedition, was not published until 1959. Of secondary accounts, by far the most thoroughly researched and impartially presented is *The War on Powder River* by Helena Huntington Smith, published in 1966.

3. Penrose said that the cattlemen "selected 19 men who they thought should die for the good of the country" (Penrose, *The Rustler Business,* 22). George Dunning wrote that he was told it would be necessary to "kill off about 30 men in Johnson county" (Dunning, "Confession," reprinted in Mercer, *The Banditti of the Plains,* 160). In the special publication "The Cattle Barons' Rebellion," issued by the *Buffalo Bulletin* on April 24, 1892, editor C. M. Lingle charged that there were "forty-two men ... this expedition had marked for death and proposed to murder." A letter written from Buffalo that month and widely accepted by rustler partisans placed the number at seventy. Purportedly written by Mary S. Watkins, sister of the coroner, the letter was published in the *Laramie Boomerang* of April 18, 1892. In a story datelined Cheyenne, April 22, the *New York Times* of April 23, 1892, reported: "In the gripsack of Canton, one of the prominent men of the expedition, was found a list of seventy rustlers who were either to be shot or hanged. Also a list of ranch houses that were [to be] burned." The *Cheyenne Daily Sun,* always a champion of the cattlemen, in its issue of April 28, 1892, scoffed at the figure and alleged that the letter was the work of Red Angus.

4. David, *Malcolm Campbell, Sheriff,* 167.

5. *Chicago Herald,* April 19, 1892.

6. Watkins's letter in *Laramie Boomerang,* April 18, 1892; *Cheyenne Daily Sun,* April 28, 1892.

7. Canton, *Frontier Trails,* 87–88.

8. After the invasion debacle, many of these men denied prior knowledge of the plan, and there is no clear proof that they did have any such knowledge (Smith, *The War on Powder River,* 298).

9. Flagg wrote that Canton and cattleman Lafayette H. Parker "were sent to Texas to hire all of the bad characters, who, for five dollars a day, would be willing to join a raid to kill settlers in Johnson County" (Flagg, *A Review of the Cattle Business,* 68). Mercer alleged that Canton was dispatched on this mission with cattlemen George W. Baxter and R. M. Allen and detective Tom Smith (Mercer, *The Banditti of the Plains,* 46).

10. McLaird, "Ranching in the Big Horns."

11. John N. Tisdale served in the senate of the first state legislature. David ("Bob") Tisdale, who ran the TTT Ranch on Willow Creek with his brother, was an incredibly cruel and brutal man, according to Owen Wister, who spent some time at the ranch in the summer of 1891. As recorded in his journal, Wister saw Tisdale ride his horse to complete exhaustion and then deliberately gouge out the animal's eye because it could move no farther (Wister, *Owen Wister Out West,* 108–9).

12. The Texas gunmen identified in the court records and contemporary literature were William Armstrong; Robert Barling (Barlin, Barlings); J. K. Barling (Barlin, Barlings); J. M. Benford (Buford, Beuford); D. E. Booker (alias D. E. Brooke, alias the Texas Kid); Jim Dudley (alias Gus Green); Buck Garrett; J. A. Garrett; Alex Howerton (alias Hamilton); J. C. Johnson; William Little; Alex Lowther; M. A.

McNally; Jeff D. Mynett; K. Pickard (Rickard); B. C. Schultz (Schultze); S. S. Tucker; George R. Tucker; Bill Wiley (Wille, Willey); and W. A. Wilson. There may have been others. Robert B. David, drawing on the recollections of his father, Edward David, and invasion participants Mike Shonsey and W. E. Guthrie, said there were three Texans--one Calhoun and two others unnamed--who were wounded during the fight at the KC Ranch, left to get treatment, and were never arrested (David, *Malcolm Campbell, Sheriff,* 209, 234).

13. Quoted in Penrose, *The Rustler Business,* 23–24.

14. Ibid., 24.

15. Dunning, "Confession," reprinted in Mercer, *The Banditti of the Plains,* 179.

16. Shonsey said there were fourteen rustlers at the KC, according to William Irvine (in a November 2, 1913, letter to Charles Penrose, quoted in Penrose, *The Rustler Business,* 22), but David wrote that there were five: Nate Champion, Nick Ray, Billy Hill, Ed Starr, and Jack Long (David, *Malcolm Campbell,* Sheriff, 178).

17. The dispute at the Tisdale ranch was related in detail in a letter from Sam Clover to Henry A. Blair dated May 15, 1892 (reprinted in *Westerners Brand Book, Chicago Corral,* for February 1953).

18. Mercer, *The Banditti of the Plains,*60–61.

19. David said Canton was throwing the rope from the stable toward the cabin, "either in an unsuccessful attempt to attach the knob and tear away the door and frame, or to cause Champion to show himself (David, *Malcolm Campbell, Sheriff,* 198).

20. Thirty-four years later Canton was asked how the invaders allowed Flagg to escape. "We were not sure it was Jack," he said, "until he crossed the bridge and he went so fast we could not get him then. We did not want to make any mistakes" (William E. Hawks to Anna Canton, January 7, 1928, CC-WHC, Box 1, Folder 54).

21. Quoted in Penrose, *The Rustler Business,* 28.

22. *Chicago Herald,* April 16, 1892. Even Frank Canton appreciated Champion's bravery: "He came out fighting and died game. If he had been fighting in a good cause he would have been a hero" (Canton, *Frontier Trails,* 92).

23. Baber, *The Longest Rope,* 138. Champion's dramatic notes were first published in full in Sam Clover's story of the raid, printed in *Chicago Herald,* April 16, 1892, and have been reprinted in virtually every account of the Johnson County Cattle War since. Clover kept the original notebook, which has since disappeared.

24. Baber, *The Longest Rope,* 134.

25. *Chicago Herald,* April 16, 1892.

26. Agnes Wright Spring note in CC-AHC; author interview with Tom Tisdale, July 28, 1992.

27. *Cheyenne Daily Sun,* April 27, 1892.

28. Smith, *The War on Powder River,* 253; unidentified clipping, CC-WHC, Box 2, Folder 15.

29. Sam Clover to Henry A. Blair, May 15, 1892.

30. Mercer, *The Banditti of the Plains,* 83.

31. A variant on the tradition of vigilantism in America, the phenonemon of the whitecaps began in Indiana in 1887 and spread across the nation in the last years of the nineteenth century. Originally defined as "a movement of violent moral regula-

tion by local masked bands," whitecapping developed "in the realm of human be-havior where the authority of the law was either not clear or non-existent" (Brown, *Strain of Violence,* 150–51).

32. Canton claimed the fortifications were constructed at his suggestion (*Frontier Trails,* 94). Joe Elliott also took credit for the idea: "I've got to say that it was me that forced the building of those fortifications there" (Hope, "Joe Elliott's Story," 159).

33. The messenger, whose identity was never disclosed, was probably one of the TA cowboys. Canton said the call for help went out from well-meaning "friends in Buffalo and Cheyenne [who believed] they were doing the only thing to save our lives . . . , but they made a very serious mistake, which resulted in the ruin of many of us financially and completely broke up all our plans for the campaign against the rustlers" (Canton, *Frontier Trails,* 103).

34. Moreton Frewen quoted the telegram in a March 29, 1922, letter to S. P. Panton of Casper. The letter was reprinted in an unidentified April 13, 1922, news-paper clipping, "An Echo from the Past," Grace R. Hebard Collection, American Heritage Center, University of Wyoming, Laramie).

35. Quoted in full in Smith, *The War on Powder River,* 224.

36. Ibid.

37. Ibid., 225.

38. David, *Malcolm Campbell, Sheriff,* 252.

39. Quoted in Penrose, *The Rustler Business,* 31.

40. Ibid., 33.

41. Bard, *Horse Wrangler,* 44.

42. Hope, "Joe Elliott's Story," 161.

43. Quoted in Penrose, *The Rustler Business,* 32.

44. Canton, *Frontier Trails,* 99.

45. Mercer, *The Banditti of the Plains,* 69–71.

46. The various accounts are in conflict on even so basic a point as the time of the cavalry's arrival. Mercer said the troops arrived "a little after sunup (ibid.). Van Horn reported reaching the scene at precisely 6:45 <sc>a.m. (Smith, *The War on Powder River,* 225). Will Irvine remembered seeing the soldiers coming at "about 10 o'clock" (Penrose, *The Rustler Business,* 32), and Canton thought it was "about noon" (*Frontier Trails,* 102).

47. Quoted in Smith, *The War on Powder River,* 226.

48. Irvine is quoted in Penrose, *The Rustler Business,* 32–33; Clover is quoted in Mercer, *The Banditti of the Plains,* 71.

49. Canton, *Frontier Trails,* 102–3.

50. Smith, *The War on Powder River,* 226. The fifty-two men who started on the expedition had been joined by Mike Shonsey, Phil DuFran, and Sam Sutherland. Roster reductions included Jim Dudley, who was wounded and taken to the fort, and the defectors: newspapermen Towse and Clover, Dr. Penrose, and ranchers H. W. Davis and Dick Allen. The three teamsters--William Collum, George ("Tex") Helm, and Charles ("Shorty") Austin--were captured with the wagons.

51. *Cheyenne Daily Sun,* April 28, 1892.

52. Hope, "Joe Elliott's Story," 161. In May of the following year Dudley Cham-

pion was shot and killed by Mike Shonsey (*Cheyenne Daily Leader*, May 24, 1893).

53. Hope, "Joe Elliott's Story," 161. As the column passed Haywood's Gulch, according to a story in the *Chicago Herald* of April 25, 1892, Al Allison rode up to the column, "and leaning toward Canton, said quietly, 'Do you remember this, Frank?' Canton deigned no notice and calmly pulled away at his brierwood pipe."

54. *Buffalo Bulletin*, May 12, 19, 1892. Deputies employed by Rankin included Thomas G. Smith, T. Jeff Carr, Frank Grouard, Baptiste ("Little Bat") Garnier, and Tom Horn, going by the name "Thomas H. Hale." The list of those enjoined was virtually the same as that published in the *Chicago Herald* of April 19, 1892, and, presumably, duplicated the cattlemen's "death list" (Subpoenas, *Henry Blair et al. v. O. H. Flagg et al.*, May 4, 1892, Circuit Court of the United States, for the District of Wyoming).

55. Charles H. Burritt to F. M. Canton, May 17, 1892.

56. *Cheyenne Daily Sun*, May 25, 1892; Smith, *The War on Powder River*, 254–58. Members of the Red Sash Gang are said to have worn crimson sashes around their waist to protect their clothing from oily cartridges in their loop belts. Nate Champion reportedly led the gang until his death (David, *Malcolm Campbell, Sheriff*, 127). A prolific crime "historian" has made the preposterous statement that the Red Sash Gang "was headed at times by gunslinger Frank M. Canton and Major Frank Wolcott." This writer also invented the fiction that Canton's "nerves began to come apart" after the killing of Champion: "Between fits of insomnia, he had fearsome nightmares, screaming in his sleep for his confederates to get their guns and horses" (Nash, *Bloodletters and Badmen*, 323–24; Nash, *Encyclopedia of World Crime* 1:601–2, 3:2555.

57. Smith, *The War on Powder River*, 259. Wellman's revolver is now on display in the Gatchell Museum in Buffalo.

58. *State of Wyoming v. Frank M. Canton et al.*: Number 365.

59. *Cheyenne Daily Sun*, August 5, 1892; *Cheyenne Daily Leader*, August 5, 1892; Smith, *The War on Powder River*, 263. In a long, violence-filled life, this was the only gunshot wound Canton ever suffered.

60. *Cheyenne Daily Sun*, August 7, 1892; David, *Malcolm Campbell, Sheriff*, 341.

61. *State of Wyoming v. Frank M. Canton et al.*: Number 365; *State of Wyoming v. Frank M. Canton et al.*: Number 379.

62. George B. McClellan, "What I Know about the Invasion," *Worland Grit*, June 6, 1935.

63. *State of Wyoming v. Frank M. Canton*: Number 21.

64. *Buffalo Bulletin*, October 6, 27, 1892.

65. Ibid., November 3, 1892.

66. *State of Wyoming v. Frank M. Canton*: Number 21; *Cheyenne Daily Sun*, January 22, 1893; *Cheyenne Daily Leader*, January 22, 1893.

67. *State of Wyoming v. Frank M. Canton*: Number 21.

68. Ibid.

69. *Evanston Register*, April 8, 1893.

70. *State of Wyoming v. Frank M. Canton*: Number 21.

71. Baber, *The Longest Rope*, 216–66.

72. Reported in the *Lusk Herald* and reprinted in the *Cheyenne Daily Leader,* March 23, 1893.

73. Even the rumor mills of Buffalo ground out little to corroborate Basch's story. "A German washer woman" is said to have come forward and sworn that she saw Canton ride in on a lathered horse the day of the Tisdale murder (author interview with Tom Tisdale, July 28, 1992).

74. *Cheyenne Daily Sun,* December 25, 1891.

75. *Cheyenne Daily Leader,* March 8, 1893.

76. In a 1938 interview, Basch said he was confronted on the road to Douglas by "Quick Shot" Davis and another man, who told him to keep moving south: "I went to Fort Collins, Colorado, where I worked on a ranch; my wife was terribly worried." But this was in the winter of 1891–92, according to Basch, who said he was back in Johnson County at the time of the invasion and did not mention fleeing again in 1893 (McPherren, "Charles Basch"). John Washbaugh, the grandson of Basch, said that sometime after the Tisdale murder, the Washbaughs heard that his enemies "were going to get Mr. Basch one night," so they had Basch and his wife stay with them. Returning to the Basch home in the morning, they found it had been broken into and articles were scattered about. "My grandfather was very lucky that he was not at home. He left here a short time after that and we did not know where he was for a long time" (Washbaugh, "The Murder of John A. Tisdale").

77. Handwritten statement of C. F. Basch in CC-AHC. In another version of the story, Basch said "he recognized Canton by his walk" (Washbaugh, "The Murder of John A. Tisdale").

78. "Testimony of Charles Franklin Bash [*sic*], May 11, 1935."

79. McPherren, "Charles Basch."

80. Nash, *Encyclopedia of World Crime* 1:187.

81. Kittrell, introduction to Mercer, *The Banditti of the Plains,* xxxiv–xlvi.

82. Horan, *The Authentic Wild West,* 233.

83. Drago, *The Great Range Wars,* 262–63.

84. Horn, *Life of Tom Horn,* 225.

85. Monaghan, *The Legend of Tom Horn,* 146.

86. Baber, *The Longest Rope,* 109–10.

87. Siringo, *Two Evil Isms,* 44. Siringo is often in error, however, as in his assertion that Tom Horn and Frank Canton were half-brothers (ibid., 45).

88. *Buffalo Bulletin,* May 12, 19, 1892; *Daily Nevada State Journal,* April 10, 1891, quoted in Nunis, *The Life of Tom Horn Revisited,* 51.

89. Tom Horn was subpoenaed to appear at a hearing charging Henry Smith, Clayton Crews, and Ed Starr with "conspiring to waylay and kill" Wellman (documents in Johnson County War File, American Heritage Center, University of Wyoming, Laramie).

90. Hanson, *Powder River Country,* 427–28.

91. The Horn "confession" has been quoted many times, most recently in Nunis, *The Life of Tom Horn Revisited,* 67.

Chapter 7. The Undersheriff, 1894–1895

1. *National Cyclopedia of American Biography* 10:475.

2. These letters are in *Ex parte Horner,* July 17, 1894, Governor's Pardon Papers.

3. P. B. Weare to George Shoup, January 17, 1894 (cc-whc, Box 1, Folder 16).

4. J. Sterling Morton to Richard Olney, January 23, 1894 (*Ex parte Horner,* July 17, 1894, Governor's Pardon Papers). Morton is credited with originating Arbor Day.

5. P. B. Weare to Walter Q. Gresham, January 27, 1894 (*Ex parte Horner,* July 17, 1894, Governor's Pardon Papers).

6. *Ex parte Horner,* July 17, 1894, Governor's Pardon Papers.

7. J. Sterling Morton, Secretary of Agriculture, to Benjamin P. Moore, Collector of Customs, Sitka, Alaska, April 9, 1894, and T. C. Power, U.S. Senator, to B. P. Moore, with an added endorsement from John M. Carey, U.S. Senator, April 9, 1894 (*Ex parte Horner,* July 17, 1894, Governor's Pardon Papers.

8. U.S. Indian Agent at Ponca Agency, O.T., to M. F. Lake, April 4, 1893 (Indian and Pioneer Records, Ponca Agency, 22:294); U.S. Agent at Ponca Agency, O.T., to Commissioner of Indian Affairs, Washington, August 5, 1893 (Indian and Pioneer Records, Ponca Agency, 24:10); *Portrait and Biographical Record of Oklahoma,* 50–51.

9. *Pawnee Agency Scout,* September 6, October 10, 1893; *Pawnee Times-Democrat,* December 28, 1893.

10. Frank Canton is erroneously named as one of the officers in the Ingalls raid by Drago in *Outlaws on Horseback,* 242, 246. In September 1893 Canton was still in Nebraska City.

11. In *Heck Thomas,* Shirley had the posse led by "Sheriff Frank Lake and his chief deputy, Frank Canton" (215). The error is repeated in Hanes, *Bill Doolin,* 129. In late January 1894, Frank Lake had not yet assumed the office of sheriff, and Frank Canton was in Washington, D.C., campaigning for appointment as U.S. marshal of Alaska.

12. *Pawnee Agency Scout,* February 9, 1894.

13. *Pawnee Times-Democrat,* April 27, 1894; *Pawnee Agency Scout,* May 4, 1894.

14. *Pawnee Agency Scout,* May 11, 1894. Fred Hesse accompanied Canton to Pawnee. The *Pawnee Times-Democrat* of May 25 noted that "Fred Hess, of Omaha, Nebraska, has been here for two weeks disposing of a carload of fine roadster horses."

15. There is a single mention of George Horner in Canton's memoirs and then with no indication that the man was his brother, only that he was "one of the gamest deputies on the sheriff's force." The name appears as George "Hanner" in *Frontier Trails* (117). This was probably an error by editor Edward Everett Dale in deciphering Canton's scrawl and not a deliberate effort to obscure the Horner relationship.

16. Canton, "Memories of the Border." This section of Canton's memoirs was unaccountably omitted by editor Dale in *Frontier Trails.*

17. *Pawnee Times-Democrat,* May 18, 1894.

18. Ibid., June 1, 1894.

19. Ibid., June 22, 1894.

20. Webb, *Handbook of Texas* 2:386.

21. Frank Kell to J. Elmer Brock, September 10, 1936. Kell knew Canton in later years and presumably got this story from him.

22. From an undated *New York Sun* clipping (Canton File, Tisdale Collection). Some verification that Canton and Hogg did hunt together appears in an Oklahoma newspaper item in September 1927, at the time of Canton's death. Two nephews of Burk Burnett's who attended the funeral recalled that Hogg and Canton had hunted together on the Burnett ranchland (CC-AHC).

23. *Ex parte Horner,* July 17, 1894, Governor's Pardon Papers.

24. Ibid.

25. Ibid.

26. Ibid.

27. Ibid.

28. Ibid.

29. Ibid.

30. This was a lie. They were married under his Canton alias (Territory of Wyoming, County of Johnson, Marriage License, Frank M. Canton and Anna M. Wilkerson, January 19, 1885).

31. *Ex parte Horner,* July 17, 1894, Governor's Pardon Papers. Horner's pardon came just four months after Governor Hogg pardoned John Wesley Hardin, who served sixteen years of his twenty-five-year sentence.

32. Ibid.

33. *Pawnee Times-Democrat,* July 27, 1894.

34. Ibid., May 25, 1894.

35. Ibid., June 29, 1894.

36. Ibid., July 6, 1894.

37. Ibid., August 17, 1894.

38. *Pawnee Agency Scout,* December 7, 1894.

39. Harman, *Hell on the Border,* 403.

40. *Pawnee Times-Democrat,* August 24, November 16, 30, December 7, 1894, February 1, April 19, 26, 1895; *Pawnee Appeal,* November 30, 1894; *Pawnee Agency Scout,* December 12, 1894.

41. *Pawnee Times-Democrat,* July 6, 1894.

42. Ibid., August 21, 1894. Canton stated in his memoirs that the Shelleys used a revolver smuggled in by Bill's wife to effect their escape (*Frontier Trails,* 122). No mention of a weapon is made in the news account.

43. Canton, *Frontier Trails,* 122.

44. Ibid., 122–23. Horton was a Kentuckian who went to the Cherokee Nation in 1868. He settled in Stillwater in 1889 and in the run of 1893 moved on to Pawnee, where he opened the first saloon in town. He was a deputy sheriff for five years. In 1937 he told an interviewer that he worked for Frank Canton in a store that Canton ran in Stillwater before moving to Pawnee. Of course Canton never was a shopkeeper in Stillwater or elsewhere, and Horton must have confused him with someone else (Interview with Cook Horton by Goldie Turner, April 16, 1937, Indian-Pioneer History, Foreman Collection 5:187–89).

45. Canton, *Frontier Trails,* 123.

46. *Pawnee Times-Democrat*, February 8, 1895. The *Guthrie Daily Leader* of February 5, 1895, said that John and Robert "McCane" joined the posse at Checotah.

47. Canton, *Frontier Trails*, 124. The house reportedly belonged to a man named Sterling Hood, who claimed to know nothing of the criminal activities of the Shelley brothers (*Guthrie Daily Leader*, February 5, 1895).

48. A more serious injury was described in the February 8, 1895, issue of the *Pawnee Times-Democrat*: "McCann received a ball which entered near the nipple and came out the back." The paper made no mention of McCann receiving medical attention and reported that he poured a volley of eight shots into the door of the cabin after being shot, so Canton's version appears more credible.

49. Ibid.

50. Canton, *Frontier Trails*, 129. Canton said it was John Shelley who was wounded; the Guthrie and Pawnee newspapers reported that it was Bill.

51. Canton, *Frontier Trails*, 130. W. F. Jones, a deputy U.S. marshal at this time, later claimed to have participated in this gunfight and capture with Bill Tilghman, Dr. Bland, Heck Bruner, Bill Robbins, and John McCann, who received "a slight shoulder wound." Jones said that it was he who devised the go-devil to smoke out the Shelley brothers (Jones, *The Experiences of a Deputy U.S. Marshal*, 18). The Canton account is supported by the contemporary newspaper reports.

52. Canton, *Frontier Trails*, 130.

53. *Pawnee Times-Democrat*, February 8, 1895.

54. Ibid., February 22, 1895. The name of the county was changed from "Q" to "Pawnee" at the beginning of 1895.

55. Canton, *Frontier Trails*, 131; Shirley, *Henry Starr*, 135. There is some confusion regarding the first name of Lou's husband. He is identified as "Ed" in the *Pawnee Appeal* (April 12, 1895) and as "Edward" by Harman in his history of the court at Fort Smith: *Hell on the Border* (436–38). Canton and the *Pawnee Times-Democrat* consistently call him "Bill."

56. Harman, *Hell on the Border*, 417; Drago, *Outlaws on Horseback*, 185.

57. *Pawnee Times-Democrat*, August 3, 1894.

58. *Pawnee Republican*, August 24, 1894.

59. *Pawnee Times-Democrat*, November 2, 1894. Lake's face was hardly like a woman's: he sported a luxurious beard.

60. Lake received 548 votes in the official count to Republican R. Veatch's 544 and Populist P. Warnock's 495 (*Pawnee Times-Democrat*, November 16, 1894). The Democratic paper on November 9 ruefully noted that it looked as if Lake and County Attorney C. A. Houston were "the only democrats elected in the U.S."

61. Canton, *Frontier Trails*, 116–17.

62. Ibid., 117–18.

63. Ibid., 119.

64. *Pawnee Times-Democrat*, November 2, 1894.

65. Undated clipping from a Pawnee paper (CC-WHC, Box 2, Folder 15).

66. *Pawnee Times-Democrat*, November 9, 1894.

67. Ibid., February 15, 22, 1895; *Pawnee Appeal*, February 22, 1895.

68. Canton, *Frontier Trails*, 118–19.

69. *Pawnee Appeal*, February 22, 1895.

70. *Pawnee Times-Democrat*, February 15, 1895.

71. Interview with T. Clyde Vandruff by Charles H. Holt, February 25, 1938, Indian-Pioneer History, Foreman Collection 68:357–61.

72. *Pawnee Times-Democrat*, March 15, 1895.

73. CC-WHC, Box 1, Folder 3.

74. Ibid.

75. Siringo, *Riata and Spurs*, 184.

76. Carlson, *Tom Horn*, 20.

77. Shirley, "Killer with Two Faces," 14–15.

78. J. S. ("Steve") Burke was one of the deputy marshals in the deadly shootout at Ingalls in September 1893. Will M. Nix was a brother of U.S. Marshal E. D. Nix.

79. Nix, *Oklahombres*, 137–41.

80. Shirley, "Killer with Two Faces," 14. In an earlier work, *Buckskin and Spurs*, published in 1958, Shirley had repeated Nix's version of the capture of Cravens.

81. Canton, *Frontier Trails*, 225.

Chapter 8. The Deputy Marshal, 1896

1. F. M. Canton to Oklahoma Governor Frank Frantz, January 15, 1906 (GRDJ, File 1896-3654), and F. M. Canton to Fred E. Sutton, August 8, 1925 (CC-WHC, Box 2, Folder 5).

2. *Pawnee Times-Democrat*, May 10, 1895.

3. Canton credited Deputy U.S. Marshal C. L. ("Loss") Hart and Ardmore Police Officer D. E. ("Dave") Booker, one of the Texas mercenaries in the Johnson County invasion, with the killing of Bill Dalton (*Frontier Trails*, 141). Booker was a member of a posse trailing Dalton at the time of his death, but the outlaw was apparently shot and killed by Deputy Marshals Selden Lindsey and Hart (McCullough, *Selden Lindsey*, 98–102). The argument has been made that no strong evidence exists that Bill Dalton led the gang or even participated in the crimes for which he was blamed and may have been hounded to his death by the officers and the press (Samuelson, *The Dalton Gang Story*, 132–48).

4. F. M. Canton to Fred E. Sutton, August 8, 1925.

5. Colcord, *Autobiography*, 170.

6. *Pawnee Times-Democrat*, June 15, 1894.

7. Canton, *Frontier Trails*, 111. Some of the Dunn brothers' nervousness and willingness to cooperate with the officers may have been triggered by news of Bill Dalton's death, news that reached Pawnee the week Bolton was arrested.

8. Ibid., 111–12.

9. Ibid., 111–13. Canton is the only source for this story. Nix did not mention the arrangement in his book *Oklahombres*. According to Canton, at least five copies were made of this remarkable document, one for each of the signers, but none have survived.

10. *Pawnee Times-Democrat*, August 3, 1894.

11. *Pawnee Appeal*, March 1, 1895.

12. *Pawnee Times-Democrat*, March 8, 1895.

13. Ibid.

14. F. M. Canton to Fred E. Sutton, August 8, 1925.

15. Canton, *Frontier Trails*, 113.

16. Canton said that this money amounted to one thousand dollars (ibid., 114). Other reports put the total at "several hundred dollars" (Shirley, *Gunfight at Ingalls*, 109; Shirley, *Guardian of the Law*, 248).

17. Canton, *Frontier Trails*, 115.

18. In *Frontier Trails* (115), Canton names all of these with the exception of Raidler as participants in the Dover robbery. Shirley, *West of Hell's Fringe* (273), adds Raidler's name.

19. Canton, *Frontier Trails*, 116.

20. Ibid.

21. *Pawnee Times-Democrat*, May 10, 1895; Shirley, *Guardian of the Law*, 248.

22. Nix is silent regarding "Sam Shaffer." He said he made "Will" Dunn a special deputy and dispatched Tilghman, Thomas, "and a substantial posse" to the Dunn ranch (Nix, *Oklahombres*, 195). Tilghman said he first learned of the arrangement between the Dunns and Canton and Lake when John Dunn appeared in Guthrie disguised as "Sam Shaffer" (Shirley, *Guardian of the Law*, 248).

23. *Guthrie Daily Leader*, May 3, 1895.

24. Ibid.

25. Canton, *Frontier Trails*, 119.

26. Ibid., 119–20. This story is repeated by Charles Colcord in his autobiography (Colcord, *Autobiography*, 171).

27. *Guthrie Daily Leader*, May 3, 1895.

28. Nix, *Oklahombres*, 195–98.

29. *Pawnee Times-Democrat*, May 10, 1895.

30. Ibid.

31. Ibid. Concurrent with all the outlaw excitement, normal life went on in Pawnee. This issue of the paper reported that Master Clarence Jacobs celebrated his twelfth birthday with a grand party of his friends. Among the guests were Frank Lake's son, Clyde, and nine-year-old Ruby Canton.

32. Undated clipping, CC-WHC, Box 2, Folder 14.

33. Shirley, *Gunfight at Ingalls*, 115.

34. *Pawnee Times-Democrat*, May 10, 1895.

35. Shirley, *Guardian of the Law*, 251.

36. Frank Canton is not even mentioned in the biography of Bill Tilghman written by his widow, Zoe (Tilghman, *Marshal of the Last Frontier*).

37. *Oklahoma State Capital*, May 16, 1895. This story appeared under the headline "REVENGE LYNCHINGS" in the *San Antonio Daily Express* on the same day.

38. *Oklahoma State Capital* item reprinted in the *Pawnee Times-Democrat*, June 21, 1895. There were false reports of the demise of the Dunns six months later. The *Guthrie Daily Leader* of December 26, 1895, said that the brothers "were killed near Stillwater by the explosion of a magazine."

39. *Pawnee Times-Democrat*, June 28, 1895.

40. A copy of a communication written on this letterhead and dated May 17, 1895, is in the Indian and Pioneer Records, Sac and Fox Agency.

41. Quoted in Holland, *Oklahombres Revisited,* 129.

42. *Pawnee Times-Democrat,* May 24, 1895.

43. *Oklahoma State Capital,* July 6, 1895.

44. *Pawnee Times-Democrat,* July 12, 1895.

45. *Oklahoma State Capital,* July 6, 1895.

46. Nix, *Oklahombres,* 132.

47. *Oklahoma State Capital,* August 20, 1895.

48. *Blackwell Times-Record,* August 29, 1895, and *Payne County Populist,* September 5, 1895, quoted in Shirley, *West of Hell's Fringe,* 307. These contemporary newspaper accounts, as well as the *Pawnee Times-Democrat,* August 23, 1895, all reported the capture of the wayward girls by deputy marshals led by Frank Canton. Nix, *Oklahombres* (132–34), credits Bill Tilghman and Steve Burke for the difficult arrest. Tilghman's foremost biographer, Glenn Shirley, rejects Nix in favor of the contemporary accounts (*Guardian of the Law,* 242).

49. *Pawnee Times-Democrat,* August 30, 1895; Shirley, *West of Hell's Fringe,* 308.

50. *Pawnee Times-Democrat,* July 12, 1895.

51. *Oklahoma State Capital,* quoted in the *Pawnee Times- Democrat,* July 12, 1895. The *Guthrie Daily Leader* of July 11, 1895, also reported that Canton suffered a broken leg.

52. *Guthrie Daily Leader,* August 21, 1895.

53. Colcord, *Autobiography,* 179.

54. Ibid., 179–80.

55. Ibid., 180–82.

56. *Pawnee Times-Democrat,* July 12, 1895.

57. Ibid., August 23, 1895.

58. Ibid., September 20, 1895. The deeply religious Burke later became an evangelist and died while delivering a sermon in Paris, Texas (Holland, *Oklahombres Revisited,* 130).

59. Shirley, *West of Hell's Fringe,* 333–38.

60. Nagle to Attorney General, April 21, 1896, GRDJ, File 1896-3654, No. 1896-6839.

61. Ibid., July 25, 1896, GRDJ, File 1896-3654, No. 1896-12165.

62. Hanes, *Bill Doolin,* 123.

63. F. M. Canton to Fred E. Sutton, August 8, 1925.

64. Shirley, *West of Hell's Fringe,* 349–52. Strangely, Frank Canton had arrest warrants for Waightman and was still looking for him in October 1896, seven months later (Sworn statement of Frank M. Canton, June 10, 1897, GRDJ, File 1896-3654, No. 1897-9534).

65. Canton, *Frontier Trails,* 132–33.

66. Ibid., 133–34.

67. *Daily Ardmorite,* June 22, 1896.

68. Canton, *Frontier Trails,* 134.

69. The amount was two thousand dollars according to the report in the *Daily Ardmorite* (June 22, 1896); Canton remembered it as twenty-five hundred (*Frontier Trails,* 133).

70. Shirley, *West of Hell's Fringe*, 358.

71. Canton, *Frontier Trails*, 134. Four of the escapees--Walter McLain, Lee Killian, William Crittenden, and Kid Phillips--were Pawnee County criminals (Shirley, *West of Hell's Fringe*, 358–59).

72. Colcord, *Autobiography*, 178.

73. Shirley, "Killer with Two Faces," 16–17. Canton said the dead man was "Dick Ainsley" (*Frontier Trails*, 227). Colcord called him "Skeeter Dick" (*Autobiography*, 178). He has also been identified as "Three-Fingered Jack" (Lamb, *Tragedies of the Osage Hills*, 44).

74. Canton credited Deputy Marshal Bud Ledbetter with dispatching Clifton "some time after" in the Creek Nation (*Frontier Trails*, 135). The circumstances of Clifton's death have been inaccurately described in many accounts, most notably Nix's *Oklahombres*, 198–99. Shirley has clarified the story in *West of Hell's Fringe*, 406–7.

75. Rose (Rosa) Dunn, described as "a beautiful girl with coal black hair," was probably the legendary "Rose of Cimarron" often referred to in the accounts of the Battle of Ingalls, although she was only thirteen at the time. She later married Charlie Noble (Shirley, *West of Hell's Fringe*, 368).

76. Ibid., 363–69.

77. Ibid., 366–67.

78. F. M. Canton to Fred E. Sutton, August 8, 1925.

79. Canton, *Frontier Trails*, 135.

80. Shirley, *West of Hell's Fringe*, 370.

81. Ibid.

82. Canton captured a man named George Taylor, wanted in Missouri for murder, at about this time and reportedly received a sizable reward, but his bitterness toward the Dunns was not assuaged (*Guthrie Daily Leader*, October 8, 1896).

83. In 1924 Canton told this story to a reporter who was writing a feature story on Canton's experiences. It appeared under the title "First Aid to Law and Order" in the Sunday, October 19, 1924, issue of the *Daily Oklahoman*. Canton also included the story in his handwritten memoirs, but editor Edward Everett Dale deleted it from the published *Frontier Trails*.

84. Ibid.

85. Harman, *Hell on the Border*, 677.

86. Ibid., 680; *Pawnee Times-Democrat*, November 1, 1895.

87. Harman, *Hell on the Border*, 673–82.

88. Canton, *Frontier Trails*, 136.

89. Ibid., 136–37.

90. "Dunn . . . had just been given a commission as deputy by United Sates Marshal Nagle" (*Guthrie Daily Leader*, November 7, 1896). The *Annual Report of the Attorney-General of the United States for the Year 1897* (280–81) indicates that Dunn took the oath of office as an "emergency" deputy on November 6, 1896, and that his service was "terminated" (an apt word choice) the same day. The report shows that a claim was entered for $126.00 to cover subsistence and travel for Bee's single day of service and that the claim was approved.

91. Cook Horton interview, April 16, 1937, Indian-Pioneer History, Foreman Collection 5:188.

92. This remark was reversed in a special dispatch to territorial papers from Pawnee: "Canton, I understand you have it in for me, by G----" (*Guthrie Daily Leader*, November 7, 1896).

93. Canton, *Frontier Trails*, 137.

94. "First Aid to Law and Order." The breastplate allegedly worn by Dunn was mentioned in another newspaper interview with Canton, who said it was made "by the best blacksmith in Oklahoma" (Undated and unidentified clipping, cc-whc, Canton Scrapbook).

95. Colcord, *Autobiography*, 171.

96. August 3, 1994, statement of Bill R. Boyd, whose great-aunt was Bee Dunn's wife. Boyd said that as a youngster, he handled the derby hat Bee had been wearing when killed and that he stuck his finger through the hole just above the brim.

97. Colcord, *Autobiography*, 171–72.

98. "First Aid to Law and Order."

99. *Guthrie Daily Leader*, November 7, 1896.

100. The files of the *Pawnee Times-Democrat* are missing for the year 1896. The quotation is from a clipping in cc-whc, Box 2, Folder 15.

101. John W. Hunter interview, November 23, 1937, Indian-Pioneer History, Foreman Collection 85:353.

102. *Guthrie Daily Leader*, November 7, 8, 1896. The story appeared on the front page of the *Kansas City Star* of November 8, which reported that Dunn was a former resident of the city.

103. "Frank Canton Vindicated," undated and unidentified newspaper clipping, cc-whc, Box 2, Folder 16; *El Reno News*, November 20, 1896; *Guthrie Daily Leader*, November 12, 1896.

104. Shirley, *West of Hell's Fringe*, 373.

105. Quoted in Shirley, *Gunfight at Ingalls*, 115–16.

106. Undated clipping, cc-whc, Box 2, Folder 16.

107. "Frank Canton a Famous Johnson County Sheriff," *Wyoming News*, April 4, 1936.

108. *El Reno News*, November 20, 1896; *Guthrie Daily Leader*, November 12, 14, 1896.

109. *Kansas City Star*, November 12, 1896.

110. Canton, *Frontier Trails*, 138. In December, Thomas secured a temporary appointment as deputy marshal for C. D. Dunn, who took the oath on December 9 and held the commission until December 31. For this three-week period he claimed no arrest fees but filed for and received $202.00 for subsistence and travel (*Annual Report of the Attorney-General of the United States for the Year 1897*, 280–81).

111. Canton, *Frontier Trails*, 139–40.

112. Ibid., 141.

Chapter 9. The Cheechako, 1897

1. Colcord, *Autobiography*, 189–91.

2. Flynn's request to Attorney-General Joseph McKenna "for information as to

accts. of Mar. Nagle for March quarter 1896" was dated December 22, 1896 (GRDJ, File 1896-3654, No. 1896-19661). T. C. Taylor's report to the attorney-general was dated June 24, 1897 (GRDJ, File 1896-3654, No. 1897-10381).

3. Sworn statements of F. M. Canton, June 10, 1897, covering fourth quarter 1896 and first quarter 1897 process-serving activities, GRDJ, File 1896-3654, No. 1897-9534.

4. The certificate of appointment is in CC-WHC, Box 1, Folder 5.

5. CC-WHC, Box 1, Folder 4.

6. Shirley, *West of Hell's Fringe,* 377.

7. Referenced in Marshal Williams's response of June 21, 1897 (CC-WHC, Box 1, Folder 16).

8. GRDJ, File 1896-3654, No. 1897-9534. For the 1896 fourth quarter, Canton's claims for reimbursement totaled $541.65. His sworn statement of June 10 lists unsubstantiated claims totaling $168.94. For the 1897 first quarter his claims totaled $572.30, of which $149.77 was unjustified. The other deputies required to file sworn statements were Harry Callahan, Samuel Large, George G. Stormer, Daniel Ryan, George H. Mouser, John R. Wisby, Isaac A. Steel, Charles F. Colcord, Clarence R. Young, and T. H. Mitchell.

9. GRDJ, File 1896-3654, No. 1897-10381.

10. GRDJ, File 1896-3654, No. 1897-11195.

11. Nagle to Attorney General, August 14, 1897, GRDJ, File 1896-3654, No. 1897-12318.

12. Glenn E. Husted, U.S. Department of Justice, to Charles W. Russell, Assistant Attorney General, April 17, 1906, GRDJ, File 1896-3654.

13. CC-WHC, Box 1, Folder 16.

14. Ibid.

15. Canton's last official act was the transportation of ten convicted prisoners from the jail at Perry to Guthrie to serve their sentences. His arrival was reported in the *Guthrie Daily Leader* of July 20, 1897.

16. CC-WHC, Box 1, Folder 15.

17. *Buffalo Bulletin,* August 26, 1897; F. M. Canton to Annie Canton, November 26, 1897, reprinted in the *Buffalo Bulletin,* March 31, 1898; Canton, *Frontier Trails,* 154.

18. Kress had chased the Dalton gang back in 1891 (Shirley, *West of Hell's Fringe,* 59, 80). Painter served two terms as sheriff of Logan County headquartered at Guthrie, from 1892 to 1896 (*Lawton Constitution,* May 20, 1981; Louis N. Baker interview, March 21, 1938, Indian-Pioneer History, Foreman Collection 99:373; Canton, *Frontier Trails,* 154).

19. Canton, *Frontier Trails,* 155; "Letter from Alaska: Frank Kress, of Guthrie, Writes His Experiences" (undated, unidentified clipping, CC-WHC, Box 2, Folder 15.

20. Canton, *Frontier Trails,* 155–56.

21. "Letter from Alaska."

22. Canton, *Frontier Trails,* 159; "Letter from Alaska"; Hunt, *Distant Justice,* 69.

23. Undated clipping from a Pawnee paper in CC-WHC, Box 2, Folder 15. The steamer *Cleveland* arrived at St. Michael on August 18 (Thrapp, *Encyclopedia of Frontier Biography* 4:439).

24. Berton, *The Klondike Fever*, 208.

25. Canton, *Frontier Trails*, 157–61.

26. Canton said he was a member of a miners' meeting that named the new camp Rampart City (*Frontier Trails*, 167), but the town was named before he arrived. In early September a recorder's court was established. On September 8, F. G. Kress recorded Lot 9 in Block E, townsite of Rampart City, and received certification that fees were paid. This document is in CC-WHC, Box 1, Folder 22.

27. Berton, *The Klondike Fever*, 207.

28. Canton, *Frontier Trails*, 156.

29. Berton, *The Klondike Fever*, 208–9.

30. Original assignment is in CC-WHC, Box 1, Folder 22.

31. Canton, *Frontier Trails*, 163–66.

32. Ibid., 167.

33. GRDJ, File 1897-12126, No. 1899-2977; Hunt, "Deadly Frank Canton," 244.

34. Original handwritten penciled documents, all witnessed by N. P. R. Hatch, are in CC-WHC, Box 1, Folder 22. Austin had recorded the Julia Creek claim only two days before.

35. Ibid. Al. H. Mayo, unofficial mayor of Rampart City, on October 10 accepted a $2.50 recorder's fee from Canton for an unspecified claim on Russian Creek. On October 15 Canton recorded "Claim No. 60 above Discovery" on Russian Creek. On October 18 he recorded "Claim No. 7" on Alder Creek and paid a $2.50 recorder's fee as well as a $7.50 road and house tax. He recorded a claim on Little Minook Creek, at the "right hand fork of Peterson Creek," on November 24. On November 28 he recorded "Claim No. 2 on Hunter Creek, Hunter Creek Mining District." He recorded and certified "Lot No. 10, Block L in the Town site of Rampart City" on December 8 (CC-WHC, Box 1, Folder 22).

36. It was four months before Annie Canton received this letter. She gave it to the *Buffalo Bulletin*, which printed it in full in its edition of March 31, 1898. Quotations in this and the following four paragraphs are from this letter.

37. Canton, *Frontier Trails*, 168–82.

38. Ibid., 173.

39. Ibid., 175. Painter, born in July 1836, was sixty-one years old in the fall of 1897 (U.S. Census, Guthrie City, Logan County, Oklahoma, 1900).

40. Canton, *Frontier Trails*, 176. Canton's rescue of Painter is related briefly in a 1907 newspaper account ("Adjutant General a True Westerner," CC-WHC, Canton Scrapbook). Painter was not available to confirm or deny the story, since he had died the previous year.

41. Canton, *Frontier Trails*, 182.

42. Ibid., 186–87

43. Beach, *Personal Exposures*, 46–47.

Chapter 10. The Sourdough, 1899

1. Hunt, *Distant Justice*, 69–70.

2. Ibid., 70.

3. Shoup to Canton, February 19, 1898, CC-WHC, Box 1, Folder 13; Weare to Shoup, March 3, 1898, GRDJ, File 1897-12126, No. 1899-2977.

4. Canton, *Frontier Trails*, 187. Back at Rampart on April 19, Canton recorded the first claim as "Claim No. 17, above discovery on Quail Creek in Quail Creek Mining District," and the second on April 25 as "a placer mining claim near the forks of the main stream above Quartz Creek and bounded by D. Waterman on lower end in the mining district of Troublesome Creek, Alaska" (CC-WHC, Box 1, Folder 22).

5. Canton, *Frontier Trails*, 187–89.

6. Berton, *The Klondike Fever*, 138.

7. Ibid., 206–7.

8. Canton devoted an entire chapter of his autobiography to the events at "Suckerville" in April–May 1898 (see *Frontier Trails*, 193–209, the source of the quotations in the following paragraphs). His story has slight independent corroboration. One of those present, he said, wrote a humorous account of the fur theft trial presided over by an unnamed deputy U.S. marshal and published it some time later in the *Chicago Herald* (*Frontier Trails*, 200). Rex Beach wrote a short story based on the rescue of the couple by the outlaw but used fictitious names (Canton to Mark Goodwin, July 24, 1914, CC-WHC, Box 1, Folder 51).

9. Canton to Mark Goodwin, July 24, 1914.

10. Hunt, *Distant Justice*, 78.

11. Berton, *The Klondike Fever*, 207.

12. Rex Beach to F. M. Canton, December 6, 1924 (CC-WHC, Box 1, Folder 34).

13. Boyer, *I Married Wyatt Earp*, 166–67.

14. *Yukon Midnight Sun*, June 11, 1898. This edition reported, "The steamer *Seattle No. 1* is on a bar down the river, and is badly damaged, if not entirely wrecked."

15. Canton, *Frontier Trails*, 210.

16. Berton, *The Klondike Fever*, 318. Captain Wilds Richardson characterized Dawson as a "most orderly and law-abiding town," in contrast to the American camps on the Yukon, which were "without any semblance of law, civil or military" from St. Michael to the border (Thrapp, *Encyclopedia of Frontier Biography* 4:440).

17. Unidentified clipping, datelined Dawson City June 25, 1898 (CC-WHC, Box 2, Folder 15).

18. CC-WHC, Box 1, Folder 7.

19. Canton, *Frontier Trails*, 215–16.

20. Ibid., 216–17.

21. William Hertz to F. M. Canton, July 28, 1898, CC-WHC, Box 1, Folder 10.

22. Painter to Canton, August 5, 1898, CC-WHC, Box 1, Folder 11.

23. Oath of Office, July 10, 1898, CC-WHC, Box 1, Folder 18.

24. The bills for materials to repair the jail are in CC-WHC, Box 1, Folder 20; Canton to Shoup, December 31, 1898, CC-WHC, Box 1, Folder 13.

25. Canton, *Frontier Trails*, 218.

26. Canton to Steele, March 28, 1899, CC-WHC, Box 1, Folder 14; Canton to J. J. McCook, U.S. consul at Dawson, March 28, 1899, CC-WHC, Box 1, Folder 9.

27. Canton, *Frontier Trails*, 219–20.

28. *Yukon Press*, January 15, 1899; Canton to Shoup, December 31, 1898, CC-

WHC, Box 1, Folder 13.

29. *Yukon Press,* January 15, 1899. Mittimus dated December 28, 1898, and signed by U.S. Commissioner John E. Crane, CC-WHC, Box 1, Folder 19.

30. Canton to Shoup, December 31, 1898.

31. *Yukon Press,* January 15, 1899.

32. Canton to Shoup, January 2, 1899, CC-WHC, Box 1, Folder 13.

33. Ibid.

34. Canton to Shoup, December 31, 1898.

35. According to the *Yukon Press,* this was not true. The issue of January 21, 1899, reported that there were sixteen bags of mail at Dawson, waiting to be delivered to Circle. In early February Del McCord, the mail carrier, arrived from Dawson in a sledge pulled by reindeer, bringing this mail and two hundred pounds of moose meat (*Yukon Press,* February 15, 1899). Delivery of the mail was a major event in remote camps like Circle City and could not have gone unnoticed by Canton. It was too soon to expect an answer to his letters of December 31 and January 2, but he obviously expected a response in the mail received March 22.

36. Canton to Shoup, March 28, 1899, CC-WHC, Box 1, Folder 13.

37. *Yukon Press,* January 15, 1899.

38. Ibid., January 21, 1899.

39. *Yukon Press,* January 21, 1899; Canton to Shoup, December 31, 1898, January 2, 1899, CC-WHC, Box 1, Folder 13.

40. *Yukon Press,* February 15, 1899. Notice of deputizing by Mayor J. C. Brown of Eagle City and oath of office of Tyler and Burton is in CC-WHC, Box 1, Folder 19.

41. *Yukon Press,* February 15, 1899.

42. Canton, *Frontier Trails,* 220–21.

43. Ibid., 221.

44. U.S. Attorney C. P. Brooks to Attorney General, March 23, 1898, and U.S. Attorney S. L. Overstreet to Attorney General, April 28, 1898, GRDJ, File 1896-3654; National Archives to Glenn G. Boyer, September 30, 1966, CC-AHC. Crossthwaite had been sent to Cheyenne in 1892 to investigate Marshal Rankin and the efforts of the Wyoming cattlemen to use the U.S. Marshal Service to achieve their ends in Johnson County (Smith, *The War on Powder River,* 162–63).

45. Harry Callahan, Thomas H. Mitchell, and Isaac A. Steel were convicted of "making and presenting false statements as United States officers" and fined fifty to one hundred dollars and costs. Daniel Ryan was fined three hundred dollars and costs. George H. Mouser, also convicted, went to jail when he could not pay his fine (*Guthrie Daily Leader,* November 29, 1898, February 17, 1899; *El Reno News,* December 2, 1898).

46. All the quotations of Annie Canton are from Mrs. F. M. Canton's statement received by P. B. Weare, October 1898, GRDJ, File 1897-12126, No. 1899-2977.

47. Weare to Shoup, October 28, 1898, GRDJ, File 1897-12126, No. 1899-2977.

48. Shoup to Canton, February 6, 1899, GRDJ, File 1897-12126, No. 1899-2622.

49. Shoup to Attorney General, February 6, 1899, GRDJ, File 1897-12126, No. 1899-2622.

50. Shoup to Crane, February 6, 1899, GRDJ, File 1897-12126, No. 1899-2622.

51. Shoup to Weare, February 9, 1899, GRDJ, File 1897-12126, No. 1899-2977.

52. Canton to Shoup, May 24, 1899, CC-WHC, Box 1, Folder 13.

53. Canton, *Frontier Trails*, 221–22. Wyatt and Josephine Earp were also on the *Cleveland*. Josephine said that because of the storm the ship was nine days late and the authorities at Seattle gave the ship up for lost (Boyer, *I Married Wyatt Earp*, 196).

54. Canton, *Frontier Trails*, 223.

Chapter 11. The Bounty-Hunter, 1900–1906

1. CC-WHC, Box 1, Folder 13. The total account, excluding Canton's salary, for the three quarters amounted to $3,898.32.

2. Chief of Division of Accounts to Rechtin, March 3, 1899, GRDJ, File 1897-12126, No. 1899-2622.

3. Ibid.; Rechtin memo dated March 8, 1899, GRDJ, File 1897-12126, No. 1899-2622.

4. *Annual Report of the Attorney General of the United States for the Year 1899*, 318–19. Canton was never paid by the government for work performed before taking his oath of office in July 1898. His service at Suckerville and the guarding of the bullion on board the *P.B. Weare* were presumably paid for by the NAT&T Company.

5. Rechtin to Canton, October 7, November 6, 18, 1899, CC-WHC, Box 1, Folder 12. It is unclear how the termination date of April 11 was determined. Canton did not receive notice of his dismissal until May 24 and was attending to his duties up to that time.

6. Shoup to Attorney General, October 27, 1899, GRDJ, File 1897-12126, No. 1899-16743. Marshal Shoup wrote that there would be "a shortage of $42.12 in the payment of the orders" claimed by Canton if there were "no disallowances made . . . by the Auditor." Shoup had disallowed $13.50 in fees and $192.75 Canton had claimed for support of prisoners; "Some of the items of the account should be paid by the owner of the building, and authority must first be given me by the Department, and proper vouchers furnished, before I can pay any of the bill." Amazingly, Shoup had disallowed the cost of "articles furnished the jail consisting of cooking utensils, knives, forks, spoons, etc., which are not proper charges against the appropriation for support of prisoners but are personal expenses of the deputy who fed the prisoners." He graciously acknowledged, "The expense of a heating stove, lamp and blankets for the jail are proper charges against the Government, [but only] if authority had been obtained before they were purchased." There were the ubiquitous government forms for Canton to fill out and return before any funds could be released for payment after the ruling of the auditor (Shoup to Canton, January 16, 1900, CC-WHC, Box 1, Folder 13). In April 1900, Shoup wrote Canton that he had just learned that there was an error of one dollar in Canton's favor made in the final resolution of the accounts, and he enclosed a check to cover the amount (CC-WHC, Box 1, Folder 13).

7. Author interviews with Martin Tisdale's son, Tom, June 21 and July 28, 1992. Tom Tisdale heard his father relate this story many times. Martin A. Tisdale

cowboyed until 1923, when he became a stock inspector for the Wyoming Stock Growers Association in Johnson County, a position once held by the hated Frank Canton. In 1926 he took another job formerly filled by Canton: he was elected sheriff of Johnson County and held the office for sixteen years. Following his long tenure, he managed the TTT Ranch for ten years. He never fully recovered from the shock of his wife's death in a January 1952 automobile accident, retiring from his job the following June and following her in death on December 28, 1952 (ibid.; *Buffalo Bulletin*, January 1, 1953). The *Bulletin* of October 12, 1899, reported Annie's trip to Sheridan but never mentioned Canton's return.

8. From a tape transcription made by J. Elmer Brock in the 1950s, published in Hanson, *Powder River Country*, 467–69.

9. Ibid.

10. Author interview with Tom Tisdale, July 28, 1992.

11. "Mrs. W.H. Wilkerson's Private Boarding House, one door south of Post Office, board by the month, week or meal," was advertised in the *Buffalo Bulletin* of April 20, 1900.

12. U.S. Census, Johnson County, Wyoming, 1900.

13. Wilbur Holt interview, April 4, 1975 (Oral History Tape H-74, Johnson County Library, Buffalo).

14. Lawmen investigating the Wilcox robbery case were confused as to the identity of all the participants, and historians to this day do not agree. It is generally believed that Robert LeRoy Parker (alias Butch Cassidy), Harvey Logan (alias Kid Curry), and "Flat Nose George" Curry were among the robbers (Patterson, *The Train Robbery Era*, 155–56).

15. Fraser to Canton, October 18, 1899, CC-WHC, Box 1, Folder 30.

16. McParland to Canton, November 25, 1899, CC-WHC, Box 1, Folder 30.

17. The *Buffalo Bulletin* of January 18, 1900, reported that "Deputy United States Marshal Tom Horn" had been in Casper for ten days "in search of law breakers" and that he was "on the trail of the Wilcox train robbers." Horn, described as "the famous detective," was interviewed in Cheyenne in early February. He confirmed reports that he and an officer named Ed Taxbury had killed two "notorious cattle thieves and criminal raiders" named Monte and Blair in the Jackson Hole country but that they were not the Wilcox train robbers. Those criminals, he said, had fled into British Columbia, and he was going up there after them. "We know who they are and the Union Pacific will pursue them to the end" (*Buffalo Bulletin*, February 8, 1900).

18. "Harvey Ray" was an alias of outlaw Harvey Logan, known better by his alias "Kid Curry" (Lamb, *Kid Curry*, 108).

19. Carr to Canton, December 12, 1899, CC-WHC, Box 1, Folder 24.

20. McParland to Canton, January 13, 1900, CC-WHC, Box 1, Folder 30.

21. Ibid.

22. McParland to Canton, February 3, 1900, CC-WHC, Box 1, Folder 30.

23. *Buffalo Bulletin*, December 7, 1899, March 22, July 12, 1900.

24. O'Neal, *Encyclopedia of Western Gunfighters*, 80. Canton and his brother missed out on the reward but perhaps saved themselves much grief later. Curry's killer, Sheriff Jesse M. Tyler, and a deputy, Sam Jenkins, were ambushed and killed a

month later, reportedly by Harvey Logan in retaliation (Thrapp, *Encyclopedia of Frontier Biography* 1:358).

25. H. S. Anderson to Canton, December 22, 1899, CC-WHC, Box 1, Folder 8.

26. H. S. Anderson to Canton, March 4, 1900, CC-WHC, Box 1, Folder 23.

27. "I suppose you are back in the U.S. by this time" (J. H. Havighorst to Canton, September 1, 1900, CC-WHC, Box 1, Folder 27).

28. Canton's trip to China with the army is mentioned in the *Shawnee Herald* of November 8, 1907, the *Beaver Journal* of November 21, 1907, the *Blackwell Morning Tribune* of September 28, 1927, and a number of unidentified news clippings in the Canton Scrapbook. In a letter to Job Ingram dated November 5, 1913, Canton said he "joined the American expedition as Chief Packer to go to China & suppress the Boxer uprising; was at the relief of Tientein [*sic*] and Pekin [*sic*]" (CC-WHC, Box 1, Folder 552).

29. There is no record in the Military Reference Branch of the National Archives of service by Canton as a civilian employee of the army. Among the records searched were records of the War Department, Quartermaster General, and Office of the Adjutant General including the appropriate records of the Ninth U.S. Infantry. Also searched was the official Register of the United States (William E. Lind, Military Reference Branch, Textual Reference Division, National Archives, Washington, D.C., to the author, May 11, 1993).

30. Mrs. V. M. Grainger to Canton, November 2, 1900, CC-WHC, Box 1, Folder 26.

31. Baber, *The Longest Rope*, 276.

32. *Buffalo Voice*, March 30, 1901; Eloise Brown, "Murder of `Arapahoe' Brown, Bold Johnson County Bad Man," *Buffalo Bulletin*, August 18, 1949; "Arapahoe Brown," manuscript in Johnson County Library, Buffalo. Rap Brown had many enemies, including "Red" Angus. The two former leaders of the rustler army had several clashes, including a gunfight in front of the Occidental Hotel in November 1893, in which Brown was wounded (*Buffalo Bulletin*, November 16, 1893).

33. F. M. Canton to Oklahoma Governor Frank Frantz, January 15, 1906.

34. Canton to Willis Van Devanter, April 10, 1901, CC-WHC, Box 1, Folder 31.

35. Ibid.

36. F. M. Canton to Oklahoma Governor Frank Frantz, January 15, 1906.

37. *Pawnee Times-Democrat*, April 12, 1901.

38. Ibid., March 29, 1901.

39. During his long criminal career, Cravens never operated alone or with gangs but took as partners a succession of young unmarried men, behavior suggesting possible homosexuality. Welty's wearing of female attire adds weight to that suspicion.

40. *Pawnee Times-Democrat*, March 22, 1901.

41. Shirley, "Killer with Two Faces," 18–19.

42. *Pawnee Times-Democrat*, March 22, 1901; Canton, *Frontier Trails*, 231–32.

43. *Pawnee Times-Democrat*, April 5, 1901.

44. Ibid., March 29, 1901; English, "A Wily Customer," 290.

45. English, "A Wily Customer," 291–93; Shirley, "Killer with Two Faces," 19; Canton, *Frontier Trails*, 233–34. Al Jennings, the outlaw turned lawyer, defended

Cravens at his trial in January 1912.

46. *Pawnee Times-Democrat,* May 10, 1901.

47. Ibid., May 3, 1901, quoting the *Guthrie Daily Leader.*

48. *Pawnee Times-Democrat,* May 10, 1901.

49. Shirley, *Heck Thomas,* 255.

50. Fugate and Fugate, *Roadside History of Oklahoma,* 366.

51. Ibid., 380–81.

52. Canton, *Frontier Trails,* 223–24.

53. Meeks, *Heck Thomas, My Papa,* 40.

54. LeFors, *Facts As I Remember Them,* 84, 97, 103.

55. Texowa, a combination of the words "Texas" and "Kiowa," was the original name for the present town of Davidson in Tillman County, Oklahoma (Shirk, *Oklahoma Place Names,* 204).

56. *Lawton Daily Republican,* September 9, 1902; *Lawton Weekly News,* September 11, 1902; undated, unidentified newspaper clippings in cc-whc, Canton Scrapbook.

57. *Lawton Weekly News,* November 13, 1902, February 19, 1903; unidentified newspaper clippings in cc-whc, Canton Scrapbook.

58. "Indians Won First Lawton Election Row," undated clipping from the *Daily Oklahoman* in cc-whc, Box 2, Folder 15.

59. Ibid. As Canton said, the Democrat Party was victorious in Comanche County--Cross defeated McGuire in the county election by more than 500 votes--but in the territorial balloting, McGuire defeated Cross by less than 500 votes out of 94,000 cast (*Lawton Weekly News,* November 13, 1902; Litton, *History of Oklahoma* 1:471).

60. Canton, *Frontier Trails,* 225; LeFors, *Facts As I Remember Them,* 103; *Lawton Weekly News,* November 13, 1902. Under the heading "Old Officers Are Out," the *Lawton Weekly News* of January 8, 1903, reported that assisting Sheriff Hammonds were Office Deputy Elmer Jaynes, Jailer S. A. Elrod, and Field Deputies Frank Canton and Frank Carter.

61. *Lawton Weekly News,* February 26, 1903.

62. *Buffalo Bulletin,* December 5, 1901.

63. cc-whc, Box 1, Folder 46.

64. Certification signed by John T. Lytle, secretary of the Cattle Raisers Association of Texas, is in cc-whc, Box 1, Folder 25. Canton also held appointments as deputy sheriff of Pawnee County and constable on the Osage reservation.

65. Ruby had graduated from high school in 1903. She worked as an operator at the Buffalo central telephone exchange that summer until she and her mother joined Frank in the fall (*Buffalo Bulletin,* May 21, July 23, August 6, 1903).

66. Canton, *Frontier Trails,* 225; F. M. Canton to Oklahoma Governor Frank Frantz, January 15, 1906; John T. Lytle to Canton, November 23, 1903, cc-whc, Box 1, Folder 25. When the Santa Fe Railroad extended its line from Pawnee to Newkirk in the winter of 1902–3, a forty-acre townsite was established on Gray Horse Creek and named Fairfax. A post office was opened on February 16, 1903 (Fugate and Fugate, *Roadside History of Oklahoma,* 232; Shirk, *Oklahoma Place Names,* 76).

67. Undated clipping from cc-whc, Canton Scrapbook.

68. Ibid.

69. F. M. Canton to Oklahoma Governor Frank Frantz, January 15, 1906.

70. Gard, "Teddy Roosevelt's Wolf Hunt"; Shirley, *Guardian of the Law*, 319–21. Roosevelt reportedly offered the Oklahoma marshalship to another celebrated western lawman, W. B. ("Bat") Masterson, but he declined. See DeArment, *Bat Masterson*, 374–75.

71. John T. Lytle to "Whom it may concern," March 24, 1906, GRDJ, File 1896-3654.

72. William F. Smith to Governor Frank Frantz, April 10, 1906, GRDJ, File 1896-3654.

73. Glenn E. Husted to Charles W. Russell, April 17, 1906, GRDJ, File 1896-3654.

74. Bird S. McGuire, delegate to Congress from Oklahoma, was a former resident of Pawnee who knew Canton well. His disparaging remarks may have been his way of getting even for Canton's work against him in the campaign of 1902.

75. Glenn E. Husted to Charles W. Russell, April 17, 1906, GRDJ, File 1896-3654.

76. Charles W. Russell to Glenn E. Husted, April 19, 1906, GRDJ, File 1896-3654.

77. *Oklahoma State Capital*, December 7, 1906; *Arapaho Bee*, April 23, 1909; Shirley, *Shotgun for Hire*, 66–73, 114–15.

78. National Archives to Glenn G. Boyer, September 30, 1966.

Chapter 12. The General, 1907–1916

1. Litton, *History of Oklahoma* 1:489–99.

2. Ibid., 501–6.

3. Ibid., 509.

4. "Life of Frank Canton Rivals Fiction for Thrills," undated clipping from an Oklahoma paper in CC-AHC.

5. *Shawnee Herald*, November 8, 1907.

6. "Adjutant General a True Westerner," clipping, CC-WHC, Canton Scrapbook.

7. *Pawnee County Outlook*, November 14, 1907.

8. Undated clipping, CC-WHC, Box 2, Folder 15. This reporter estimated Canton's age with accuracy; he was fifty-eight in September 1907. Canton was still misrepresenting his true age, however. When the Canton family was enumerated at Guthrie on May 2, 1910, he was sixty but gave his age as fifty-five (U.S. Census, Logan County, Oklahoma, 1910).

9. CC-WHC, Canton Scrapbook.

10. Canton, *Frontier Trails*, 234.

11. John Hutchins to the author, September 24, 1992.

12. *Thermopolis Independent*, December 20, 1907.

13. Canton, "Memories of the Border."

14. Litton, *History of Oklahoma* 2:347, 422–23.

15. *Pawnee County Outlook*, November 28, 1907.

16. Canton, *Frontier Trails*, 234–35.

17. Franks, *Citizen Soldiers*, 13; Canton, "Memories of the Border."

18. Canton, "Memories of the Border."

19. Ibid.

20. Ibid.; Litton, *History of Oklahoma* 1:511, 555, 2:38.

21. Canton, "Memories of the Border."

22. Undated and unidentified clipping, CC-WHC, Canton Scrapbook.

23. Ibid.

24. CC-WHC, Box 1, Folder 35.

25. J. P. Tumulty, secretary to Woodrow Wilson, to F. M. Canton, February 14, 1916, CC-WHC, Box 2, Folder 1.

26. "Police Force for State Is Needed," undated, unidentified clipping, CC-WHC, Box 2, Folder 17.

27. Ibid.

28. Starr and Hill, *Footprints in the Indian Nation*, 31–37.

29. *Oklahoma State Capital*, April 18, 1909.

30. Starr and Hill, *Footprints in the Indian Nation*, 38–41.

31. "For First Time True Story of the Last Oklahoma Indian Uprising Is Told by Man Who Put It Down," *Tulsa World*, June 13, 1915.

32. Ibid.; Bolster, "The Smoked Meat Rebellion," 47.

33. *Oklahoma City Times*, March 30, 1909.

34. "True Story of the Last Oklahoma Indian Uprising," *Tulsa World*, June 13, 1915; Tilghman, *Marshal of the Last Frontier*, 274.

35. Starr and Hill, *Footprints in the Indian Nation*, 47.

36. "Adjutant General Canton and the Band Incident," undated, unidentified clipping, CC-WHC, Box 2, Folder 15; "Canton Threatened Governor Haskell But Was Disarmed," undated, unidentified clipping, CC-WHC, Box 1, Folder 16.

37. "Canton Threatened Governor Haskell But Was Disarmed."

38. Ibid.

39. Ibid.

40. "The Governor under Guard," undated, unidentified clipping, CC-WHC, Box 2, Folder 14.

41. The Canton family lived at the boardinghouse of Mrs. S. K. Van Voorhees, 117 East Noble Avenue in Guthrie ("Canton Threatened Governor Haskell But Was Disarmed"; U.S. Census, Logan County, Oklahoma, 1910).

42. "The Governor under Guard."

43. "Canton Threatened Governor Haskell But Was Disarmed."

44. "Denies He Intended to Shoot Haskell," unidentified clipping, CC-AHC.

45. "Will Not Accept the Resignation of Canton," unidentified clipping, CC-AHC.

46. Litton, *History of Oklahoma* 1:526–27.

47. Ibid., 532.

48. Ibid., 534.

49. Colcord to Cruce, December 30, 1910, CC-WHC, Box 1, Folder 39.

50. Wrightsman to Cruce, December 27, 1910, CC-WHC, Box 2, Folder 11.

51. Doyle to Cruce, December 21, 1910, CC-WHC, Box 1, Folder 43.

52. Canton to Cruce, June 22, 1911, CC-WHC, Box 1, Folder 40. The official document of appointment was dated January 9, 1911, the day of Cruce's inauguration. Apparently Cruce held it six months before making the announcement (CC-WHC, Box 3).

53. Colcord, *Autobiography*, 211.

54. Clipping, CC-AHC.

55. Casey, "Governor Lee Cruce," 436.

56. Ibid., 451.

57. *Daily Oklahoman*, February 6, 1913; Casey, "Governor Lee Cruce," 451–52.

58. *Buffalo Bulletin*, March 20, 1913; undated clipping from the *Daily Oklahoman*, CC-WHC, Canton Scrapbook.

59. Undated clipping from the *Tulsa World*, CC-WHC, Canton Scrapbook.

60. *Daily Oklahoman*, October 5, 1914; Casey, "Governor Lee Cruce," 449.

61. Frank M. Canton to the editor of the *Daily Oklahoman*, September 12, 1923, CC-WHC, Box 1, Folder 41.

62. *Daily Oklahoman*, April 15, 1914.

63. Ibid.

64. Ibid.

65. Ibid., April 16, 1914; Casey, "Governor Lee Cruce," 455; Haser-Harris, "Horse Racing in Early Oklahoma," 16.

66. Unidentified clipping, CC-WHC, Box 2, Folder 18.

67. Ibid.; Casey, "Governor Lee Cruce," 455.

68. "Verdict against Allison Is Given," *Daily Oklahoman*, June 10, 1915.

69. Smith, "Swanson County," 420–21.

70. Ibid.; Litton, *History of Oklahoma* 1:536.

71. Canton to the editor of the *Daily Oklahoman*, September 12, 1923.

72. Myers, "The Delaware County Fight," 34–35.

73. Undated, unidentified clipping, CC-AHC.

74. Ibid.

75. Canton to the editor of the *Daily Oklahoman*, September 12, 1923; "Written Report of Canton Today," undated, unidentified clipping, CC-WHC, Canton Scrapbook.

76. "Hostilities Cease at County Seat," undated, unidentified clipping, CC-WHC, Canton Scrapbook.

77. Ibid.

78. Ibid.

79. Canton to the editor of the *Daily Oklahoman*, September 12, 1923.

80. "Jay Fight Off for All Time," undated, unidentified clipping, CC-WHC, Canton Scrapbook.

81. "Moving a County Seat," undated, unidentified clipping, CC-WHC, Canton Scrapbook.

82. "Frank Canton as a Diplomat," undated, unidentified clipping, CC-WHC, Canton Scrapbook.

83. "Draw Straws for Gen. Canton," undated, unidentified clipping, CC-WHC, Canton Scrapbook.

84. Litton, *History of Oklahoma* 1:536–37.

85. Ibid., 538.

86. Ibid., 539.

87. Cruce to Canton, January 9, 1915, CC-WHC, Canton Scrapbook.

88. "Rex Beach Hero Will Retire Soon," clipping, CC-AHC.

89. G. R. Gilmore to Robert L. Williams, December 26, 1914, CC-WHC, Box 1, Folder 50.

90. Shirley, *Henry Starr*, 167–74.

91. Merle Blakely, "Emergencies Kept State's Guardsmen Busy in 1915," undated *Oklahoma City Times* clipping, CC-AHC.

92. Ibid.

93. Ibid.

94. Ibid.

95. Ibid.

96. Franks, *Citizen Soldiers*, 19–20. Hoffman led the Oklahoma National Guard during the Mexican border affair and later when it was combined with Texas units to become the Thirty-Sixth Division during World War I. He was promoted to brigadier general, later major general, and commanded the Forty-Fifth Infantry Division, formed in 1920 from units of the Oklahoma National Guard, during the period between the world wars. The Forty-Fifth went on to distinguish itself in the European theater of operations during World War II and in Korea. It was deactivated on February 1, 1968 (ibid., passim).

Chapter 13. The Legend, 1917–1927

1. Wright, "Necrology"; undated, unidentified clippings, CC-AHC.

2. In 1907 the adjutant general of Oklahoma was paid the munificent sum of five hundred dollars a year (Franks, *Citizen Soldiers*, 4).

3. "F.M. Canton Bucks Oil Game in Tulsa," undated, unidentified clipping, CC-WHC, Box 2, Folder 16.

4. "Famed Fighter Plays Oil Game," undated, unidentified clipping, CC-WHC, Box 2, Folder 16.

5. Green, *Grass-Roots Socialism*, 359–61; Burbank, *When Farmers Voted Red*, 133–34.

6. Frank Lake to F. M. Canton, August 11, 1917, CC-WHC, Box 1, Folder 57.

7. The nine were J. H. Graham, W. B. Slaughter, M. V. Brownfield, John N. Simpson, Luther T. Clark, D. B. Gardner, J. H. Paine, S. B. Burnett, and Frank Canton. A photographer, wanting to capture the pioneers on film after the meeting, could round up only six: Slaughter, Burnett, Gardner, Canton, Graham, and Clark (*Cattleman*, April 1917, 7).

8. Copy of the resolution is in CC-WHC, Box 1, Folder 38.

9. "Pioneer Day `Bad Man' Hunter Here," undated clipping, CC-WHC, Box 2, Folder 15.

10. "Returns to Bandit Hunt," unidentified clipping, November 20, 1921, Lamborn Collection, Kansas State Historical Society, Topeka.

11. The *Breeders Gazette* article is in CC-WHC, Canton Scrapbook.

12. Canton, *Frontier Trails*, 36–42.

13. *Breeders Gazette*, July 4, 1906, CC-WHC, Canton Scrapbook.

14. *Cattleman*, March 1918.

15. Canton, *Frontier Trails*, chapter 3: 49–73.

16. Edward Everett Dale, January 15, 1930, introduction to Canton, *Frontier Trails* (1930 edition); Bell, "Frontier Lawman," 6.

17. The original manuscript is in CC-WHC.

18. Frank Canton to Job Ingram, November 5, 1913.

19. Beach to Canton, May 12, 1910, CC-WHC, Box 1, Folder 34.

20. The Jennings story, written by Will Irwin, was originally published under the title "Beating Back," in seven installments of the *Saturday Evening Post,* September-November 1913. It appeared in book form under the same title a year later (Adams, *Six-Guns and Saddle Leather,* 352). A movie version of "Beating Back" was filmed in 1913 at a farm near Ogdensburg, New Jersey, and at the New Rochelle studios of the Thanhouser Film Company (Shirley, *West of Hell's Fringe,* 423).

21. Beach to Canton, February 2, 1915, CC-WHC, Box 1, Folder 34.

22. Beach to Canton, February 16, 1915, CC-WHC, Box 1, Folder 34.

23. Warfield to Lillie, April 14, 1916, CC-WHC, Box 2, Folder 8.

24. Ibid.

25. Warfield to Canton, December 4, 1916, CC-WHC, Box 2, Folder 8.

26. Wohlers to Canton, June 20, 1916, CC-WHC, Box 2, Folder 10.

27. Wohlers to Canton, September 21, 1916, CC-WHC, Box 2, Folder 10. Both the envelope and the letter were addressed to "Major" Canton, an error that did nothing to improve Wohlers's chances of acting as the agent for Major General Canton.

28. Irvine to Canton, March 12, 1913, CC-WHC, Box 1, Folder 56.

29. Richardson to Canton, March 12, 1915, CC-WHC, Box 2, Folder 2.

30. *Cattleman,* March 1919.

31. Ibid., May 1923.

32. "Simplicity Marks Last Sad Rites of Texas Cattle King," "General Canton Here," "Granddaughter of S.B. Burnett Gets Bulk of Big Estate," undated, unidentified clippings, CC-WHC, Box 2, Folders 15 and 16.

33. Tad Moses to Edward Burnett, March 12, 1937, CC-AHC.

34. Ibid.

35. DeArment, "Bloody Easter," 18.

36. Tad Moses to Edward Burnett, March 12, 1937.

37. Ibid.

38. F. M. Canton to Fred E. Sutton, August 8, 1925. Sutton, in collaboration with Kansas City newspaperman A. B. MacDonald, published his book in 1927 under the title *Hands Up! Stories of the Six-Gun Fighters of the Old Wild West.* Canton was not mentioned.

39. William E. Hawks, self-proclaimed "Historian of the Plains," came to Oklahoma from his Vermont home in April 1926, and visited with Canton, Wylie Haynes, Ransom Payne, and other veteran lawmen. "I had not seen Frank since 1892 and the colored glasses changed him so," he told Anna Canton in a letter dated January 7, 1928 (CC-WHC, Box 1, Folder 54).

40. "Veteran Peace Officer and Adventurer Retires from Texas Association to Spend Last Days in Quiet," clipping, CC-WHC, Box 2, Folder 15. J. Elmer Brock was advised on May 29, 1935, by the secretary of the Texas cattlemen's association that Frank Canton drew a pension up until the time of his death (Canton File, Tisdale Collection).

41. Ruby Canton to Frank Canton, August 22, 1925, CC-WHC, Box 1, Folder 47.

42. Oklahoma State Department of Health, Bureau of Vital Statistics, Oklahoma City, Certificate of Death, Frank Melvin Canton.

43. William S. Key later served as warden of the state penitentiary and was a candidate for governor in 1938. As a major general in the U.S. Army, he commanded the Forty-Fifth Infantry Division in the early days of World War II (Franks, *Citizen Soldiers*, 40).

44. *Blackwell Morning Tribune*, September 30, 1927; *The Daily Oklahoman*, September 30, 1927; undated, unidentified clippings, CC-AHC.

45. A. D. Dailey, "Some Observations by the Editor," undated, unidentified clipping, CC-AHC.

46. "Those Who Made the West," undated, unidentified clipping, CC-AHC.

47. *Cattleman*, November 1927.

48. Barrett, "Necrology." It is curious that the man who had preceded him as adjutant general and whom he had praised so highly in 1927 was virtually ignored in Barrett's monumental four-volume history of Oklahoma published in 1941: *Oklahoma after Fifty Years: A History of the Sooner State and Its People, 1889–1939*. In this work Barrett gave Canton only cursory mention as one of the many deputy U.S. marshals who fought the outlaws during territorial days.

Afterword

1. Wright, "Necrology."

2. "Edward Everett Dale, A.B., M.A., Ph.D.," in Barrett, *Oklahoma after Fifty Years* 3:1106.

3. Canton, *Frontier Trails* (1930 edition), xii–xiii.

4. Edward Everett Dale, introduction to Canton, *Frontier Trails*, xiv.

5. Berton, *The Klondike Fever*, 318.

6. Canton, *Frontier Trails*, 237.

7. "Book Reviews," *Chronicles of Oklahoma* 8 (1930): 446.

8. Quoted in "Oklahoma Writers," undated and unidentified clipping, CC-AHC.

9. Ibid.

10. Canton, *Frontier Trails*, xiv.

11. Ibid., xiv–xv.

12. "Oklahoma Pioneer Inspired Wister to Create the Popular 'Virginian,'" unidentified July 22, 1938, clipping, CC-AHC. Even Canton's death certificate erroneously cited Virginia as his place of birth.

13. Beach to Canton, May 12, 1910.

14. Canton, *Frontier Trails*, xiii.

15. Ibid., ix.

16. Anna Canton to E. E. Dale, December 4, 1928, CC-WHC, Box 1, Folder 42; "Last of Distinguished Family Leaves Edmond," undated clipping from an Edmond paper, CC-AHC.

17. Wright, "Necrology."

18. Annie M. Canton to Elmer Brock, August 31, 1947, quoted in Hanson, *Powder River Country*, 224–25; Hanson, "Five Women of One Hundred Years Ago."

19. The headstones of Frank and Ruby are side by side. That of Annie is at the foot of their graves.

20. Secrest, "The Best of the Bad Men"; Mrs. R. L. Askew to William B. Secrest, January 24, 1972, and William B. Secrest to the author, July 13, 1992.

Bibliography

Unpublished Materials

Adjutant General's Files [A.G.F.], Archives Division, Texas State Library, Austin.

Mrs. R. L. Askew to William B. Secrest, January 24, 1972. Provided to the author by William B. Secrest.

Bailey, Rebecca Williamson Carter. "Wyoming Stock Inspectors and Detectives, 1873–1890." Master's thesis, University of Wyoming, 1948.

Bancroft, Ashley. "Interview with Sheriff Frank M. Canton, Buffalo, Wyoming, September 16, 1885." Manuscript Collections, Bancroft Library, University of California, Berkeley.

Barber, Amos. "Scrapbooks." American Heritage Center, University of Wyoming, Laramie.

Rex Beach to Anna Canton, November 30, 1928. CC-WHC, Box 1, Folder 34.

Billy M. Birmingham, Texas Department of Corrections, to the author, November 18, 1992.

Boise City, Idaho, U.S. Penitentiary. Records. Boise City.

Boyd, Bill R. "Statement about the Death of Bee Dunn Passed on by Members of Bee Dunn's Family." August 3, 1994. Provided to the author by Dale Chlouber, Ripley, Oklahoma.

Donaly E. Brice to the author, October 26, 1992.

Burnett, Edward. "Frank Canton, the Sheriff." Local History Collection, Johnson County Library, Buffalo, Wyoming.

Minnie Belle Burnett to Anna Canton, n.d. CC-WHC, Box 1, Folder 47.

Charles H. Burritt to F. M. Canton, May 17, 1892. cc-ahc.

T. A. Campbell Collection, Wyoming State Historical and Publication Division, Cheyenne.

Canton, Frank M. "Memories of the Border." CC-WHC, Box 3, Folder 14.

Frank M. Canton Collection, American Heritage Center, University of Wyoming, Laramie (cc-ahc).

Frank M. Canton Collection, Western History Collections, University of Oklahoma Libraries, Norman (CC-WHC).

Frank M. Canton File, Thomas Tisdale Collection, Cheyenne, Wyoming.

Frank M. Canton to Job Ingram, November 5, 1913. CC-WHC, Box 1, Folder 55.

Frank M. Canton to Josie Newman, January 2, 1885. Thomas Tisdale Collection, Cheyenne, Wyoming.

Lelia Vene Cozart, District Clerk, Jack County, Texas, to the author, January 29, 1992.

Gene M. Gressley to the author, September 28, 1992.

Guthrie, W. E. "The Johnson County Invasion; or, The Wyoming Rustler War: Observations of One of the 'Invaders' Forty Years After." Burton S. Hill Collection, American Heritage Center, University of Wyoming, Laramie.

Hanson, Margaret Brock. "Five Women of One Hundred Years Ago." Local History Collection, Johnson County Library, Buffalo, Wyoming.

Grace R. Hebard Collection, American Heritage Collection, University of Wyoming, Laramie.

Ethel Horner to Anna Canton, February 15, 1928. CC-WHC, Box 1, Folder 47.

John Wesley Horner. Interview with Ethel Horner, February 1928. CC-WHC, Box 2, Folder 12.

Indian and Pioneer Records, Ponca Agency, Sac and Fox Agency, Oklahoma Historical Society, Oklahoma City.

Indian-Pioneer History, Foreman Collection, Oklahoma Historical Society, Oklahoma City.

Thomas H. Irvine Papers, Montana Historical Society Library, Helena.

Frank Kell to J. Elmer Brock, September 10, 1936. Thomas Tisdale Collection, Cheyenne, Wyoming.

Lamborn Collection, Kansas State Historical Society, Topeka.

William E. Lind, Military Reference Branch, Textual Reference Division, National Archives, Washington, D.C., to the author, May 11, 1993.

McPherren, Ida. "Charles Basch." 1938 interview. Wyoming Stock Growers Association File, American Heritage Center, University of Wyoming, Laramie.

Tad Moses to Edward Burnett, March 12, 1937. CC-AHC.

Murdock, Jerry. "Law History of Johnson County." May 18, 1954. Local History Collection, Johnson County Library, Buffalo, Wyoming.

Oral History Tapes, Johnson County Library, Buffalo, Wyoming.

"Pioneer Peace Officers." T. A. Campbell Collection, Wyoming State Historical and Publication Division, Cheyenne.

Rietz, Minnie. "Johnson County." WPA manuscript. Local History Collection, Johnson County Library, Buffalo, Wyoming.

Mary Jane Sams to Anna Canton, December 14, 1927. CC-WHC, Box 1, Folder 47.

William B. Secrest to the author, July 13, 1992.

Floyd Shock to Frank M. Canton, September 29, 1915. CC-WHC, Box 2, Folder 3.

Stock Brand Certification No. 144. Local History Collection, Johnson County Library, Buffalo, Wyoming.

Tanner, Francis Henry. "The Disposal of the Public Domain in Johnson County, Wyoming, 1869–1890." Master's thesis, University of Wyoming, 1967.

Tom Tisdale. Interviews with the author. June 21, 1992, Buffalo, Wyoming; July 28, 1992, Cheyenne, Wyoming.

"Testimony of Charles Franklin Bash [sic]." May 11, 1935. Collection of Thomas Tisdale, Cheyenne, Wyoming.

B. H. Turk. Interview, March 1978. Local History Collection, Johnson County Library, Buffalo, Wyoming.

Washbaugh, John. "The Murder of John A. Tisdale." Local History Collection, Johnson County Library, Buffalo, Wyoming.
Webb, J. R., Papers. Research Center, Hardin-Simmons University, Abilene, Texas.

Newspapers

Arapaho Bee, April 23, 1909
Beaver Journal, November 21, 1907
Big Horn Sentinel, September 27, October 18, November 8, 29, December 13, 1884; January 1885 through December 1886; April 23, September 3, 24, 1887; July 7, September 8, 22, November 10, 1888; January 12, 19, February 16, March 23, April 20, July 6, 13, 1889
Blackwell Morning Tribune, September 28, 30, 1927
Blackwell Times Record, August 29, 1895
Buffalo Bulletin, October 23, December 11, 1890; January 1891 through December 1892; November 16, 1893; August 26, 1897; March 31, 1898; October 12, December 7, 1899; January 18, February 8, March 22, April 20, July 12, 1900; May 21, July 23, August 6, 1903; March 20, 1913; August 18, 1949; January 1, 1953; August 21, 1958; July 2, 1959
Buffalo Echo, December 5, 12, 1891
Buffalo Voice, March 30, 1901
Cheyenne Daily Leader, October 22, 1885; December 8, 1891; August 5, 1892; January 22, March 8, 23, May 24, 1893
Cheyenne Daily Sun, December 25, 1891; April 24, 27, 28, May 25, August 5, 7, 1892; January 22, 1893
Cheyenne Tribune, December 5, 7, 1907
Chicago Blade, March 12, 1892
Chicago Herald, April 16, 19, 25, 1892
Daily Ardmorite, June 22, 1896
Daily Nevada State Journal, April 10, 1891
Daily Oklahoman, February 6, 1913; April 15, 16, October 5, 1914; June 10, 1915; September 12, 1923; October 19, 1924; September 28, 30, 1927
Edmond Enterprise, November 12, 1925
El Reno News, November 20, 1896; December 2, 1898
Evanston Register, April 8, 1893
Fort Worth Democrat, April 22, 1876
Frontier Echo, September 11, 18, October 16, 1875; February 11, March 10, April 14, 1876; February 22, March 15, 1878
Galveston Daily News, February 29, 1876
Guthrie Daily Leader, February 5, May 3, July 11, August 21, December 26, 1895; October 8, November 7, 8, 12, 14, 1896; July 20, 1897; November 29, 1898; February 17, 1899
Houston Daily Telegraph, February 4, 1876
Kansas City Star, November 8, 12, 1896
Kerrville Mountain Sun, November 5, 1925

Laramie Boomerang, February 19, 1884; September 22, 1891; April 18, 1892
Laramie Daily Sentinel, August 18, 1883; September 19, 1885
Lawton Constitution, May 20, 1981
Lawton Daily Republican, September 9, 1902
Lawton Weekly News, September 11, November 13, 1902; January 8, February 19, 26, 1903
Lawton Weekly Republican
New York Times, September 28, 1927, April 23, 1892
Northwestern Livestock Journal, October 15, 1892
Oklahoma City Times, March 30, 1909
Oklahoma State Capital, May 16, July 6, August 20, 1895; December 7, 1906; April 18, 1909
Pawnee Agency Scout, September 6, October 10, 1893; February 9, May 4, 11, December 7, 12, 1894
Pawnee Appeal, November 30, 1894; February 22, March 1, April 12, 1895
Pawnee County Outlook, November 14, 28, 1907
Pawnee Republican, August 24, 1894
Pawnee Times-Democrat, December 28, 1893; April 27, May 18, 25, June 1, 15, 22, June 29, July 6, July 27, August 3, 17, 21, 24, November 2, 16, 30, December 7, 1894; February 1, 8, 15, 22, March 8, 15, April 19, 26, May 10, 24, June 21, 28, July 12, August 23, 30, September 20, November 1, 1895; March 22, 29, April 5, 12, May 3, 10, 1901
Payne County Populist, September 5, 1895
St. Louis Republican, December 12, 1914
San Antonio Daily Express, September 16, 1875; February 4, March 14, 1876; March 16, April 3, 6, 18, 19, 20, 21, May 1, 2, 3, 9, 15, 22, 25, July 27, 1877; May 16, 1895
San Antonio Daily Herald, March 2, 1876
Shawnee Herald, November 8, 1907
Sheridan Enterprise, January 2, 1892
Sundance Gazette, April 29, September 16, 1887
Thermopolis Independent, December 20, 1907
Tulsa World, June 13, 1915
Wichita Daily Times, November 22, 1925
Worland Grit, June 6, 1935
Wyoming News, April 4, 1936
Wyoming State Tribune, December 22, 1941
Yukon Midnight Sun, June 11, 1898
Yukon Press, January 15, 21, February 15, 1899

Government Documents

Annual Report of the Attorney-General of the United States for the Year 1894. Washington: Government Printing Office, 1894.
Annual Report of the Attorney-General of the United States for the Year 1897. Washington: Government Printing Office, 1897.

Annual Report of the Attorney-General of the United States for the Year 1898. Washington: Government Printing Office, 1898.

Confederate Records, Military Service Branch (NNMS). National Archives, Washington, D.C.

Ex parte Horner, July 17, 1894, Governor's Pardon Papers, Texas State Archives, Austin.

General Records of the Department of Justice (GRDJ). File 1893-6271, File 1896-3654, File 1896-19661, File 1897-10381, File 1897-12126. Record Group 60, National Archives, Washington, D.C.

Illinois State Board of Health, Cook County. Certificate of Death, Helen Canton.

Johnson County, Wyoming, Assessment Rolls, 1883, 1884, 1885, 1889, 1890. Wyoming State Archives, Cheyenne.

Johnson County, Wyoming, Commissioners' Books, 1882–92. Johnson County Courthouse, Buffalo, Wyoming.

Johnson County, Wyoming, Sheriff's Day Book, 1883–84. Wyoming State Archives, Cheyenne.

Oklahoma State Department of Health, Bureau of Vital Statistics, Oklahoma City. Certificate of Death, Frank Melvin Canton.

Records of the Adjutant General. Record Group 94, National Archives, Washington, D.C.

State of Texas v. Joe Horner: Number 327, Jack County, July 10, 1874, aggravated assault and battery.

State of Texas v. Joe Horner: Number 332, Jack County, July 10, 1874, theft of cattle.

State of Texas v. Joe Horner: Number 335, Jack County, July 10, 1874, theft of cattle.

State of Texas v. Joseph Horner: Number 361, Jack County, November 6, 1874, assault to murder.

State of Texas v. Joe Horner: Number 368, Uvalde County, April 23, 1877, robbery.

State of Texas v. Joe Horner: Number 374, Uvalde County, April 30, 1877, breaking telegraph wires.

State of Texas v. Joe Horner et al.: Number 379, Jack County, June 8, 1876, bond forfeiture.

State of Texas v. Joe M. Horner, George Horner, and Wageman alias Redding: Number 384, Comanche County, March 1, 1876, assault and battery, robbery.

State of Texas v. Joseph Horner: Number 415, Jack County, February 27, 1875, theft of cattle.

State of Texas v. Joe Horner: Number 416, Jack County, February 27, 1875, theft of cattle.

State of Texas v. Joe Horner and George Horner: Number 1690, Bexar County, March 15, 1877, theft.

State of Texas v. W. Z. Redding, A. H. Murchison, T. R. Redding: Number 388, service of bond.

State of Wyoming, Plaintiff, v. Frank M. Canton, Defendant, Information Charging the Said Defendant with the Murder of John A. Tisdale: District Court

Journal No. 3, Johnson County, Wyoming.

State of Wyoming v. Frank M. Canton: Number 21, Johnson County, November 19, 1892, murder in the first degree.

State of Wyoming v. Frank M. Canton: Number 21, Uinta County District Court, Criminal Case Docket 2.

State of Wyoming v. Frank M. Canton et al.: Number 365, Laramie County District Court, Criminal Case Docket 3.

State of Wyoming v. Frank M. Canton et al.: Number 379, Laramie County District Court, Criminal Case Docket 3.

State of Wyoming v. Frank M. Canton, Frank Wolcott, Thomas Smith, and Buck Garrett: Motion to Continue, First District Court, County of Laramie, January 2, 1893.

Subpoenas, *Henry Blair et al. v. O. H. Flagg et al.*, May 4, 1892, Circuit Court of the United States, for the District of Wyoming.

Territory of Wyoming, County of Johnson. Marriage License, Frank M. Canton and Anna M. Wilkerson, January 19, 1885.

Texas State Penitentiaries. "Description of Convict When Received: Joe Horner, No. 5920, May 5, 1877."

Texas State Penitentiary, Huntsville. Records of Joe Horner.

U.S. Census Reports. 1850: Henry County, Indiana; Williamson County, Texas. 1860: Benton County, Arkansas; Denton County, Texas; Williamson County, Texas. 1870: Denton County, Texas; Washington County, Arkansas. 1880: Denton County, Texas; Wichita County, Texas; Williamson County, Texas; Young County, Texas. 1900: Johnson County, Wyoming; Knox County, Texas. 1910: Logan County, Oklahoma.

Books

Abernathy, John R. *In Camp with Roosevelt; or, The Life of John R. (Jack) Abernathy, Author.* Oklahoma City: Times-Journal Publishing Co., 1933.

Adams, Ramon F. *The Adams One-Fifty: A Check-list of the 150 Most Important Books on Western Outlaws and Lawmen.* Austin, Tex.: Jenkins Publishing Co., 1976.

————. *Burs under the Saddle: A Second Look at Books and Histories of the West.* Norman: University of Oklahoma Press, 1964.

————. *More Burs under the Saddle: Books and Histories of the West.* Norman: University of Oklahoma Press, 1979.

————. *Six-Guns and Saddle Leather: A Bibliography of Books and Pamphlets on Western Outlaws and Gunmen.* Norman: University of Oklahoma Press, 1969.

A List of Fugitives from Justice, from Records in the Adjutant-General's Office. Austin, Tex.: Adjutant General's Office, 1878.

A List of Fugitives from Justice, Indicted for Felonies in the State of Texas and a Descriptive List of Escaped Convicts. Austin, Tex.: John P. Kirk, 1886.

A List of Fugitives from Justice, 1891: Part VII, Compiled from Reports of Sher-

iffs Received at the Adjutant General's Office. Austin, Tex.: Henry Hutchings, State Printer, 1891.

A List of Fugitives from Justice for 1900. Austin, Tex.: Texas State Library, 1900.

Baber, D. F. *The Longest Rope.* Caldwell, Idaho: Caxton Printers, 1959.

Baker, Pearl. *The Wild Bunch at Robbers Roost.* New York: Abelard-Schuman, 1971.

Bancroft, Hubert Howe. *History of the Pacific States of North America: Nevada, Colorado, Wyoming, 1540–1888.* San Francisco: History Co., 1890.

Bard, Floyd C., as told to Agnes Wright Spring. *Horse Wrangler: Sixty Years in the Saddle in Wyoming and Montana.* Norman: University of Oklahoma Press, 1960.

Barnard, Evan G. *A Rider of the Cherokee Strip.* Boston: Houghton Mifflin Co., 1936.

Barrett, Charles F., ed. *Oklahoma after Fifty Years: A History of the Sooner State and Its People, 1889–1939.* 4 vols. Hopkinsville, Ky.: Historical Record Association, 1941.

Barrows, John R. *U-Bet: A Greenhorn in Old Montana.* 1934. Lincoln: University of Nebraska Press, 1990.

Battey, Thomas C. *The Life and Adventures of a Quaker among the Indians.* Norman: University of Oklahoma Press, 1968.

Beach, Rex. *The Barrier.* New York: Harper and Brothers, 1908.

———. *Personal Exposures.* New York: Harper and Brothers, 1940.

———. *The Spoilers.* New York: Harper and Brothers, 1906.

Berton, Pierre. *The Klondike Fever: The Life and Death of the Last Great Gold Rush.* New York: Alfred A. Knopf, 1958.

Bolster, Mel Hallin. *Crazy Snake and the Smoked Meat Rebellion.* Boston: Branden Press, 1976.

Boyer, Glenn G. *I Married Wyatt Earp: The Recollections of Josephine Sarah Marcus Earp.* Tucson: University of Arizona Press, 1976.

Breihan, Carl W. *Gunslingers.* Wauwatosa, Wis.: Leather Stocking Books, 1984.

———. *Lawmen and Robbers.* Caldwell, Idaho: Caxton Printers, 1986.

Brown, Dee. *Hear That Lonesome Whistle Blow: Railroads in the West.* New York: Holt, Rinehart, and Winston, 1977.

Brown, Richard Maxwell. *Strain of Violence: Historical Studies of American Violence and Vigilantism.* New York: Oxford University Press, 1875.

Burbank, Garin. *When Farmers Voted Red: The Gospel of Socialism in the Oklahoma Countryside, 1910–1924.* Westport, Conn.: Greenwood Press, 1976.

Burroughs, John Rolfe. *Guardian of the Grasslands.* Cheyenne, Wyo.: Pioneer Printing and Stationery Co., 1971.

Burt, Struthers. *Powder River, Let 'Er Buck.* New York: Farrar and Rinehart, 1938.

Calkins, Frank. *Jackson Hole.* New York: Alfred A. Knopf, 1973.

Canton, Frank M. *Frontier Trails: The Autobiography of Frank M. Canton.* Boston: Houghton Mifflin Co., 1930.

———. *Frontier Trails: The Autobiography of Frank M. Canton.* Reprint. Norman: University of Oklahoma Press, 1966.

Capps, Benjamin. *The Warren Wagontrain Raid: The First Complete Account of an Historic Indian Attack and Its Aftermath.* New York: Dial Press, 1974.

Carlson, Chip. *Tom Horn: "Killing Men Is My Specialty."* Cheyenne, Wyo.: Beartooth Corral, 1991.

Carter, Captain Robert G. *The Old Sergeant's Story: Winning the West from the Indians and Bad Men.* New York: Frederick H. Hitchcock, 1926.

Chrisman, Harry E. *Fifty Years on the Owl Hoot Trail: Jim Herron, the First Sheriff of No Man's Land.* Chicago: Sage Books, 1969.

Clay, John. *My Life on the Range.* 1924. Norman; University of Oklahoma Press, 1962.

Colcord, Charles Francis. *Autobiography of Charles Francis Colcold.* N.p.: Privately printed by C. C. Helmerich, 1970.

Crouch, Carrie J. *A History of Young County, Texas.* Austin: Texas State Historical Association, 1956.

Croy, Homer. *Trigger Marshal: The Story of Chris Madsen.* New York: Duell, Sloan, and Pearce, 1958.

Cummins, Jim. *Jim Cummins' Book, Written by Himself.* Denver: Reed Publishing Co., 1903.

David, Robert B. *Malcolm Campbell, Sheriff.* Casper, Wyo.: Wyomingana, 1932.

DeArment, Robert K. *Bat Masterson: The Man and the Legend.* Norman: University of Oklahoma Press, 1979.

Douglas, C. L. *Cattle Kings of Texas.* 1939. Austin, Tex.: State House Press, 1989.

Douthitt, Katherine Christian. *Romance and Dim Trails: A History of Clay County.* Dallas, Tex.: William T. Hardy, 1938.

Drago, Harry Sinclair. *The Great Range Wars: Violence on the Grasslands.* New York: Dodd, Mead, Co., 1970.

———. *Outlaws on Horseback.* New York: Dodd, Mead and Co., 1964.

———. *Road Agents and Train Robbers: Half a Century of Western Banditry.* New York: Mead and Co., 1973.

Driggs, B. W. *History of Teton Valley, Idaho.* Caldwell, Idaho: Caxton Printers, 1926.

Dugan, Mark. *Knight of the Road: The Life of Highwayman Ham White.* Athens, Ohio: Swallow Press/Ohio University Press, 1990.

Dykstra, Robert R. *The Cattle Towns.* New York: Atheneum, 1968.

Edgar, Bob, and Jack Turnell. *Brand of a Legend.* Cody, Wyo.: Stockade Publishing, 1978.

Elman, Robert. *Badmen of the West.* Secaucus, N.J.: Castle Books, 1974.

Flagg, Oscar H. *A Review of the Cattle Business in Johnson County, Wyoming, since 1882, and the Causes That Led to the Recent Invasion.* New York: Arno Press and the New York Times, 1969.

Flannery, L. G. (Pat), ed. *John Hunton's Diary, Volume 1, 1873–75.* Lingle, Wyo.: Guide-Review, 1956.

———. *John Hunton's Diary, Volume 2, 1876–77.* Lingle, Wyo.: Guide-Review, 1958.

———. *John Hunton's Diary, Volume 3, 1878–79.* Lingle, Wyo.: Guide-Review, 1960.

———. *John Hunton's Diary, Volume 4, 1880–82.* Lingle, Wyo.: Guide-Review, 1963.

———. *John Hunton's Diary, Volume 5, 1883–84.* Lingle, Wyo.: Guide-Review, 1964.

———. *John Hunton's Diary, Volume 6, 1885–89.* Glendale, Calif.: Arthur H. Clark Co., 1970.

Franks, Kenny. *Citizen Soldiers: Oklahoma's National Guard.* Norman: University of Oklahoma Press, 1984.

Frink, Maurice. *Cow Country Cavalcade: Eighty Years of the Wyoming Stock Growers' Association.* Denver, Colo.: Old West Publishing Co., 1954.

Frye, Elnora. *Atlas of Wyoming Outlaws at the Territorial Penitentiary.* Laramie, Wyo.: Jelm Mountain Publications, 1990.

Fugate, Francis L., and Roberta B. Fugate. *Roadside History of Oklahoma.* Missoula, Mont.: Mountain Press Publishing Co., 1991.

Gage, Jack R. *The Johnson County War.* Cheyenne, Wyo.: Flintlock Publishing Co., 1967.

Gard, Wayne. *The Chisholm Trail.* Norman: University of Oklahoma Press, 1954.

———. *Frontier Justice.* Norman: University of Oklahoma Press, 1949.

Gibson, A. M. *The Life and Death of Colonel Albert Jennings Fountain.* Norman: University of Oklahoma Press, 1965.

Green, James R. *Grass-Roots Socialism: Radical Movements in the Southwest, 1895–1943.* Baton Rouge: Louisiana State University Press, 1978.

Haley, James L. *The Buffalo War: The History of the Red River Uprising of 1874.* Garden City, N.Y.: Doubleday and Co., 1976.

Hall, Charles ("Pat"), ed. *Documents of Wyoming Heritage.* Cheyenne: Wyoming Bicentennial Commission, 1976.

Hamilton, Allen Lee. *Sentinel of the Southern Plains: Fort Richardson and the Northwest Texas Frontier, 1866–1878.* Fort Worth: Texas Christian University Press, 1988.

Hanes, Colonel Bailey C. *Bill Doolin: Outlaw, O.T.* Norman: University of Oklahoma Press, 1968.

Hanna, Oliver Perry. *An Old-Timer's Story of the Old Wild West.* Casper, Wyo.: Hawks Book Co., 1984.

Hanson, Margaret Brock. *Powder River Country: The Papers of J. Elmer Brock.* Cheyenne: Frontier Printing Co., 1981.

Hardin, John Wesley. *The Life of John Wesley Hardin as Written by Himself.* 1896. Norman: University of Oklahoma Press, 1961.

Harman, S. W. *Hell on the Border: He Hanged Eighty-Eight Men.* 1898. Lincoln: University of Nebraska Press, 1992.

Heald, George D. *Wyoming Flames of '92.* Vermillion, S.D.: Hill's Creative Printing, 1972.

Hendricks, George D. *The Bad Man of the West.* San Antonio, Tex.: Naylor Co., 1941.

Henry, Stuart. *Conquering Our Great American Plains.* New York: E. P. Dutton and Co., 1930.

Heritage Book Committee, Wyoming Pioneer Association, Converse County, Douglas, Wyoming. *Pages from Converse County's Past.* Casper, Wyo.: Historical Press, 1986.

Hinton, Harwood P., ed. *History of the Cattlemen of Texas.* 1914. Austin: Texas State Historical Association, 1991.

Holland, Thomas R. *Oklahombres Revisited.* N.p., 1992.

Horan, James D. *The Authentic Wild West: The Outlaws.* New York: Crown Publishers, 1977.

Horan, James D., and Paul Sann. *Pictorial History of the Wild West.* New York: Crown Publishers, 1954.

Horn, Tom. *Life of Tom Horn, Government Scout and Interpreter, Written by Himself.* 1904. Norman: University of Oklahoma Press, 1964.

Horton, Thomas F. *History of Jack County.* 1932. Centennial Edition. N.p., 1975.

Huckabay, Ida Lasater. *Ninety-Four Years in Jack County, 1854–1948.* Jacksboro, Tex.: Texian Press, 1974.

Hufsmith, George W. *The Wyoming Lynching of Cattle Kate, 1889.* Glendo, Wyo.: High Plains Press, 1993.

Hunt, William R. *Distant Justice: Policing the Alaska Frontier.* Norman: University of Oklahoma Press, 1987.

Hunter, J. Marvin, ed. *The Trail Drivers of Texas.* 1920–23. Austin: University of Texas Press, 1985.

Jones, Ralph F. *Longhorns North of the Arkansas.* San Antonio, Tex.: Naylor Co., 1969.

Jones, W. F. *The Experiences of a Deputy U.S. Marshal of the Indian Territory.* 1936. Muskogee, Okla.: Starr-Hill Associates, 1976.

Jordan, Arthur J. *Jordan.* Missoula, Mont.: Mountain Press Publishing Co., 1984.

Kelly, Charles. *The Outlaw Trail.* New York: Devin-Adair Co., 1959.

Lamb, Arthur H. *Tragedies of the Osage Hills.* Pawhuska, Okla.: Osage Printery, 1935.

Lamb, F. Bruce. *Kid Curry: The Life and Times of Harvey Logan and the Wild Bunch.* Boulder, Colo.: Johnson Books, 1991.

Larson, T. A. *History of Wyoming.* 2d ed., rev. Lincoln: University of Nebraska Press, 1978.

Leckie, William H. *The Buffalo Soldiers: A Narrative of the Negro Cavalry in the West.* Norman: University of Oklahoma Press, 1967.

Ledbetter, Barbara A. Neal. *Fort Belknap Frontier Saga: Indians, Negroes, and Anglo-Americans on the Texas Frontier.* Burnet, Tex.: Eakin Press, 1982.

LeFors, Joe. *Wyoming Peace Officer.* Laramie, Wyo.: Laramie Printers, 1953.

LeFors, Rufe. *Facts As I Remember Them: The Autobiography of Rufe LeFors.* Austin: University of Texas Press, 1986.

Litton, Gaston. *History of Oklahoma at the Golden Anniversary of Statehood.* 2 vols. New York: Lewis Historical Publishing Co., 1957.

McCoy, Joseph G. *Historic Sketches of the Cattle Trade of the West and Southwest.* 1874. Edited by Ralph P. Bieber. Lincoln: University of Nebraska Press, 1985.

McCullough, Harrell. *Selden Lindsey, U.S. Deputy Marshal.* Oklahoma City: Paragon Publishing, 1990.

McIntire, Jim. *Early Days in Texas: A Trip to Hell and Heaven.* 1902. Edited by Robert K. DeArment. Norman: University of Oklahoma Press, 1992.

McLoughlin, Denis. *Wild and Woolly: An Encyclopedia of the Old West.* Garden City, N.Y.: Doubleday and Co., 1976.

Meeks, Beth Thomas, with Bonnie Speer. *Heck Thomas, My Papa.* Norman, Okla.: Levite of Apache, 1988.

Mercer, A. S. *The Banditti of the Plains; or, the Cattlemen's Invasion of Wyoming in 1892.* 1894. Norman: University of Oklahoma Press, 1954.

Miner, H. Craig. *Wichita: The Early Years, 1865–80.* Lincoln: University of Nebraska Press, 1982.

Mokler, Alfred James. *History of Natrona County, Wyoming, 1888–1922.* 1923. New York: Argonaut Press, 1966.

Monaghan, Jay. *The Legend of Tom Horn, Last of the Bad Men.* New York: Bobbs-Merrill Co., 1946.

Murray, Robert A. *Military Posts in the Powder River Country of Wyoming, 1865–1894.* Buffalo, Wyo.: Office, 1968.

Myers, Patty, ed. *Buffalo's First Century.* Buffalo, Wyo.: Buffalo Bulletin, 1984.

Myers, Patty, and Nancy L. Jennings. *With Winchesters and Determined Hearts: A Bibliography.* Buffalo, Wyo.: Johnson County Historical Society, 1992.

Nash, Jay Roberts. *Bloodletters and Badmen, Book 1.* New York: Warner Books, 1975.

———. *Encyclopedia of World Crime.* 6 vols. Wilmette, Ill.: Crime Books, 1989.

National Cyclopedia of American Biography. New York: James T. White and Co., 1921.

Nix, Evett Dumas. *Oklahombres, Particularly the Wilder Ones.* St. Louis: Eden Publishing House, 1929.

Nunis, Doyce B., Jr. *The Life of Tom Horn Revisited.* Los Angeles: Westerners Los Angeles Corral, 1992.

Oklahoma Department of Libraries. *Short Biographies of Governors, Oklahoma Territory, State of Oklahoma.* Oklahoma City: Oklahoma Department of Libraries, 1977.

O'Neal, Bill. *Encyclopedia of Western Gun-Fighters.* Norman: University of Oklahoma Press, 1979.

Paine, Lauran. *Tom Horn: Man of the West.* Barre, Mass.: Barre Publishers, 1963.

Parsons, Chuck, and Marjorie Parsons. *Bowen and Hardin.* College Station, Tex.: Creative Publishing Co., 1991.

Patterson, Richard. *The Train Robbery Era.* Boulder, Colo.: Pruett Publishing Co., 1991.

———. *Wyoming's Outlaw Days.* Boulder, Colo.: Johnson Books, 1982.

Payne, Darwin. *Owen Wister: Chronicler of the West, Gentleman of the East.* Dallas: Southern Methodist University Press, 1985.

Pence, Mary Lou. *Boswell: The Story of a Frontier Lawman.* Cheyenne, Wyo.: Pioneer Printing and Stationery Co., 1978.

Penfield, Thomas. *Western Sheriffs and Marshals.* Grossett and Dunlap, 1955.

Penrose, Charles B. *The Rustler Business.* Douglas, Wyo.: Douglas Budget, [1959].

Perkins, Doug, and Nancy Ward. *Brave Men and Cold Steel.* Fort Worth: Texas and Southwestern Cattle Raisers Foundation, 1984.

Pointer, Larry. *In Search of Butch Cassidy.* Norman: University of Oklahoma Press, 1977.

Portrait and Biographical Record of Oklahoma. Chicago: Chapman Publishing Co., 1901.

Potomac Corral of the Westerners. *Great Western Indian Fights*. Lincoln: University of Nebraska Press, 1966.

Prassel, Frank Richard. *The Western Peace Officer: A Legacy of Law and Order*. Norman: University of Oklahoma Press, 1972.

Raine, William MacLeod. *Guns of the Frontier*. Boston: Houghton Mifflin Co., 1940.

Raymond, Dora Neill. *Captain Lee Hall of Texas*. Norman: University of Oklahoma Press, 1940.

Reed, Paula, and Grover Ted Tate. *The Tenderfoot Bandits: Sam Bass and Joel Collins, Their Lives and Hard Times*. Tucson: Westernlore Press, 1988.

Rollinson, John K. *Wyoming Cattle Trails*. Caldwell, Idaho: Caxton Printers, 1948.

Samuelson, Nancy B. *The Dalton Gang Story: Lawmen to Outlaws*. Eastford, Conn.: Shooting Star Press, 1992.

Sandoz, Mari. *The Cattlemen: From the Rio Grande across the Far Marias*. New York: Hastings House, 1958.

Shirk, George H. *Oklahoma Place Names*. Norman: University of Oklahoma Press, 1965.

Shirley, Glenn. *Buckskin and Spurs: A Gallery of Frontier Rogues and Heroes*. New York: Hastings House, 1958.

———. *Guardian of the Law: The Life and Times of William Matthew Tilghman*. Austin, Tex.: Eakin Press, 1988.

———. *Gunfight at Ingalls: Death of an Outlaw Town*. Stillwater, Okla.: Barbed Wire Press, 1990.

———. *Heck Thomas, Frontier Marshal*. 1962. Norman: University of Oklahoma Press, 1981.

———. *Henry Starr, Last of the Real Badmen*. New York: David McKay Co., 1965.

———. *Shotgun for Hire: The Story of "Deacon" Jim Miller, Killer of Pat Garrett*. Norman: University of Oklahoma Press, 1970.

———. *Six-Gun and Silver Star*. Albuquerque: University of New Mexico Press, 1955.

———. *West of Hell's Fringe*. Norman: University of Oklahoma Press, 1978.

Siringo, Charles A. *Riata and Spurs*. Boston: Houghton Mifflin Co., 1927.

———. *Two Evil Isms*. 1915. Austin, Tex.: Steck-Vaughn Co., 1967.

Smith, Helena Huntington. *The War on Powder River*. New York: McGraw-Hill Book Co., 1966.

Spring, Agnes Wright. *Seventy Years: A Panoramic History of the Wyoming Stock Growers Association*. Cheyenne, Wyo.: Wyoming Stock Growers Association, 1942.

Starr, Helen, and O. E. Hill. *Footprints in the Indian Nation*. Muskogee, Okla.: Hoffman Printing Co., 1974.

Stone, Elizabeth Arnold. *Uinta County: Its Place in History*. Laramie, Wyo.: Laramie Printing Co., 1924.

Streeter, Floyd B. *Prairie Trails and Cow Towns: The Opening of the West*. New York: Devin Adair Co., 1963.

Strong, Henry W. *My Frontier Days and Indian Fights on the Plains of Texas*. N.p., [1926?].

Stuart, Granville. *Pioneering in Montana: The Making of a State, 1864–1887.* 1925. Lincoln: University of Nebraska Press, 1977.

Sutton, Fred E., and A. B. MacDonald. *Hands Up! Stories of the Six-Gun Fighters of the Old Wild West.* Indianapolis: Bobbs-Merrill Co., 1927.

Thrapp, Dan L. *Encyclopedia of Frontier Biography.* 4 vols. Glendale, Calif.: Arthur H. Clark, 1988–94.

Tilghman, Zoe A. *Marshal of the Last Frontier: Life and Services of William Matthew (Bill) Tilghman.* Glendale, Calif.: Arthur H. Clark Co., 1964.

Time-Life Books. *The Gunfighters.* New York: Time-Life Books, 1974.

Tise, Sammy. *Texas County Sheriffs.* Albuquerque, N.M.: Oakwood Printing, 1989.

Walker, Donald R. *Penology for Profit: A History of the Texas Prison System, 1867–1912.* College Station: Texas A&M University Press, 1988.

Walker, Tacetta B. *Stories of Early Days in Wyoming: Big Horn Basin.* Casper, Wyo.: Prairie Publishing Co., 1936.

Waller, Brown. *Last of the Great Western Train Robbers.* South Brunswick, N.Y.: A. S. Barnes and Co., 1968.

Watson, John. *The Real Virginian.* Tucson: Westernlore Press, 1989.

Webb, Walter Prescott, ed. *The Handbook of Texas.* 3 vols. Austin: Texas State Historical Association, 1952–76.

Whisenhunt, Donald W. *Fort Richardson: Outpost on the Texas Frontier.* El Paso: Texas Western Press, 1968.

White, Virgil D. *Index of U.S. Marshals, 1789–1960.* Waynesboro, Tenn.: National Historical Publishing Co., 1988.

Wister, Fanny Kemble, ed. *Owen Wister Out West: His Journals and Letters.* Chicago: University of Chicago Press, 1958.

Woods, Lawrence M. *British Gentlemen in the Wild West: The Era of the Intensely English Cowboy.* New York: Free Press, 1989.

Yost, Nellie Snyder. *The Call of the Range: The Story of the Nebraska Stock Growers Association.* Denver: Sage Books, 1966.

Articles

Ackenhausen, Chas. A. "Frank Canton: A Famous Johnson County Sheriff." *Wyoming News,* April 4, 1936.

Barrett, Charles F. "Necrology: Requiescat En Pace." *Chronicles of Oklahoma* 5 (1927): 422.

Bell, William Gardner. "Frontier Lawman." *American West* 1, no. 3 (Summer 1964): 5–13, 78.

Bolster, Mel H. "The Smoked Meat Rebellion." *Chronicles of Oklahoma* 31 (1953): 37–55.

"Book Reviews." *Chronicles of Oklahoma* 8 (1930): 446–48.

Boyer, Glenn G. "Alias General Canton." *Real West,* February 1985, 16–22.

Brayer, Herbert O. "New Light on the Johnson County War." *Westerners Brand Book, Chicago Corral* 9, no. 12 (February 1953): 1–2.

Canton, F. M. "The Capture of Samuel and Beaver." *Cattleman,* March 1918.

———. "Reminiscences of a Veteran Officer." *Cattleman*, May 1923.

———. "The Wyoming Cattle War." *Cattleman*, March 1919.

Carroll, Murray L. "Tom Horn and the Langhoff Gang." *Annals of Wyoming* 64, no. 2 (Spring 1992): 34–44.

Carson, John. "Frank Canton, Gunfighter." *Frontier Times* 40, no. 5 (August-September 1966): 34–35.

———. "They Didn't All Die with Their Boots on." *True West* 18, no. 5 (May-June 1971): 16–19.

Casey, Orben J. "Governor Lee Cruce and Law Enforcement, 1911–1915." *Chronicles of Oklahoma* 54 (1976–77): 435–60.

Christy, Mort. "King of the Rustlers." *Real West*, August 1958, 17, 61–64.

Conant, Lora M. "Frank Canton: Lawman!" *Wyoming*, June 1972, 6–8.

DeArment, R. K. "Bloody Easter." *Old West* 30, no. 3 (Spring 1994): 12–19.

———. "'Hurricane Bill' Martin: Horse Thief." *True West* 38, no. 6 (June 1991): 38–45.

———. "Joe Horner, Desperado." *Old West* 29, no. 1 (Fall 1992): 28–39.

———. "Teton Jackson." *True West* 40, no. 3 (March, 1993): 14–19.

———. "Wyoming Range Detectives." *Old West* 30, no. 1 (Fall 1993): 14–21.

DeMattos, Jack. "Gunfighters of the Real West: Frank Canton." *Real West*, May 1979, 22, 54–55.

Drago, Harry Sinclair. "The Battle of Ingalls and the 'Cimarron Rose' Legend." *Brand Book of the New York Posse of the Westerners* 10, no. 3 (1963): 49–50, 56, 60–64.

English, Paul. "A Wily Customer: The Life and Crimes of Ben Cravens." *Chronicles of Oklahoma* 62 (1984): 284–95.

Fraser, Hugh Russell. "Crime of the Age." *Overland News* 1, no. 11 (June 1958): 9.

Gard, Wayne. "Teddy Roosevelt's Wolf Hunt." *True West* 9, no. 6 (July-August 1962): 34–35, 52.

Gooddell, G. B. "Gratitude Twenty Dollars Bought." *Cattleman*, March 1917.

Gordon, Bill. "The Bare-Handed Coyote Catcher Who Became Marshal." *True Frontier*, June 1967, 8–11, 44.

Gould, Lewis L. "A. S. Mercer and the Johnson County War: A Reappraisal." *Arizona and the West* 7, no. 1 (Spring 1965): 5–20.

Haines, Joe D., Jr. "The Log of a Frontier Marshal." *Chronicles of Oklahoma* 59 (1981–82): 295–303.

Haley, J. Evetts. "Book Reviews and Notices." *Southwestern Historical Quarterly* 35, no. 4 (April 1932): 331–32.

Haser-Harris, Diane B. "Horse Racing in Early Oklahoma." *Chronicles of Oklahoma* 64 (1986–87): 5–17.

Hawthorne, Roger. "Conflict and Conspiracy." *True West* 31, no. 6 (June 1984): 12–17.

Henderson, Sam. "The Careers of Sheriff Buck Garrett." *The West* 9, no. 2 (July 1968): 16–19, 66–70.

Hill, Burton S. "Buffalo: Ancient Cow Town." *Annals of Wyoming* 35, no. 2 (October 1963): 125–54.

———. "A Girl Called Nettie." *Annals of Wyoming* 37, no. 2 (October 1965): 147–56.

Holding, Vera. "He Bagged 'Em Bare-Handed." *Golden West* 1, no. 2 (January 1965): 20–21, 46–48.

Hope, B. W. "Joe Elliott's Story." *Annals of Wyoming* 45, no. 2 (Fall 1973): 143–75.

Hunt, William R. "Deadly Frank Canton." *Alaska Journal*, 1986 Collection, 244–49.

Hunter, J. Marvin. "Colonel C. C. Slaughter." *Frontier Times* 8, no. 10 (July 1931): 433–37.

Hutchins, John M. "The Jekyll-Hyde Gunman of the Johnson County War of 1892." *Denver Westerners Roundup* 48, no. 2 (March-April 1992): 3–14.

Koch, Anna Elaine. "Cowtown Merchant, Cattle War Santa Claus." *True West* 38, no. 1 (January 1991): 20–25.

Lingle, C. M., ed. "The Cattle Barons' Rebellion against Law and Order." *Buffalo Bulletin*, April 24, 1892.

Lott, Howard B. "The Old Occidental." *Annals of Wyoming* 27, no. 1 (April 1955): 25-30.

McConnell, H. H. "Five Years a Cavalryman." *Frontier Times* 11, no. 2 (November 1933); 11, no. 6 (March 1934): 63–80.

McElwee, Pat. "Blood Brothers." *Frontier Times* 33, no. 4 (Fall 1959): 31, 58.

McLaird, James D. "Ranching in the Big Horns: George T. Beck, 1856–1894." *Annals of Wyoming* 39, no. 2 (October 1967): 157–85.

Milek, Dorothy G. "Who Killed Bob McCoy?" *True West* 14, no. 2 (November-December 1966): 24–27.

Murray, Robert A. "The United States Army in the Aftermath of the Johnson County Invasion." *Annals of Wyoming* 38, no. 1 (April 1966): 59–75.

Myers, Olevia E. "The Delaware County Fight." *Frontier Times* 47, no. 2 (February-March 1973): 34–35, 63–64.

Rescorla, Richard. "Frank M. Canton, Johnson County Raider." *Golden West*, January 1971, 42–43, 68–70.

Rickards, Colin. "The Old West Speaks: Nate Champion Tells about the Wyoming Range War." *Real West*, March 1970, 58–60.

Ryland, Lee. "Deep Ran the Blood in Buffalo." *True West* 9, no. 3 (January-February 1962): 16–17, 64–66.

Secrest, William B. "The Best of the Bad Men." *Real Frontier*, November 1971, 32–33, 46–49.

Shirley, Glenn. "Killer with Two Faces." *True West* 36, no. 6 (June 1989): 14–19.

Smith, Emily B. "Swanson County." *Chronicles of Oklahoma* 9 (1931): 412–22.

Smith, Helena Huntington. "George Dunning: Mystery Man of the Johnson County Invasion." *Montana Magazine*, Autumn 1963.

Trenholm, Virginia Cole. "Last of the Invaders." *True West* 9, no. 3 (January-February 1962): 18–20, 59–60.

"Twenty-Seven Years a State." *Chronicles of Oklahoma* 12 (1934): 393– 401.

Waida, Marilyn. "Jack Abernathy, Oklahoma Legend." *Old West* 6, no. 2 (Summer 1969): 34–37.

Walker, Wayne T. "Burk Burnett and the Four Sixes." *Real West,* January 1981, 40–43, 50.

———. "Legend of the Four Sixes." *Golden West* 8, no. 3 (March 1971): 10–13, 57–60.

Wiltsey, Norman B. "The Saga of Nate Champion," parts 1 and 2, *Real West,* April 1968, 22–23, 53–55; May 1968, 48–51.

Wright, Muriel H. "Necrology: Anna May Wilkerson Canton." *Chronicles of Oklahoma* 26 (1948–49): 489–90.

INDEX

Saufley, Micah C., 87–88
Sayers, Joseph D., 255
Sayres, W. O., 168
Schmerer, Jacob, 59, 61
Schooley, Elmer, 259
Schroeder, George, 38
Schultz, B. C., 336 n. 12
Schultze, B. C. *See* Schultz, B. C.
Scott, Dr. Hugh, 266
Scott, Winfield, 285, 291, 293
Searight brothers (cattlemen), 86
Seattle, Wash., 148, 204–7, 209, 211,
    218, 219, 235, 239, 249, 352 n. 53
Seattle No. 1 (steamship), 218, 219–21,
    223, 350 n. 14
Secrest, William B., 314
Selig Polyscope Company, 300
Seminole, Tex., 303
Sentinel, Okla., 279
Sequoyah County, Okla., 296
Service, Robert W., 215
71 Ranch (Wyo.), 88, 89
76 Ranch (Wyo.), 71
Shackelford County, Tex., 39, 321 n. 51
Shadley, Lafayette, 150, 189
Shaffer, Sam. *See* Dunn, John E.
Sharp Nose, 67–68, 327 n. 71
Shaughnessy (prizefighter), 283
Shaw, A. S. J., 306
Shawnee, Okla., 265, 275, 279
Sheehan Ranch, Wyo., 88
Shelley, Bill, 160–63, 341 n. 42, 342
    nn. 47,50,51,55
Shelley, Edward. *See* Shelley, Bill
Shelley, John, 160–63, 341 n. 42, 342
    nn. 47,50,51
Shelley, Lou, 160–63, 341 n. 42, 342
    n. 55
Shephard, T. A., 197
Sheridan, Wyo., 58–59, 82, 83, 86, 117,
    241, 242, 258, 353 n. 7
Sheridan County, Wyo., 109, 328
    n. 104
Sherman, Tex., 35
Shirley, Glenn, 169, 340 n. 11, 343

n. 80, 345 n. 48, 346 n. 74
Shock, Floyd, 34, 321 n. 53
Shonsey, Mike, 98–100, 122, 124, 133,
    331–32 nn. 72,74, 336 n. 12, 337
    n. 50, 338 n. 52
Shoshone Indians, 67, 68
Shoup, George, 149, 211
Shoup, James M., 211, 212, 217,
    228–30, 232–34, 239, 240, 250, 352
    n. 6
Silver Republican Party, 206
Simpson, John A., 271
Simpson, John N., 260, 359 n. 7
Simpson, Sloan, 260
Sines, "Old Man," 82
Sioux Indians, 15–16, 318–19 n. 44
Siringo, Charles A., 143, 168, 339 n. 87
Sitka, Alaska, 203, 204, 205, 228, 230,
    231, 233
6666 Ranch (Tex.), 10
Sixth Cavalry, U. S. Army, 130
"Skeeter Dick." *See* McGregg,
    Buck
Skiatook, Okla., 198
Slack, A. J. ("Jack"), 66–67
Slaughter, C. C., 14, 318 n. 34
Slaughter, W. B., 359 n. 7
"Slaughter's Kid." *See* Newcomb,
    George
Smith, Al, 121
Smith, "Black Henry," 93, 121, 135,
    143, 339 n. 89
Smith, Drew, 74, 76
Smith, Elias R., 73–74, 76
Smith, Frank, 121, 135
Smith, Pvt. George, 30, 31, 32
Smith, Helena Huntington, 130, 335
    n. 2
Smith, Jack. *See* Tregoning, John
Smith, John R., 116, 121
Smith, Terence ("Coyote"), 121, 126,
    127
Smith, Thomas G., 89, 121, 330 n. 45,
    332 n. 74, 338 n. 54
Smith, Tom, 121, 122, 123, 128, 131,
    335 n. 9

Terry, Mose, 19
Teschemacher, Hubert E., 130, 334
n. 56
Texas and Southwestern Cattle
Raisers Association, 259, 260–61,
266, 295–96, 299, 303, 305, 313
Texas Fugitive Lists, 38
"Texas Kid." See Booker, David E.
Texas Military Institute, Austin, Tex.,
86
Texas National Guard, 273
Texas Rangers, 11, 29, 153, 273, 313,
316 n. 17, 317 n. 19, 323 n. 85
Texas State Penitentiary, Huntsville,
Tex., 18, 43–46, 50, 153, 155, 323
n. 97
Texas Street, Abilene, 15
Texowa, Okla., 255, 355 n. 55
Thanhouser Film Company, 360 n. 20
34th Regiment, C.S.A., 8
Thirty-Sixth Division, U.S. Army, 359
n. 96
Thomas, Albert, 190
Thomas, Charles. See Welty, Albert
Thomas, Henry Andrew ("Heck"), 176,
178, 179, 186–87, 188, 190–91, 193,
197–98, 254–55, 304, 344 n. 22, 347
n. 110
Thomason, Bud, 287–88
Thompson, Frank M., 202
Thompson, Leslie, 39
Thompson, Sanford ("Zang"), 121
Thorp, Russell, 326 n. 54
"Three-Fingered Jack." See McGregg,
Buck
"Three Guardsmen," 179
Tilghman, William M., 20, 176, 178,
179, 186–88, 190, 191, 275, 277, 304,
342 n. 51, 344 n. 22, 344 n. 36, 345
n. 48
Tilghman, Zoe, 344 n. 36
Tillman County, Okla., 355 n. 55
Tisdale, David Robert ("Bob"), 122,
123, 334 n. 56, 335 n. 11, 336 n. 17
Tisdale, John A., 86, 97, 98, 100,

101–103, 104–14, 116, 119, 122, 128,
130, 138, 139, 140–43, 241–42, 334
nn. 51,56, 339 nn. 73,76
Tisdale, Mrs. John A., 104, 106, 139
Tisdale, John N., 122, 123, 334 n. 56,
335 n. 11, 336 n. 17
Tisdale, Martin A. (son of John A.),
103, 104, 106, 241–43, 352–53 n. 7
Tisdale, Martin Allison (brother of
John A.). See Allison, Al
Tisdale, Tom, 352 n. 7
Tisdale Gulch. See Haywood's Gulch
Toddy, Jack, 121
Tongue River (Wyo.), 51
Tonkawa Indians, 39
Topeka, Kans., 8, 14
Towse, Ed, 122, 337 n. 50
Trafton, Edwin B., 91
Travis County, Tex., 38, 40
Tregoning, John, 88–89, 95, 167–68
Troublesome River Mining District,
Alaska, 218, 350 n. 4
TTT Ranch, 225 n. 11, 353 n. 7
Tucker (Cheechako), 213–14
Tucker, George R., 336 n. 12
Tucker, S. S., 336 n. 12
Tulsa, Okla., 160, 161, 162, 188, 282,
283–85, 287, 292, 296
Tulsa County Fair Association, 284
Tulsa Jockey Club, 284
Turner, Edward P., 39
Turner, John B., 288
Turner, Martin L., 273
Tway, Ed ("Eat-Em-Up-Jake"), 116, 121
28 Ranch (Wyo.), 103, 122
Tyler, George, 231, 351 n. 40
Tyler, Jesse M., 353 n. 24

U Cross Ranch (Wyo.), 118
Uinta County, Wyo., 79, 139
Union Pacific Railroad, 16, 72, 121,
245, 247, 248, 353 n. 17
U.S. Army Department of the Platte,
130
University of Oklahoma, 306, 311, 315

University of Oklahoma Press, 312
University of Wyoming, 315
Upson, Perry, 41–42
Uvalde, Tex., 43
Uvalde County, Tex., 42, 43, 323 n. 84

Valdez, Alaska, 302
Valentine, Colin, 306
Van Devanter, Willis, 114, 121, 137–40, 142, 148, 250–51
Van Horn, J. J., 130, 132, 133, 337 n. 46
Van Tassell, R. S., 118
Van Voorhees, Mrs. S. K., 357 n. 41
Van Zandt County, Tex., 49
Veatch, R., 342 n. 60
Vernon, Tex., 150
Victoria (steamship), 231
Victoria, Tex., 86
Villa, Pancho, 293
Virginian, The (Wister), 91, 312
VR Ranch (Wyo.), 122

Waggoner, Thomas J., 89, 96, 98, 121, 330 n. 45
Wagman, Tom. See Redding, William Z.
Wagner (deputy sheriff), 74
Wagner, John. See Redding, William Z.
Waightman, George ("Red Buck"), 171, 176, 178, 188, 345 n. 64
Wales, William, 321 n. 51
Walker, Bill, 114, 124, 127, 140, 143, 249–50
Wallace, J. L. See Walton, J. L.
Wallace, W. B., 122
Walling, Crowell, 17
Walrus. See Seattle No. 1
Walsenburg, Colo., 70
Walters, Joseph, 56
Walters, Okla., 257
Walton, J. L., 72, 328 n. 89
Ward, Dewey, and Company, 44
Warden, George Francis, 56
Warfield, T. O., 300–302
Warnock, P., 342 n. 60

Warren, Francis E., 59, 66, 121, 130, 136, 148, 149
Warren, Henry, 17
Washakie (Shoshone), 68, 327 n. 71
Washbaugh, George, 93
Washbaugh, John, 339 n. 76
Washbourne, Jay, 286
Washington, D. C., 68, 129, 149, 186, 204, 211, 233, 234, 256, 260, 262, 263, 292, 340 n. 11
Washington County, Ark., 30, 150
Waterman, D., 350 n. 4
Watkins, Mary S., 335 n. 3
Watson, Ellen, 88, 89, 96, 330 n. 42
Watson, Joe, 22, 30, 33, 39
Watson, Sally, 39
Watson, Tom, 188
Watt, Cullen, 108
Weare, Portus B., 147–49, 203, 204, 206, 211, 212, 217, 225, 232–34, 239
Weare Land and Live Stock Company, 147
Weatherford, Tex., 25
Webb, L. A. ("Lew"), 86, 103, 108, 116, 121, 241–42, 331 n. 66
Webber, Sarah E., 330 n. 47
Webber, T., 326 n. 60
Webster, Miss (Buffalo, Wyo.), 109
Wellman, George, 135, 143, 338 n. 57, 339 n. 89
Welty, Albert, 251–52, 354 n. 39
West, Charles, 282
West, George B., 331 n. 58
Western History Collections, University of Oklahoma, 315
Western Union Beef Company, 124
Weston County, Wyo., 89, 117, 138
Wharton, West, 160
Wheeler County, Tex., 73
Whitcomb, Elias W., 334 n. 56
White, Ham, 322 n. 77
Whitecaps. See Johnson County Invaders
Wichita, Kans., 14
Wichita Indians, 253